THE WEAKNESS OF GOD

T0366497

Indiana Series in the Philosophy of Religion

Merold Westphal, general editor

The Weakness of God

A Theology of the Event

JOHN D. CAPUTO

Indiana University Press
Bloomington & Indianapolis

This book is a publication of

Indiana University Press
601 North Morton Street
Bloomington, IN 47404-3797 USA

http://iupress.indiana.edu

Telephone orders   800-842-6796
Fax orders   812-855-7931
Orders by e-mail   iuporder@indiana.edu

The paper used in this publication meets the minimum requirements of
American National Standard for Information Sciences—Permanence of
Paper for Printed Library Materials, ANSI Z39.48-1984.

MANUFACTURED IN THE UNITED STATES OF AMERICA

Library of Congress Cataloging-in-Publication Data

Caputo, John D.
The weakness of God : a theology of the event / John D. Caputo.
p. cm. — (Indiana series in the philosophy of religion)
Includes bibliographical references and index.
ISBN 978-0-253-34704-6 (cloth : alk. paper) — ISBN 978-0-253-21828-5
(pbk. : alk. paper)   1. God.   I. Title.   II. Series.
BT103.C37 2006
231—dc22
2005024892

2 3 4 5 11 10 09 08 07

To Sabrina, Joel, and Natalie
and to all those to come

"Mes amis, je vous remercie d'être venus. Je vous remercie pour la chance de votre amitié. Ne pleurez pas: souriez comme je vous aurais souri. Je vous bénis. Je vous aime. Je vous souris, où que je sois."

"My friends, I thank you for coming. I thank you for the good fortune of your friendship. Do not cry: smile as I would smile at you. I bless you. I love you. I am smiling at you, wherever I am."

The final words
of Jacques Derrida (1930–2004),
read by his son at his graveside

CONTENTS

PREFACE

As I put the finishing touches on this book, the world reels under the overwhelming violence of the tsunami ("sea wave") that occurred on the day after Christmas 2004, which destroyed the lives and property of hundreds of thousands of people in south Asia.

Predictably, many religious leaders have been rushing to the nearest microphone or camera to explain that, while these are all innocent victims, we cannot hope to explain the mystery of God's ways—implying that this natural disaster is something God foresaw but for deeper reasons known only to the divine mind chose not to forestall. Others are telling us that God has taken this terrible occasion to remind us that we are all sinners and to dish out some much-needed and justifiable punishment to the human race.

Tell that to the father who lost his grip on his three-year-old daughter and watched in horror as she was carried out to sea.

Those are blasphemous images of God for me, clear examples of the bankruptcy of thinking of God as a strong force with the power to intervene upon natural processes like the shifting movements of the crustal plates around the Pacific rim as our planet slowly cools—the decision depending upon what suits the divine plan.

One can look upon the book that follows as an attempt to think of God otherwise.

January 2005

ACKNOWLEDGMENTS

My thanks to Villanova University for several research leaves during which the work on this book was completed, and in particular to Dean Kail Ellis, O.S.A., and Dr. John Johannes, Vice-President of Academic Affairs, who have been so supportive of my work over the years. Anna (Misticoni) Monserrate, the secretary to the David R. Cook Chair, has as always been an indispensable aid to me. I am grateful to Steven Jungkeit, Catherine Keller, and B. Keith Putt who have been especially helpful readers of various stages of sections of this manuscript. I have also benefited from several comments by my new colleagues in the Religion Department at Syracuse University.

While the great majority of this manuscript is previously unpublished, some sections of the following chapters appeared in earlier versions, most of which have been so completely revised and reinscribed in a new context that I hesitate even to mention them. But for the sake of the official record, antecedent versions of some sections of the following chapters can be located as follows:

Chapter 1: "In Search of a Sacred Anarchy: An Experiment in Danish Deconstruction," in *Calvin Schrag and the Task of Philosophy after Postmodernity,* ed. William McBride and Martin Matuskik (Evanston, Ill.: Northwestern University Press, 2002), 226–50.

Chapter 5: "The Poetics of the Impossible and the Kingdom of God," in *The Blackwell Companion to Postmodern Theology,* ed. Graham Ward (Oxford: Blackwell, 2001), 469–81.

Chapter 7: "Metanoetics: Elements of a Postmodern Christian Philosophy," *Christian Philosophy Today,* ed. Francis Ambrosio (New York: Fordham University Press, 1999), 189–223.

Chapter 8: "Reason, History and a Little Madness: Towards an Ethics of the Kingdom," in *Questioning Ethics: Contemporary Debates in Philosophy,* ed. Richard Kearney and Mark Dooley (New York: Routledge, 1999), 84–104.

Chapter 10: "The Time of Giving, the Time of Forgiving," in *The Enigma of Gift and Sacrifice,* ed. Edith Wyschogrod, Jean-Joseph Goux, and Eric Byonton (New York: Fordham University Press, 2002), 117–47.

Chapter 11: "No Tear Shall be Lost," in *Ethics of History,* ed. David Carr and Thomas Flynn (Evanston, Ill.: Northwestern University Press, 2004), 91–117.

Chapter 12: "Adieu sans Dieu: Derrida and Levinas," in *The Face of the Other and the Trace of God: Essays on the Thought of Emmanuel Levinas,* ed. Jeffrey Bloechl (New York: Fordham University Press, 2000), 276–311.

THE WEAKNESS OF GOD

Introduction:
A Theology of the Event

I confess I have a weakness for theology.

Against the sound advice of my attorneys, my investment counselors, and my confessor, and after holding out for as long as possible against my inner *daimon,* I have finally succumbed to the siren call of this name. I do not know how to avoid speaking of theology. So be it. I am prepared to face the consequences. *Hier stehe ich.*

Whatever may be the fortunes of the word *theology* at present, and even if I have tended in the past to avoid it,[1] I cannot deny that what I am doing here is theological. Almost. The word *theology* has always been for me a double bind, a promise of my youth that I could never quite make, yet never quite break. I have never been able to resist theology, even as I have never had the immodesty to presume that I could get as far as theology. I have tended to defer the flow of this desire and send it rushing down other channels, letting it sail under foreign flags. I am wounded by theology, unhinged and uprooted by the blow it has delivered to my heart. Theology is my weakness, the way one has a weakness for sex or money, what I secretly desire, or maybe not so secretly, even as it desires everything of me. Still, with all due deference, like Johannes Climacus speaking of being a Christian, I would say that on my best days I am working at becoming theological.

All power to knowledge and to the scholarly study of religious beliefs and practices as an object. That is a fascinating study, the way alchemy and ancient Roman coins are fascinating, and I support including religion in the core curriculum. But theology signifies a passion in which everything is at stake,[2] the logos of a passion, the logos of a desire for God, the logos of a prayer. The desire for God—that is the root of the trouble I have bought for myself. *I have taken God, the name of God, what is happening in the name of God, as my subject matter.* With or without religion,[3] with or without what ordinarily passes for theology, the name of God is too important to leave in the hands of the special interest groups. That is why I freely own up here to a certain theological gesture, to a theological desire and a "desiring theology," as Charles Winquist would have put it,[4] which is undeniably a desire for God, for something astir in the name of God, a desire for something I know not what, for which I pray night and day.

I am praying for an event.

NAME AND EVENT

The modest proposal I make in this book is that the name of God is an event, or rather that it *harbors* an event, and that theology is the hermeneutics of that event, its task being to release what is happening in that name, to set it free, to give it its own head, and thereby to head off the forces that would prevent this event. My subject is theology and the event, a theology of the event, and a prayer for the event of theology. Obviously, then, everything turns on explaining what I mean by an "event" and how it is related to a name.[5]

(1) *Uncontainability.* Names contain events and give them a kind of temporary shelter by housing them within a relatively stable nominal unity. Events, on the other hand, are uncontainable, and they make names restless with promise and the future, with memory and the past, with the result that names contain what they cannot contain. Names belong to natural languages and are historically constituted or constructed, whereas events are a little unnatural, eerie, ghostly things that haunt names and see to it that they never rest in peace. Names can accumulate historical power and worldly prestige and have very powerful institutions erected in or under their name, getting themselves carved in stone, whereas the voice of events is ever soft and low and is liable to be dismissed, distorted, or ignored.

Although a name contains an event, an event cannot in principle be contained by a name, proper or common. There is always something uncontainable and unconditional about an event, whereas names, like "God," belong to conditioned and coded strings of signifiers. The event is the open-ended promise contained within a name, but a promise that the name can neither contain nor deliver. No name—the name of God being the particular case in point in this study—can enjoy more than a contingent privilege relative to the event, a privilege generated by the particular historical circumstances of a language and a culture. Traditionally, the name of God has enjoyed a very special privilege vis-à-vis the event. But it is always possible for the forces gathering in the event to be discharged or released under other names, other conditions, other times and cultures, including the names that are still to come, the very idea of the "to come" being constitutive of the event. Whether the name of God enjoys a merely passing historical privilege relative to the event it harbors, whether it can be bypassed or surpassed, is a question of which I will be mindful as I proceed.

It is especially important to see that a name does not house an event the way the body houses the soul in Platonism. On the contrary, it would be better to say that the event is the offspring of the body of the name and that without names there would be no events. The event is conceived and born within the body of the name. But names outstrip themselves and come undone just in virtue of their capacity to link up with other names, which gives rise to the event they themselves nurture. Names set off chains of promise and aspiration or chains of memories that outstrip themselves, in the face of which the name itself collapses and soon gives out, being unable to sustain the memory/promise it itself engenders. A name is a promissory note that it cannot itself keep. In the "democracy to come," for example, "democracy" is a name that may someday collapse under the strain of the "to come," which is the force of the event that will force the name beyond itself. In the "democracy to come," the "to come" is more important than the "democracy."[6] A name is conditioned, coded, and finite, whereas the event it shelters is unconditional and infinite in the sense of being capable of endless linkings and endlessly productive dissemination. One is a nominalist about names because of one's respect for the event.

(2) *Translatability.* An event is distinguished from a simple occurrence by reason of its polyvalence, complexity, and undecidability, by its endless nameability by other names equally eventful. Names are endlessly translatable, whereas events are what names are trying to translate, not in the sense of an inner semantic essence to be transferred, but in the sense of carrying (*ferre*) themselves toward (*trans*) the event, like runners thrusting themselves toward a finish line that never appears. Events are what names "mean" in the sense of what they are getting at, what they are trying to actualize, the source of their restlessness, the endless ends toward which names reach out, hurling themselves forward toward something, I know not what, toward God knows what. Names are asked to carry what they cannot bear toward a destination they do not know. Names are trying to help make things happen, while events are what is happening.

(3) *Deliteralization.* Because the name is never the equal of the event that stirs within it, the name can never be taken with literal force, as if it held the event tightly within its grip, as if it circumscribed it and literally named it, as if a concept (*Begriff*) were anything more than a temporary stop and imperfect hold on an event. That is why the name of an event is continually subject to a "reduction" to the event it harbors, which displaces the name, replacing it with other names, deliteralizing the name, subordi-

nating the grammar of the name to what I call the poetics of the event. The reduction of an event to a name, on the other hand, would be precisely the dangerous reductionism I am trying to avoid. By a *poetics* I mean a non-literalizing description of the event that tries to depict its dynamics, to trace its style, and to cope with its fortuitous forces by means of felicitous tropes. The event harbored in these names must not be trapped inside them. Accordingly, I want to impede the closure of these names, to block their literalization or ontologization, however sacred these names may be. The more sacred, the better, for their sacredness does not merely tolerate but demands deliteralization, and this is in virtue of the event they shelter.

That is also why an event cannot be held captive by a confessional faith or creedal formula. An event cuts across the distinctions among the various confessions, and even across the distinction between the confessional faiths and secular unbelief, in order to touch upon a more elemental, if ambiguous, quality of our lives, however this quality is given words or formulated, with or without what is conventionally called religion or theology, with or without what is called literature or politics. It would be better to say that the event is the subject matter, not of a confession, but of a *circumfession* in which we "fess up" to being cut and wounded by something wondrous, by something I know not what.

(4) *Excess*. Events happen to us; they overtake us and outstrip the reach of the subject or the ego. Although we are called upon to respond to events, an event is not our doing but is done to us (even as it might well be our undoing). The event arises independently of me and comes over me, so that an event is also an *advent*. The event is visited upon me, presenting itself as something I must deal with, like it or not.

The event requires a horizon of expectation or anticipation, not in such a way that it must abide within it, but in order precisely to shatter and overflow it. That is why one cannot speak of an absolute event, because every event occurs against a horizon of expectation that it breaches. But if it is nothing absolute, an event is an excess, an overflow, a surprise, both an uncontainable incoming *(l'invention)* on the side of what philosophy calls the "object," and something that requires a response from us, soliciting an expenditure without an expectation of return on the side of what philosophy calls the "subject." That is because an event is not part of an economic chain; it cannot be contained within a balanced equation, is not held in equilibrium by counterbalancing considerations. An event is an irruption, an excess, an overflow, a gift beyond economy, which tears open the closed circles of economics.

Moreover, if horizons demarcate zones of possibility, what Kant would call the conditions of possible experience, then an event belongs to what philosophy calls (the) impossible, constituting an experience of *the* impossible.

(5) *Evil.* The excess of the event is not necessarily good news. Evil, which I will describe as irreparably ruined time, without the possibility of compensation, also exhibits this excess. There are no guarantees about the course that events follow. An event is not an inner essence, like a Hegelian *Wesen,* the essential being of a thing that is unfolding more or less inevitably in time, but it is the endless possibilities of linking of which the name is capable. Events set off a chain or series of substitutions, not a process of essentialization or essential unfolding. Accordingly, an event can result in a disintegrating destabilization and a diminished recontextualization just as well as it can create an opening to the future. Nothing guarantees the success of the event. Its links are not assured of asymptotic progress toward some goal. Every promise is also a threat, and the event to come can be either for better or for worse. The promise of the democracy to come is menaced by the threat of the National Socialism to come. The event is not an essence unfolding but a promise to be kept, a call or a solicitation to be responded to, a prayer to be answered, a hope to be fulfilled. The event is subject to all the contingencies of time and tide, of chance and circumstance, of history and power—in short, to all the forces of the world that conspire to prevent the event, to contain its disruption, to hold in check its bottomless disseminative disturbance, to betray its promise.

(6) *Beyond Being.* An event refers neither to an actual being or entity nor to being itself, but to an impulse or aspiration simmering within both the names of entities and the name of being, something that groans to be born, something that cannot be constricted to either the ontic or ontological order at all. Rightly understood, the event overflows any entity; it does not rest easily within the confines of the name of an entity, but stirs restlessly, endlessly, like an invitation or a call, an invocation ("come") or a provocation, a solicitation or a promise, a praise or benediction (like Elohim's "good, very good"), whether or not the occurrences on the plane of being are promising or good, whether or not they are the match for what is stirring in the event of the call. An event is not an ontico-ontological episode on the plane of being but a disturbance within the heart of being, within the names for being, that makes being restless.

(7) *Truth.* The event constitutes the "truth" of a name. But I am not speaking of truth in the Platonic sense of the sunlight of the Good, of the absolute being underlying the sensible appearances, or in the Hegelian sense of its essential being and *Aufhebung,* or in the Heideggerian sense of its unconcealment. By the truth of the event, I mean what the event is capable of, the open-ended and unforeseeable future that the name harbors, its uncontainable possibilities, which may contain bad news. Because they

are uncontainable, events are essentially unforeseeable, which means their truth is more like a night than a light, and the event itself is as risky as it is promising. On that accounting, the truth is something one needs to have the heart for, the courage to cope with or expose oneself to, as when we speak of a hard truth or a harsh one, or when we speak of honestly facing the truth. That is also why the truth for me is a matter of prayer, not of epistemology.

(8) *Time.* An event has an irreducibly temporal character, so that living with the event is a way of living in time, a way of temporalizing, but one that is more kairological than chronological. The movement of the event cannot be clocked by the ticktock of ordinary time but has to do with a transforming moment that releases us from the grip of the present and opens up the future in a way that makes possible a new birth, a new beginning, a new invention of ourselves, even as it awakens dangerous memories.

Taking this little sketch of name and event as a point of departure, let me say that my interest in theology is a function of my interest in the name of God, and my interest in the name of God is a function of my interest in the event, and my interest in the event is a function of my interest in prayer (I am always praying for an event). To say that *theo*logy is the logos of the name of God means to say that it is the hermeneutics of the event that is astir in that name, for the event is what that name "means." By a "meaning" I do not mean a semantic content but what a name is getting at; what it promises; what it calls up, sighs and longs for, stirs with, or tries to recall; what we are praying for. The event of theology is the theology of the event. By the same token, the event of theology could also be called a deconstruction of the name of God, insofar as deconstruction is the deconstruction of the conditioned name in order to release the unconditional event that is sheltered by the name. The event that is promised by a given name is what Derrida calls "the undeconstructible." The event is always undeconstructible because it is always promised or called for, always to come, whereas whatever actually arrives has arrived under present conditions and so is deconstructible. Events are not what is present but what is coming.

To think *theo*logically is to make the mind's ascent toward God, which means toward whatever event is astir in the name of God, where the name of God is not a linguistic object that can be stretched out on the table for analysis. To use the name of God is an unstable, destabilizing act that exposes us to whatever event is transpiring in that name, to whatever chain of events this name provokes. The name of God comes first, while thinking theologically comes as a response, the way one responds to a knock at the door that interrupts your work. Theology comes in answer to the call that issues from the event harbored in the name of God, as a way to hear it, heed it, and hearken to it; to pray over it; and to set the music of this event to words.[7] Theology tries to follow the tracks of the name of God, to stay on the trail it leaves behind as it makes its way through our lives. The name of God, it should be insisted, is not a term of art, a technical or lifeless word coined by philosophers for their speculative purposes, but it is a word forged in the fires of life, in the joys and sorrows of ordinary life, a word we invoke on the most casual as on the most solemn occasions, signaling something familiar, even commonplace, yet bottomless, always on the tip of our tongue yet incomprehensible. That is because it shelters an event.

THE WEAKNESS OF GOD

But I am duty bound to warn the reader in advance not to expect too much. With all this talk of the stirring of event, I do not mean to stir up expectations of power. For however much prestige and power a name may accumulate, an event is a more wispy and willowy thing, a whisper or a promise, a breath or a spirit, not a mundane force. As such, this hermeneutics of the event will at best offer a somewhat undernourished theology as opposed to the hearty and robust ones that populate the tradition. I am tendering something in the spirit of what Derrida calls "a non-dogmatic doublet of dogma."[8] This theology of the event lacks corpulent articles of faith, a national or international headquarters, a well-fed college of cardinals to keep it on the straight and narrow, or even a decent hymnal. Think of it as a "theology without theology" that accompanies what Derrida calls a "religion without religion," as a "weak theology" that accompanies Vattimo's "weak thought," or perhaps even as the weak messianic theology that should accompany Benjamin's "weak messianic force."[9] In advocating weakness I am patently running together Derrida, Vattimo, and Benjamin, but I am also shamelessly citing St. Paul on the "weakness of God" (1 Cor. 1:25), all in the hope of inciting a holy riot, as Paul himself was sometimes wont to do. If Slavoj Žižek is in search of robust and pulpy theological orange juice, he must do his shopping elsewhere.[10] I confess, this theology of the event does not serve up the *Sache selbst* in all its palpable presence, which I love as much as the next chap, but only a tearful concession that the *Sache selbst* always slips away.[11]

But is it not obvious that God is the Father Almighty, the Creator of Heaven and Earth? Where were you and I when he created the heavens and the earth? Has not the name of God from time out of mind been associated with unlimited power so that "God Almighty" is practically a redundant expression? That I would never deny. I am not saying that power has not been a defining feature of theology right from the start; theology has been strong theology and religion has been strong religion, in love with strength, right from the gate.[12] But I am suggesting that theology is a house divided against itself and that it lacks self-understanding to the point that it is intellectually bipolar, vacillating wildly between the heights of power and the depths of weakness. It is, on the one hand, the locus of the most divine discourses on the weakness of God, even as, on the other hand, it is too much in love with power, constantly selling its body to the interests of power, constantly sitting down to table with power in a discouraging contradiction of its own good news. The more it talks about weakness, the more we can be sure it has power up its sleeve. If theology were somebody, a person, the solution would be to find a good analyst to help him or her work through this conflict.

This bipolarity is a function of the distinction between name and event. For the name belongs to the world and can gather worldly prestige, which is why it can be taken to be a strong force; whereas the event belongs to the order that disturbs the world with the possibilities of being otherwise, and this by means of its weak but unconditional force. A name can accumulate an army and institutional power, semantic prestige and cultural authority. But the event is not a natural thing, not a part of a natural language; it is more like a ghost, the specter of a possibility. The event belongs to the order of the poor "perhaps," the *peut-être,*[13] suggesting and soliciting another possibility in a still-silent voice that is all but drowned out by the mundane force of the name.

So suppose we think of the name of God, not as picking out the *ens realissimum* or the almighty creator of the universe, but as a "weak force," an *ens diminutum,* to use the language of Duns Scotus? Suppose all the trouble theology causes to itself and to others is brought about by sitting in the window "all rouged and powdered" waiting for a virile power to come striding by hoping to get lucky?[14]

I cannot avoid thinking these anarchic thoughts of a weak God and a rouged and powdered theology. *Hier stehe ich—noch einmal!* I am compounding what up to now might have been charitably construed as nothing more than an entirely orthodox expression of modesty about the frailty or weakness of our theological discourse, with the idea of a God of frailty or weakness. It is one thing to declare the debility of theology—but to project such debility upon God Almighty? How irreverent and impious! Still, I offer no apologies. I, who am against ethics, am likewise against piety. I do not want to be caught dead being pious, especially when such serious matters are at stake, like God, the event, and truth.

A theology of the "event" is inevitably a thin thing, taking the name of God as the name of a call rather than of a causality, of a provocation rather than of a presence or a determinate entity. But in a "strong" theology—which is pretty much what "theology" *tout court* always is or wants to be, including negative theology—God is the highest being in the order of presence (overseeing and insuring the presence of order), who presides over the order of being and manifestation. In a strong theology, the name of God has historical determinacy and specificity—it is Christian or Jewish or Is-lamic, for example—whereas a weak theology, weakened by the flux of un-decidability and translatability, is more open-ended. A theology of the event is in part a second-order act that maintains a certain ironic distance from strong theologies, which in a certain sense are the only theologies that "exist," that are found in concrete historical communities. I love the strong theologies that I know the way I love great novels, but I maintain an ironic distance from them occasioned not only by the fact that they are invariably in league with power but also by my conviction that the *event* that is astir in the name of God cannot be contained by the historical contingency of the names I have inherited in my tradition. There are many traditions, many forms of life, and on Pauline grounds I hold that God is not partial. On this point, I dare to expand the teachings of Johannes Climacus on the question of the historical point of departure for eternal happiness: not only is it pos-sible, but there may be several such points.

In a strong theology, God is the overarching governor of the universe, but in what follows I will endeavor to show that the weak force of God set-tles down below in the hidden interstices of being, insinuated into the ob-scure crevices of being, like an *ordo non ordinans,* the disordering order of what disturbs being from within, like an anarchic interruption that refuses to allow being to settle firmly in place. The name of God is the name of an event transpiring in being's restless heart, creating confusion in the house of being, forcing being into motion, mutation, transformation, reversal. The name of God is the event that being both dreads and longs for, sighing and groaning until something new is brought forth from down below. The name of God is the name of what can happen to being, of what being would become, of what rising up from below being pushes being beyond itself, outside itself, as being's hope, being's desire. The name of God is being's aspiration, its inspiration, its aeration, for God is not being or a being but a ghostly quasi-being, a very holy spirit.

A HYPER-REALISM
OF THE EVENT

The abstention that constitutes the diminished state of my theology—God is neither a supreme being nor being itself, neither ontic nor ontological, neither the cause of beings nor the ground of being—represents not a loss but a gain. Blessed are the weak! By untying the name of God from the order of being, it releases the event, sets free the provocation of this name, which disseminates in every direction, setting it free as a vocative force, as an evocative, provocative event, rather than confining its force to the strictures of naming a present entity. I approach God neither as a supreme entity whose existence could be proven or disproved or even said to hang in doubt, nor as the horizon of being itself or its ground, either of which would lodge God more deeply still in the onto-theological circuit that circles between being and beings. Being loves to hide, and being loves to cling to itself, but what is going on within the name of God turns the well-rounded sphere of being inside out, prying it open and exposing it, throwing the house of being into holy confusion, into a sacred anarchic disorder.

By pulling the plug on the name of God in the ontological order, I disconnect the energy source that supplies power to the debate about whether there is or is not an entity called God somewhere, up above or here below, inside or outside, here and now or up ahead. Hearing this talk of "disconnecting" *(ausschalten)* Husserlians will—rightly—suspect that there is an *epoche* afoot in a theology of the event. About God as an entitative issue, I offer no final opinion. I leave you on your own, twisting slowly and all alone in the winds of that ontico-ontological conundrum. Translating or transferring the affirmation of the event that takes place in the name of God, which is the heart of a theology of the event, into the order of an existential affirmation of a determinate and identifiable someone or something who somewhere answers to the name of God, inside or outside, with or without what is called "religion" in Latin or Greek, Hebrew, or Arabic, may or may not be the best way to give this affirmation life and breath. It is certainly one way, and I have not come to try to put a stop to it. God forbid! It is vital for some, but not for those for whom God is otherwise than an entity, or for those who rightly pass for atheists, not to mention those for whom this all remains a matter of some confusion. An affirmation such as that is something to be decided by each one for oneself in the existing, *in actu exercitu.* I have not been authorized from on high to settle that venerable debate. I am more interested in answering to the provocation of the *event* of this name than in adjudicating whether there is an entity somewhere who answers to that name. Answering to the name of God is our business, not God's. The name of God is rather more something that calls upon us than an identifiable entity called up or named by us.

I am praying for this theology of the event to come true the way I pray for peace. Imagine the nightmare if there were a *definitive proper name* for the event, one that would be accompanied by the strong force to enforce it. With whom could we trust this name? Would not a war break out among those who claimed to be its authentic representatives, between the spokesmen or vicars of the one true Sacred Name and the infidels? Would we not witness a veritable firestorm of orthodoxies, neo-orthodoxies, radical orthodoxies, heresies, and schisms? Would not the dissidents from the Sacred

Name be persecuted mercilessly, even if all they did was to offer a different interpretation or gloss on the Name or point out its historical provenance? In whose language would the Name be housed? Heidegger would insist on Greek (but his fallback position would be German), the Catholics on Latin; and there would be fervent advocates aplenty for Hebrew, Arabic, and San-skrit, while the negative theologians would present a long, verbose, and par-ticularly perplexing discourse on behalf of silence. Where would its sacred city be located? If, in an effort to stop all the fighting, we called for a round of negotiations, how would we agree on the shape of the table? The Chris-tians would demand something triangular, while others would want to form a circle, and still others would insist that we all sit on a rug.

But make no mistake about the *existential intensity* of weak theology. Do not confuse the modesty of this proposal with a lack of passion or en-gagement in existence. The weakness of this theology of the event has to do with the undecidability of the name and with our notion of God as a weak force, but do not underestimate its passion. Indeed, as an event, the name of God overtakes us and overturns us, uprooting and unhinging us, and leaves us hanging on by a prayer. The more undecidable it is, the more our passion is intensified, just as that sage Johannes Climacus said that the pas-sion of faith is directly proportionate to its objective uncertainty. We toss about in the grips of something we desire and something that desires us, something we know not what. That is why, despite the fact that I have un-plugged or disconnected the ontical and ontological connections of the name of God, this name does not undergo a diminution for me but an in-tensification, an enhancement, even a magnification, which even provides, *mirabile dictu,* all the makings of an odd sort of postmodern Magnificat, a postmodern way to magnify the name of the Lord. I am just following the Beatitudes in virtue of which weakness is construed as a blessing.

For by allowing this name to fluctuate in all its undecidability and provocativeness, by releasing it from its servitude to being in order to free it as a promise, we free it from its service as the name of a *res,* even the most real of all real beings, but we do not deny thereby that it has any reference to reality at all. Rather, we enlist it in the service of a certain "hyper-reality," of a reality promised beyond what is presently taken to be real, the hyper-reality of the beyond, the reality of the *hyper-* or *über.* Accordingly, weak theology takes the form neither of theological realism nor of anti-realism, but of a magnifying *hyper-realism of the event,* one whose passion and exis-tential intensity are correspondingly magnified by this very undecidabil-ity.[15] By this hyper-realism I mean the excess of the promise, of the call, of the endless provocation of an event that calls us beyond ourselves, down unplotted paths and into unexplored lands, calling us to go where we can-not go, extending us beyond our reach. Hyper-reality reaches beyond the real to the not-yet-real, what eye has not yet seen nor ear yet heard, in the open-endedness of an uncontainable, unconstrictable, undeconstructible event.[16]

SHORT CIRCUITS: ST. PAUL
AND ST. JACQUES

About God I confess to two heterodox hypotheses. First, the name of God is the name of an event rather than of an entity, of a call rather than of a cause, of a provocation or a promise rather than of a presence. Secondly, and this follows from the first, we will do better to think of God in terms of weakness rather than of outright strength. So in sum, I shift from the register of strength to that of weakness, from a robust theology of divine power (all rouged and powdered!) and omnipotence to a thin theology of the weakness of God, from the noise of being to the silence of an unconditional call.

For advancing the celestial cause of this weak theology I am sure that there will be at least some hell to pay. So if the police of orthodoxy descend upon me, I will assume no responsibility—I was just following orders!—and I will blame the waywardness of this theology on St. Paul (a revered saint much admired by Žižek, whom I may thus have found a way to satisfy) and Jacques Derrida (who is in certain circles known as Saint Jacques, albeit a monkey of a saint![17]). As to which of these two saintly figures has a higher place in the hier(an)archy of this book, gets to have more say, and has the more hallowed halo, I will wait for the reviews to come out. But my idea is to produce a "short circuit"—that would make Žižek happy and qualify me for a place in his book series[18]—in which I read St. Paul through Derrida, thus short-circuiting a strong voice through a weak one, that is, a classic text through a "minor" voice. Of course, I treat Derrida as a major figure with a "minor" voice, where minor (like a minor chord in music) does not mean of little quality but is used in a Deleuzian sense, that a dash of devilish derring-do from Derrida contributes a subversive or disseminating effect vis-à-vis the mainstream or strong theological tradition that stands guard over St. Paul.

I am doing my best to read both texts at once, both the sacred one and the devilish one, to write with both my left hand and my right, composing both an edifying discourse with my right and a comic-ironic pseudonymic satire with my left. I am all along exploring the paradoxical consequences of St. Paul's proclamation about the "weakness of God" (1 Cor. 1:29) at the same time that I pursue what Derrida calls the "weak force" of the unconditional that lacks sovereignty.[19] Paul is distinguishing the power and the wisdom of the world from the power of God's powerlessness, which is foolish-

ness to the world. Derrida is discussing the unconditionality of an unconditional claim, like the call of and for the justice to come (or the gift or the
hospitality to come), which he calls a weak force and which he distinguishes
from sovereign power, the strong force or raw power to enforce what one is
calling for, whether it is just or unjust. Derrida wonders if there is or might
be something unconditional without sovereignty, that is, without a strong
force; if there is, it would be something of which we would say not that it
"is" but that it "calls." If I can pull this off before I am hauled away by the
Grand Inquisitor, the result will be nothing short of a short-circuiting of the
name of God itself, or of the word of God, or at least of St. Paul. Instead of
producing a strong theology that describes a great onto-theological genera-
tor supplying endless energy to the world, I produce a charged field where
sparks are thrown off in every direction, constituting the divine disturbance
I will shortly describe as a "sacred anarchy." My idea is to stop thinking
about God as a massive ontological power line that provides power to the
world, instead thinking of something that short-circuits such power and
provides a provocation to the world that is otherwise than power.

To cross the wires of Paul and Derrida, I require what I call a kind of
quasi-phenomenological "reduction" from the name to the structure of the
event, that is, to the vocative (evocative, provocative) force sheltered by the
name of God. That *epoche,* referred to above, interrupts the power supply
to the question of being as presence, to the existential debate about an entity answering to the name of God, in order to release the event harbored
by this name. The structure of the call is precisely to call from below being
to what is beyond, to call us forth to what is promised up ahead, and to call
us back to the long-forgotten. The weak force of a call is something we can
(posse) or have the power to ignore—at our peril, perhaps, but just so. The
call comes packing only a vocative power—not power pure and simple, but
the powerless power of a provocation or a summons, a soliciting, seductive
power—but it does not have an army to lend it support, and nothing stops
us from turning a deaf ear to it. It lacks the sheer brawn to coerce or to
translate what it calls for into fact. It must make do with the power of powerlessness, not the power of pure strength.

SACRED ANARCHY

In the New Testament the event goes under the name "kingdom of God,"
while the forces that conspire to prevent the event are called "the world."[20]
The event is embodied in the "kingdom of God," filled in or fleshed out,
given a kind of phenomenological fulfillment, in soaring parables and
mind-bending paradoxes. You get an idea of what is happening in the name
of God when you see what kind of kingdom opens up under the impact of

God's name. The meaning of the idea of God is carried out, *in actu exercitu,* in God's kingdom. You see the weak force that stirs within the name of God only when someone casts it in the form of a narrative, tells mad stories and perplexing parables about it, which is what Jesus did when he called for the kingdom of God. Of this event that is called for in the Scriptures and that calls upon us, we say, "May your kingdom come," *viens, oui, oui.* I will follow the way that event was recorded with full amplification and orchestrated with a heavenly cosmology in the Christian Scriptures, which were not only written down afterwards in memory of Jesus but also with an eye on the future, on the establishment of a church here below, in the interim, where the church assumes an uneasy place in that very "world" it was bent on disturbing.

The event that takes place under the name of the kingdom of God is an anarchic field of reversals and displacements. So rather than identifying the highest entity or nominating the supreme governor who everywhere brings order, my anarchic suggestion is to think of the name of God as the name of a disturbance or a holy disarray. That is what I call a "sacred anarchy,"[21] another of my crossed wires, this time wiring up the sacred, not with the *arche,* but with the *anarche,* producing a kind of hier*an*archy. The kingdom of God that is called for in the New Testament[22] is an anarchized field, produced by exposing being to the provocative name of God, like a field of forces that have been scrambled under the influence of some electronic disturbance or interference. In the kingdom, weak forces play themselves out in paradoxical effects that confound the powers that be, displaying the unsettling shock delivered to the reigning order by the name of God. The kingdom is the embodiment of the turmoil caused in being by the good. Indeed, were I coerced by the police of orthodoxy into coughing up an argument for the existence of God, I would offer, not a teleological argument, but an ateleological one. I would point to all the disturbances in being and ask, What is the anarchic *arche* at the heart of all this disorder? And instead of asking whether some intelligent being must not have designed it, I will ask whether something amorous must not have loved it!

The kingdom of God is a domain in which weakness "reigns," where speaking of a "kingdom" is always an irony that mocks sheer strength. The kingdom is not the simple weakness that lacks the power of faith or the courage for action, but the provocative and uplifting weakness of God, a sublime weakness that, however weak, should not be underestimated because it is a divine force, capable even of inflicting a divine trauma. The kingdom of God obtains whenever powerlessness exerts its force, whenever the high and mighty are displaced by the least among us. The kingdom of God obeys the law of reversals in virtue of which whatever is first is last, whatever is out is in, whatever is lost is saved, where even death has a certain power over the living, all of which confounds the dynamics of strong forces. When the Romans posted "King of the Jews" above the head of Jesus on the cross, they meant to mock him with a cruel joke. But there is something deeply true about this bitter Roman irony that backfires on such brutality and is visited on Roman power itself. The kingdom that Jesus called for was a kingdom ironically, one that was itself mocking the business-as-usual of the powers that be, one in which a divine madness reigned, even as it was, from the point of view of the Roman Empire, of the brutality of the world, simple foolishness, outright stupidity.

The kingdom calls. A call is as weak as a word, as a breath of air, a trace, or a sigh, while the world is as tall as a mountain. Thus, in the kingdom of God, weak will-of-the-wisp words move mountains, provoking deep seismic shifts in the movements of continents and the toppling of empires. (This is the subversiveness of the New Testament that worried Nietzsche.)

The kingdom of God is the rule of weak forces like patience and forgiveness, which, instead of forcibly exacting payment for an offense, release and let go. The kingdom is found whenever war and aggression are met with an offer of peace. The kingdom is a way of living, not in eternity, but in time, a way of living without why, living for the day, like the lilies of the field—figures of weak forces—as opposed to mastering and programming time, calculating the future, containing and managing risk. The kingdom reigns wherever the least and most undesirable are favored while the best and most powerful are put on the defensive. The powerless power of the kingdom prevails whenever the one is preferred to the ninety-nine, whenever one loves one's enemies and hates one's father and mother while the world, which believes in power, counsels us to fend off our enemies and keep the circle of kin and kind, of family and friends, fortified and tightly drawn.

Because theology is bipolar—beneath all its talk about weakness it conceals a love of power—I expend every effort to preserve the purity of the element in which the call for the kingdom sounds, to preserve the purity of the weak force of God, to keep the peal of its appeal safe from the harsh and withering lights of being, and to safeguard it on the plane of the event. Otherwise the love of power packaged as weakness takes over, and the call dissipates into resentment, priestcraft, a wily way to wend one's way to the top of the heap, which is the bit that Nietzsche got right. Or it descends into thaumaturgy and magic. In the kingdom, death turns into life, but that amazing transformation should not be confused with a strong theology of magical resuscitations or supernatural interventions upon natural processes. For that would rivet the kingdom to the order of being instead of releasing the event that invites—and an invitation is a weak force—another way to be, a way to be below being just in order to move beyond being's chains. The kingdom of God belongs to the sphere of invitation, of invocation, to the poetics of proclamation, of *kerygma*. The kingdom is proclaimed in narratives whose truth is not to be measured by the standards of historiographical accuracy, of truth as correspondence or *adequatio,* for in the kingdom, the meaning of truth is *facere veritatem*. The truth of the event is a deed, something to do, to translate into the flesh of existence. To be in the truth means to be transformed by a call, to have been turned around, to have been given a new heart. The kingdom's truth, the truth of these biblical narratives, is a truth that we are called upon to make come true, to realize, *facere veritatem,* not the truth of a record or a journal kept by eyewitnesses of magical events transpiring in the world, in being, *in re*. The narratives of the New Testament are more true, not less true, because their truth is beyond the truth of correspondence. Truth is not a correspondence with being but its parabolic intensification beyond being's achievements.

Jesus does not merely tell parables; he *is* a parable,[23] forged by the followers of "the way" who linked onto the event of which he was the locus. That is how and why he can walk on water or pass through solid walls, call Lazarus out of his grave, cleanse lepers, and straighten the lame and how he came eventually to have a virgin birth, having come down from a heavenly dwelling to be born in an earthly womb. The kingdom of God is like that, like Jesus, who gives the kingdom body and blood. The kingdom of God releases us from evil the way Jesus releases paralyzed limbs, the way he released his executioners on the cross. Dead bodies rise, substances are transmuted, impermeable walls are permeated. But none of this is to be confused with a strong force, with the power of a super-being or a super-hero to bend natural forces to his almighty will with a display of awe-inspiring power. In such deadening literalism, God becomes the ultimate laser show at Disneyworld, an exercise in world-weary fantasizing that, when we awake from our reveries, leaves us face to face with the grim visage of ineluctable reality, with the dead bodies of the tsunami or the victims of ethnic cleansing. The kingdom narratives are meant to hold up to us the possibility of the impossible, the possibility to be otherwise than being. The power of the kingdom is the powerless power to melt hearts that have hardened, to keep hope alive when life is hopeless, to revive the spirits of the dispirited and the despairing, to pray for something otherwise than the world that is closing in around us on every side, to pray for the possibility of something coming, in short, in a paradigmatically religious expression, the possibility of the impossible (Derrida), for with God all things are possible (Luke 1:37), one of the most fetching short circuits of all!

Death is turned into life, not by a power that overpowers things, like the God of omnipotence-theology, but by the power of powerlessness. The kingdom is a field of weak forces, like forgiveness, which does not trade force for force and thereby feed the cycle of retaliation, or like the kiss with which Jesus subdues the Grand Inquisitor after the Cardinal makes a great show of how much power he has over Jesus in *The Brothers Karamazov.* Like the lilies of the field, which neither sow nor reap; like the dead, deprived of all power and agency, whose dangerous memory constitutes an infinite provocation; above all, like Jesus' own death, around which the weak forces of the kingdom are galvanized.

The opposite of a sacred anarchy is the profane order that the New Testament calls the "world," whose forces conspire to prevent the event. The profanity of the world is the business-as-usual of power, of a field of strong forces, in which the strong have their way with the weak, in which the weak but unconditional force of justice is a joke unless you get caught, in which everything is for sale and everything has a price, in which time is money and nothing is sacred. The world punishes the trespass—but the kingdom forgives; the world wants children to behave like the adults (not always such a good idea)—but the kingdom wants the adults to be like children; the world bars strangers or makes them present their papers—but the kingdom offers them hospitality and invites them to the wedding feast.

The kingdom is as mad as any hatter's party, but it is divinely mad.

A MAP

This contribution to a theology of the event is divided into two parts: first God, and then God's kingdom; first the divine *anarche* and then the anarchic kingdom that issues from the exposure of the world to the divine *anarche;* first the weak force of God, then the mad and scrambled character of the kingdom where the power of powerlessness reigns.[24]

In Part One, I mount as strong an argument as I can on behalf of the weakness of God, starting with an account of God and creation, which is also where Thomas Aquinas began his more orthodox, stronger, and more straight-up sort of *Summa Theologica.* In chapter 1, which runs together Paul's idea of the weakness of God with Derrida's idea of something "unconditional without sovereignty," I form the notion of God as a weak force that lays claim to us unconditionally but has no army to enforce its claims. Since the bipolarity that I constantly attribute to rouged theology shows up in St. Paul's account of what he calls the "logos of the cross," his brilliant discourse on weakness that is also clearly in the service of power, I then clarify my use and abuse of St. Paul (chapter 2).

I spend the next two chapters trying to recover from the knee-bending blow of the perfectly obvious objection that God is, on the orthodox accounting, the Father Almighty, Creator of Heaven and Earth, *ex nihilo, om-*

nipotens deus. Here I try to establish a beachhead for a theology of the event by finding an alternate reading of the doctrine of creation which, in the Scriptures, is nothing exnihilatory at all, but very much a matter of Elohim giving life and fruitfulness to preexisting but barren elements. I hold that the Genesis account does not presume later ideas of divine omniscience or omnipotence, here entering into dialogue with the groundbreaking theology of creation to be found in Catherine Keller's *Face of the Deep.*[25] I am not trying to dodge but to redescribe the idea of creation and re-creation, of making all things new and fruitful, and to insist that creation is a risk, for God as well as for us, albeit a beautiful risk, as Levinas says.

Given theology's inveterate confusion of weak forces with strong ones, it is important to keep an eye on the methodological issues, which I do during a kind of hermeneutical interlude between Parts One and Two. Here I introduce what might be regarded as the two hermeneutic keys to the kingdom that we are about to enter. First, I pose the idea of a "poetics of the impossible" (baldly borrowed from deconstruction), which describes how things happen in the narratival space of the kingdom, as distinguished from a "logic of omnipotence," which belongs to strong metaphysical theology (chapter 5). Next I spell out the "hermeneutical situation" of this book in terms of a "hermeneutics of the call" (chapter 6), which turns on what I call the "reduction to the call," that is, the disconnecting of the order of presence and power in order to take the name of God as a provocation or a call without causality. While my faith in the possibility of the impossible is not to be confused with giving credence to thaumaturgy or magic, still my de-literalizing reduction is not a diminution but a magnification, a releasing of the event in the full range of its genuine effects. Weak theology is neither magical realism nor cynical anti-realism but a "hyper-realism of the event," a little Magnificat I offer after Gabriel announces the impossible.

In Part Two I get down to details about the kingdom of God, down to its nuts and bolts—or rather to its lilies of the fields and its birds of the air—moving from the event of God as a weak force to the blessed events effected in God's name. Now one of the sub-arguments that circulates throughout this text is a certain thesis I am maintaining about prayer: that prayer is not the private property of the faithful but a common passion, indeed, the common lot of us all, for we are all praying and weeping for the coming of something, even if, especially if, we know not what, which leaves us praying to be able to pray. The Lord's Prayer, which prays for the coming of the kingdom, is particularly close to my heart. Thus, the second half of this study may be viewed as a kind of Franco-American gloss on the *pater noster,* filled with lost postcards and unscientific postscripts that together make up a loose and running commentary on the Lord's Prayer, a venerable medieval tradition toward which I dare to make my own weak theological contribution. (I refuse to grant the Radical Orthodoxists exclusive rights to the Latin liturgy, even though they have the advantage over me in vestments, hymnals, and candles.)

I kick off this unscientific, short-circuiting quasi-commentary on the Lord's Prayer in chapter 7 with what I call "metanoetics," by which I mean the utter transformability that transfixes things by exposing the "world" to the call for the coming of the "kingdom." In a kingdom of events, everything turns or overturns on *metanoia,* to which, following Hannah Arendt, I give the more upbeat translation "being of a new heart" (leaving "repentance" to the Baptist editions), which is just the sort of thing we are praying for when we pray to the *Abba* to let the kingdom come, which means to let the event happen. In chapter 8 I take up the model of the lilies of the field, whose model trust in God sees them through the day, or the birds of the air, who neither sow nor reap, which I call "quotidianism," the special time they keep in the kingdom. This is an impossible model, of course, because nothing is more certain in this post-Edenic *quid pro quo* world of ours than that we must sow in order to reap, that there is no free lunch. At the end of this discussion, I face the problem of what it means to trust in the rule of God if we have also delimited the power of God.

Chapters 9 and 10 have to do with forgiveness, a theme to which I return repeatedly in several chapters, and one of the most topsy-turvy events in the kingdom. Chapter 9 is devoted to an excursion into the history of metaphysical theology and to the figure of Peter Damian, whose argument that God's power is such that God could change the past, were God so minded, is a kind of fascinating limit case of the bipolarity of theology. Peter Damian represents the other side of attributing the power of *creatio ex nihilo* to God, namely, the converse power of *reductio ad nihilum.* While dramatically underlining the sense of time and transformability in the kingdom—what more effective way to be forgiven our trespasses than to have the trespass entirely wiped away?—Damian is also, tellingly, a fierce authoritarian who coined the word *sodomy,* an ominously Foucauldian gesture (constituting what it wants to condemn). In chapter 10 I take up the more sensible idea that in the event of forgiveness the past trespass is not wiped out but is left standing *sous rature* with a new meaning as "forgiven." Turning to Jesus, who consorted with sinners and told them they were forgiven, I ask whether Jesus was teaching the traditional theory of *teshuvah* or an idea of *teshuvah* with an anarchic twist, a radical and unconditional forgiveness that helped buy Jesus trouble from the powers that be, who suspected that he was an anarchist (they were right).

If we have conceded a certain powerlessness in God, how is it possible to be "saved" and what would being saved even mean? Here (chapter 11) I take my point of departure from the story of the raising of Lazarus read, not as an exercise in a magical resuscitation of a corpse, but as an event, as a story of rebirth and resurrection in the sense of the giving of a new time (you see the bite my "reduction to the event" has), of being saved from irreparably ruined time but not of being saved *from time*. Chapters 10 and 11 also turn to evil, which is an "event" that is not good news, asking how we can be released both from the evil that we do (forgiveness) and from the evil that befalls us (salvation).

In chapter 12 I raise the question of the hospitality of the kingdom of God—who gets in and who gets left out. Of course, the results are delightfully anarchical: the insiders are out and the outsiders are given pride of place, as in the story of the wedding feast, a gathering that is as mad as any hatter's party imagined by Lewis Carroll (a Deleuzian comparison I do not hesitate to use several times in this book). I am interested in displacing distinctions between believer and infidel, theist and atheist, the subscriber to a particular confession and everybody else. We are all in this weak theology together, all exposed to the event under whatever name, all afloat on rafts large and small in an endless sea, all wondering who we are and what is what and who is calling and what is being called for in the name of God.

I conclude—and what could be more fitting?—with a prayer: for theology, for the truth of theology, for the truth of the event, which is also a prayer for prayer itself. By the "truth of the event" I mean the cold truth, the truth we have to be bold enough to face, which is the open-ended, uncertain, and unforeseeable future of the event. I am praying with both hands: with my right hand, making a passionate profession of the name of God, of the unhinging and uncontainable event that makes the world tremble with possibility; with my left hand, making a confession that is also a concession of the name of God, preparing for the possibility that we must surrender the name of God itself. For if this name harbors an unforeseeable future, what is to ensure that the event that is coming will go, or come, under the name of God? In the end, I hold, the truth of the event is not a name but a deed.

So let us have the heart to ask, What is being called for when we call out, when we say and pray the name of God? What are we calling up when we call for the coming of God's kingdom? Are we asking for more trouble than we can handle?

Part One

THE WEAKNESS
OF GOD

ONE

God without Sovereignty

> Nothing is less sure, of course,
> than a god without sovereignty,
> nothing is less sure than his coming, of course.
> (Jacques Derrida)[1]

> For God's foolishness is wiser than human wisdom,
> and God's weakness is stronger than human strength . . .
> But God chose what is weak in the world to shame the strong;
> God chose what is low and despised [*ta agene*] in the world,
> things that are not [*ta me onta*],
> to reduce to nothing things that are [*ta onta*].
> (1 Cor. 1:25, 27–28)

All this talk about the stirring of the event within the name of God should not stir up expectations of power. On the contrary, precisely insofar as it is the locus of an event, and not the nominator of an entity, the name of God indicates a certain weak force, at most a power of powerlessness, even though it is addressed to us in unconditional terms. Let us venture further down this risky road.

Suppose we dare to think about God otherwise than metaphysics and metaphysical theology allow? Suppose we say there is at least this much to the death of God: that the God of metaphysical theology is a God well lost and that the task of thinking about God radically otherwise has been inescapably imposed upon us? Suppose we say that metaphysical theology has been given enough time to prove its case and that the time has come to think about God in some other way? What then?

Might it be that God, contrary to the hopes and expectations of theology (not to mention of His Reverence, who depends upon God to earn a living), that there is indeed something "unconditional" about God, but that

God is not a sovereign power? Accordingly, might any possible "kingdom" of God turn out to be an unlikely kingdom without a sovereign or a royal army, where those who are strong are weak, and those who are weak are strong—in short, a land where reversals more wondrous than anything Alice ever imagined transpire?

That at least is the present hypothesis and the modest premise of the following little experiment.

DIFFÉRANCE, EVENT, AND A KINGDOM
WITHOUT KINGDOM

I will speak, then, of God, theology's most famous protagonist. But to do so, I will first call upon the help of *différance*, philosophy's most famous misspelling. Here I commence my little experiment in short-circuiting, of reading a strong and major voice—and what could outrank the name of God, the Logos itself?—by wiring it up to a minor one—and what is more measly, weak, and minor than a mere misspelling?

Différance is a word Derrida uses to describe the general condition that besets us all, believers and nonbelievers alike—"nonbelievers" simply being people who believe something different than the "believers"—in virtue of which we must all make our way by way of the differential spacing of signifiers. Boy/toy/joy, king/ring/sing, and so forth, produce the significant effect they do by reason of the differential spacing, either phonic or graphic, of these signifiers. Whether you say king or *roi* does not matter so much as whether, inside the language game you are playing, the rest of us can discern the difference (or the "space between") king/sing or *roi/loi*. In general, this sort of thing holds, *mutatis mutandis,* not only for linguistic signifiers but also for the concepts they signify, and more generally still for the whole range of our beliefs and practices, cultural and institutional, all of which come under and are structured by this differential spacing.

The difference between Derrida and the structuralists who proceeded him is that the structuralists took these signifying chains to be rigorously systematic and rule-governed, while Derrida—this is what the name "Derrida" first meant in the 1960s and 1970s—argued that these chains formed, not closed formalizable systems, but open-ended, uncompletable networks, like the contemporary Internet, in which any element could link on anywhere with some other element and in that fashion spread endlessly and "rhizomatically" (like crabgrass) across the surface. One could no more get to the end of these chains than one could point and click on every link in the virtual space of the World Wide Web. Sustaining such claims entails a lengthy argument that is not my current business.[2] Suffice it to say that by defending the idea of *différance,* Derrida meant to say that we make sense

under conditions that threaten to undo the sense we make, and that our beliefs and practices enjoy only a provisional unity and tentative stability that
is in principle liable to unravel at the most inconvenient times. I think Derrida is right about this. From a religious point of view, I think this does not
undermine faith but explains precisely why we need faith, we believers and
nonbelievers (or believers-otherwise) alike, and why in every believer there
is a bit of an unbeliever (and conversely). In the reflections that follow I will
not pursue Derrida's earlier articulation of *différance* but its ethico-politico-
religious implications in his later writings. *Différance,* we might say to Alice,
is not so much the "foundation" as the *agent provocateur* for everything that
follows in this wonderful upside-down land.

Différance* is a seemingly secular word[3]—actually, it is the quasi-tran-
scendental condition of possibility for distinguishing "secular/sacred," or
"theism/atheism," constituting the slash between them—coined for a secular philosophical world by a philosopher who says of himself "I quite rightly pass for an atheist."[4] Still, for reasons that I hope to spell out here, God
and this misspelling *différance* keep up what must seem to many of the
Saved and Righteous an unholy communication with each other, which
Derrida seems not to have intended but with which he has constantly had
to deal. Many years ago, in the famous essay *"Différance,"* Derrida said that
différance "everywhere comes to solicit, in the sense that *sollicitare,* in old
Latin, means to shake as a whole, to make tremble in entirety." For that reason, he went on to say, *différance* should not be construed as some sort of
primum ens sent into the world to set things straight, some principle of
order and governance:

> It governs nothing, reigns over nothing, and nowhere exercises any author-
> ity. It is not announced by any capital letter. Not only is there no kingdom
> of *différance,* but *différance* instigates the subversion of every kingdom.
> Which makes it obviously threatening and infallibly dreaded by everything
> within us that desires a kingdom, the past or future presence of a kingdom.
> And it is always in the name of a kingdom that one may reproach *différance*
> with wishing to reign, believing that one sees it aggrandize itself with a capi-
> tal letter.[5]

In other words, although many of its admirers have come to expect quite a
lot of it, *différance* is not our Redeemer, and it does not set up court in
something like a kingdom of God, constituting as it does, not a strong
steely framework of hard structures, but a looser assembling of weaker,
more watery ensembles. So, far from having the status of God or a king, of
any sort of *arche,* divine or otherwise, far from being a prince, a principle,
or a *principium,* empirical or transcendental, that orders and stabilizes, *dif-*

férance is, if not downright disorderly, slightly subversive of such orderliness inasmuch as it exposes the contingency of any constituted order. Its "natural" tendency, if it had a nature, is to destabilize stable natures, not by an active assault, but by seeing to it that the warp and woof of every woven fabric (text) is marked by unravelability. Not only is there no *royaume de différance,* the very idea of *différance,* if it is an idea, is the idea of no more reigning, no more sovereigns, no more kingdoms, not now, not ever. *Différance* is the very idea of instigating the subversion of kingdoms wherever they appear.

Unless, of course, in the best spirit of deconstruction—and the very idea of deconstruction is that there is always, structurally, a "but" or an "unless" or a "perhaps"—one might speak, in all perversity, of the possibility of a kingdom of the kingdom-less, a kingdom where there is no sovereignty and no one reigns—or if they do, they have no power—an un-kingly, anarchic kingdom, a kingdom where the only power that is permitted is the power of powerlessness, where the very condition of power is that it be without power.

Damnable deconstructive trickery, sheer relativistic and nihilistic wordplay, thunders His (Right) Reverence from the pulpit! Yes, of course, no doubt. But unfortunately for the defenders of the True and the Good, I am practically quoting an apostle, verbatim, in a revelatory document that is one of deconstruction's first epiphanies on earth. The apostle dares to speak of the "weakness of God" *(asthenes tou theou),* where God chose the weak to confound the strong and the things that are not to reduce to nothing the powers that be (1 Cor. 1:27–29). When the Roman soldiers mocked the so-called "king of the Jews," telling him to come down from the cross, the irony was instead visited on them. To speak of a "kingdom" in a case like that would indeed be an irony, but one in which a mighty kingdom like the Roman Empire was being mocked by declaring a bedraggled bunch of low-born and powerless people a "kingdom." If this is a kingdom, it is not the sort the world is used to seeing. That is the possibility that interests me in these pages, to identify such a reign of powerlessness, drawing upon several spirits—of St. Paul and Derrida, of the Gospels and of what Derrida has recently been calling the structure of something, God, for example, that is "unconditional" but "without sovereignty," all in the name of God's kingdom come and of the "democracy to come,"[6] which suggests, as political principles go, a slightly anarchical *arche,* an *arche* without *arche.* This link between Paul and Derrida, between deconstruction and First Corinthians, a scandal to the faithful and a stumbling block to the deconstructors, is a central point in this study, to which I will return shortly.

So the first ingredient in my heretical experiment is this anarchico-deconstructive idea (which humbly seeks the protection of an apostle!), which seems to be internally tensed and torn apart from within, a kingdom *without* kingdom, a kingdom without sovereignty, where there is no capital city and where the only rule is the rule of the unruly, of the weak and foolish. Here I am applying the theorem of the *sans* in Derrida, that you get the best results with our favorite words, not by unleashing their full semantic force, which will eventually send them crashing into a wall, but by maintaining them in their weak mode, their weak force, by striking them through but not quite altogether effacing them—as in religion *without* religion, community *without* community, and so forth, a formula that, like every formula, requires a bit of art and would be degraded were we to repeat it by rote or formulaically.

To be sure, by advocating *différance* Derrida does not advocate outright chaos. He does not favor a simple-minded street-corner anarchy (nothing is ever simple) that would let lawlessness sweep over the land, although that is just what his most simplistic and anxious critics take him to say. For that would amount to nothing more than a simple counter-kingdom, a reign of lawlessness, where lawlessness and unchecked violence rule. Just like a simple totalitarianism, which is simply violent in the opposite way, a simple anarchy would break the tension between the *arche* and the *an-arche,* erasing the slash between power and powerlessness; pure life would spell death. The power of powerlessness is neither pure power nor pure powerlessness. That is why, twenty years later, in "Force of Law," Derrida made it plain that deconstruction is not a matter of leveling laws in order to produce a lawless society, but of deconstructing laws in order to produce a just society.[7] To deconstruct the law means to "negotiate the difference" between the law and justice, where the law is thought to be something finite, and "justice" calls up an uncontainable event, an infinite or unconditional or undeconstructible demand. Deconstruction is—this is the spin I am giving it in these pages—a negotiation undertaken between a conditioned name and an unconditional event. To deconstruct the law is to hold the constructedness of the law plainly and constantly in view so as to subject the law to relentless analysis, revision, and repeal, to rewriting and judicial review, in the light of the unconditional demand of justice. To feel the sharp tip of what deconstructing the law means, imagine if some relativistic deconstructor somewhere were reckless enough to say that the law concerns the ninety-nine, while justice goes off in search of the missing one! Of course, in virtue of *différance,* even *justice* is a coded, conditioned word, in whose name much innocent blood has been spilled. No name is safe.

When something is said to be "deconstructible," then, contrary to the received view, that is not bad news—in fact, if Derrida were of a more evangelical frame of mind, he might even call it (the) "good news"—for that means it has flexibility and a future, and it will not be allowed to harden over. To deconstruct something, in the terms I am using in this study, is to release the event that is harbored by a name, to see to it that the *event* is not trapped by the *name*. The deconstruction of the law is made possible by the structural and necessary gap between the name of the law, which is constructed, and the event of justice, which is undeconstructible, between the law, which is conditioned, and the event of justice, which is an unconditional demand. Deconstruction resists the closure of the law in the name of the event that laws close off and exclude, namely, the singularity of what Kierkegaard called the "poor existing individual."

That points to the other hybrid that I am all along cultivating, what we might dare to dub "Danish Deconstruction," by which I mean to suggest that Kierkegaard and Derrida are collaborators (co-conspirators!), an intrepid team of supplementary clerks, hilarious bookbinders, and pseudonymous agents. Kierkegaard is a kind of double agent for me, doubling back between deconstruction and St. Paul, carrying messages back and forth between Holy Scripture and devilish *écriture,* infiltrating both lines at once.[8] (For years now I have been working on an essay to be entitled "On the Difference between a Deconstructor and an Apostle.") Deconstruction, which settles itself into the gap between the singularity of the poor existing individual and the universality of the law, breeds justice, even as deconstruction is born and bred of justice; indeed, to invoke one of Derrida's most startling formulations, "deconstruction is justice." That is not an act of public narcissism, of embarrassing public self-congratulation, of idolizing one's own handiwork, but the name of an *infinite task* and of a *confession* that we live our lives on call, under the call of an unconditional claim that will not let up, day or night. Deconstructing the law means to hold the law in question, to solicit the law, to hire a radical solicitor who will make the law tremble, while always letting oneself be solicited and troubled by the event of justice that is trapped inside, by the need to let the event of justice come, to let justice flow like water over the land, to let justice rule, as they say in Prophetic Deconstruction (Amos), still another experimental hybrid on which I am at work here.[9]

But if the event of justice "rules," then, by the most rigorous semantic laws, is there not a "kingdom" of this event, a "kingdom of justice?" I mean this, not in the sense of some central sovereign ministry of justice that keeps the peace with the aid of a royal army and police force, nor in the sense of some identifiable locale where justice is factually found to obtain. I mean the rule of some sort of *unconditional summons* that justice issues, the rule of a *call* to let justice reign, of the *demand* that holds sway to stay steadily open to the call of justice, to stay tuned or on call to justice's address, to the *claim* or *appeal* that the event of justice makes on all of us. That is what I mean by an event—a summons, call, demand, claim or appeal, as well as a promise and a lure—whose structure is on display in what Derrida calls a "sovereignty without force." By this Derrida means the unconditional authority exerted by the undeconstructible event—which goes under an endlessly translatable string of names like justice, the gift, forgiveness, hospitality—which of itself lacks force or worldly power, lacks an army or an armature, the material means to enforce its will, that is, to forcibly bring about what it is calling for. Such an unroyal, unkingly power, like the power of "justice," the power of what is sounding in that word from time out of mind, lies in the majesty of its claim, which settles particularly upon the brow of the weakest and most vulnerable and most powerless. When and where that claim is heard, justice reigns. The power of powerlessness, the power of a weak force, is the force without power exerted by an unconditional claim. So then, there are kingdoms and there are kingdoms, and "kingdom" is not, in itself, altogether a "bad name,"[10] and deconstruction has not been authorized to ban this word from our vocabulary. Indeed "kingdom" is nothing in itself, apart from the differential space in which it is deployed (which is a Parisian way of saying "context," so that it depends on what's reigning). Just so long as what reigns in this kingdom is justice and not terror, and no one enjoys special royal privileges or privileged access in the corridors of power, and there is not a purple or royal robe anywhere to be found, then I will be the first to step forward and declare myself a royalist who is dreaming of a kingdom to come. May this kingdom come, *oui, oui.*

Could we not say, then, that for deconstruction the rule of justice, the reign or kingdom of justice, constitutes a world or social order in which the sails of the law are trimmed close to the winds of justice? Could there not be a "kingdom of *différance*" after all—this is just an experiment, a hypothesis I am idly, wildly, entertaining of a rainy afternoon—contrary to Derrida's most literal assertion? I would be the first to concede that this would be a very strange sort of Alice in Wonderland kind of kingdom where everything is upside down, a counter-kingdom or a kingdom set on countering the business as usual of kingdoms. Here things are governed, not by a powerful and overarching *arche,* not by a positive, princely *principium* decked out in purple that holds all things mightily in its sovereign sway, but rather the opposite. This kingdom is organized around the power of the powerless, by forces that are weak, not strong, by a sustained sensitivity for the exceptional and singular, for the different and the left out, the foreigner and the immigrant, for what Derrida called the "*voyous,*" the "rogues" that American power is harnessed to stamp out, to which the *arche* is systematically blind. Now, I ask you, would not a kingdom of rogues be something of an an-archic kingdom, a kingdom whose ear is cocked for the different, whose *Stimmung* is tuned to those who stand outside the law? Could there not be a kingdom, not of law but of justice, not of unbending rule but of the holding sway of the outlaws and the losers, the left out and the lost, of the homeless and the street people, which keeps an ear perked and an eye peeled for poor existing individuals of every stripe? Could there not be a kingdom reigned over, not by the rule of the law, but by the gratuity of grace, the graciousness of the gift, of chance, of the serendipitous, of what Derrida calls the "event"? Has anyone ever heard of such a thing, or is it simply unheard of?

Would such a kingdom as that even be possible? Or impossible? Or the possibility of the impossible? (More about such im/possibilities later.)

This kingdom of *différance* would constitute an anarchic kingdom of cast-offs and cast-outs, of the ill-born and the low-down, of everyone un-royal and unkingly, uncourtly and disreputable, a kingdom of everyone who amounts to nothing or who is nobody from the point of view of worldly power, a "kingdom of nuisances and nobodies," as John Dominic Crossan puts it, speaking of another kingdom about which more shortly.[11] In this very peculiar kingdom, everything odd and out of step would enjoy a special *strategic* favor,[12] would capture justice's anarchic heart and eye, watched over in the vigil that justice keeps for the anarchical individual who slips beneath the radar of the *arche* of the law, for the law watches out for the ninety-nine and fails to notice the one-hundredth. If the law is blind, then deconstruction takes its stand with the glance of the eye of jus-tice upon the singularity to which the law blinds itself, in the face of which the law must continually be reconfigured, which we might call, in the lan-guage of a certain Prophetico-Danish Deconstruction, the *Augen-blick* of justice's event.

With this mention of the prophetic, the sounding of the name of God can be heard off in the distance, the sounding of the Major Word we are reading through the minor voice of a misspelling in order to produce a sub-versive, odd, or hybrid hymn, or maybe a rap, that they will never be able to sing in church. Like *différance,* the prophetic is an operation of solicitation, and this because of their common commitment to *sollicitare,* to disturbing the peace, to raising hell, to troubling the tranquility of the present. In prophetic space, we are less inclined to dream of the "tranquility of order," which was Augustine's dream,[13] than of the justice that disturbs an oppres-sive order and sleepy tranquility, which is why Derrida once said that de-construction is "produced in a space where the prophets are not far away."[14] We take a "prophet" in the biblical sense, not as one who tries to the see the future, which is what the blind Greek prophet and seer has his eye on, for that would confine everything to the plane of being, to predicting the fu-ture present on the basis of present being. But a prophet belongs, not to the order of being but to the order of the event of the call, not to presence but to provocation, as one who speaks for *(prophetes)* justice, who calls for justice, who warns us about ignoring justice. The kingdom of justice calls to me, putting me in the accusative, on the spot, called on the carpet about the privileges "we" currently enjoy under the law and in the present order. In prophetic grammar, the idea is to reconstitute the "I" as a "me," under accusation, *me voici:* here I am on the receiving end of a call, called on the carpet!

According to this schema, the present order is the prevailing kingdom for which deconstruction is designed to instigate trouble. The present order is the "euphoria of liberal democracy" and the "new world order"[15]—where Disneyworld and the free market economy masquerade as the parousia—and now, after 9/11, the still more divisive world of us and them, of American "democracy" pitted against undifferentiated "terrorists," as if those were the only categories available to analyze this terrible situation and as if that were the only lesson to be drawn from that tragic day. St. Paul called for resistance to the *aion,* not to "conform to the present age" *(to aioni touto)* (Rom. 12:2). That fed Kierkegaard, who was as usual following Paul, with the line for a very good book in which he claimed that the "present age" is always under the "revolutionary" gun,[16] which means this counter-kingdom packs a revolutionary punch.[17] A prophet is a troublemaker, who speaks for justice now, in the present, which is why he usually ends up getting killed, another thing that distinguishes Jewish prophets from Greek ones. For every king (like Jeroboam), there is a prophet (like Amos) to give him grief and prick his conscience, a point that interests Jacques Ellul in his little book on anarchy; and for every prophet, there is a king to give him trouble and sometimes death.[18]

A prophet is a functionary of the event. A prophet is not someone who sees the future but someone who warns about the consequence in the future of a present evil because he senses the gap between the present state and the event of justice. So he comes to deliver the message to the king, to the powers that be, to the present age, to spread the word that "we" in the present do not want to hear, to tell us what is urgently demanded of us now, in the present, because to defer the event of justice is to deny it.[19] The prophet lets us know what we do not want to know; he troubles and solicits us, makes us tremble, decentering the "I," the *arche*/self, which has a tendency to organize everything around itself and to ensure that everything that it gives out is returned with interest. The "present age" is not a fixed date in calendar time, like Paul's Rome or the Republican Right's America, but a floating structure of human existence, a structure that, like the poor, you always have with you, that is always already in place, that permanently trembles under the stirring of the event. So the short circuit I am proposing here crosses the following wires: to the present age in Paul's letters, link the structure of the authority of "presence" and of the prestige of the present in de-construction. The spark thereby given off is the standing need of solicita-tion, that is, of deconstruction, of not conforming to the present age. The live wire of prophetico-anarcho-Danish deconstruction, which crosses four wires (= the Prophets + Paul + Kierkegaard + Derrida), is always the decon-struction of the power and prestige of what pretends to presence and would prevent the event. Do you think, when we say deconstruction is justice, that this means deconstruction has come to bring peace? No, it brings the sword!

GOD WITHOUT SOVEREIGNTY

Now I turn to God (a lifelong task), to the name of God, and to my hy-pothesis that the event that this name shelters is a weak force.

Suppose we grant all this business about a kingdom without kingdom, of disturbing the prestige of the present by means of an event—what has any of this to do with God or with a kingdom of God? Does not *différance* spell big trouble for God? Does not *différance*'s subversive misspelling spell the end of religion and the death of God? *Différance* steadfastly resists be-coming a "master word or master concept" and accordingly "blocks every relationship to theology,"[20] since the discourse on God is a discourse on the master word *par excellence,* the Lord of history and the master of the uni-verse, the royal power omnipotent. Is not God the dream of power aplenty, of omnitude and plenitude and plenipotentiarity, of exnihilatory and an-nihilatory power, "of being as presence, as parousia, as life without *dif-férance*"? And is not "theology" the very name, the very model, of the logo-centric love of presence and the effacement of the trace?[21] Can one imagine a more permanent presence or a more prestigious *ousia* or a more powerful *parousia* than the "God" under whose protection the religious powers that be huddle for protection?

Can one imagine any more sovereign power than God's? Can one imag-ine anything more supportive of the established order, anything more top-down, more entrenched in the *status quo,* anything more immobilized, ac-tualized, contented, and *nunc stans* than religion and religion's "God"? *Pro deo et patria:* is that not a lethal combination, literally a deadly, ultra-divi-sive call to arms in whose ungodly name more blood has been spilled than just about anything else we can imagine? What has founded and grounded top-down orders of sovereign power more firmly than such a "God"? Is not the very idea of God as the sovereign lord of the universe the very model after which every terrestrial sovereignty is designed? Is not the sovereign Fa-ther Almighty, Creator of Heaven and Earth, the very model of every earthly patriarchy? How often has the "reign of God" meant a sovereign

reign of theocratic terror? What has been more violent than theocracy? What more patriarchal, more hierarchical? What more authoritarian, inquisitorial, misogynistic, colonialist, militaristic, terroristic?

But suppose all this power mongering is just rouged and powdered theology?

Suppose—and this is the working hypothesis of a theology of the event—as a regular reader of essays like "*différance,*" Kierkegaard's "The Present Age," and St. Paul, we raise the possibility of a "God" who belongs, not to the fixed order of presence, but to the (dis)order of the deconstruction of presence? Suppose we abandon the top-down schema of one Father Almighty, one king to rule the land (another father), in favor of a paradigm where such sovereign power slips out of favor? Suppose we say that the event that is sheltered in the name of God does not belong to the order of power and presence, but rather withdraws from the world in order to station him or herself (Godself is the gender-neutral word, if you can get used to it) with everything that the world despises?[22] Suppose we think of God as someone who prowls the streets (a *voyou*) and disturbs the peace of what Kierkegaard called "Christendom?" Suppose we imagine God as a street person with a definite body odor, like Lord Shiva living as a beggar?[23] Suppose our thought of God is not domesticated by Sunday sermons by His Reverence or co-opted by ecstatic visions of a great military show of arms in a massive square, visions of the supereminent power of the supreme creator of heaven and earth, of the hyper-eminence of the *arche*? Suppose instead we take our lead in thinking about God from images of the most powerless remnants and marginalized bodies and nobodies, the little *me onta,* the obscure pockets and folds and hovels of the world? Suppose God most especially pitches his tent among the homeless, so that God has no place on which to lay his head?

Suppose, further, that "religion" and "theology," which are human, all too human and not to be confused with God, tend systematically, structurally, regularly to forget this, and to associate themselves with a discourse of power, which is what we mean by strong theology? Suppose that we reverse these gears and thrust theology in the direction of weakness and the disavowal of power? Suppose that the God of religion and theology, which is also our invention, might almost be defined by its prevention of the event that is sheltered by the name of God, by its oblivion of this event, so that the first step that would be required, as Meister Eckhart said, is to pray God to rid us of this God? To which we might add, "I pray God to rid us of religion," since, according to Isaiah (1:11–17), Amos (5:21–24), and Hosea (6:6), God can do *without* religion if religion means only cultic sacrifice and ritual, but not without the event of justice, which is not always what religion means,[24] a point also frequently made by Karl Barth.[25] Suppose we add the prophets to the list that Derrida composes of those who advocate a religion *without* religion and what we called a theology without theology or a weak theology? Suppose, indeed, that the event that is astir within the name of God is stationed, not on the side of the *arche* and the *principium,* or of timeless being and unchanging presence, or of the true, the good, and the beautiful, but on the side of the an-archic and subversive, as the driving force of a divine subversion? Suppose God is the prime mover unmoved not of physical movement but of justice, and that God moves not by force but by attraction, like a call, by drawing us on and luring us? Suppose the name of "God" harbors an event of solicitation, that it solicits us by being situated, not inside the churches on the high altars, but with the beggars with outstretched hands on the church steps?

Suppose God is not to be conceived as the overarching and sovereign governor of the *ordo universi,* of the *cosmos,* but as what disorders such orders, de-worlds such worlds, and subverts and polyverts such universes, all for the chaosmic ends of justice? Suppose God is not conceived as the rock-solid ground on which the onto-theo-political edifice of sovereignty is erected but is systematically associated with the different, the marginal, the outsider, the left out; with the naked ones, not the long robes in the sanctuary within; with the least among us, the destitute, the *anawim,* those who are plundered and ground under (Amos 8:4), and hence as a subversive and "revolutionary" impulse? Suppose God is to be found hidden in a subversive corner of a revolutionary age, not as the stabilizing center of the present age?

Suppose the event that is sheltered by the name of God is not identified with timeless infinite power invested in an *omnipotens deus,* but with the powerless who suffer the ravages of time? Suppose the sense of "God" is to interrupt and disrupt, to confound, contradict, and confront the established human order, the human, all too human way and sway of doing business, the authority of man over man—and over women, animals, and the earth itself—human possessiveness and dominion—to pose, in short, the contradiction of the "world"? Suppose God has no time for the hierarchical power structures that human beings impose on one another and even less time for the power of God over human beings, which is actually the power that human beings exert "in the name of God"? Suppose the event that simmers in the name of God, if it were to be written out, would read: "No God, No Master?" Suppose that God's power over human beings is limited by love and that God takes up a place beside them in their powerlessness?[26]

Suppose the idea behind the "rule of God" is not to back up human authority with a divine fist but to turn the eye of the law to the widow, the orphan, and the stranger, which is the *Augen-blick* of justice? Suppose the idea behind calling God a father is not to set up an oppressive patriarchal model of sovereign power but the relativization of worldly power: "Do not call any man on earth father, for you have one Father, and he is in heaven . . . the greatest among you must be your servant" (Matt. 23:8–12). Then repeat and update that with a sexual difference, and say that you have one mother in heaven, and for the same reason (which should make us worry about some of these mothers here on earth). Then generalize it in terms of parents and human authorities.

Suppose we associate God with disseminating tongues and deconstructing towering edifices, with confusion and profusion, the way God interrupted the plans of the Shemites (Gen. 11:1–9), who wanted to build the tower of Babel, and then disseminated their language into a profusion of mutually unintelligible tongues so that they could no longer build up a consensus, no longer construct an ideal speech community, and no longer build their transcendental tower?[27]

Suppose we stop thinking about God onto-theo-logically as *prima causa,* as some sort of ontological power plant or power source, the first mover of the motions of the firmament, as if we need God to explain why the heavens move, and onto-theo-politically as the foundation of political sovereignty, "one nation under God," the backup for the established order, and begin to think of "God" in terms of what is left out and ground under by the whole economy of causes, orders, and nations, in terms of what groans for freedom in all these establishments. Suppose "God" stands for an event that confounds, confuses, contradicts, and scandalizes this economy, these crusts of power and privilege, this order of presence, *not,* I hasten to add, in order to throw us to the wolves of lawlessness, but in order to let the lamb lie down with the wolf (Isa. 11:6), not in order to level institutions and structures, but precisely in order to open them up, to keep them just, to let justice reign? Suppose, then, the international politics that accompanies the theology of this event is a community of nations without individual sovereignty?

Suppose, when you cross the wires of *différance* with the name of God, the result is to have crossed out the name of God in order to release the event this name contains? That is a move made by Jean-Luc Marion, which he has adapted from Heidegger's crossing out of the name of Being[28] and which here, in these pages, deforms the name of God in conformity with the deforming *a* in *différance.* Suppose we do this just in order to save the name of God, saving the event sheltered by the name of God, from the God of religion and strong theology, which is an idol, a graven image, an instrument of institutional power, of moral melancholy, of top-down authoritarianism, and confessional and identitarian divisiveness? Suppose we cross out the name of God, not in the spirit of a mystical theology, where

God is the *nomen innominabile* of a *hyperousios,* or of Heideggerian *Denken,* where it signifies the mystery of the great power of Being, but in the name of a weak theology, which is composed of graffiti that defaces standard theological writing, like a body that is scratched, scarred, and defaced, marred by lines of hunger or persecution, wounded and bleeding? Suppose we imagine weak theology as a meditation upon God crossed out, cut and bruised, bleeding and bent in pain, like the crucified God of which Moltmann speaks?

Suppose we think of God, not as the *hyperousios* of negative theology, the purity of/from being *(puritas essendi),* the God of eminence and supereminence, who towers tall *beyond* being—negative theology, for all its modesty is very strong; it is the tall, strong, silent type—but as the one who lies down with nullity and insignificance, who clings steadfastly with the nothings of the world, the lowly bodies and nobodies *below* being.[29] Suppose this anarchic God is not to be found high above the seventh heaven in the realm of Neoplatonic *hyperousios,* but down below in the bowels of the earthly khoral kingdom of the *me onta*?

Suppose we imagine God, not as a prime mover unmoved, but as removed from the order of cosmic movements and cosmological explanations, removed from the onto-causal order altogether, from being, presence, power, and causality? Suppose we imagine God otherwise, not really having a seat in being at all, but below being and beings, simmering beneath the ontico-ontological difference, as the heart of a heartless world? Suppose we think of God not so much in terms of everything that we desire, which seems a little acquisitive, but in terms of everything that desires us, everything that draws us out of ourselves and calls upon us, calling from below being to what is beyond, that summons up what is best in us, that asks us to go out of our creaturely way of being and live generously, to live and love, to live and let live, to love and let love, to live by loving, unconditionally? Suppose we hold that whatever has being can come to be only under certain conditions, while the unconditional would somehow be free from being, otherwise than being, a kind of demi-being, almost like a ghost, a very holy one, no doubt, and almost nothing?

Suppose, then, in short, and contrary to the expectations of religion, mainstream theology, and the vested interests of His Reverence, the name of God harbors an event that is at best a "weak force" *(force faible),* and that the "weakness of God" is, nonetheless, the only thing that is strong enough to save us, which is why we want to save this name?

What then?

Then the wires of the "kingdom of God" would be crossed with this so-called "kingdom without kingdom" of *différance,* and we would find ourselves with just the short circuit we desired. Then we would have the sparks of anarchy on our hands, sacred sparks and a sacred anarchy. Then, instead of a great onto-theological power supply surging from on high, we would have a short circuit, where the wires of the kingdom of God, which threatens and subverts the "world" *(kosmos),* are crossed with the wires of *différance,* which threatens and subverts the order of presence. This little bit of cross wiring—a transference that is neither an *analogia fidei* nor an *analogia entis,* but at best an *analogia non-entis*—is crucial to my experiment. In the New Testament, the "world" means the holding sway of the real power of this world, the *strong force* of the power of the present age, of the *aion,* to which the weak force of the kingdom is opposed. The "world" is what really exists, whereas the kingdom *calls for* something else. The world stands for the business as usual of the powerful and privileged, the oppressive order of presence that builds wealth on the backs of the poor and the outcast, that builds privilege on the backs of the despised and the different, while the kingdom contradicts the world, which means it calls for something contrary to the world. The kingdom calls the world out, calls it what it is, and calls for something else. The kingdom belongs to a different order, a different plane, than that of being or presence. Make no mistake, there is only one world, in the sense of what Heidegger calls "being-in-the-world," but within it the kingdom and the "world" are its tensions. (We will come back to this kingdom in more detail in the second part of this study.)

THE TRANSCENDENCE OF GOD

But let us not shirk our duty and run from the paradoxes and improbabilities provoked by speaking about the "weakness of God." If God is weak, how can God still be God at all? How, for example, on such anarchical terms, can we still speak of what has always been called the "transcendence" of God?

One quite classic way to explain the transcendence of God in strong theology is to adapt the Platonic way of eminence, of the Good beyond being, the Good for which being is not good enough. God is "without being" where "without" signifies an excess beyond, not a lack, that than which nothing that is can be greater. But that is not good enough for a weak theology, because the Good in the *Republic* is the ultimate sovereign power, a king *(kurios)* in its own kingdom *(basileia),* the very knowledge of which entitles the philosopher to be a king, a real king not an ironic one, because knowledge rules.[30] The Good in the *Republic* is the most powerful and superlative power, which imposes a hierarchical order upon lower being, just in accord with the model of sovereignty, which is not what I mean by the power of powerlessness. The Good is the father of all, the *arche,*[31] the *hy-*

perousios, the hyper-being beyond being, the Godhead beyond God *(Gott-heit über Gott),* not the power of powerlessness, not the weak force of a powerless solicitation or promise or provocation. Strong theology loves the order of the *Republic,* whereas a theology of the event, as we will see, is happy down below with *khora.*

I treat God, not as an eminent omnipotent onto-power capable of leveling tall buildings and reducing his enemies (no need for gender-neutral language here) to ashes, but as the weak force of a call. If pressed by the Lord Cardinal, His Eminence the Grand Inquisitor, to say what then God "is," I would nervously defer because I prefer to say not that God "is" but that God "calls," that God promises, not from beyond being but from below, without being or sovereignty. If I were then pressed further by His Awful Eminence to say what God's transcendence is, I would again defer because I prefer to say, not that God is a transcendent super-essential hyper-being towering over other beings, but that God's transcendence is that of a call, of an address that, while arising from the hinter regions below being, lays us low. God's transcendence is a matter of the transcendence of the event that transpires in the name of God. God's transcendence means that we are laid low by a call arising from on high, but whose heights are event-ful, provocative, and arise from someone who, lacking the wherewithal to lay down his head, pitches his tent among the lowly bodies and nobodies below in the bodily bowels of hypo-being. The transcendence of God is not that of a fist that smashes, but of a Spirit who breathes, who inspires, and whose gentle breath urges us on.

God's transcendence is the power of a spirit, not of the sword. The transcendence of God is not at odds with the weak force of God; it *is* the weak force of God. Otherwise it would not be transcendence of God but the transcendence of the world, which is a strong force, one with a real army and the real power to enforce its word. The word of God, the God of the word. The promise of God, the God of the promise. If it is true that we can hardly resist God's promise, it is not less true that this irresistible force is weak—for on our premise, God can only promise.

The weak force of God is to lay *claim* upon us—*uns in Anspruch nehmen,* as Heidegger would say—but not the way a sovereign power in the domain of being invades and then lays claim to territory, overpowers its native population and plants a foreign flag, but in the way of a summons that calls and provokes, an appeal that incites or invites us, a promise that awakens our love. The name of God harbors an unconditional appeal without the sovereign force to enforce it. God is, without being, of unconditional import and the stuff of unconditional desire.

To say, as is said in strong theology, that God is the judge is to say in weak theology that it is in the *name* of God that we judge that the kingdom is hardly here, has hardly begun, is still to come, even as it is urgently required now and we cannot wait any longer. It is in the name of God that the kingdom is called for; the kingdom of God is the event that is called by the name of God. That is how God can be God. That is how to prevent the event from being trapped by the name of God. Considered in terms of the event, the issue is not so much with what name we are to call God, but what the name of God calls for, what it calls upon us to do. To live "before God" *(coram deo),* as Augustine put it so beautifully, is to live on call, under the call, always already solicited, called upon, pressed by the weak force of the call, called by the call to let the kingdom come, which is what is called *for.* Let the kingdom come, in the name of God.

God's transcendence is not to be taken onto-theo-logically as a *summum ens* towering over finite beings, nor is it to be taken onto-theo-politically as a sovereign master who supplies the paradigm for the human mastery over everything else. That is rouged theology. As Derrida says, the "unavowed theologeme" of the power politics of sovereignty is the sovereignty of God.[32] I do not think of God as some super-being who outknows, out-wills, out-does, out-powers, and out-exists every entity here below, a higher super-entity, a hyper-presence dwelling in a higher world. I do not think of God as a an omnipotent onto-theo-cosmo-logical power source for the universe, but as the unconditional demand for beneficence that shocks the world with a promise that is not kept, as the heart of a heartless world, as the call from below being that summons us to rise beyond being, beyond ourselves. I think of the world as addressed by a call, not produced by a cause, as an addressee, not an effect, and of God as a call, not a cause, as a beneficence, not a sovereign power.[33]

Another way to put all this is to say that, in my vocabulary, the world is there, being is there, and there we are, there, in the world, being right there along with the world. By "God," on the other hand, I do not mean a being who is there, an entity trapped in being, even as a super-being *up there,* up above the world, who physically powers and causes it, who made it and occasionally intervenes upon its day-to-day activities to tweak things for the better in response to a steady stream of solicitations from down below (a hurricane averted here, an illness averted there, etc.). That I consider an essentially magical view of the world. I do not mean anything that is *there,* because what is *there* belongs to the order of being and power; to the strong force of the world, where you solve problems by raising money—or an army. I mean a call that solicits and disturbs what is there, an event that adds a level of signification and meaning, of provocation and solicitation to what is there, that makes it impossible for the world, for what is *there,* to settle solidly in place, to consolidate, to close in upon itself. By the name of "God" I mean the event of this solicitation, an event of deconsolidation, an electrifying event-ing disturbance, the solvent of the weak force of this spectral spirit who haunts the world as its bad conscience, or who breathes lightly and prompts its most inspired moments, all the while readily conceding that there are other names than the name of God. I am trying to save the name of God, not absolutize it.

Whether over and beyond what we might call the hermeneutics of the event, the lived experience of the call and of being on call, there is some entitative cause calling, some entity or hyper-entity out there with a proper name, verifiable by a metaphysical argument or certifiable by a divine revelation, is no part of my hypothesis, one way or the other (for or against). I leave that stock to fluctuate on the open market of existence. I leave that question to fluctuate in that domain of undecidability wherein all concrete decisions are made, which has the effect of intensifying this decision, not attenuating it. About that decision I have no inside-trader information to pass along. About God, God alone knows. That is a matter for each poor existing individual to work out, and no part of the trouble we are buying for ourselves with this experiment. No one has authorized us to settle that question. We are not a party to that dispute. Although I have my opinions, I have not the least firsthand information to convey about that. Relative to that sort of strong decision, a theology of the event is but a prolegomenon aimed at keeping that decision out of trouble.

The trouble rouged theology buys for itself is the result of selling the body of theology to power. The very core of the mistake made by onto-theology derives from conceiving God on the horizon of being, power, and causality, as if God were a cosmic power supply. In the weak and colorless theology whose cause I am promoting, it is profane magic, thaumaturgy, to think of God as an omnipotent meteorological onto-power who could stop (or start) hurricanes, landslides, and floods, or as an omni-historical superpower who can stop or start wars or prevent holocausts and put an end to pornography, obesity, junk TV, computer spam, crime in the streets, and the ruining of the environment. When we see an athlete praying for victory in a game, blame the strong theologians, for the athlete simply makes the logic of this onto-theo-cosmo-interventionism embarrassingly visible, right on national TV, as if God were a party to a Final Four office pool.

The thoroughly onto-theological project of "theodicy," of getting God off the causal hook, whether for the vagaries of natural disasters or for the disasters caused by human vagary and malice, is no less profane. The authentically religious way to think about God, on my slightly heretical hypothesis, which keeps holy the idea of the anarchical, is in terms of the power of powerlessness, which is what I mean by the weak force of God. That is the sense described by St. Paul in First Corinthians 1 even as it picks up on what Levinas means when he says that those who are destitute and laid low come to us from on high and lay claim to us.[34] The voice of God, the Word of God, the Spirit of God, is the call that calls to us without causality, power, or prestige, calling upon what is best in us.[35]

In the end, I am just proposing a theology of the cross. That is what I will now try to show—and in the process, settle an outstanding account or two with an apostle.

TWO

St. Paul on the
Logos of the Cross

WAS JESUS HOLDING BACK?

Wherever possible, I invoke the authority of St. Paul, from whose protective cover I never stray any more than necessary. I am above all in Paul's debt for what he calls the "logos of the cross" (*logos tou staurou,* 1 Cor. 1:18), which is quite central to the idea of the weakness of God.[1] But Paul inscribes his idea of the weakness of God that is revealed in the cross in a larger economy of power—"for whenever I am weak, then I am strong" (2 Cor. 12:10) and "God's weakness is stronger than human strength" (1 Cor. 1:25)—from which I will, with fear and trembling, take my leave as circumspectly and inconspicuously as possible so as not to attract the attention of the authorities.

The strong point about weak theology is that it is a theology of the cross. In the Christian tradition, the force of the event that calls to us and overtakes us in the name of God arises crucially from the cross, where all the lines of force in Christianity intersect (cross). The life and death of Jesus are interwoven with defeat and death, and not simply death, but a humiliating public execution reserved for the worst criminals. God's mark is upon an executed man, suffering an agonizing death, taunted as a king and dressed mockingly in purple, his "kingdom" being, from Rome's point of view, a joke, which is not to say that Rome did not wish to cruelly crush it all the same. God crossed out by the cross, the kingdom of God as a kingdom of the crucified. Surely there is as much askew in an unnuanced celebration of God's power in Christian theology as there is in the gold-and-diamond-studded crucifixes worn by corpulent clerics or the luxurious life styles of the televangelists. That is so much rouged theology. The notion that Jesus could come down from the cross had he wished belongs to the unbelieving, uncomprehending Romans who taunted him, as if Jesus were a magician, whereas the genuine divinity of Jesus is revealed in his distance from this request for magic, in his helplessness, his cry of abandonment, and above all, in the words of forgiveness he utters.

Žižek is only half right to say that the perverse core of Christianity lay in Jesus' being abandoned and that what we should learn from his death on the cross is that there is no Big Other to save us, so we should get on with our lives.[2] The other half, what Žižek leaves out, is that in this abandonment there lies the weak force of God. I agree that we should not think of God as a source of magical effects or as a master manipulator of mundane powers and that in that sense we should get on with our lives. But the divinity of the truly divine God is to be displayed neither in a display of magic by Jesus or his heavenly Father, nor in the secret hope that the Father is going to square the accounts for him in an afterlife and give these Roman soldiers their comeuppance in the world to come. The divinity is rather that his very death and humiliation rise up in protest against the world, rise up above power. Under power, I include both Roman power and a God of power who has the power to intervene, as if God is like a hurricane who could descend on the scene and send the Roman soldiers hurtling through the air were he of such a mind. The perverse core of Christianity lies in being a weak force. The weak force of God is embodied in the broken body on the cross, which has thereby been broken loose from being and broken out upon the open plane of the powerlessness of God. The power of God is not pagan violence, brute power, or vulgar magic; it is the power of powerlessness, the power of the call, the power of protest that rises up from innocent suffering and calls out against it, the power that says *no* to unjust suffering, and finally, the power to suffer-with *(sym-pathos)* innocent suffering, which is perhaps the central Christian symbol.[3]

The question is, when it comes to that defining scene of the crucifixion, how Christian we are willing to be and how radical our theology of the cross will be. How genuinely, how seriously are we to take this central Christian vision? Is Jesus *really* unable to come down from the cross, or does he only *seem* to be *(dokein)*? Remember, the world is what is *there,* in all its violence and strength. Are we to think that behind this helpless mortal frame, he is holding his infinite power in check? Are we to think that he *can* come down but that he just does not want to because he is trying to make a point? Is he *really* nailed there, or is that just an appearance or semblance *(dokesis)*? Is his weakness voluntary, in which case it is a mask for strength, an even greater show of strength? In the world, there are real (Roman) nails and real (Roman) crosses and real imperial power. The Romans are the real. If the kingdom Jesus preached were a kingdom of real power, he could, by a mighty roar—nay better, by a soft word—from his mouth, spring the nails from his hands, thrust away the spears from the hands of the soldiers, heal the wounds of his flesh, and shatter the cross into a million splinters in a dazzling display of sheer might. But his kingdom did not belong to the world, to the realm of meeting power with power. His strength was the weak power of powerlessness—my God, my God, why have you abandoned me?—not the real power of the world, and so he was killed, quite against his will and against the will of his Father. But in the powerlessness of that death the word of God rose up in majesty as a word of contradiction, as the Spirit of God, as a specter, as a ghostly event that haunts us, but not as a spectacular presence.

That is God's transcendence.

On the classical account of strong theology, Jesus was just holding back his divine power in order to let his human nature suffer. He freely chose to check his power because the Father had a plan to redeem the world with his blood. But if his Father *had* changed his mind, those Roman soldiers would rue the day they were born, as they will certainly rue it in eternity. On my accounting, that is to misconstrue this scene solely in terms of power, mundane power pitted against celestial power. On my accounting, Jesus was being crucified, not holding back; he was nailed there and being executed very much against his will and the will of God. And he never heard of Christianity's novel idea that he was redeeming the world with his blood. His approach to evil was forgiveness, not paying off a debt due the Father, or the devil, with suffering or with anything else. His suffering was not a coin of the realm in the economy of the kingdom.[4] The kingdom is not an economy, and God is not in attendance at this scene as an accountant of divine debts or as a higher power watching the whole thing from up there and freely holding in check his infinite power to intervene. That is more rouged theology, weakness fantasizing about an orgasm of power—if not power now, then power later, when we can really get even with those hateful Romans. That is not the weakness of God that I am here defending. God, the event harbored by the name of God, is present at the crucifixion, as the power of the powerlessness of Jesus, in and as the protest against the injustice that rises up from the cross, in and as the words of forgiveness, not a deferred power that will be visited upon one's enemies at a later time. God is in attendance as the weak force of the call that cries out from Calvary and calls across the epochs, that cries out from every corpse created by every cruel and unjust power. The logos of the cross is a call to renounce violence, not to conceal and defer it and then, in a stunning act that takes the enemy by surprise, to lay them low with *real* power, which shows the enemy who really has the power. That is just what Nietzsche was criticizing under the name of *ressentiment*.

The effect of situating God on the side of vulnerability and unjust suffering is not, of course, to glorify suffering and misery, but to prophetically protest it, to give divine depth and meaning to resistance to unjust suffering, to attach the coefficient of divine resistance to unjust suffering, which is why suffering is the stuff of dangerous memories. The call, the cry, the plaint that rises up from the cross is a great divine "no" to injustice, an infinite lamentation over unjust suffering and innocent victims. God is with Jesus on the cross, and in standing with Jesus rather than with the imperial power of Rome, God stands with an innocent persecuted for calling the powers that be to task. The name of God is the name of a divine "no" to persecution, violence, and victimization. Accordingly, as we have just argued, God's traditional top-down "transcendence" must be reconceived in such a way that all of its resources are deployed on behalf of lowliness and the despised. The effect of speaking of God's transcendence is not to support and top off presence with a hyper-presence, but to disturb presence with difference and to allow the lowliest to rise in divine splendor.

On this scheme—and this is the point of weak theology, of the religion of an anarcho-prophetico-deconstructionist—the transcendence of "God" does not mean God towers above being as a hyper-being. Rather, God pitches his tent among beings by identifying with everything the world casts out and leaves behind. Indeed, rather than speaking of God's transcendence at all, it might be better to speak of God's in-scendence (incendiary inscendence!) or "insistence" in the world. The essence of God's transcendence lies in God's insistence. In God, essence and insistence are the same. By this I mean that God withdraws from the world's order of presence, prestige, and sovereignty in order to settle into those pockets of protest and contradiction to the world. God belongs to the air, to the call, to the spirit that inspires and aspires, that breathes justice. God settles into the recesses formed in the world by the little ones, the nothings and nobodies of the world, what Paul in First Corinthians calls *ta me onta*. I am trying to displace thinking about God as the highest and best thing that is *there* by starting to think that God is the call that *provokes* what is there, the specter that haunts what is there, the spirit that breathes over what is there.

FIRST CORINTHIANS 1: THE LOGOS
OF THE CROSS

It is precisely the soaring brilliance of Paul that has thematized the weakness of God, the scandal of God made manifest in weakness. But at the same time that Paul champions the idea of the weakness of God, he does so precisely in the service of the genuine power of God. So we need now to look at both sides of the argument and see Paul's whole view.

Paul tells the Corinthians that there are two ways to make sense of their lives, the law and wisdom, the Torah and Greek philosophy, signs and *sophia.* But, Paul argues, the first will make them slaves to its prescriptions, while the second is folly, for the wisdom of Greek philosophy is foolishness before God. So they should give up trying to make sense and follow the folly of the cross. No hard-nosed philosopher can fail to be impressed by the depth and brilliance with which Paul taunts Greek philosophy in First Corinthians, a text that belongs to his authentic corpus, unlike the speech to the philosophers that Luke stages in Acts 17:16–34. When Paul says that God chose "the things that are not *(ta me onta)* to reduce to nothing the things that are" (1 Cor. 1:28), he flies in the face of Greek philosophy on the very issue that is constitutive of it, the search for *ousia* and true being. Paul flaunts the scandal of the cross: God chose everything foolish *(moria,* moronic) to solicit the wisdom *(sophia)* of the wise, which, according to Isaiah (29:14), God means to "destroy" *(apolo),* to confound and scatter. When human rule is displaced by the rule of God, foolishness is favored over the *sophia* and *philosophia* of the present age *(aion)* (1 Cor. 1:18–20). Those whom God calls upon are not wise, not powerful, not well-born *(eugeneis):*

> God chose what is weak in the world to shame the strong; God chose what is low and despised *[ta agene]* in the world, things that are not *[ta me onta]* to reduce to nothing things that are *[ta onta].* (1 Cor. 1:27–28)

That is the key to what is called the kingdom in the Synoptics: God chose the "outsiders," the people deprived of power, wealth, education, high birth, high culture. Theirs is a "royalty" of outcasts, so that, from the point of view of the *aion,* the age or the world, the word *kingdom* is being used ironically, almost mockingly, to refer to those pockets of the despised that infect and infest the world.[5] For this is a kingdom of the low-down and lowborn, the "excluded," the very people who are precisely the victims of the world's power.

Paul's heightened sense of God's insistence in the obscure pockets of the world is the almost perfect "inversion" (Nietzsche would say, with a Greco-German sneer, while holding his nose, the *Umwertung,* the "transvaluation") of Greek *sophia* or *phronesis,* subverting, threatening the world's wisdom, making it tremble, which is why Nietzsche was so mean to Paul.[6] In contrast to Greek philosophy, the divine is not to be found in the highest, in the most brilliant and beautiful realm of being, but in the lowliest and most unsightly. Aristotle describes the man of *arete,* of "excellence," the smart, moderate man who knows what is best for himself and for the *polis* generally, a virtuous gentlemanly man of reason, that well-heeled, high-brow, aristocratic sort of chap you run across in the novels of Jane Austen or Anthony Trollope. Plantagenet Palliser has *arete* aplenty. In contrast, Paul says that God chose people who are not well-born and well-bred, who are fools from the world's point of the view, people who do not act in their own best interest, who are of "no account," no *logos, a-logos*. Things are judged, not in terms of the logic of excellence, but of what Paul calls the *"logos tou staurou"* (1:18), the message, the mad logic, the word of the cross that crosses out the logos of the world and in the process gets crucified by the world; whereas the Aristotelian *logos* means staying on top of what is going on around you, knowing how to hit the mark, and hoping to get lucky.

The Aristotelian comparison is instructive on another point: Aristotle wanted to cultivate the virtues of the mind, of the intellect or reason *(nous, logos)*. His *phronimos* "sees" something, has "insight" into the particularities of the case, whereas the Corinthians are to be bowled over, overcome, touched by the needs of one another, which is what should rule in their hearts. In the Scriptures, the "rule of God" is associated with the rule of what Aristotle called the *a-logos;* whereas for Plato and Aristotle, the *logos* is the divine part, which is what should rule, not the *alogos,* which is the part that should follow.

But Paul's solidarity with *ta me onta* (1:28) makes a mockery of the central concept in Greek philosophy.[7] Being *(to on, ousia)* has the sense of what really and truly is, what is enduringly and permanently present, as opposed to all that is fleeting and apparent. Rhetorically and conceptually associated with sun, light, and gleaming manifestation, the essence of Greek wisdom is to ascend to the element of Being and to avoid the black holes and dark corners of non-Being or the shifting sands of becoming. The wise man is wired up to Being, knows his way around what is, can perspicuously sort through what is and what is not, and can always hit the mark of what is. But the kingdom of God is populated with shadowy semi-beings, with half-real nobodies of no worldly account. By choosing "what is not" *(ta me onta),* being is short-circuited and God can "cross out" (again following Jean-Luc Marion and Heidegger) the distinction the Greeks make between being and non-being, between wisdom and foolishness. God crosses one sort of "kingdom," a worldly kingdom, a kingdom in the straightforward sense, with another paradoxical, irregular, even ironical kingdom in which the rule of everything human, all too human has been shattered.

Paul cites Isaiah, who says, as we saw above, that God "will destroy" *(apolo,* 1:19) the wisdom of the wise. In Latin, *apollumi* is *destruere, destructio.* John van Buren has suggested that Heidegger's *"Destruktion"*—of which, of course, Derrida's *"déconstruction"* is a paraphrase and translation —derives from Luther, who spoke of the need for a *destructio* (in Latin) of medieval scholasticism; and Van Buren suggests that Luther may possibly have had this citation of Isaiah from First Corinthians in mind.[8] One could, then, by a certain retrofitting, render this text of Isaiah, "I will deconstruct the wisdom of the wise." Or, more boldly still, "I will deconstruct the metaphysics of presence of the strong onto-theologians, sayeth the Lord God."

The "kingdom of God" is the contradiction of the "world" *(cosmos),* which is the order of power and privilege and self-interest, of the business as usual of those who would prevent the event. Kierkegaard could not have been more biblical and more prophetic when he insisted that Christianity stands in permanent structural opposition to this world, to the kingdom of this world, and that it is a sign of decadence in Christianity, a mark of rouged theology, to have sat down to table with the world, to have made peace with that *cosmos* upon which it is called to make war. Such an unholy compromise he called "Christen*dom,*" a word that emphasizes the worldly king*dom* of a Christian establishment, the power of a worldly *domi*nion or *domi*nation. In Christendom, the call that issues from the bent body on the cross is converted into the coin of being and presence. He could not have been more biblical than when, in *Works of Love,* he described a love that is nonexclusionary, that is not reserved for a closed circle of friends but is extended to the "neighbor," which means everyone, including our enemy, describing something more topsy-turvy than anything ever dreamt of by Alice. Kierkegaard also said that the way to contradict Christendom was simply to walk through its streets (or shopping malls) holding over one's head the New Testament, in which the call for the kingdom glows white hot, for all to read.

The kingdom of God is a kingdom of base, ill-born, powerless, despised outsiders who are null and void in the eyes of the world, dropouts measured by the world's *arche* and the present *aion,* tax collectors and prostitutes, and yet precisely for that reason the ones whom God called *(kletos)* and set apart, whom God chose, even favored, singling them out for all their singularity and exceptionality.[9] They are the people of God, and it is hard for the rich to be a part of it. What God calls for, the event that is called for in and by the name of God, is justice, *sedaqah,* breaking the rule of power and privilege, which is what the prophets announced when they call for the rule of God, a call that often costs the prophets their heads (whereas academics get tenure and endowed chairs).

ROMANS 13: ALL POWER IS FROM GOD

But we should not be misled; one needs to keep on reading and get to the second chapter of First Corinthians, for Paul's hymn to the weak and low-born, his eulogy of the weakness of God, belongs to a larger economy of power and wisdom. That is why is it always necessary to read the stronger voice of Paul via the minor voice of *différance*, to keep crossing their wires. "Yet among the mature [*teleiois*] we do speak wisdom, though it is not a wisdom of this age [*aionos*]," a "secret and hidden" wisdom (2:6). If you are ripe and mature enough and have reached a certain stage of development and perfection, you will see that this foolishness really is wisdom and this weakness really is power. Worldly weakness is a good long-term investment in real power that is not deceived by the fool's gold of worldly power. So Paul's hymn to weakness is, in the long run, a tribute to the power of God. God *makes* the wisdom of the world foolish by outfoxing the wisdom of the philosophers with faith in the foolishness of the cross. God outplays the philosophers, outsmarts them at their own game of wisdom and power, trumps them with the paradox of the cross that confuses the Jews and is a laughing stock to the philosophers. So "God's foolishness [*really*] is wiser than human wisdom [*which is not really wise*], and God's weakness [*really*] is stronger than human strength [*which is not really strong*]" (1 Cor. 1:25). So what counts in the long run is *real* power and strength, not counterfeits, and having the superior spirit (or having been given the secret) to discern the difference between the power that "is doomed to perish" (1 Cor. 2:6) and the real thing, the power that is for keeps. The faith of the Corinthians rests on the "power of God," based as it is upon a secret wisdom kept hidden from the age, a wisdom that the rulers of this world simply cannot understand, that will *appear* to be foolish to them just so long as they have not been given the spirit to understand that it is really the true wisdom, the true power. Now as a dyed-in-the-wool lover of weak theology and the weak force of the event, I am of a mind to think that the cause is ill-served if you have all along had a secret power up your sleeve. As a believer in the logos of the cross, I am inclined to think that Jesus really *was* crucified, that he could not avoid it, and that it was not part of a long-term power play.

Paul thinks of God as holding the real power, and he even thinks that this translates into investing human power with divine authority. The most famous text in this regard is Romans 13, a text that has become even a bit notorious in the light of the use that has been made of it over the last two millennia:

> Let every person be subject to the governing authorities; for there is no authority except from God, and those authorities that exist have been instituted by God. Therefore, whoever resists authority resists what God has appointed, and those who resist will incur judgment. For rulers are not a terror to good conduct but to bad. . . . For the same reason you pay taxes, for the authorities are God's servants. (Rom. 13:1–3)

However suggestive a document it may be, the New Testament does not offer a blueprint for a radical social and political philosophy. In contradiction to everything I have been saying, Paul here advocates a top-down hierarchical order that backs up the powers that be with divine authority, one that has been used by the supporters of the status quo ever since Constantine put Christians in the driver's seat. That is why Derrida thinks an unavowed theologeme lurks in national sovereignty.

Various things can be said on behalf of Paul in this text, chief among them Günther Bornkamm's point that it was probably ad hoc advice given to the Christians at Rome to keep a low profile in the wake of the earlier expulsion of the Jews from Rome (49 C.E.). Paul is not trying to formulate a general theory of church and state, especially since he thinks that the second coming is around the corner and that with states we have no lasting cities.[10] Of course, that did not prevent this from becoming the dominant interpretation of the text once the Christians got the power. Paul is also telling authorities to behave in a manner that reflects their divine authority. Finally, the text is framed before and afterward by the primacy of love, so Paul might even be saying that though we do not love the authorities, we should at least respect them.

Be that as it may, I think there is a tendency in the New Testament to separate the real freedom of the children of God as an inner reality from the external world. As Thomas Ogletree argues, the egalitarian radicalism of the New Testament communities was more of an internal affair of the community of faith, while the surrounding social and political structures were taken as more or less given and beyond their pale.[11] There may indeed be neither Greek nor Jew, male nor female, master nor slave, in the inner sphere of the spirit, but that has nothing to do with inciting rebellion against real laws that enslave actual men and women. Paul was a Roman citizen and proud of it, and he had no brief about Roman power. His work as an apostle did not amount to resisting it, if only because he thought it was all about to end anyway. But we should not be led by texts like these into a two-worlds theory in which a sacred circle of beautiful souls saves itself while letting the real world circle the drain.[12] To the extent that such a notion is present in the New Testament, and I do not deny it is there, it is a mistake.

So on that point, I think we need to push the authors of the New Testament beyond themselves and make them a little more true to their vision. For after all, what Paul says here does not square well with the other things he says—he had just gotten done telling us not to conform to the present age (Rom. 12:2)—or with his own defiant practices that regularly landed him in jail or started a riot or both. Paul routinely put up stiff "resistance" to authorities, whom he clearly did not regard as expressing the will of God whenever they interfered with his right to do what he was called to do, the work of an apostle to preach the gospel. As to those interpretations of Romans 13:1–3 that conclude that he means that we should only obey just mandates (the ones we agree with), not unjust ones (the ones we don't agree with), or with the interpretations of Barth and Ellul, which stress the relativization of human authority, I wish them well and I will pray for their success.[13] I myself am inclined to treat Romans 13 as at best an *ignoratio elenchii,* an argument that, even if you concede it starts out well (which I do not), draws the wrong conclusion.[14] From the fact that there is no authority but God's, it follows, not that all human authorities are divinely appointed, but that all human authorities are contingent and relative, that they have only what Derrida calls a certain "mystical force," the force that comes from the fragile fact that they are there and that they assert themselves (like cartoon characters who walk off a cliff but do not fall until they notice that nothing is holding them up). Beyond their mystical force, nothing deep holds them up; no divine or hyper-presence undergirds their presence. The lack of archical depth is indeed one of the principal planks of my anarchical ark, *pace* Romans 13. Laws are always deconstructible, but justice in itself, if there is such a thing, is not deconstructible. The way to justice—justice/Yahweh: "you that seek justice, you that seek the Lord" (Isa. 51:1)—is to insist upon the pliability and relativity of the law, which, *pace* Romans 13, should never be confused with the authority of God, who calls for justice.

To be sure, on the point of paying taxes, Paul is repeating what Jesus said (in Mark). In part, I think that Jesus was, as usual, making a clever riposte to whoever was trying to trap him (I doubt it was the Pharisees—that sounds like a later Christian slander of the Jews). But I also concede that when Jesus said, "Render to Caesar the things that are Caesar's, and to God the things that are God's," he may well have meant that the children of Israel should keep themselves pure as an internal community of the circumcised while outwardly conforming to the ways of the world, which are beyond repair. If so, that is one of the human limitations of Jesus' views. The best I can do is to try to hear the double bind here: even while conceding the world's arche, we must always refuse the totalizing grip of the world, always find room to resist, always understand that there is something that shatters the horizon of the world. There is no simple exterior to the world, and for the most part you have to pay your taxes. We need apostles on the outside, at their computers, not in jail. But it could well be a good idea once in a while not to pay your taxes and to tell Caesar what he can do with his taxes and then to go to jail—like Martin Luther King or Nelson Mandela or Dietrich Bonhoeffer or for that matter Paul himself—in the name of the very kingdom that Jesus announced.

However you read what Mark has Jesus say about Caesar, it would be a mistake to conclude that it provides a basis for a wholesale withdrawing from political engagement, or that it undermines the need to offer resistance to unjust political power. I steadfastly oppose a two-worlds theory, in which the kingdom of God is one thing and the world is something entirely separate to be left to itself to run its bloody course. That may well have been the way the first Christians thought, especially if they thought that the second coming, and hence the end of the world, was coming soon. But we can have nothing to do with such unworldliness. The kingdom is the salt of the earth, the leaven of the world's bread—and you only need a little leavening to make the whole bread rise—the outside that insists and insinuates itself inside the world and saves the world from itself. Everything that Jesus did say about the kingdom of God during his short life, and everything about his death, cries out for the remedy of the social injustices that systematically efface the image of his kingdom; everything he said cries out for a translation into a social and political actuality. When Jesus said, "Do not call any man on earth father, for you have one Father, and he is in heaven . . . the greatest among you must be your servant" (Matt. 23:8–12), he was clearly teaching the relativization of worldly power and of earthly patriarchy.

There is certainly nothing in what Jesus said or did to suggest that he thought the Roman occupiers were divinely appointed to exploit the Jews (although the prophets sometimes thought the "nations" were assigned that task as a punishment for the sins of the Jews).[15] If Jesus did not think that the high priests of the temple were divine appointees who should not be subverted, it is hard to imagine that he could have thought the bloodthirsty rulers of the Roman Empire who occupied his land were divine appointees, even if he did think they were a given and immovable fact of life. Jesus was not a Zealot, and he appears to have shown no interest in overthrowing the Roman occupation; but he did overthrow the money-changers' tables in the temple, and he did offer a revolutionary view of the kingdom of God:

> I came to bring fire to the earth. And how I wish it were already kindled! . . .
> Do you think that I have come to bring peace to the earth? No, I tell you,
> but rather division! (Luke 12:49–51)

In the world in which Jesus moved about and that he took as his field of action, the "system" was for him, as for Jeremiah (7:4), embodied in the temple—and when Jesus attacked the temple, he was quickly killed. As Daniel Maguire writes:

He [Jesus] was fussing with the system, and scholars now think he may have been killed within hours of his attack on the temple. Jesus was attacking the law and order that preserves unjust privileges and exploitative social arrangements. Had he and Jeremiah contented themselves with urging private charity and a depoliticized piety, they could have died in their beds at a ripe old age. Neither did, because they were prophets of Israel and agents of the subversive reign of God.[16]

But beyond an *ignoratio elenchi,* an argument that starts out well but draws the wrong conclusion, I do not think that Romans 13 even starts out well. For while it may not follow logically, it is very tempting psychologically to transfer the authoritative power of God to worldly authority, to pass from the paradigm of the celestial sovereignty of the "Father" in heaven to the terrestrial sovereignty of earthly fathers. It is not enough to relativize temporal sovereignty while maintaining divine sovereignty. The problem lies with the paradigm of sovereignty itself, with conceiving of God in terms of sovereign power and authority.

A more radical conception of the weakness of God, of the weak force of God, of the sort we cultivate in a theology of the event, would cling more tenaciously than does Paul to the power of powerlessness, and it would find in the name of God the event of an unconditional appeal, a word or a call that lays claim to us unconditionally but without sovereign power. Not all "power and authority" *(exousia),* but every unconditional appeal is from God, and no authority may be rightfully exercised except in response to the call for justice for the least among us. In a theology of the event, we cling more tenaciously to the tenuous structure of the call and to the response elicited by this call, which is its best and only testimony. God is taken to be, not the reason things are *there* or the cause that makes them *happen* or the power supply that can intervene when things go wrong, but the reason that they are or can be *good,* the verdict or judgment reached by Elohim when he concludes that what he has made is good, very good.

The name of God, the word of God, the event that is astir in this name, is the *call* to goodness, beyond or below or without being. God is an event, not in the order of power or being, but in the order of the good, the order of the order or command or call or appeal for the good, which calls for the good even when, especially when, things are going badly. The rule of God, the kingdom of God, are names for the solicitation by which we are visited and which regularly disturbs the world with a word from afar. The word issues from the lowliest and least likely places, from the nothings and nobodies, and above all, for Paul, from the abject and crucified body on a Roman cross. The more radical conception of the rule of God and the power of

God is to say that the power of God is embodied in the helpless body whose flesh is nailed to the cross. A theology of the event, which takes the form of a weak theology, takes its lead from the *logos tou starou*.

But to do so *without* pulling a power play, *without* adding that if you have been given the Spirit to discern the Secret Word, you will know that this is Really-the-Royal-Road-to-Real-Power, that the cross belongs to a long-term economy in which God is going to show us all who *really* has the power around here. That is not the foolishness of the kingdom of God. That's just smart, and no mundane power broker, no bait-and-switch marketer, no stockbroker of the finite, could fail to be impressed by such a powerful and cunning use of weakness.

THREE

The Beautiful Risk of Creation:
On Genesis ad literam *(Almost)*

> Twenty-six attempts preceded the present genesis,
> all of which were destined to fail.
> The world of man has arisen out of the chaotic heart
> of the preceding debris; he too is exposed
> to the risk of failure, and the return to nothing.
> 'Let us hope it works' *(Halway Sheyaamod)*
> exclaimed God as he created the world,
> and this hope, which has accompanied the subsequent history
> of the world and mankind, has emphasized
> right from the outset that this history is
> branded with the mark of radical uncertainty. (Talmud)[1]

With the mention of the majestic words of Elohim presiding over creation in the opening verse of Genesis, I raise a touchy subject. For truth to tell, while all this talk about a sacred anarchy or the "weak force of God" may have an appeal to a select few party radicals, it is not a proposal likely to win mainstream votes in a general election. So I cannot proceed without first dealing with a problem that threatens to inundate me before my campaign is barely started. For one of the most powerful images in Western literature, one of the most archical ideas in the cultures of the great monotheisms, one of the most memorable verses in world literature for anyone who can read, or who can look up at the ceiling of the Sistine Chapel, undoubtedly the greatest show of sheer force in the history of everything, the most hierarchical, patriarchal exercise of pure omnipotence ever thought up, in comparison with which everything else, biblical miracles included, is small potatoes indeed, is surely the majestic opening verses of Genesis: "In the beginning *(en arche),* God created heaven and earth."

Out of nothing, simple as that. Where there was nothing, now there is something—nay, everything. In an instant, the first one, which he also created. Sheer, clean, lean, perfect, stunning, uninhibited power. Absolute archical omni-power, perfect sovereign power, pure and simple. *Fiat!*

How in heaven's name could my poor hypothesis of a "sacred anarchy" and the "weak force" of God stand up to that? Is not my modest proposal of a theology of the event shown the door, ignominiously driven out of town, disgraced and discredited, by this mighty display of cosmic power on the part of the Father Almighty, Creator of Heaven and Earth?

That is the biblical music I must face, in fear and trembling, to say the least, knowing full well that if the election were held today, I wouldn't stand a chance. In the process I will, from lack of imagination, try the same old trick, still another short circuit or sacred double cross. This time I will run a deconstructive current through the book of Genesis, in order to double-read or overload or short-circuit the creation narrative(s). I will call up Derrida's analysis of "*khora.*" "Khora," says Derrida, "before the 'world,' before creation, before the gift and being—and *khora* which *there is* perhaps 'before' every '*il y a*' as '*es gibt.*'"[2] If I succeed in crossing Derrida's *khora* (itself the result of his rewiring of Plato's *Timaeus*) with the book of Genesis, *khora* will get a biblical or quasi-biblical touch, and Genesis will look a little khoral.

I have never denied that a dominant drift of the name of God, one event that can dominate other events whenever this name is heard, is the event of power. Indeed, that is part of my hypothesis about the bipolarity of theology. But the drift of my rereading of Genesis will be to show that even in the creation narratives, where there is power aplenty, things are not all that they seem, and there is room for me to pitch the tent of my little hypothesis about the weak force of God, which is, if not the centerpiece, at least the crucially decentering and disruptive short circuit of a theology of the event.

TOHU WA-BOHU AND TEHOM

Let us read slowly, even literally, for while I have no love for the literalism of the evangelicals and fundamentalists, I am a great lover of the literalism of a close literary reading, which gives us access to the site of the events harbored by words.

In the beginning, *en arche*—things had *already* begun. That is easily forgotten in all the good press this text has gotten over the centuries. In the beginning, something was always already there, before the beginning began. In the beginning, *when* God created, *when* God *began* to create—those are the alternatives the NRSV proposes as translations of this text.

These alternatives, which ultimately go back to the Middle Ages, especially to the suggestion of Rabbi Rashi, a medieval rabbinic commentator, have gained the ascendancy in the literature.[3] In beginning with this rabbinic parsing of Genesis 1:1–3, I am in a special way, however, following the lead taken in theologian Catherine Keller's *Face of the Deep.*[4] I am engaging in a kind of partnership with her groundbreaking work on a new theology of creation, with which, as will become plain, the present chapter is very much a creative dialogue. Keller's theological breakthrough has the great advantage for me of being itself deeply marked by post-structuralist and Derridean openings. Keller has given my own Derridean intuitions about these texts theological guidance and scriptural flesh and bones, and she has greatly aided and abetted my work of short-circuiting. So we read, all of us, the entire corporate partnership, Rabbi Rashi and Reb Rida, Keller and I:

v. 1 "*When* God began to create": *in medias res,* in the midst, not of "things," exactly, for that is what God was beginning to create.

v. 2 *at that time* (1) the earth was a *tohu wa-bohu:* this is best understood as something desolate, like a desert, something arid, barren, uninhabited, and more abstractly as an emptiness. In one view, it actually "has nothing to do with 'chaos' and simply means 'emptiness' and refers to the earth which is an empty place."[5] It sounds a bit like the "wild" in English, but a barren wild, not wildlife. It is not the opposite of creation but the not-yet inhabited earth, and it is not quite a desert either because it seems to be covered by the waters of the deep. (2) And darkness covered the *tehom,* the deep, the ocean, the face of the churning salty waters, (3) over which a wind *(ruach)* swept,

v. 3 and *then* God said, "Let there be light."

Thus, in the beginning, things had already begun. As the rabbis like to point out, the Tanach does not open with the first letter "A" (aleph, alpha) but with the second letter "B" (bet, beta), *bereshit,* "in the beginning," something was already there. Even in English, "beginning" begins with a "b" not an "a." Something has already eluded the "*bereshit,*" gotten there before it. As André Neher writes, history is open not only on this end, as we head into the future, but on the other end as well, in the beginning, stretching back to time immemorial. So Genesis does not begin at an absolute beginning. Elohim begins where he finds himself, with co-everlasting but mute companions: a barren earth, lifeless waters, and a sweeping wind. Elohim has to play the cards he is given, to work with the materials at hand, after which it will turn out he will even need a rest. He must work with these elements, with wind and water and wilderness, first to differentiate and then to populate them. So first he separates off the empty expanse of earth and sky and water, and then he fills them up with living things. And time, too, was also already there—not the time of day and night, of course, but the primeval time of the immemorial ticktock *when* God presided over the elements, when he began to create, according to this grammar of creation. The beginning had *always already* begun, before the first verse of Genesis began. One begins where one is, in the middle of a (con)text, and there is no outside-the-context *(hors-texte),* even for the Creator God of Genesis. The pure beginning, an absolute "origin,"[6] is an ever-receding horizon; the *arche* is inevitably haunted by an irreducible *an-arche.* (You can already see where this gloss is going.)

Let us try to imagine the mythopoetic scene.[7] In the beginning, *they are there,* wind and waters and land, barren and lifeless, the wind sweeping over the deep, everywhere darkness, like the dark side of some distant desolate planet. There they are, just there, without a word, the only noise being the heaving of the seas, the blowing of the wind. It is almost as if they are sleeping, as if they are laid out like some great giant, some massive body whose only sounds and movements are the heaving and sighing of a sleeper, and Elohim seems to be just watching them sleep. Then Elohim was moved to speak to them, and by addressing them *to bring them to life,* to awaken life in them, to make life stir through their massive limbs the way one calls a sleeper to awake. *He calls them into life; he does not bring them into being,* for the whole point is that they were *there* all along, from time out of mind, in a somnolence deeper and more dreamless than any sleep we can imagine. Genesis is not about being, but about life.[8] Bare barren being is there, what was already there. The astonishing thing is that God *brings being to life.* That is the wonder, and that life that God breathes in them is what God calls "good," which goes a step beyond being.

In the sharpest contrast to what a later metaphysical theology would say, the primeval elements have been there from the beginning, from time immemorial, from time out of mind. "Anonymously," Levinas says, by which he means that they do not speak, that while the deep has a face, it is only a surface *(face),* not a countenance *(visage).* (We will come back to Levinas on creation in chapter 11.) Hence, while there is a kind of rumble or roar of the wind, or the chopping of the sea, there is no language there.

In these narratives, the elemental stuff of the world is *there,* like it or not. *Il y a, es gibt,* "there is." It always was. No one disputes that, certainly not Elohim. The elements are his everlasting, aboriginal companions, silent partners, wordlessly pre-given, presupposed, from time out of mind. God is not responsible for the fact that the elements are *there,* but for making them *stir,* making them *live,* by staking out great expanses that God fills up with living things. Creation is not a movement from non-being to being— which is what makes the hearts of metaphysicians everywhere skip a beat—

but from being to beyond being, from a mute expanse of being to the bustle of living things, from barrenness to the bloom of life, from silence to the word that makes the empty full and the barren buzz with life. Where there was once a dumb factuality, a mute "there"—there was certainly a "there," there—now there is meaning, signification, interpretation, valuation, differentiation, and above all—life. Where there were facts, now there is an articulation and an interpretation.

In other words, as soon as we start reading a little more literally, we find a different story, not the usual metaphysical yarn, the official story put out by a later theological orthodoxy that Catherine Keller calls the "power discourse of creation from nothingness," which has, alas, taken these narratives by storm and turned them into a tale told by a metaphysician. Metaphysical theology has turned this Hebrew narrative into the tale of a pure, simple, clean act of power carried out on high by a timeless and supersensible being, a very Hellenic story that also goes along with a top-down social structure of imperial power flowing down from on high. There is order and majesty here no doubt, but the story is, upon closer reading, "much messier," as Keller says, more complicated—not *creatio ex nihilo* but *"creatio ex profundis,"* not a single clean power acting *ex nihilo,* but a concert of forces, one active and formative and the other more open-ended, free-floating, fluid and unformed. A poetics of creation from primal, untamed, unwieldy, watery elements, as wily as the wind and as slippery as water, elements that tend to resist fixed order. In all, a tricky business. It took twenty-six tries to make it stick, the Talmudic author quips, and even then, all God could do was hope for the best.

But what has become of the *tohu wa-bohu* and the *tehom* in the official story put out by orthodox theology? Alas, these great sleeping bodies, these slippery, suspicious characters, did not make it into the official theology books, despite their prominence in this famous scene.[9] They were dropped by the later theological *creatio ex nihilo* tradition, which did not emerge until the second half of the second century, on the grounds of a metaphysical interpretation that maintained that such a conclusion is the most logical implication of the logic of God's power in the Scriptures. Maybe, maybe not. But these are not logic books or metaphysics books, and this development of what would become the standard "orthodoxy" looks very suspicious to us for the following reason.

We ever-suspicious sacred anarchists, we who have a strong affection for weak theology, suspect foul play.[10] We are always worrying about rouged and powdered theology. We suspect a cover-up, that the strong theologians, who (like everyone else) have an unnerving taste for power and sovereignty, were themselves unnerved by these two signifiers of barrenness and indeterminacy, with the result that they dropped them from the official story, and not on the basis of logic, or at least not of logic alone (or maybe the logic was the cover). Did violence play any part in the demise of these elemental stuffs? Were they killed off, like Abel by Cain, literally annihilated or reduced to nothing, the onto-theo-logical record being expunged of their very trace, so that not a hint of them would remain? We radical hermeneuts of suspicion are worried at the way, as Luce Irigaray says in *The Forgetting of Air,* a man makes a foundation of and for himself by annihilating that (uterine) foundation from which he proceeds.[11] Emerging erect in the world, hard(y) and upright, he wants to shake off his watery origin like a furry creature shaking dry after a swim in the lake. So the *tohu wa-bohu* and the *tehom* have our sympathies from the start. They are the "nothings and nobodies" of this story, *ta me onta,* literally, and this because they seem to bear all the marks of the riskiness—the element of unforeseeability and chance—that is built right into what Levinas would call this "beautiful risk" called life.[12] They appear to be the bearers of what in the story from the Talmud was called the "radical uncertainty" in things, which goes to the heart of the beautiful risk of creation. Everything that we have been saying about the "kingdom" of nothings and nobodies tells us to keep an eye out for them. For these are the elements in the priestly narrative that the tradition has excluded and repressed: the exiles, the veritable hermeneutical lame and the lepers of this story, the insidious outsiders who menace and unnerve the theological powers that be who have in the meantime sat down to table with Neoplatonic metaphysicians. Might the long-forgotten waters, wind, and wild, the very stuff of this biblical poetics, turn out to be valuable witnesses whom we must protect lest the authorities get their hands on them and prevent them from testifying? If their part of the story gets told, will it contradict the official line and embarrass the theological powers that be? For all these reasons, we suspect a cover-up and an official plot.

Indeed, suppose it turns out that we human beings were made not *simply* in the image of God, which is surely a central part of the story, but that we are also made of an unimaginable, or hardly imaginable, unmanageable, and unstable stuff, something that is neither icon nor idol, that is prior to both, reducible neither to Elohim nor to a demon or false god? Suppose we are offspring jointly of a divine image-maker and of something unimaginable, or of something that can only be imaged in provocative and stunning visual images? Or better still, suppose that being the image of God is completely compatible with being made of some sort of unimaginable khoral corporeality (khora-poreality) and that we are the stuff of some sort of khoral incarnation? Suppose our corporeal being is deeply interwoven with, or immersed in, these wild, watery, and windy conditions? And suppose that was one of the elemental things these stories were insisting upon, if we would be just a little more just, a little more loyal, to their letter, a strong metaphysical theology to the contrary notwithstanding? Suppose the flux, which has been deprived of its papers by *theology,* has veritably *biblical* credentials and is not an invention of Nietzschean or post-structuralist nihilism, as Radical Orthodoxy likes to comfort itself? Suppose the flux is neither as wicked as the devil himself, as Barth liked to imagine,[13] nor able to be simply transcribed into a beautiful "mystery" that we should just "trust," but is rather the figure of "radical uncertainty," of a beautiful but risky business.[14] What then?

Our suspicions deepen when we are told by Catherine Keller that one of these elements is a woman whose name has been smeared. The plot of the primal soup thickens. *Tehom,* a feminine noun, used without an adjective, like a proper name, meaning the "ocean" or the "deep," has etymological links to Tiamat, the feminine goddess in the Babylonian theogony *Enuma elish.*[15] Tiamat is the principle of salt water—salt, we know by now being a very important seasoning in a sacred anarchy—of ocean and desert, who mates with Apsu, fresh water, and their progeny constitute the theogony of Babylonian gods. Tiamat is of course a fierce dragon woman, but Keller suspects a cover-up: that over a series of redactions, a mother or a grandmother has been turned into a great monster; that her name has been blackened; and that she had, at least in the beginning or in earlier redactions, a kinder, gentler side, wanting only to protect her grandchildren from Apsu's plan to kill them for disturbing his rest.[16] Tiamat is eventually slain by Marduk (her grandson), the hero of the story, who creates the world by dividing up her body parts. So does the *Enuma elish* represent a bit of "tehomophobia"? Is it the story of a matricide arising from demonizing the deep, from a fear of the watery uterine beginning that turns a mother into a monster? Perhaps.

But what is interesting about the priestly narrative with which Genesis starts off is the serenity and nonviolence of the tale. Wind and water and wild are just *there,* mute and wordless, the wind blowing, the seas chopping. There is no battle with warring chaos *(Chaoskampf);* Elohim is not a warrior; the *tehom* is not a dragon or a terrible beast, just waters over whom the spirit *(ruach)* of Elohim sweeps.[17] She is not evil but simply, in her still unprocessed state, not yet good. The elements are not enemies of God but a mutable and transformable stuff, like clay for a potter. The *tehom* is channeled, or separated off, not killed. She is not a god or goddess but an element to be fashioned by Elohim and then called good, for it is the cosmos (cosmogony), not the gods (theogony), who are generated in Genesis.[18] But *tehom* is still an important part of the story, even in the redaction that is finally handed down to us; no telling what *tehom* was in the earliest tellings. So too is the *tohu wa-bohu,* which is a figure not of a watery womb but of earth as desolate, wild, lifeless, like a desert but covered with water, a deserted, lifeless sea-bottom, like a *khora* (which is a surname for *différance*).[19] The work of Elohim is not to make war on the elements but to section them off from one another and populate them by making them fertile. God makes the deep into a place aswarm with living things, including "sea monsters," a Leviathan, "sporting" in the sea (Ps. 104), whom God feeds rather than hunts and kills, *pace* Captain Ahab. God makes the desolate sea-bottom dry and transforms it into fields full of vegetation, and God fills the air with birds and the sky with sun and moon and stars. Elohim prepares a *Lebenswelt* for us by filling the empty, hanging up lights in the dark, separating the mixed, and making the barren fertile.[20]

The entire narrative turns on the *life-giving transformations* that Elohim has wrought *in and with the elements,* the transformations of the darkness *(pne choshekh),* of the deep *(tehom)* and of the void *(tohu wa-bohu),* not from nothing to something, the dream of metaphysical theology, but from the barrenness of being to the ebullience of life, which takes a more poetic turn. It is a narrative of transformation and of metamorphosis and, as they say in Paris, of an *événement,* an event—an event not to end all events but one to start them off. To say that Elohim makes something out of nothing[21] is to change the subject and produce a dazzling distraction and a very puzzling notion indeed to anyone in Babylonia, to anyone at all before the second century C.E. The opening verses of Genesis make no use whatever of a meta-physical distinction between an eternal, infinite, and supersensible being creating finite, temporal being, which is an un-Hebraic conception that is not conceivable outside of the two-worlds schema that Christianity inherited from Hellenistic metaphysics. The binarity at work in the story is not between sensible and supersensible, or finite and infinite, or eternal and temporal, or being and non-being. It turns instead on a series of sensuous transformations in and of the elements: empty/filled, mixed/separated, barren/living, dark/light. Elohim's transcendence is not that of an omnipotent supersensible being but that of a more mundane type, like that of an artist fashioning materials. The artistic paradigm carries weight on two fronts. First, God creates by his word, not by his hands, which does not mean *ex nihilo,* but the way a master artist is the genius and inspiration in his studio, who directs the work of the underlings, or the way a king gives the "word" and others carry it out: so I have spoken, so it will be done. Secondly, the narrative does not present a scientific logic of how the seas or birds would actually have been formed; rather it proceeds like a painter filling in a canvas, first marking off broad spaces for the sky, the air, the earth and the sea, and then filling them in with their inhabitants.[22]

In the first Genesis narrative, the elements are "there," but they are clearly not "evil." If anything, they are potentially good, though not yet good, having as they do all the makings of something (soon to be) good. They are neutral or, as Hyers says, "ambiguous," marked, shall we say, by a kind of "khoral undecidability." Water tends to run anywhere unless it is banked and channeled; the wind tends to blow anywhere it will unless it is directed; and the formless void to spread out indefinitely unless it is shaped and filled. They flex and flow, heave and sigh, and slip and slide, but they are not evil.[23] They are pre-creational materials, bodies without members, spaces that are being prepared for inhabitation: the *tohu wa-bohu* is the not-yet-productive earth about to be made productive. They are on the brink of good, able to be brought to good. The dark deep is the empty waters before they become a sea aswarm with frolicking fish, even as they harbor the potential for trouble, as when the waters rise or the winds are not held in check. The elements can go both ways; they are astir with multiple and mutable possibilities. In fact, it would be logically incoherent, not just exegetically questionable, to suggest that the elements are evil in their still-unformed state, inasmuch as it is the very act of creation by Elohim that introduces the category of "good," and by implication the distinction between good and evil. Before creation, before their formation, they are a threat to no one, to neither God nor human nor beast. When Cain slays Abel, that is evil, because it reverses the action that God has taken in filling the barren earth with living creatures, but in the primal elements before creation there is no murder, because there is no life to take away, as there was no theft, no lying, no violence of any sort at all. There cannot be a "flood" before creation; floods are problems only after there is something to flood. The primal desert and the deep are completely nonviolent. If ever there were an "innocence of becoming," an innocent "play of forces," to use Nietzsche's phrases, it was here, not because the primal elements are "beyond good and evil" but because they are "before" them, "before creation," as Derrida says, although, in the telling of the priestly narrative at least, they seem to simmer on the edge of good. That is why Elohim does not make war on them but regards them rather the way a potter regards clay.

We might be tempted to declare the elements good with a kind of anticipatory or proto-goodness that preceded the creation of what is to be actually declared good. That is the tack taken by Catherine Keller, who wants to counter "tehomophobia"—a fear of the deep, of the monsters of the deep, a fear of the flux—in all its forms, not only in the *Enuma elish* but also when it makes its way into the Hebrew scriptures and into Christian theology—the culmination of which for her is the literal annihilation of the elements in the theology of *creatio ex nihilo*. Keller has forged an independent and unique voice by cultivating a dialogue between American process thought, including Irigaray's lyrical accounts of sea and air, recent chaos theory, and—something for which I am particularly grateful—Derrida and post-structuralist theory generally.[24] Keller sings a song to the primal elements and above all to the *tehom,* as to the depths from which all life springs. Now we radical anarchists have always fancied ourselves lovers of the flux, at the least as ones who say that we get the best results, not from flight but from trying to face up to the facelessness of the flux, which is the task of what I have called "radical hermeneutics."[25]

Anxious to avoid at all costs any anxious flight from the flux, my aim in the present chapter is precisely to show that even here, in Genesis, there is a recognition of something like a *khora* or *différance* that is an ingredient in the creation stories themselves, delimiting the later power-metaphysics of creation and making room for chance and happenstance. There is an element of irreducible indeterminacy and instability built right into creation, so that creation is going to be continually exposed to re-creation. What God has formed is able both to come unformed, to break down or come unstrung—that is the bad news, the downside of the risk—but by the same token and for the same reason, things are also able to be reformed, reconfigured, and reinvented, which is the upside, the more creative and re-creative side in things. There is a deep structural mutability and transformability inscribed in things by these narratives that works both ways, which is what we mean by a risk. It can undo the best-laid plans of God and humankind, even as it keeps the future open. Things are deconstructible just because they are constructed from a mutable stuff to begin with. That is why life is a risky if bracing business, and why the Talmudic author points to the "radical uncertainty" in things, while God is keeping the divine fingers crossed, hoping that it all works.

Einstein once said that God does not play dice. On that point the great man should have stuck to physics and left God to the theologians—that is, to theologians of the event, or sacred anarchists, who are better at betting and have more of an appetite for dice. For the creation is nothing if it is not a dicey business, both for God and for us. Life, existence, creation are nothing if not a risk; but for anyone worth their salt, they are what Levinas would call a "beautiful risk." The beautiful risk of creation is also an elemental ingredient in what we have been calling here a "sacred anarchy," which we will discuss before taking up our account of the "kingdom." First we talk about creation, then we talk about sacred anarchy.

But Keller takes this argument one step further by arguing, in the spirit of Irigaray, that beyond learning not to fear the face of the deep, we should learn to love it; beyond avoiding tehomophobia, we should embrace tehomophilia, a celebration of the elements, and she gives brilliant readings of Genesis, Psalm 104, and the book of Job to document this as at least a subtendency, albeit not the dominant tendency of the Hebrew scriptures.[26]

The onto-theological repression of the *tohu wa-bohu* and the *tehom* represents a deep-set phallic fear of our oceanic uterine beginnings, she thinks, a masculine unease before a watery cosmic womb. The *tehom* and the *tohu wa-bohu* are reduced to nothingness or beaten into semi-nothingness by a highly "hysterectomic" and masculinized onto-phallo-theological tradition, and in their place is put an omnipotent masculine father creator who draws all things from a pure and absolute nothingness by the sheer power of the word of his mouth, without a trace of the void or the deep (or a woman!) in sight. Men just cannot tolerate the thought of their aquatic origin, of floating around helplessly in a sea of utter uterine dependence, so they have tried to shake it off and purge the official record, utterly effacing this uterine beginning. Strong theology has from of old worked with the model of fathers generating sons, of generation by a father without a mother, or by divine fathers with merely human mothers, and with fathers almighty with as little input from the material/maternal side as possible, so that where the Genesis narratives speak of something, a wild or a watery deep, onto-phallo-theology reads "nothing," leaving a big erect masculine will to do it all by himself. Keller rewrites these narratives with the aid of a feminine imaginary and the resources of a positive and productive idea of the *tohu wa-bohu* and the *tehom* as equal partners in the deal. It is better to be ready-for-anxiety, as Heidegger put it, than to take flight. But Keller has shown that, beyond all that being-ready-for-anxiety, the void and the deep (she tends to talk more of the deep than the void) signify the matrix or womb from which we all have been formed, a positive spring of life, not simply an ominous and threatening vortex. The deep is not something to fear but to love, the way we love the mother and matrix of us all, the way we love wind and sea and earth, the stuff from which we are formed and into which we return. Beyond the Heideggerian idea of squaring off with thrownness and blind facticity, she embraces what Arendt called "natality," being grateful for being born.[27]

ELOHIM AND *YAHWEH*

The way to see how this insistence on the elements cashes out is to contrast the priestly narrative with the equally famous story of Adam and Eve that follows it. As everyone knows nowadays, there are two creation narratives in Genesis, written for two very different audiences. Up to now we have spoken only of the first one, attributed to "P," by the best accounts a sixth-century "priest" writing during the time of the Babylonian exile, who speaks of *"Elohim"* (Gen. 1–2:4), usually translated as "God." P is composing a rival and distinctively Hebrew narrative meant to counter the *Enuma elish,* and he is trying to tell an uplifting story to boost the spirits of a people in exile and make sense of their exiled condition.[28] The second but much earlier story, of Adam and Eve in the Garden of Eden (perhaps going back to the time of the Davidic kingdom, but placed second by the Redactor), is attributed to "J," because this ninth- or tenth-century author speaks of "*Jahweh*" (with the German spelling), usually translated as "Lord."[29] This story, which belongs to quite a different world, long before the exile, is being told by an agriculturalist who dreamed of a lush garden in Eden where the land readily yielded its fruits to our labor, in sharp contrast with the rocky soil with which the Israelites had to contend and which demanded backbreaking work and the sweat of one's brow. The Yahwist is warning the people about their imperial ambitions and trying to remind them of their humble, earthly origins. So the two stories are addressing opposite audiences and making opposite points. Without at all sacrificing the differences uncovered by rigorous historical-critical work, Jack Miles has artfully articulated these two rather different narratives by adopting the literary artifice of taking the Bible as a story starring God as a protagonist who is a single character with a number of different personalities.[30]

In the first story the work of Elohim is portrayed as majestic, serene, benign, almost effortless, although at the end God does require a Sabbath rest, because that was an important part of P's theological agenda and perhaps because the Sabbath rest looked especially good to the forced labor the Hebrews suffered under in exile. The dominant mark of the narrative is clearly a rule of beneficence and of what Milan Kundera called our "categorical agreement with being."[31] The rhythmic refrain of the originary benediction, "And God saw that it was good," portrays Elohim as the master craftsman of this immense and beautiful world. God looks at what God did and says "good," which we might translate as "yes," as Rosenzweig says.[32] *Oui, oui,* Derrida would say. Having made all things great and small, Elohim (the noun is plural) makes us in his (or their) image, which means to be fertile and creative as Elohim is, and to have dominion, let us say, stewardship, over the earth.[33] That means to work hard tending the earth, make love, have families, eat well, live to see your children's children, and take the time to enjoy the flowers on the weekends, for which Elohim also provides a model. Death and sex, work and play, are all part of life on God's green earth. The greatness of Elohim is the greatness of an artist/poet who has designed and fashioned a stunning landscape out of wild and unwieldy materials. The first narrative is a poem to *poiesis,* where the emphasis is on the beautiful design and bountiful goodness of the world Elohim has fashioned.

It is very important to see that in this narrative Elohim creates by the word of his mouth, whereas the primal elements are quite silent. Elohim is not responsible for the fact that the elements are *there* but for the fact that they are fashioned and *called good.* Creation is not a movement from non-being to being, but from being to the good, from the mute being to speech and categoriality. That is what the preexistence of the elements in the narratives signify, what the elements are "saying" in their silence and wordlessness, what they say by saying nothing, what the narrative is saying by means of the fact that the elements do not say a thing. They are not absurd or chaotic, just silent and wordless; they are not *de trop* or absurd or an anonymous rumbling—all of which would constitute an anachrony, a retrospective illusion. They are just there, like it or not. Elohim, on the other hand, does all the talking. Elohim is the "word," the one who speaks, who introduces meaning, articulation, intelligibility. In a rigid monotheism, Elohim is technically speaking to himself, speaking a divinely private language (something that philosophers will tell you is technically impossible for several perfectly good reasons, which is an objection only if you think that matters when you are reading poetry!). In fact, there is some evidence of a residual polytheism in which Elohim is consulting with a divine council and they all agree to create something in "our" image. Be that as it may, God is responsible for the "word," the work of language, meaning, *sens* in the dual sense of both sense and direction. Elohim pronounces a judgment, word, a verdict, *vere dictum,* upon things, which is a benediction; God pronounces them "good." Elohim draws vast and sprawling expanses of sky and air and sea, and that is good; then God fills them with living things, and living things are good, and God hangs lights like lanterns in the sky-dome, and light is good. And God makes human living things and makes them fruitful just like him, and human fruitfulness is good.

We might think of this as Elohim's contract with creation, his first, last, and constant covenant, the oldest and the newest covenant, that creation is good.

Good, good, good, good, good—very good. Yes, I said, yes, yes. That's the word. That's the world.

Then "J," the author of the second but earlier creation myth (2:4–24), is led on to the stage by the Redactor to read his lines, and he will give a different verdict—not "evil," exactly, not a malediction, exactly, but "guilty!" First the good news, the Redactor seems to think, then the bad news. The Yahwist's story is darker and more distrustful, earthier and more complicated, more tempestuous and with more overt sexual overtones. If Elohim is a calm, distant, celestial, hands-off creator, Yahweh is very nervous about what he is getting himself into and is much more of a hands-on micromanager, down in the dust with humankind, talking, arguing, caring for, and growing angry with humankind. If Elohim made humankind in general and made them male and female, both equitably in the image of God, like a kind of royal pair,[34] the first couple in the Yahwist story is regarded more like a pair of servants or gardeners. Yahweh makes the man not in God's image but from dust, vividly reminding us of the mortal dust to which man will return, an evident effort to humble the pretensions of the glories of David and Solomon. Then, after a search for a companion for man, Yahweh makes the woman from the man's rib, pointedly reminding her that she is clearly a derivative and junior partner. If there is a kind of grand munificence and beneficence about Elohim, Yahweh seems both *distrustful* of his creatures and *jealous* of his own superior knowledge and immortal life. If Elohim was in search of images of himself (themselves) and enjoined humankind to be fertile and creative just like himself, Yahweh seems very worried about their becoming *too much* like him. The Yahwist is trying to warn us that we human beings must avoid *hybris,* must avoid wanting to exalt our own mortal status. And as a historical-critical matter, rather like the prophets after him, he is telling the Hebrews to curb their imperial ambitions, and that is surely a point well made. But what interests me about this Yahweh is that he has little taste *for the risk of creation, for the risk of parenting.* He does not so much give the first couple life as he gives them a *test* to see if they are worthy of life; he gives them life on a kind of conditional trial loan to see if they are going to abuse it and try to become like him, in which case he is prepared to withdraw from the deal and wipe —or wash—them out.

High above in heaven, making deft strokes on a cosmic canvas, Elohim, who does not seem to be worrying about anything, gives humankind in general the whole world over which to roam, with no prohibitions, just a positive command to multiply and be fruitful, that is, to be creative like himself. But down here on earth, somewhere in the vicinity of the Tigris and the Euphrates, Yahweh gives the first couple only a garden, albeit a very lovely and fruitful one, the sort of which can only be dreamt of by anyone who makes a livelihood off the land only with great difficulty. But this garden is from the very start constituted as a confined place of trial, temptation, and even a bit of trickery, little more than a trap calculated to deceive them. Yahweh knows better than anyone that these beings are fashioned from earth, but he immediately sets out to see what they are made of! He moves in swiftly at their first misstep, less like a loving parent than like a stern, distrustful, and short-tempered stepparent. When Elohim speaks from on high, the waters and the land, the light and the dark answer with a joyful *yes;* but the Yahwist is worried that, down here on earth, these unreliable human beings might very well answer back and disobey, that the divine address is liable to be countered with a human *no,* a point that did not seem to concern the first narrative.

Yahweh tells them to make themselves at home and enjoy everything *except* the tree of the knowledge of good and evil. An impartial observer would have to say that this is a little disingenuous; it is like telling them that they may let their minds roam freely over any object of thought at all, but they are definitely not to think of a giant pink elephant. That *constitutes* the tree precisely as an object of forbidden desire—is there any other kind?—which seems to have been planted there in the first place just to tempt them. Yahweh tells them that they shall die if they eat this fruit, which turns out to be not quite true: they eat it and do not die. What the "crafty" serpent says, however, is straightforwardly true: Yahweh knows that they will not die but that by eating this fruit they will become like him, godlike, because they too will know good and evil, that is, they will have a full range of human and adult experiences, for better and worse, which is just what Yahweh does not want. So the very thing that Elohim seeks, to have images of himself, full and mature, productive and reproductive, adult images of himself, is just what Yahweh wants to avoid. The serpent became famous as the crafty one who deceived our first parents, but truth to tell, the serpent was telling God's honest truth, which is confirmed by Yahweh himself (3:22), and Yahweh seems to be not a little crafty himself. J has Yahweh banish them from the garden because they might become emboldened to eat of the tree of life and live forever, which would have made them like gods. But by now we are asking, what is wrong with that? Would that not have made them more perfectly in his "image" (P) and given God everlasting companionship? Then the exile is enforced, but only after a somewhat surprising and unbecoming outburst (3:14–19) in which both P and J (and hence the Redactor) have the "Lord God" curse his own creatures and promise to make their lives miserable, although Yahweh, showing another side, does yield to a moment of parental tenderness by providing Adam and Eve with leather garments made from skins for life in the cruel world outside the garden.

The upside of the Yahwist's narrative is that he portrays a more corporeal down-to-earth God, who gets down in the dirt with us, talks familiarly with us, enjoys an evening breeze, and is clearly involved with and concerned about us. But Yahweh seems to have a bit of a short fuse, seems inordinately suspicious of his own creation, and is far too nervous about his offspring for a good parent. Creating, like procreating, is risky business, and one has to be prepared for a lot of noise, dissent, resistance, and a general disturbance of the peace if one is of a mind to engage in either.[35] There may have been confusion before, but the wind blowing over the deep was relatively peaceful compared to the mayhem that follows creation! Still, at least Yahweh cares about us, while we worry that Elohim seems so celestial that he couldn't care less. But by the end of the third chapter of Genesis, the effect of the majestic Elohist narrative is checked by a tempestuous Yahweh; what was called good in the opening Elohist narrative is now cursed. The desire to make humankind in "their" own image expressed in the opening story is frustrated on every side by a God who sees to it that human life is short, brutal, nasty, un-godlike, and Hobbesian. Yahweh has, in no short order (by the sixth chapter), decided that his creatures are wicked, their every inclination evil, and he is sorry he made them (6:5–7). He decides to wipe them all out, except for Noah, to send them all back to kingdom come, if I may say so, that is, back to the primal *tehom* from which Elohim fashioned the world in the first place, and to start all over again. This the Lord God does (the Redactor is now running both narratives together) by opening the floodgates in the dome that held back the dark swirling waters of the first day (rather the way the Tigris and Euphrates would periodically flood the surrounding plains).

Having been unable to foresee what he was getting into—something that Marcion would later on hold against him!—and having little heart for this dicey experiment called creation, the Lord God decides that he made a mistake in creating at all and decides to cut his losses and start all over, making a New No(ah)etic Deal, and ultimately striking a final deal with Abraham. If Abraham is to be the fertile fore-father of generations as numerous as the stars in the heaven, which would be an excellent image of God's creativity, an endless human fertility to image the divine creativity, it will be entirely at the Lord God's pleasure, by God's doing, in God's own good time and on God's terms, in unmistakable token of which Abraham, then ninety-nine years old, and his house and line should all be so kind as to at once return the foreskins God has given them, thank you very much. Ouch! Then, after being put through all that, Abraham and Sarah are finally given a son. But Abraham is tested still one more time, this time to see if he would be willing to return not his foreskin but his long-awaited son to God in sacrifice to God's unconditional authority over fertility and life.

In the first story Elohim creates adult beings like him- and herself, while the Yahwist, worrying about their aspiring to a rank beyond themselves and in his desire to cut down their *hybris,* would have Yahweh satisfied to bring forth eternal children, naked Edenic innocents who were good because they did not know the taste of evil, good the way little children are good who don't even know that they are naked. But in the first narrative, in which Elohim wants to produce an *eikon* and is not worrying about *hybris,* God has also given us the rope with which to hang ourselves, which we do quite regularly (the rope is called history). Elohim wants images who are not children but adults, not faint images but robust ones, not bad copies but true ones; but all that worries Yahweh half to death, if I may say so. Creation is a risk for which Yahweh has little appetite; it is easy to get angry but hard to be patient. Yahweh shows little heart for the risk that any parent takes, which is that their offspring will outstrip their intention and spin out of control, and things will not turn out as the parents planned. In Genesis, it is rather the opposite of the old adage: here God proposes, humankind disposes. Right from the start, Yahweh is hedging his bet, trying to test what he has made, trying to minimize the risk he is taking, and he has no tolerance for failure. The original setting of creation is not a garden of delight but a minefield of tricks, traps, tests, trials, and temptation for such fallible and unstable things as humus/humans. Anyone who knew what these khoral creatures are made of would understand that they were bound to fail such ordeals sooner or later. Yahweh should have known better. If Adam and Eve were disobedient, this early rendering of Yahweh was hardly of a perfect parent. The original sin is a two-way street.[36] Not only were Adam and Eve tested, but so was Yahweh, and, as they say, Yahweh was the adult in the room (garden).

But instead of simply opposing the two stories, we do better to try to fit them together, as the Redactor is trying to do, and to see in them a good news/bad news sequence. In the first narrative, P announces the original covenant that Elohim makes with creation, which is that what he has made is good; and in the second narrative, that judgment is put to the test by showing us to what extent things go wrong. But the second narrative is framed by the first, and the Redactor's intention seems to be to enjoin us to keep the faith that creation is good, very good (=P's narrative), *no matter what* (=the Jahwist narrative). The result is that the "good" becomes in part descriptive and in part prescriptive; in part a judgment of what Elohim has done, and in part a promise of what is possible, of what he has in mind for creation. Good—now let's hope it works.

But what does all this have to do with the *tohu wa-bohu* and the *tehom*? The elements, from our point of view, are hermeneutic keys. These stories tell, not of an omnipotent creator creating *ex nihilo,* which stretches our credulity, but of a maker making something over which he has only so much control and no more—and at times not quite enough patience— which is highly believable. The myth makes more sense than the metaphysics. That is signified by the mythic elements out of which things are formed—the deep, the dark, the wind, and the earth—which God shapes and then "hopes for the best," according to the amusing but wise story from the Talmud, which claims that twenty-six previous attempts at creation had failed! "History," the Talmudic author suggests, "is branded with the mark of radical uncertainty." Humankind is woven from the elements and is ever liable to fall back into them, to come unstrung; and the Creator, blessed be his name, is just going to have to come to grips with this. The Lord made things, but things sometimes kick back; that's the way gifts work. The Lord God, like any good parent, must learn to deal with the unpredictability and the unforeseeability, the foolishness and even the destructiveness of his children, in the hope that they will grow up and eventually come around. For after all, they are formed of an indeterminate and fluctuating stuff that can work for good or for ill; it is this indeterminacy that makes them unpredictable and inventive—creative in their own way, not in his way—for better or for worse. They are made of *humus,* of *tohu wa-bohu* and *tehom,* so there is an element in them which is not precisely God's image but in which God is trying to fashion his image, a certain irreducible alterity that God wants to cultivate, fertilize, plant, order, and bring around to the divine way of doing things but whose irreducibility and resistance the Lord God is just going to have to learn to live with and hope for the best. Nothing is perfect.

Creation is quite an "event," which means it opens up a long chain of subsequent and unforeseeable events, both destructive and re-creative ones, and the creator is just going to have to live with that undecidability that is inscribed in things.

The thrust of the Genesis narrative, as opposed to the *Enuma elish,* is that the elements from which things are made are not evil, just fluid; they are not wicked, just unwieldy; they are not demonic, just determinable, flexible and unprogrammable (like Derridean *khora*). They are not opposed to God's purposes diabolically; they are just loose, runny, and slippery, and so it is difficult to hold them fast. The elements signify a certain limit on God's power and call for God's patience, for the God of Genesis was not the *omnipotens deus* created by second-century onto-theology. The several authors of Genesis—that is, the generations of underlying oral tradition—understood that creativity and unpredictability, inventiveness and instability, having an open-ended future and uncertainty, go hand in hand. The two creation stories do not differ on that point, but differ on the attitude God takes to creation: Elohim is cool; Yahweh, a nervous wreck. The pre-existent elements, then, are signifiers, or mythologemes, not of evil but of uncertainty, not of rival or opposing gods but of undecidability. They are a little like the *khora* in Derrida, which is a surname for *différance,* which, devilish critter though it be, is not a demon and ought not to be demonized. (Or from another point of view, the echo of these ancient biblical figures is bouncing around in Derrida's head.) These are just names, or nonnames, for the limits under which we all labor, whether in the six days of creation or thereafter, in our own mortal works and days.

By making room for the three elements of the primeval wild or desert, the deep, and the wind, the original creation narratives, indeed the prevailing accounts of creation before the second century c.e., have inscribed a coefficient of contingency into life, a placeholder for the unpredictability and uncertainty and creativity that is constitutive of historical life. Yahweh is indeed almighty, for who else could have fashioned earth and sea, and blessed be his name? But however the "almighty" power of Yahweh is understood, it is not understood to mean that every element of chance and misfortune has been purged from life, or that God's plans are not exposed to failure, or that he so thoroughly and omnipotently dominates human existence that nothing happens unless he has arranged it and is responsible for it or has permitted it.[37] God is the source of good and its warrant. That is the stamp or the seal that God puts on creation; that is God's covenant with us. But God is not the power supply for everything that happens. In the beginning, they are there, and then God made them good; that is, God fashioned them and started them out well, but who knows how it will turn out! On the contrary, he very frequently vents his anger at just how many things go wrong and how little influence he has on the world. God is a voice, a law, a word, a command, a call—but the people have a mind of their own, and they can shut up their ears and harden their hearts. Like every author of every similar tale we know of in the ancient world, both authors include primeval elements with which the Creator must work, and in Genesis these signify the irreducible chance and indeterminacy in things over which God must attempt to exert his influence. It is not so much that this limits God's power as that no one ever imagined that God's power was ever supposed to include such things. God is what God is supposed to be, but that does not mean that everything is perfect or that God is responsible for everything that is not.

In a lovely little book James Kugel has shown how different the early picture of God—the "God of old"—was from the one that emerged at the end of the biblical period and in the beginning centuries of the Common Era.[38] One need only think of the image of God strolling in the Garden of Eden to catch an evening breeze, looking for Adam and Eve (because he doesn't know where they are), or wrestling with Jacob through the night, to see what Kugel means. God is not omniscient, omnipresent, omnipotent, eternal, or supersensuous. God gets into a scuffle with humankind, grows angry, regrets what he has done and starts over, and has to be talked down off the edge by humans trying to dissuade him from acting rashly. He is not at all transcendent, but he frequently appears in sensuous form, the very distinction between physical and spiritual being very tenuous and shaky. That is a God whose act was to be cleaned up by metaphysics and made into pure act, with the very considerable help of Hellenistic metaphysics, the upshot of which was a God blended from biblical poetry and Platonic and Aristotelian metaphysics. Having removed the "anthropomorphisms," theology would then devote its remaining energies to trying to resolve the speculative paradoxes it thereby engendered for itself. It would, for example, become a problem in medieval theology to explain how God, an infinite, eternal, and supersensuous being, could have knowledge of finite, temporal, and sensuous individuals like us, or could feel passion, which are difficulties that early biblical writers would have found comically absurd. I am, in keeping with my idea of a theo-poetics of the event, trying to keep my ear close to the ground of the poetry of the Scriptures and to crawl beneath the firepower of metaphysics flying overhead, trying to form an idea of the event that rings in the name of God, that rings true to experience, which is, on my improbable hypothesis, best formulated by my ideas of a "sacred anarchy" and the "weak force of God." It is all a question of what to make of these stories. Metaphysical theology has made one thing of them, and, as Johannes de Silentio says of the System, I wish it well; but I am trying to make something else of them.

To sum up this part of the story: the event that rings out in the name of God in the creation stories is to announce a kind of covenant with life that we are asked to initial. We are asked to say "yes" to life by adding a second yes to God's "yes" (Rosenzweig); to countersign God's yes with our yes, and that involves signing on to that risk; to embrace what God has formed *and* the elemental undecidability in which God has formed or inscribed it. God does indeed have a plan for creation, but God, like the rest of us, is hoping it works. The whole drama of creation follows a simple but bracing law: without the elements, there is no chance in creation; and without chance, there is no risk; and without risk and uncertainty, our conception of existence is an illusion or fantasy. The phenomenological perspicacity of the authors of the creation narratives lies in their provision for the uncertainty and unpredictability of the human drama, including the undecidable link between gratuity and grace.

Walter Benjamin once said that history is "one single catastrophe which keeps piling wreckage upon wreckage," and that we are driven through time by "a storm blowing from Paradise," which "drives [us] irresistibly" into the future.[39] Benjamin clearly has the second narrative in mind, and by the "storm," I would hazard he means Yahweh's outburst in Genesis 3:14–19. Here Yahweh curses the serpent, childbirth, and work, after which he expels the first couple from Paradise and sends them hurtling through history, consigning them to a Hobbesian existence, lurching from one catastrophe to the next.

Benjamin was right enough. In the very next chapter, Cain murders Abel and the bloody course of history is launched. But it is worth noticing that the Redactor put the Yahwist narrative second so that it is framed in by the first one, which tells the story of the agreement that Elohim made with the world, the contract that he signed for us in our absence, that everything that he made is good, very good, yes, yes. The two narratives have a kind of good news/bad news structure: "Good, yes, yes—but." The overarching idea is, however, that the dirge that issues from the Yahwist is not enough to suppress the dance of P, the majestic hymn of praise that P is singing to Elohim about the stunning beauty of the world and the joy of life. So there is another wind blowing out of Paradise, one that Benjamin misses, this one a gentler breeze that pronounces all things "good." P's creation narrative gives the world significance, not a cause, a meaning, not a metaphysical explanation. By placing P's narrative first, the Redactor does not mean to suppress evil, or deny it, or declare that it is an illusion, or to say that every evil ultimately works out for the best. The Redactor is simply saying that for all of its violence and ferocity, we cannot let the storm of the catastrophe, the history of ruins, overwhelm us. Keep hope alive and listen for the quiet, gentle listing of the spirit of Elohim, which breathes "good, good, good, good, good—very good," which are so many ways to say "yes" that we are asked to counter-sign with a second yes. *Oui, oui.* God's creative yes, then our yes, which is our word of faith and hope.

CREATIO EX NIHILO

By the end of the second century c.e., the delicate balance between God's lordship and the chanciness of creation found in these Hebrew stories is upset by an excess of metaphysical zeal, by an overzealous extension of the concept of God's power to an "omnipotence" that had a tin ear for life's contingencies and would thereafter have the effect of laying the horrors of this life squarely at the feet of God. The concept of God's limited power, forged with the sweat and tears of historical experience, is detached from its historical matrix and allowed to lead an artificial life of its own as a conceptual "free radical." Paradoxically, by making God responsible for everything, such conceptual zeal limits God in another way, not by limiting God's power, but by compromising God's goodness. Were one equally zealous about God's goodness, one would show more care about creating exorbitant metaphysical structures that expose God to being blamed for everything. The preoccupation with a hyperbolic doxology, the contest to see just how far one can go conceptually in ratcheting up metaphysical praise of God, ends up distorting God and distorting human experience and leaving us aswarm with irresoluble paradoxes. How or why can anything possibly go wrong without God being responsible? How can God be God if things go wrong? On the older paradigm, God is not the one who is utterly responsible for everything[40] because there is an element of indeterminacy in things that frustrates us all, God, human, and beast.

The ancient narratives know that things have a way of working them-selves out otherwise, because there is an unprogrammability and uncer-tainty in things, an elemental undecidability with which we all have to cope. That indeed is the salt of life, the risk, but also the chance of the "event." They provide for that by the widespread notion, the seemingly self-evident idea in the ancient world—stretching from Babylon to the Bible to the *Timaeus*—of the preexistent deep (Genesis) or stuff (the pre-Socratics) or container (Timaeus) or matter (Aristotle) of the world. Along with the divine *arche,* the ancient stories provided for an element of *anarche,* which is the element that needed to be worked and fashioned. An utterly pro-grammed world would have to be created *ex nihilo;* a world created *ex nihilo* should have been utterly programmed if the programmer knew what he was doing. The upshot of the Genesis narratives is to show both the majesty of the world that we have been given and its limits, and hence to demonstrate a kind of tragic split in, or structural sundering of, human ex-istence, which is the downside of the story but also the chance for creativity and re-creativity, which is the upside. It would be nihilistic to want to sim-ply wipe it all out because of its flawed nature—Genesis 6–7 is Yahweh's (or the Yahwist's) most nihilistic moment. But it would also be a nihilism of another sort to want to reduce the *tehom* and the *tohu wa-bohu* to nothing, to say that the world is utterly and completely God's doing. That is literally too much of a good thing, and it leaves us wondering why and how things can ever go wrong, like Descartes in the Fourth Meditation, who lurches from the first day of worrying that he is deceived by everything to the fourth day where he finds himself having to explain how it would be possi-ble to be deceived at all. (The life of poor existing individuals is somewhere in the middle!) Omnipotence leaves God holding the bag and forces us to offer lame excuses for God to the effect that evil is a little nothing that has leaked into being and that God is only responsible for the being, not the leak, while we, wicked things that we are, are almost all leak, so that a flood is a fitting way to end it all. We keep shifting the blame between God and humankind, having not noticed that the creation narratives were providing for this situation all along by describing a built-in limit in things that was nobody's doing, even as it could be everybody's undoing, and even as it holds out the hope of everyone's redoing.

To the great scandal of religion and its strong metaphysical theology, the sad and tragic irony is that after the metaphysical excess of creation *ex nihilo* is proclaimed, the world goes on as before, evil continues to prolifer-ate, monstrous crimes and natural disasters prevail again and again, lives are pointlessly ruined or cut short, irredeemably lost, and all this takes place on the watch of the newly installed *omnipotens deus.* I am reminded of the nineteenth-century proclamation of papal infallibility, which did nothing to improve the judgment of the popes! History is a nightmare from which we are trying to awake, says James Joyce, or an ever-increasing heap of ruins, says Walter Benjamin (almost on the eve of his suicide). The only difference now is that God has become even more incomprehensible than before, having now been left entirely holding the bag by the strong theologians. Instead of tending to its other duties, theology will hereafter have to spend an inordinate amount of time trying to explain how God is not to be blamed for the evils of a world God created good. God is supposed to give humankind direction, hope, and meaning by planting the seed of the good in things, informing the flux with the form of the good, *viens, oui, oui,* but not to be causally responsible for every last thing that happens. But theology will hereafter have to dedicate a considerable part of its budget trying to put out a fire whose flames it has itself fanned with its idea of *creatio ex nihilo.*

Of course, one does not need a full-blown conception of metaphysical omnipotence to generate the mystery of evil, that is, of God's nonintervention in human misery. It was already enough that God be "almighty" in the sense of the Jewish scriptures, mighty enough to smite the wicked, part the waters, and come to the aid of just causes, to run into this problem. Revving up the divine power to the level of omnipotence only exacerbates the problem. The Hebrew scriptures are filled with their fair share of divine power and thaumaturgy. But right from the start, the one thing that constantly accompanied the faith in God's merciful and compassionate power of intervention in human affairs is the sense of confusion, even dumbfoundedness, at the regularity with which that compassion is contradicted by the empirical record of nonintervention in the face of violence and injustice. The one is as old as the other. It is as self-evident that God is the one who hears the cry of the victim and comforts the downtrodden as it is that the downtrodden are regularly trodden down and their cries ignored, so that on balance it is question whether "God" makes a dime's worth of difference in the empirical-historical record. The 74th Psalm wonders aloud if God is asleep at the wheel. Theology and Scripture simply throw their hands up on this one and declare the matter an inscrutable mystery. As James Kugel says, we didn't have to wait for Auschwitz to become convinced that the cry of the victim as often as not—more often than not?—goes unheeded. The Book of Lamentations is already an ample record of God's high tolerance for suffering and injustice. And God's response to this—"I will be gracious to whom I will be gracious, I will show mercy on whom I will show mercy" (Exod. 33:19)—is no help. God's miserable record of hearing the cry of the victim is so bad, as Kugel points out, that one wonders why the Bible keeps bringing up the idea.[41] To make matters worse, the idea is not only not confirmed by the historical record, it is as a conceptual matter unfalsifiable in principle and hence in the old positivist sense quite meaningless: when victims experience relief, that is because God has heard their prayers; when they do not, God is testing them or has some other mysterious purpose. If you include both *p* and ~*p* in your premises, you can prove—or believe—*anything you like.* One would do better to examine the presuppositions that are leading one into such a moral and conceptual dead end.[42]

On this account, the book of Job, which enjoys the dubious honor of inventing the genre of "theodicy," is better read as a warning to monotheism that it was heading for trouble with its conception of God's power. Job's arguments are much more cogent than are his friends'—their arguments are even dismissed by Yahweh (whose side they had taken) at the end (42:7)—but Yahweh himself has no argument at all, just a chest-thumping show of strength, a divine *argumentum ad baculum* about how he was the one who created the world, not Job, so where does Job get off complaining? That is the "might makes right" argument on a grand, indeed, a divine scale. As Keller quips, if this bullying harangue is the answer, what was the question? Better still, "the Whirlwind is a windbag," a false god and parody of a God of justice and love, and Job's sudden, complete, and uncalled-for capitulation at the end is almost humorous ("comi-cosmic," Keller quips again!)[43] Thus, the story is interpreted by Keller as a kind of parody on the simplistic piety of the last two chapters—which grabs all the attention in His Reverence's sermons—by means of the splendid retelling of the Genesis creation narrative with which the better part of the text is concerned.[44] The effect of this retelling is to concede, on the one hand, that life is rent with tragic loss, but to sustain the faith, on the other hand, that the world is nonetheless a place of majesty and beauty. All things are knotted together, the good and the bad, and life goes on, so don't let hope die. The "good" that Elohim pronounced over the world in the priestly narrative is tested and strained by the subsequent course of history, but it is not overthrown or refuted. Or if, as our Talmudic author says, "the world of man has arisen from out of the heart of the chaotic debris [of the first twenty-six attempts to make the world]," then perhaps it would not be too impudent to say that the conclusion to be drawn from the book of Job is "debris happens" (and life goes on), which is the point that Kundera missed.

One of our most fundamental and human, all too human fantasies—and certainly one of the most fundamental fantasies of religion—is the fantasy of power. That fantasy that is never far removed from religious violence, from the crown of power that religion places on its own head by imagining that it is the vicar of absolute power, that all power was handed over to it by an all-powerful God, whose will it is charged to execute (all too literally!). The model of sovereignty is contagious. It spreads from rouged theology to blood in the streets. The sovereignty of God is readily extended to the sovereignty of men over other men, over women and animals, over all creation. In this fantasy of divine omnipotence, God will (should, could) arrive on the scene and save us all—from murderous violence or from a killing disease, from invading armies or an invasive cancer. If and when that happens, as Catherine Keller points out, it will surely have been too late for everyone who in the meantime has been killed or persecuted or otherwise died a miserable and untimely death. They are dead and their loss is irredeemable. The past is irremissibly over and done with. The religious subject fantasizes about such power the way the weak and the disenfranchised fantasize about a sudden influx of strength, dreaming of a divine thunderbolt with which to smite their enemies. That is just what I am criticizing under the idea of the strong force of God, the visible power of a magical divine intervention on the forces of nature or of history that bends them to the divine will. Or so God should, so that if God does not show up, we should just chalk it up to a mystery exceeding the limits of our own intelligence, rather than to the limits of the paradigm with which we are working. That is, indeed, as Žižek says, a Big Other that we can do without.

Everything we know about nature and history teaches us that this is an illusion, a fantasy and a mystification. That is why the saints quip that if this is how God treats his friends, what must life be like for his enemies? Or why spiritual writers, invoking the unfalsifiability theorem, say that God always answers our prayers, but sometimes God just says no. Or why they say "God helps those who help themselves," meaning no one should actually wait for God to intervene. The massive omnipresence of natural destruction in this world as well as of unjust death and innocent suffering—violence too often committed in the name of God, or in the name of someone else's God, or lamented to have transpired "in the absence of God"—is testimony against this omnipotence. It is not a mystery but a mystification and a conceptual mistake. It is, moreover, an unworthy way to treat God; it is unworthy to think of God in terms of his power to deliver the goods, which is like loving a cow for its milk, as Meister Eckhart says. The player praying for victory in an athletic contest is but a comic exaggeration of the point. His only fault is to apply this idea of God to a trivial object, to waste omnipotence on an unworthy project, whereas God's omnipotence should be reserved for higher and larger stakes—shrinking a cancerous tumor, winning a war, or the triumph of one's own religious confession over the "infidels."

The very idea of "creation from nothing" and of divine "omnipotence" has the fundamental mark of idealizing, epistemological, and psychoanalytic fantasy, that is, the removal of all the limits imposed by reality, carrying out an action in an ideal space where there is absolutely perfect control and not a trace of resistance from the real. Just as in a sexual fantasy our sexual triumphs meet no resistance from, and indeed enjoy the complete cooperation of, one's fantasized partner, so in a metaphysical fantasy our abstract concepts meet no resistance from the real world, natural or historical. They are, as Kant said of the Ideas of pure reason, concepts that are allowed to proceed down the primrose path to completion beyond the limits of experience without meeting any resistance at all from experience, like wheels spinning freely off the ground.[45] Concepts like power that are valid under fixed and determinate conditions are applied unconditionally, where they lose all their traction. Divine omnipotence is a concept fulfilled in fantasy, spinning wildly in ideal space, with absolute velocity, while the brutal course of the real world proceeds at a slower, bloodier pace.

No wonder, then, that the idea of absolute omnipotence did not arise from biblical and historical experience, but rather arose from a metaphysical debate among ecclesiastical theologians in the process of consolidating institutional power who seized upon a biblical idea *(con-capere)* and set it loose into infinity in a way that neither historical nor religious experience could support. According to Gerhard May, the author of the definitive history of the doctrine, the idea of *creatio ex nihilo* arose from a speculative controversy with the gnostics in the second half of the second century.[46] The gnostics taught, on Neoplatonic grounds, that matter was uncreated because it was essentially evil and that it was beneath the goodness and dignity of God to have created such a thing. This was branded as a heresy by the leading Christian theologians of the day—first Theophilus and then Irenaeus—on the grounds that the very idea of something uncreated other than God would contradict God's omnipotence. Everything was created by God and everything that God created is good, including the material world; hence, there could be no uncreated material substratum, nothing like the *khora* found in the *Timaeus*. Indeed, as soon as theology reflected upon God's omnipotence, May contends, the notion of *creatio ex nihilo* was inevitably discovered.[47]

To be sure, a "sacred anarchy" moves in exactly the opposite direction of Gnosticism, because its whole idea is to affirm—to say "yes," *oui, oui*—to the sacredness precisely of what is lowest and anarchical, to affirm hier*an*-archically the very things that would appear on the very lowest rung of any hierarchical scale. Gnosticism, on the other hand, is a highly hierarchical way to think that holds its nose about matter. The very idea of a sacred anarchy is to say *yes* in particular to our khoral corporeality, our khora-poreality, our khoral incarnation, and by so doing to come to grips with, nay to affirm, the only world we know, which is, we maintain, a beautiful but risky place, an event and not an occasion for flight. Our emphasis on the primal elements of the story—flux and deep, darkness and wind—is made precisely in the name of recovering what the tradition considers the lowest of the low, matter/materia, what Keller calls the elements of "materiality, maternality, mortality,"[48] which are annihilated by the theology of *creatio ex nihilo* in order to allow God to create cleanly from nothing. Thus a sacred anarchy takes seriously the sensuousness of our beginnings and the sensuous artistry of Elohim, which are figures of a very earthy and earthly Hebrew imagination. The latter knows nothing of Hellenistic metaphysics or Neoplatonic dualism or the denigration of matter or trying to "escape" from the material world as if it were an essentially evil (and not merely a chancy) place. Remember, one of the first images of God with which we are presented in the Tanach is God strolling in a garden to catch an evening breeze (Gen. 3:8).

There is nothing the least bit gnostic about the *tehom* and *tohu wabohu*. These notions belonged to the mainstream tradition for centuries of Judaism, right from the start, long before Gnosticism reared its head, up through Philo and Hellenistic Judaism. They would certainly have been part of the common stock of biblical ideas inherited by Jesus himself.[49] They were never challenged in the New Testament[50] or in early Christian circles until the doctrine of *creatio ex nihilo* took hold—as a result of a theological controversy—in the second half of the second century. Before that time, eminent theologians like Justin the Martyr and Clement of Alexandria were only the most famous Christians who were completely comfortable holding to the preexistence of matter.[51] The mistake that links the primeval elements described in the opening verses of Genesis to Gnosticism lies in thinking of the essentially lush categories of the Hebrew imagination, of churning salty waters and green gardens, in terms of a Hellenistic notion of *steresis* or privation, of lower grades of being verging on unreality. There is nothing unreal or less real about the elements, just something wild, unwieldy, and barren.

Furthermore, the idea of *creatio ex nihilo* not only is *not foreign* to Gnosticism, but it both has a gnostic version and actually *arises* in part from gnostic sources. As May points out, the great gnostic theologian Basilides is, in fact, "the first Christian theologian known to us who speaks in the strict sense of a creation out of nothing."[52] Basilides defended creation *ex nihilo* against the then-orthodox teaching about the eternity of matter, which was being defended by Justin. In the beginning, according to Basilides, is pure ineffable Nothing, by which he seems to have meant the good beyond being of Plato, inasmuch as Basilides taught a rigorous *theologia negativa* that was emphatic about the transcendence of the immaterial God over material being. The world, in turn, came to be out of nothing by the sheer will and word of God. Basilides is led *precisely by his hierarchical and gnostic logic* to reject both the emanation of matter from

God (like a spider spinning a web) and any fashioning out of the world out of preexistent materials, because the latter would limit the transcendent power of God. According to May, Basilides is the first to criticize the analogy of God fashioning the world like an artist using materials. He rejects the analogy, first, because it would compromise the power of God as "almighty," and, secondly, because God so transcends the world that he creates in an exalted manner that cannot be compared to the way that human creators create, namely, by working with preexistent materials.[53] As May says, "The gnostic supreme God produces in a simply wonderful way, corresponding to his boundless might. His 'act of creation' is exalted incomparably above all earthly processes of making and therefore can only be defined negatively."[54] Is this gnostic theory of creation *ex nihilo* just a curious accident of history? asks May. Maybe, but Basilides has interwoven Christian and gnostic themes so closely that May finds himself having to argue that "the doctrine of *creatio ex nihilo* is not in itself gnostic."[55]

The elements are not evil, as the gnostics maintained, just risky business, both bracing and dangerous, like a swift ride down a steep ski slope, which is exhilarating if you do not kill yourself. The flux is simply—for better or for worse (it all depends)—the element in which things are inscribed, the space in which they are forged, the indeterminacy that is built right into whatever gets built, in virtue of which whatever is constructed is deconstructible, which means not only able to be destroyed, but also able to be remade, reconfigured, and reinvented. The flux explains the eventiveness in things. It is not only why things are able to fall apart, but why they are able to have a future, why the work of creation can be continued by humankind in a work of continuous re-creation. The ability of a thing to be reinvented and to surpass itself goes hand in hand with its vulnerability to destruction, which is all part of the risk. Without something like the flux, emblematized in the mythical *tohu wa-bohu,* or quasi-conceptualized in the *khora,* which is on my telling an echo of a very biblical idea, there would be no indeterminacy and determinability in things, and thus no explaining the open-endedness and riskiness of materiality and of life—for God or for us.[56] Without an account of the riskiness of material life, one really has no account of life at all, but a fantasy that turns its face away from reality, which would, in the end, be a lot more like nihilism and the Gnosticism that the Church rightly rejected.

CONCLUSION

So the creation narratives are about a primordial benediction, not all about being and power, not all about being bowled over by the amazing feat of a *creatio ex nihilo.* They are about a gentle breeze blowing out of Paradise that bears the word "good" across the ages, the event of a word. In them, the name of God harbors the event of a yes, while their authors make no effort to conceal that there is a dicey dimension to this thing called creation, and we hope it works. Let us now pursue this point to the point of regaining the nerve to affirm the weak force of God, while also offering a little prayer that the Inquisitors have lost our trail.

FOUR

Omnipotence, Unconditionality, and the Weak Force of God

OMNIPOTENCE

The preceding inquiry into the Genesis narratives was meant to build up our nerve to stick with our thesis about the weak force of God in the face of God's mightiest feat, creation, which, however exhilarating, is nothing exnihilatory but rather a feat of clay. We should thus have the heart to hold fast to our hypothesis to the end, and not at the last minute reveal that we have had power up our sleeve right from the start. It would be mere cunning to side with the lowly of this world in order to spring a trap on the unwary, who would then be visited by the mighty power of God Almighty, who smites his enemies. The humbling of human power in order to exalt the power of God is a ruse; it uses weakness in a bait-and-switch game, as a lure in order to spring power at the crucial moment. We should have the strength of our convictions and allow our weak theology and anarchic hypothesis to play itself out, to stretch all the way from the world to God, from *ta me onta* of the world, whom God has deployed to confound the powerful, all the way to God, to what we have been calling the weakness of God.

So let us pose again our original hypothesis: what if, in the name of a weak theology, we reconceived God as something unconditional but without sovereignty? What if the event that stirs in the name of God is the event of a weak force? What then?

I am insisting upon the gap between the original narratives, which I hold to *ad literam* (almost) and what a later post-biblical metaphysical theology has made of them.[1] In that gap there opens up an alternative possibility much more sympathetic to my anarchic sensibilities than the highly hierarchical power story that emerged in the later theological tradition. I confess a love of all deep abysses and of this original desert in the rule of

God. I am advocate of the *tohu wa-bohu* and the dust of the earth, a champion of the waters of the *tehom,* the salty deep. I also confess to a certain amount of cross-wiring. I have read about the *il y a* in Levinas,[2] which he treats as an anonymous rumbling, and about the *khora* in Derrida, which he treats as an elemental indeterminacy in things and the basis of the open-endedness of the future, and those readings have rekindled my interest in these ancient texts. The mainstream orthodox tradition has drummed the primal elements out of the discussion in order to make way for *creatio ex nihilo,* which makes for a cleaner cut, everything black and white, and gives things a firm foundation. The theological tradition thinks that God comes out ahead this way, that God is even greater and mightier, and that God is a greater giver of gifts if God's gift-giving were complete, including both form and matter, exhaustively *ex nihilo.* But while I agree that *creatio ex nihilo* might increase the *power* component in God's rule, I think the loss of the *tohu wa-bohu* and the *tehom* outweighs the gain.

So I have rewired the later mainstream theology with lines coming from a closer reading of the early creation narratives and a little bit of derring-do from Derrida.

Consider how *creatio ex nihilo* would, for example, work against the traditional idea of the "gift" that God is giving. Without the inoriginate desert and the watery deep, God cannot give a true gift because God cannot *give up* or *give over,* not in truth, and expose Godself to risk, or make Godself vulnerable. As Moltmann says, God cannot love if God cannot make himself vulnerable.[3] Without the desert and the deep, God would remain in such total annihilatory, exnihilatory absolute control of what God makes, God would retain so much possession of what God gives, with so much power over it, that it would only be by a weak analogy that we could speak of a gift or of God giving, or even of the production of something "other" than God. The word by which God lets the world *be* must also be the word by which God lets the world *go,* letting Godself in for something that God did not bargain for or see coming. When we idealize God into an ideal observer who knows and sees everything past, present, and coming, we leave behind the biblical narrative in which Yahweh lets himself in for a future that he had not planned on and in which he comes to regret his decision. The possibility of regret is a condition of the possibility of the gift. Time is not a creature in these narratives—the Hebrews did not have a Platonic idea of eternity beyond time. Rather, time is the element in which they transpire, the common horizon of God and the elements, while the unforeseeability of the future is an elemental part of time. Otherwise, creation is just more of the divine self-same, God and more God, the same engendering the same, and there would be no alterity in creation. That kind of *ex nihilo* monotheism is continually exposed to pantheism, on the one hand, where God simply suffocates the very world into which God was trying to breathe life, or, on the other hand, to the reduction of religion to the syco-phantic praise of a transcendent Power-God who would seem to enjoy such obsequiousness, of a Zeus-like oriental tyrant or a decadent Roman em-peror, to whom we pray for magical interventions on the course of history and nature.

Without the mythological *tohu wa-bohu* and the *tehom,* the horizon of the narratives is dramatically and disproportionately shifted away from that of beauty, goodness, and life and over to that of power and of being. They are turned into explanations of why the world is *there,* instead of proclama-tions that what is there is beautiful and *good.* The stories are not about being—being is there, given, mute, and barren—but about *bringing being to life.* But in what has become the orthodox account, the opening hymn to Elohim ceases to be a priestly prayer and becomes a piece of proto-meta-physics or pseudo-physics. It becomes an account, not of the wondrous de-sign and the goodness of life, but of an outburst of muscle-flexing power. The amazing thing, then, becomes, not that things are alive and flowing in differential rhythms marvelous to behold, but the astonishing metaphysical feat that something was made from nothing, that something is *there* at all rather than not, whereas the narratives assume the raw fact of being there and sing the praises of Elohim for *surpassing* mere mute being there. It starts to look as if, when Elohim beheld everything that he did, he said, "it is"; as if Elohim were a German metaphysician who looked upon the work of the six days and said, with a Yiddish accent, "*es gibt das Sein,*" "there is Being," for which the Hebrews hardly had a word. Metaphysicians, with their tin ear for poetry, throw the narratives into reverse, making them go backwards, into being. Then we come away from the story thinking that God can do anything it comes into the divine head to do, which the narra-tives never mention, while pushing God's beautiful artistry and creation's bountiful goodness into a subordinate status, which is the story's clear and pointed emphasis. That distortion is what provokes the later conundrums of a testosterone-heavy onto-theologic, where it is wondered whether God can make a rock heavier than he can lift, or change the past, a tradition to which Peter Damian, as we shall see, belongs, even as it exacerbates the problem of evil that was eating away at Job.

Without the *tehom* and the *tohu wa-bohu,* things lose their depth; the dark drops out; the sea dries up, and everything is simple, cut and dried (up).

Tehom and the *tohu wa-bohu* are mythologemes that emblematize[4] the *eventiveness* of creation in these narratives. There is no doctrine of omnipo-tence, but there is a notion that the good is what Elohim intends by creat-ing, even as what he intends is put at risk by creating. There is no *creatio ex nihilo* in these stories, but rather the fashioning of life from fragile and earthly stuff. While Elohim tells the elements to shape up, there is no telling how well it will all hold up. I take the narrative to imply clearly, if not to say explicitly, that God can do only so much with the raw materials with which he works, that the potter is limited by the clay, that creation is a certain roll of the dice.

The Yahwist account of Yahweh's unbecoming display of trickery, wrath, and frustration, while not revealing Yahweh's best side, brings out something crucially important about the biblical God that the later tradition of metaphysical theology suppresses. Yahweh did not create time, but he is in time and has to cope with an uncertain future. Things do not always turn out the way Yahweh thought they would, which leads the Yahwist to have Yahweh—rashly, in my opinion!—come to regret the whole idea of creation, which is not something that would happen if God could foresee what would happen when he created. (The Radical Orthodoxists like to call everybody else a nihilist, but truth to tell, the first really big nihilistic story in Western literature is the story of Yahweh's show of bad temper in the flood narrative.) There is an irreducible depth and uncertainty in things, an indeterminacy built right into things, which is the condition both of production and creativity as it is of self-destruction, the one and the other. Time and the turmoil are aboriginal, like God, not like demons or evil anti-gods with whom God must make war, but as the ineradicable resistance, indeterminacy, and chance in things with which God must cope. The stories very clearly provide for the constraining limits under which things transpire, which defines what the Greeks would have called the "tragedy" of the human situation, and which we are more inclined to describe by saying that life is risky business, an "event," and we hope it works.

My idea, which is deeply sympathetic with the critique of omnipotence in process theologians,[5] is to shift the emphasis of the Genesis narratives back from power to goodness, back from being to life, back from a muscle-flexing causal force to a gift-giving word who fashions life out of desert and deep.[6] In that sense, the Creator needs to be a weak force, and, *mirabile dictu,* my improbable case for the "weak force of God" is, against all the odds, getting stronger and showing signs of life.[7] That emboldens me now to make what I take to be the real point of the creation stories and to put my cards on the table, as it were, in a more interpretive and less exegetical manner.

UNCONDITIONALITY

Absolute omnipotence is a religious and metaphysical fantasy, but one that contains and displaces a powerful core truth, which is that by "God" we mean the possibility of the impossible. What, then, is the power of God? The name of God is powerful because it is the name of our hope in the contract Elohim makes with things when he calls them "good," when he calls them *to* the good, when he breathes the life of the good over them. The name of God is a name of an event, the event of our faith in the transformability of things, in the most improbable and impossible things, so that life is never closed in, the future never closed off, the horizon never finite and confining. The name of God opens what is closed, breathes life where there is desolation, and gives hope where everything is hopeless. The name of God is powerful, not with the power of brute strength, but with the power of an event. It opens up like an abyss, like a word of abyssal power—which means a groundless ground, not a grounding and foundational one—by means of which it shatters every horizon of representation or imagination, of foreseeability or programmability. But I do not mean this in the fantastic sense, as if God were a super-hero who arrives in the nick of time to save us from the brink of danger by steering the hurricane out to sea and away from populated areas, or by turning back the advancing army of our enemy, or by resuscitating those who are dead.

But then what do I mean? In the name of God, cannot God help us? Is not the name of God the name of our hope and our help? Indeed, that is exactly what it is.

The name of God, we have maintained, is the name of an event, not an entity; the name of something unconditional, the object and the subject of unconditional love and unconditional hope, which concerns us absolutely. The name of God is the name of everything that we love and desire, with a desire beyond desire, the name of our passion, which is the side that Augustine brings out in the *Confessions*. But I go further, for such desire is still in the nominative mode, as if it were a matter of a purely subjective agency on our part, of what we can do by means of our desire desiring. The name of God is also the name of everything that desires us, everything that puts us in the accusative, that desires what is best in us and desires what is best from us, that calls us out beyond ourselves, beyond our desire and our being, beckoning us beyond being to the good. God cajoles, God lures— that is the desire of God *(genitivus subjectivus)*, God's desire for us. Beyond our desire for God lies God's desire for us. The God whom we desire, so beautifully enunciated in the prayers and tears of St. Augustine, is met on the other side by the desiring God who pursues us down labyrinthine paths and with unhurrying pace.

In P's creation narrative, the name of God is the name of an unconditional benediction, an unconditional affirmation of the goodness of life. The name of God, both ancient and beautiful, belongs to a time out of mind, to an ancient beginning, to the event of a fundamental contract with life that calls life good, signed for us in advance, before we were of a legal age. The world resonates with the echo of God's ancient blessing of creation, so that every time a wind blows or a child smiles, we can, if we have the ears to hear, detect there the murmur of the "good" that Elohim pronounces over things, the movements of the spirit of God listing where it will. In the same way, the name of God is the name of everything we hope for in the future, the name of the one who is coming, or coming again, to save us, to establish a reign of messianic peace, the name of the kingdom to come, of the justice that is coming to lift us up in its arms and embrace us like a mother holding her child. Just so, the present, today, stands in the crosswinds, enjoying the breeze that blows out of Paradise and gently caresses us as it wends its way forward to the future, toward the coming of the Messiah.

The creation narratives are first and foremost religious poetry, works of religious imagination, that give expression to a faith and a hope, a love and a desire, to a religious hermeneutic that the name of God is inscribed in things from the start, that the world is marked by the hand of God, that the world bears the stamp of a great and sweeping Yes. To be sure, these stories are through and through the products of their time and do not provide the least inside information about how it was at the beginning of time, when there was no time, or when there was only time, or when there was only God knows what. They give lyrical expression to a faith that, however it was, God's word is there: good, good . . . very good. They start out with the idea that things are *there,* with a kind of mute and barren existence, and their point is to add a new layer of signification to what is simply there: beyond being, life; beyond silence, speech; beyond anonymity, the *good;* beyond neutrality, yes. That "good," that yes, is a fundamental faith in life, the fundamental agreement between Elohim and his creation, the first and last and constant covenant.

Yes—that is the bottomless promise he makes—and yes—that is our bottomless faith. Both a benediction and prediction, a blessing and a faith, God's yes and our yes. Yes, yes.

What we in the West call with our Latinate word *religion* (and are all too ready to spread around the globe) is, on my accounting, the bonds of a mutual agreement, the point where our *yes* meets God's, where our desire meets God's, where the bottomless abyss that opens up in the name of God meets the bottomless abyss of our desire for God, where abyss meets up with abyss, like two great bodies of water that are joined by a storm that inundates a narrow strip of land. Abyss calls out to abyss (*abyssus abyssum invocat,* Ps. 42:7). Abyss joined to abyss in an ever-yawning abyss. Like a deer yearning for running streams, as the psalmist says, the bottomlessness of our passion and of our restlessness, so powerfully chronicled in the *Confes-*

sions, reaches out to the waves and billows of God's bottomless goodness, to the one who calls things "good."

The power of the event that unfolds in the name of God is the unconditional, inextinguishable power of God's Yes. No matter what. Unconditionally. But to be more precise, "unconditionality" is not a property of *power* but of the *word,* not of an entity but of an event. A "condition" is the "word" *(dictum, dictio)* that accompanies *(con)* an agreement, the small print you had better read before you sign on. What is properly unconditional is a word given without conditions, with no fine print, no hidden or secret terms. A promise, an agreement, a covenant (or a command) can be unconditional. The unconditional absolute action in creation is not the magical feat of producing being out of absolutely nothing, an idea nowhere found in the narratives, but the absolutely unconditional *yes,* good, very good, pronounced six times by Elohim, his unconditional affirmation of life, no matter what. His absolute loyalty to life, his absolutely unconditional judgment—and *promise.* Good, good . . . very good.

The promise stands in the face of the worst. In the worst abandonment—"God-forsaken," we say. Why have you forgotten me—my help and my God? We call out to God, will you not be faithful to your promise? The name of God, what we call God, is God's call, the word he pronounces, the promise that he inscribes in creation, the word that calls things good. The name of God is the name of an unconditional promise, not of an unlimited power. A promise made without an army to enforce it, without the sovereign power to coerce it. *That* is what I am calling the weak force of God. That force is the power of powerlessness. Thus, the psalmist laments:

> Why must I walk around mournfully because the enemy oppresses me?
> As with a deadly wound in my body, my adversaries taunt me,
> while they say to me continually, "Where is your God?"
> Why are you cast down, O my soul, and why are you disquieted within me?
> Hope in God; for I shall again praise him, my help and my God. (Ps. 42:9–11)

The name of God is the name of our hope in something unconditional but without sovereign power. If the power of God were a strong force, a power of this world, if it possessed worldly sovereignty, God would send "twelve legions of angels" (Matt. 26:53) whenever "the enemy oppresses me," whenever injustice reared its head. But the name of God is the name of a promise, a weak force, not a worldly power. The word of God—God is a word who addresses us—declares the good in things, calls for an age of messianic joy and peace, but it does not have an army to keep the peace (and when those who speak on behalf of God *do* have an army, that only makes things much worse). When religion becomes a strong force, it becomes consummately dangerous. If you think of God in terms of power, you will be regularly, systematically confounded by—let us say, to put it politely—the unevenness of God's record on behalf of the poor and the oppressed, the irregularity of the help that God gives when my enemy oppresses me. Beyond obfuscation and mystification, it is in the end an outright blasphemy to say that God has some mysterious divine purpose when an innocent child is abducted, raped, and murdered. That is not a mystery but a misconception about God and about the power of God. God's power is invocative, provocative, and evocative, seductive and eductive, luring and alluring, because it is the power of a call, of a word/Word, of an affirmation or promise. That murder is not part of a long-term good, a more mysterious good that we just can't understand. The murder is a violation of the "good," a contradiction of God's benediction, which strains and stresses God's word, puts it to the test, puts us to the test. God is not testing us like Job with this murder, but we are all of us—Job and God, God and God's word, "good . . . very good"—being put to the test.

So if religion indulges in the fantasy of omnipotent power, the truth of religion is the genuine power of powerlessness, of the bottomless and infinite depth of the unconditional affirmation of the world, of the very stuff of things, calling the world "good," categorically, which means "amen," *oui, oui,* despite the tragic course of history. For no matter how profound our misery, the name of God runs deeper; no matter how strong our sorrow, the name of God is stronger. The *yes* to life that Elohim sprawls across the space of history, as on a great map in which the letters go unnoticed, the *yes* that echoes across the ages, is at the same time a vast and resonant *no* directed against hopelessness and meaningless suffering. The world is good, not because it was made by a super-agent external to the world who communicates his goodness to it as his handiwork and pronounces it good; its goodness speaks for itself, although it is constantly contradicted, and this narrative gives words to our faith and our hope against hope that it is good nonetheless, no matter how dangerous it also is.

The first creation narrative was written for a people in exile: it said *yes* to life when everything about life said *no;* it said good when everything about life seemed wrong. That is why the irreducible truth of religion, which rises up from an affirmation of the world, from celebration and bottomless joy, arises no less from the abyss of suffering, from the tears of the exiled and persecuted, from the lament of the lame and the leper, from the cry of the victim, and also—this is a part of today's religion—from the abyss of a suffering earth that cries out against exploitation. *De profundis clamavi ad te, Domine.* From these depths, where I am, from these depths, which I am, I cry out to you, in the depths. That is the groan of every living thing, of all creatures great and small, from the Levinasian widow, orphan, and stranger to the Leviathans sporting in the sea with whom Yahweh can no longer play because, mad as Ahab, we have slaughtered nearly all of them, as Catherine Keller has argued.

The promise that Elohim inscribes upon creation gives words to a depth of meaning in life, affirming the sacredness of the least thing, and it adds an infinite depth to the protest against violence and the violation of life. Life is sacred stuff, arising from elements of bottomless and dark depths, from deep and dark and salty seas upon which Elohim has breathed. Life springs up from an antique turmoil that trembled with possibility and the future, recorded in ancient archives of scenes long lost to memory, about which we can only tell tall, telling, and searching stories, like old salts telling stories of life upon the deep when they were young and hardy lads. The abyss signifies that life has an inviolability about it, a sacredness that it is the role of the name of God to confer and confirm, to confirm and affirm, to affirm and reaffirm, from time out of mind, and for ages upon ages. Elohim's "good" is an event resonating across the epochs, and this despite the tragic turns life takes again and again, despite the meaningless suffering and the irredeemable loss, despite the persecution of the innocent and the triumph of the wicked, in a history of ruins that mocks the "progress" of our ever-increasing technological skills.

The answer to the problem of evil involves asking the right question.[8] The problem is misconceived if we think it somehow involves arguing God off the hook. The problem of evil is in part human malice, which is as old as Cain, and for that we require ever-more-just institutions; and it is in part the vagaries of disease and natural disasters, and about that we need better medical knowledge, better meteorological forecasts, a lot more prudence in our dealing with nature, and better luck all around. But evil is part of the price we pay for life, for history and nature. Evil is half malice and half bad luck, but all trouble, an omnipresent specter that is the cost of doing business in the world. The only answer to it is to have the strength to countersign Elohim's *yes* with our own *yes*—yes invoking and provoking yes—while allowing ourselves to be haunted and disturbed by the Yahwist's *but*. There is always the *but,* but the *but* is only allowed on stage by the Redactor after the majestic hymn to creation, the opening hymn to *yes,* in the priestly narrative.

Yes, yes. . . .

but . . .

Well, then, let's hope it works.

Yes, yes.

The sovereignty we affirm is not the sovereignty of power but the sovereign beauty of the world and the sovereign joy of life, which is unconditionally affirmed and unconditionally promised in the rhythms of Elohim's "good," which we are asked to countersign, yes, yes. That is God's covenant with us, the oldest of the old and the newest of the new covenants. The name of God lays an unconditional claim upon us—that is the event that is lodged within it—because it is Elohim's unconditional verdict and benediction, his decisive declaration, his promise that everything he has made, *come what may,* is good. Our faith is a countersigning of his declaration, which is hoping it all works.

Very good.

THE WEAK FORCE OF GOD

Abyssus abyssum invocat—invocation as opposed to incantatory magic, the power of powerlessness as opposed to an omnipotent power of intervention. That is the basic acoustics or stereophonics of a theology of the event. God is a lure who draws us on, Whitehead said,[9] luring us through history, the power of an attraction, a provocation, an evocation, the power of an abyssal promise, which is more like the "final" than the "efficient" cause of Aristotle, an attracting cause but without a tidy teleology. God is the power of a promise. To this end without end, an end out of sight, we run a line to Derrida, when he says, in speaking of the "promise" that is inscribed in language, that this is what is called God in theology.[10] For Derrida, the event of the promise, the call of what is "to come," is inscribed in the name of God, but not only there, for Derrida could say whatever he has to say without the benefit of this name, because this name is endlessly translatable into other names, like justice or the gift, all of which hold out the promise of something to come. For Derrida, the promise is lodged in language itself, in words harboring events of elemental lure and allure, which draw us out beyond the present toward the future even as they stir up memories of an immemorial past, words that resonate with the past and are restless with the future and possibility, including even, especially, the possibility of the impossible.

For the word that Elohim first pronounces over creation is not only a proclamation that declares the world good, it also gives voice to a promise that keeps its fingers crossed. As the most ancient and aboriginal word in creation, it holds out to us the prospect of a messianic age in which the good will be realized, actualized, incarnated. The call calls things forth into the world and calls us forward to the promise it holds. And Elohim looked upon everything he made and said, This is good, it may just work, let's hope it does.

In the most classical language of theology, God is a spirit who inspires, who breathes upon us and draws us hence, who moves us forward by the gentle listing of its breath, who lifts us with an invisible hand, raising our spirit, who breathes upon us and makes us new. Send forth your spirit, Lord, and make us new. The Lord is the *ruach Elohim,* the spirit of Elohim, where the wind that Elohim sends over us is the spirit that Elohim is, his very breathing over the deep from which we are drawn.

Abyssus abyssum invocat. The name of God is to be thought in terms of the Hebraic model of the call calling rather than the Hellenistic model of a cause causing, of covenant rather than of causality, of undying loyalty to his word rather than of eternal being, of a primordial promise rather than a prime mover—or if a mover, then one who moves by a motivating call or a provocation or a promise rather than by the strong force of an efficient cause. Faith moves the mountain of hopelessness, while the physical mountain stays hopelessly put. Hope raises hearts dashed by the cruelty of events with the prospect of a coming day, but what is done is done; hope raises the dead by resurrecting the heart while the dead bury the dead. God is a hope, not a magician. Forgiveness changes the meaning of the past, while the being of the past is irremissible. It is because God is but a weak force that Auschwitz was possible, all the Auschwitzes, all the ethnic cleansings that have stained human history. It is because God is but a weak force that God does not intervene upon the heartbreak of a perfectly innocent child struck down by a rare disease. It is the weak force of God that kept Jesus nailed to the cross, for he was not a king in any archical sense. My God, my God, why have you forgotten me? If he is a king, why doesn't his army save him? That is what the *Romans* ask, they who understand about worldly sovereignty and imperial power. He was a king *ironice,* in a way that worldly might mocked and that in turn makes a mockery of worldly might. The Romans could extinguish Jesus but not his memory, the primal scene of suffering's most dangerous memory. The dead are the stuff of dangerous memories, constituting a weak force, harnessing all the power of powerlessness.

One of the most revealing and moving examples of the power of an unconditional claim that is without power, of the weak force of something unconditional but without sovereignty, is Benjamin's conception of a "*weak messianic power*" formulated in his famous "The Concept of History," to which I have already referred. He is speaking of the claim made upon us by those who are the weakest of all, whose voice is thus the softest: the dead, whose claim cannot be taken lightly. Benjamin describes the "angel of history," which is for him a figure of the "messianic" view of history, as opposed to what he calls "historicism," by which he means several things: a secular and Rankean science of history, one steered by an Enlightenment view of "progress," in virtue of which the dead are sacrificed to the story of progress and imbedded in a tale told by the winners. The task of the messianic historian is to save or redeem the dead. So this is a peculiar sort of messianism, one that is turned toward the past, not the future, in which we, in the present, occupy the messianic position; we are not the ones who expect but the ones who were expected.[11]

The angel is driven forward into the future, but with his back to the future, his eyes fixed on the ever-accumulating heap of ruins called history, where the ruins are the irredeemably ruined lives of the dead upon which "progress" is built. Were he turned around to face the future, the angel would presumably become himself a believer in progress, and the dead would be out of sight and soon enough out of mind. But everything in Benjamin turns on mindfulness *(Gedächtnis)* of the dead, a recollection *(Andenken)* of them, which is never far from prayer and devotion *(Andacht)*, keeping them in our "thoughts and prayers," keeping them "in mind" or "in our hearts," as we say in English. This remembrance is not a simple epistemic and historiological act, like keeping good notes, a complete chronicle, or a historical record, but it is an act that moves closely in tune with prayer, with prayers and tears, and perhaps even with love, which is why Kierkegaard said that remembering the dead is not simply a thought but a work of love.[12]

Still, this mindfulness and prayerfulness is not magic; the redemption the historian can offer is only remembrance, not resurrection, which is why it is a "weak" messianic power. The angel would like to, but cannot awaken the dead; time and the force of progress move on and leave the dead behind. Remembrance is not an incantation that brings them back to life or calls them out of their graves or restores their ruined lives. Were it a strong and not a "weak" power, it would be turned to the future, where a real Messiah who will show up later on could make a real difference. But why then is something so weak not simply another name for despair? Why is it a "messianic" power at all, even a weak one? Because a messianic force is an event, and mindfulness is itself a messianic force: "our coming was expected," and we today, in the now-point of the present, are the ones the dead were waiting for; we stand at the messianic point of redemption and remembrance. The "now-time" *(Jetztzeit)* is a door through which at any moment the Messiah may pass. We today are charged with the messianic role of redeeming the past, of seeing to it that the dead have not died in vain, and that each one, down to the smallest and most insignificant, is recalled from oblivion. The past lays claim to our "*weak* messianic power," and "that claim," he says, "cannot be settled cheaply." There we see the force of the unconditional, of an event that lacks physical power.

The limitation of Benjamin's view is that he does not say much about hope, perhaps because he does not see much room for hope. He does mention "fanning the spark of hope in the past,"[13] which is what needs to be cultivated. If there is such hope in Benjamin, it is not a point he takes any pains to emphasize.[14] "Hope in the past" is an odd expression, but it has to do with the attempt to change past time that is always at work when we raise the question of the irredeemable sufferings of the past. Hope in the past means the hope that is engendered by the mediation, the remembrance, of the past. For the act of remembrance of the dead is also an act of hope, a hope that flares up in the face of hopeless catastrophe, the hope in Elohim's "good." For hope is most authentically called for when everything is hopeless, according to the logic of the impossible. The angel is driven into the future by a storm blowing from Paradise, the storm called "progress," which is the force of history, which soon started up with Cain and Abel.[15] Backed into the future, the angel must become a figure of hope in the midst of hopeless ruin, and hence a figure of what St. Paul called hope against hope, and Benjamin should remember not only the history of ruin but the original *yes* that Elohim inscribes on history. But in what does such redemption consist? Perhaps in the resurrection of the dead at the end of time? Perhaps. "We do not know whether [Benjamin] prayed."[16] But short of that, the redemption is the remembrance, and the remembrance is the spark of hope that burns in remembrance, the breath of hope that breathes whenever we remember those whose lives were meaninglessly cut short and brutalized, which is what Johann Baptist Metz calls the "dangerous memory of suffering." That is why the weak force of Benjamin's backward-directed messianism needs to be joined with the weak force of Derrida's "come," which is a call for a justice to come, in which this spectral figure has turned around toward the future. For in Derrida's conception of the messianic, in which mourning is held in tension with hope, and remembrance with expectation—unlike Benjamin's, Derrida's is not a "tragic" view—the messianic is concerned not only with redeeming the dead, the *revenants,* but with redeeming the future, the children, the *arrivants,* the ones to come, which is the more usual meaning of hope. For Derrida, it is not a question of choosing between the two.[17]

The name of God is astir in weak messianic forces, like remembering the dead, which does not raise them out of their graves, as also in forgiving the unforgivable instead of getting even, in loving one's enemies instead of hating back, or mercifulness instead of punishing, or hospitality instead of exclusion, or saying yes in the face of bottomless despair. In every case, a weak force rather than a strong, powerful only with the power of powerlessness, each of which is a way of making the impossible possible.

In the name of God, in the name of the event that is astir in the name of God.

Abyssus abyssum invocat. I have not been authorized to probe the abyss, to decide the undecidable, to determine whether this call issues from someone identifiable or something entitative; whether the call has an ontological footing in some real being, power, or entity; whether this vocative force is likewise an entitative power, personal, pre-personal, or impersonal.[18] But as a strictly phenomenological matter, the call subsists as a call, and a call is something that is called, its only and best testimony being that it is heard. For a call, to be is to be heard; *esse est audiri.* Indeed, I would go further and say that it is a condition of our hearing it that we *cannot* identify it further. The confession that we cannot identify it is *constitutive* of it. For as soon as we would be able to identify it, as soon as we could say who and what is calling, we would have begun to master it and make it our own and put ourselves back in the nominative. We would no longer be in the accusative, put on the spot, de-posed by what it poses to us. We would have driven the abyss out of it, and we would own it entirely. But as a weak force, with no being in this world, with no worldly place to lay down its head, the physical voice of the call is faint, just a trace of a voice. Like the kiss Jesus gives the Grand Inquisitor, which is mightier than the powerful Cardinal's armed guards. We, in turn, who have been called forth from the turmoil and the abyss, drawn from the deep, we who are an abyss and a question to ourselves, we who are made of such uncertain and unstable stuff, are in no position to locate its source or identify it. Abyss calls to abyss. The call calls from I know not where, from the deep, like a wind rustling above the waters, like the rush of the *ruach Elohim* sweeping across the darkness of the deep, like another breeze blowing out of Paradise. The question, my friend, is blowing in the wind, in the cross-currents of these winds out of Paradise.

It is in or under the name of God that the event calls upon us. It is not what we call God that is at issue, but what God calls. Then again, it is not what God calls that is at issue, but the response, which is the first and only testimony to the call, which is from a worldly point of view a weak force, like a kiss.

HERMENEUTICAL INTERLUDE: TWO KEYS TO THE KINGDOM

FIVE

The Poetics of the Impossible

> The angel said to her: . . .
> For nothing will be impossible to God.
> Then Mary said, *me voici.* (Luke 1:35–38)

A HERMENEUTICAL INTERLUDE

Let us take a moment to regroup methodologically.

Theology is the logos of our passion for God, with or without religion or the churches or what is ordinarily called theology, the name of God being too important to leave to the special interest groups. The theological work undertaken here may be described as a hermeneutics of the name of God, the explication *(Auslegung)* of what is unfolding in the event of this name, or even as a deconstruction, which means to release the event that is trapped in the name. The next step in this hermeneutic, or deconstruction, this radical hermeneutic of the name of God, is to take up what the Scriptures call the "kingdom of God," which is where the name of God is incarnated, gets flesh and bones, blood and sinew, where it is stretched out in space and time. We will argue that, with a perfectly perverse symmetry, God's weakness and God's kingdom, God's powerless power and God's rule, are well and truly suited to each other, so that God's kingdom provides a perfect way to concretize or embody the weak force of God, nothing like what you would expect if you were expecting a kingdom in the royal sense, full of the paraphernalia of purple and power and princely potentates.

However, before proceeding straightaway to this analysis, we pause for a little methodological intermission or hermeneutical interlude, meant to clarify a persistent and not inconsiderable problem. For on the face of it, the very idea of the kingdom as a "sacred anarchy," which signifies the unruliness of the rule of God, a kind of divine madness that runs roughshod over the settled ways and rules of the world, seems quite at odds with "weak theology." For a sacred anarchy seems to send us hurtling down the path of omnipotence and divine interventionism, of bodies raised from the dead, of Jesus walking on water or passing through solid walls, of miraculous healings and angelic visitations—in short, of a world turned inside out and upside down by divine power. With God, all things are possible, even the impossible; and that enters into the very warp and woof of strong theology and the metaphysics of omnipotence, of miracles and divine interventions, providing all the support we would ever need for the idea that the name of God is the name of the strongest force of all. Why then is a sacred anarchy not part and parcel of, nay, the best argument yet for, a *strong* theology? That is another formidable and knee-bending objection, as least as tough as dealing with the idea of *creatio ex nihilo.*

This objection forces us to work out some general methodological is-sues about the discursive type or hermeneutical status of the event that is unfolding in the name of God, in the Word of God (Scripture). I will do this in two steps, thus offering the reader two hermeneutical keys to the kingdom of God. First, in the present chapter I will make clear that the dis-course of the kingdom rightly understood is governed, not by a "logic of omnipotence," which has to do with entities, but by what I will call a *poet-ics of the impossible,* which has to do with events (ch. 5). Then, in the next chapter, I will explicate the "hermeneutical situation" of a theology of the event as a *hermeneutics of the call,* in the process staking out the case that weak theology has to do with what I call a "hyper-realism of the event," and in this way escapes between the horns of the debate between theological re-alism and anti-realism (ch. 6). Only then will we be in a position to dive down the rabbit hole of the kingdom, to behold the exceedingly odd things that happen there in the amazing mirror of its metanoetics, its epiousiology, and all of the other astonishing adventures we encounter in this wonder-land (Part Two).

THE POETICS OF THE IMPOSSIBLE

In the kingdom, things happen *by* the impossible. To be very precise, every-thing is possible just in virtue of being impossible. In response to Mary's objection that she could not possibly be with child, Gabriel points out with angelic courtesy that with God nothing is impossible. And so begins the kingdom. And still another short circuit, another cross-wiring, for with the idea of something happening *by* "the impossible" every reader knows that I am running still another structural line between the beginning of Luke's fa-mous story of the Annunciation and deconstruction. To the way things happen when God rules, where with God nothing is impossible, I link what Derrida calls "the impossible." Jesus himself associated with sinners, so perhaps he will mind less than do his self-appointed and anointed defenders my associating the Gospels with deconstruction. But my offense is multiple. For in addition to offering a stumbling block to the secularizing deconstructors who think with Nietzsche that when you read the New Testament you should wear gloves, and in addition to presenting a scandal to religious conservatives, who think that Derrida is a messenger of the devil sent as a punishment for our sins (unless of course they think he *is* the devil himself, which is not impossible), I here risk adding the hoary ranks of the logicians to the list of those whom I am offending and who are certain to bring this up at a crucial moment in my campaign if I ever stand for public office. Be that as it may, the "poetics of the impossible" is the suitably anarchic law or lawlessness that tends to rule, or makes things unruly, in the "kingdom."

St. Paul—my sometime namesake whom I try not to betray too much—counseled us not to conform to the world. But if, under the pressure to conform to the world of the philosophers, I were forced to cough up the "logic" of a theology of the event, then I would have to insist from the start that this is a divine logic that is outright madness from the point of view of the "world," which is supposed to be as sane as Kansas, a logos that is a folly *(moria)* (1 Cor. 1:18). From the point of view of logic, for logic is the light of the world, the "kingdom of God" is impossible. But, to be quite precise, we must insist that it is not *simply* impossible—remember, nothing is simple and nothing is impossible—but rather, remembering the Derrida link, *the* impossible. By this Derrida does not mean a simple logical contradiction, like "(*p* and ~*p*)," which would be a little boring, but something unforeseeable that shatters our horizons of expectation, which is quite exciting.[1] That is why he says that the least bad definition of deconstruction is "an experience of the impossible,"[2] a way of calling *("viens")* for the possibility of the impossible, where the impossible is the event that shatters the horizons of the possible. So in the place of a "logic" of *the* impossible I have chosen instead to speak here of a "poetics," like the "poetics of obligation" I defended in *Against Ethics*.

The central and overriding reason for this decision is that a poetics is an evocative discourse that articulates the event, while a logic is a normative discourse governing entities (real or possible), which can or do instantiate its propositions. A poetics addresses the rule of the promise or of *the call,* the grammar of the *weak force of the call,* while a logic regulates the *strong force of the world.* A logic addresses real or possible occurrences in the world, while a poetics addresses the event of being addressed, not by what actually is but by what is promising. So you begin to see how I plan to elude the torpedo of omnipotence that a sacred anarchy might otherwise seem to have launched straight in my direction, namely, by replacing a logic of omnipotence with a poetics of the impossible. In a logic, things are really possible or necessary or not, and that is that.[3] But a "poetics" is meant to interrupt the workings of the real by evoking another possibility, the possibility of the event, which is here the event of the kingdom's coming, where it is weakness, not strength, that reigns, if anything reigns. A poetics describes the symbolic space that obtains in the kingdom, while a logic describes the ideal or normative rules that govern real or possible worlds. In a *poetics* of the impossible, we mean to pose the possibility of something life-transforming, not to report how an omnipotent being intervenes upon nature's regularities and bends them to its infinite will, which is an occurrence, or a super-occurrence, that would transpire on the plane of being, not an "event" of the call. In the logic of impossibility, the impossible is simply something that cannot be, whereas in a poetics of *the* impossible, we are hailing an event that is otherwise than being.

But what then does a poetics look like? A poetics gives voice to the properly symbolic discourse of the kingdom, while a logic enunciates the literal discourse of the world. As a symbolic discourse, then, a poetics is a certain constellation of idioms, strategies, stories, arguments, tropes, paradigms, and metaphors—a style and a tone, as well as a grammar and a vocabulary, all of which, collectively, like a great army on the move, is aimed at gaining some ground and making a point. We might say that a poetics is a discourse with a heart, supplying the heart of a heartless world. Unlike logic, it is a discourse with *pathos,* with a passion and a desire, with an imaginative sweep and a flare, touched by a bit of madness, hence more of an a-logic or even a patho-logic, one that is, however, not sick but healing and salvific. A poetics of *the* impossible describes the dynamics of a desire beyond desire for the kingdom, a desire beyond reason and beyond what is reasonably possible, a desire to know what we cannot know, or to love what we dare not love, like a beggar in love with a princess, whose desire is not extinguished by the impossible but fired by it. For our hearts are burning with a desire to go where we cannot go, to the impossible, praying and weeping for what eye has not seen nor ear heard, hoping against hope, as Paul said. A poetics is situated in the space where the call of the kingdom communicates with the response (come!).

Logic describes the rules of what is possible, probable, or entirely necessary.[4] But to curb our passion to the parameters of realistic expectation, so that desire remains confined by the boring borders of the real, of the inevitable, or of a carefully calculated probability—what would that amount to if not a lover without passion, which is, according to Johannes Climacus, the definition of a "mediocre fellow"?[5] So once again we enter upon the turf of anarcho-prophetico-Danish deconstruction, of the amazing short circuit we are trying to wire up. We want to think thoughts that cannot be thought, to work things up to a feverish pitch, to give life a passion, a salt, and a cutting edge that has all the marks of the kingdom, as opposed to the business as usual of the world, which is the province of logic.

Logic addresses the modally possible, whereas a poetics is always a grammar of the "perhaps," which is the prime modality of the event. In logic the "possible" has the straightforward sense of logical or metaphysical possibility and necessity, ideal or real possibility, in which everything is organized around the very prestigious category of being or reality, whereas in a poetics the possible belongs to the humble sphere of what Derrida calls the "perhaps," the *peut-être*. The *peut-être* threatens to irrupt from within and to disturb the conditions of *être*,[6] supplying the dangerous *perhaps* of the possibility of the impossible that solicits us from afar. The grammar of the "perhaps" is neither that of the incontestable "it is" nor the inexorable "it is necessary" *(chrein)* nor the imperious "thou shalt." The call of the kingdom is "unconditional," but its unconditionality is not that of an unconditionally necessary being beyond being but rather the unconditional appeal for something unconditional, a plea for something beyond being— for the kingdom—to come. As a promise without the power to enforce its promise, as a call without the force to enforce what it calls for, as a plea or an appeal whose realization is exposed to all the hazards of chance, the "perhaps" lacks both the being *(ousia)* and the authority *(exousia)* to enforce its demands. Not a booming "thou shalt" or "it is necessary," but an ever soft and mild "maybe." Not as powerful as being, or as imperious as a categorical imperative, it calls without the worldly wherewithal to realize or materialize the concrete entitative conditions in the world that its unconditional appeal requires. They are, after all, impossible. It calls in the quiet tones of the weak force of the "perhaps."

So everything in a poetics of the impossible is turned toward showing that the possibility of the impossible does not belong to the horizon of power and being, to the power trip of a metaphysics of omnipotence, to a logic of a supervening super-power that overpowers garden-variety power and performs feats of thaumaturgical intervention. The kingdom is amazing grace, not amazing magic. Everything depends upon what may seem a bit of prestidigitation, namely, inscribing the possibility of the impossible within the horizon of the power of powerlessness, of the weakness of God. The impossible does not depend upon a metaphysical heavyweight or a theological super-power but upon the weakness of its unconditional claim upon us, the strength, not of its sovereign force, but of its unconditional call. That is why it requires a poetics, why it is expressed in parables and narratives that stretch logic's credence. For the possibility of the impossible does not describe the domain of what is, but of what calls. It does not articulate what is there, but something soliciting what is there, groaning and sighing for birth, something that longs to happen, a dangerous possibility, endangering what is and the powers that be. It summons up the irruption of an event simmering in the heart of what is there. So if in a poetics someone walks on water or is raised from the dead, that is not supposed to send the physicists and the biologists scurrying back to their computers to crunch their numbers once again to check this out, but to send our hearts soaring with a desire beyond desire for transformation, renewal, rebirth, for which we pray and weep. The world is what is there; the kingdom is what calls, or is called for, or calls us. Just as in our reading of Genesis: the elements are what is there; it is up to Elohim to call them "good," which is as much a prediction as a predication, as much a benediction as a prediction, as much a provocation as a benediction.

Vis-à-vis logic, the rule of this poetics is "foolishness," which means it has a taste for the para-logical, a love for the elusive lines of the parabolic and the hype of the hyperbolic. That is why the text of the New Testament is rife with parables and paradoxes, and why you could even write a history of people who were fools for the kingdom of God.[7] Rather than a clumsy, heavy-handed logic that is all thumbs in these matters, we require just such a poetics if we are to negotiate the subtle pianissimos and fortes of the music that is played in the kingdom. This poetics does not play an Aristotelian tune; it takes its measure, not from moderation and calculation, from equilibrium and holding the center, but from excess and the recess, from the hyperbolic and the elliptical. Hence the paradoxes that punctuate this poetics are parabolic, and its parables are hyperbolic (when they are not elliptical), and its evaluations are reversals. That explains why its system of accounting, its *logos,* is so odd. The way things are counted in the "kingdom" confounds the calculations of the "world," for it demands that if your brother offends you seven times a day, you should forgive him, and that still holds even if he offends you seven times seventy, which seems excessive. There is more rejoicing over the one sheep that is found than over the ninety-nine that are safe, which is an unaccountably odd way to count, since there is more profit in the ninety-nine, and the one is not worth the risk to the ninety-nine, as we can be assured by any cost accountant.

So in the end, the disapproving look of the philosophers notwithstanding, I chose to speak, not of a logic of the possible and necessary, but of a "poetics" of "*the* impossible." We can only keep pace with what is going on in the kingdom by staying with the twists of its parables and riding out the turns of its paradoxes. The paradoxes usually take the form of reversals: the last shall be first; the insiders are out; sinners are preferred; the stranger is the neighbor; enemies are to be loved; and, as a general rule, a generally unruly rule, the impossible is possible. The parables usually take the form of outrageous stories, like the story of the wedding banquet in which the guests are casual passersby who are dragged in off the street, while the invited guests snub the host, which seems like an excessively mad party, of a sort to stretch the imagination even of a Lewis Carroll, not to mention of any parents who actually paid for their daughter's wedding.

But this love of poetic diction does not spring from a wanton fondness for poetic license or from a taste for rhetorical impishness or from authors with no head for logic. On the contrary, it is a discourse with a deadly serious and rigorous concern to give voice to the call that *contradicts* the world, as serious as Jesus himself, who evidently had a taste for this kind of sharp and paradoxical discourse, and as serious as First Corinthians, which turns on these overturning turns of phrase. And it has a prophetic concern to confound and *interdict* the hardness of heart of the world, to shame its cold-hearted logic, and to put its heartless economics on notice, which is as serious as Amos. When, as we have seen, Paul says that God sides with the foolish and weak things of the world, the nothings and nobodies, in order to *reduce to nothing* the things that boast of being and presence *(ta onta),* which means the powers that be, that pretend to be and have *ousia,* he was trying to shock the world with the impossible way things are done in the kingdom. For the kingdom comes to loosen the grip of the world, to dislodge the rule of being, to release the event that the world would prevent, which is the whole idea behind what I am calling a sacred anarchy.

In the New Testament, the "world" and the kingdom are antagonists because the logic of the world is a calculus, an economy, a heartless system of accounting or of balanced payments, where scores are always being settled. In the logic of the world, nothing is for free and nobody gets off scot-free. By the same token, in the logic of the world, everything is for sale, everything has a price, and nothing is sacred. The world will stop at nothing to get even, to settle or even a score; the world is pomp and power and ruthless reckoning. In the world, offenders are made to pay for their offense and every investor expects a return. Every equation must be balanced, with blood or money or prison time. In the world, everybody has a lawyer. So the logic of the world and the poetics of the kingdom do not describe two different places, like New York and Paris, or Athens and Jerusalem, or this world and the other one behind the clouds, except poetically, differentiating two different orders of signification that contend with each other in the only existing world we know. They describe, not two different "wheres," but two different "hows," whose differences must be negotiated in the one and only world we know.

A poetics is a discourse or diction of contradiction and interdiction, a grammar of how one "calls for" *(prophetein)* the rule of God, how it is proclaimed *(kerygma),* how one calls for things to happen in God's way, not the world's, remembering all the time the paradoxical character of this "rule," where the reign of God settles upon the brow of the powerless. The discourse of the kingdom flies up in the world's face, which is a costly business, for the world keeps strict accounts and knows how to make its opponents pay. If someone comes into the world and calls the world to account for itself, the world will receive him not (John 1:10–11), which usually means it will cost him dearly, maybe everything, not a good investment. That is why the discourse of the kingdom takes such a contrarian form, why it is so unyielding, so full of poetic perversity.

The kingdom comes to contradict the world and contest the world's ways, and it always looks like foolishness to the world's good sense, moving as it does between logic and passion, truth and justice, concepts and desire, strategies and prayers, astute points and mad stories, for it can never be merely or simply the one or the other. The whole idea of an anarchic strategy is not to break these tensions but to settle into and deploy them, negotiating the distance between them. The whole idea is to create a disturbance, to insinuate a dangerous "perhaps," to speak out in the name of justice, in the name of God, in the name of an event, of something, I know not what, to raise hell, holy hell, or to raise the roof, a sacred roof, which is what happens if you call for the coming of the kingdom, if you pray and weep for the coming of justice, right out in public. The kingdom comes to put the world in question, to put it on the spot, to put it into question. May thy kingdom come. *Viens, oui, oui.*

When I speak of the "kingdom," I should add, I am not talking about going to heaven after you die, which you are free to believe. That is one way to go where you cannot go—and I have no special travel information to offer you about that trip. I am not describing a form of death but a form of life, a life of salt and passion, of prayers and tears, whatever you may believe about cosmic geography. I do not know what happens to you after you die—we suffer from a scarcity of reliable reports from the other side—so do not ask me. The dead are good listeners and singularly good at keeping their counsel. They lie there patiently and hear us out, but they rarely reply to our inquiries, no matter how earnestly we press them. Still, they have much to teach us and I recommend their counsel. If you doubt it, take a trip to the cemetery, as Kierkegaard says in "The Work of Love in Recollecting One Who Is Dead," and consult with those "masterful thinkers" who see through every illusion and offer the shortest and most succinct summary of life. They are deadly honest brokers.[8]

We do not know who we are or where we are going, if indeed we are going anywhere. That you will have to find out for yourself. That is part of the passion of our lives. The question of existence is worked in the concrete for each poor existing individual, worked out "in the existing," as Heidegger says. The project of a theology of the event, on the other hand, is to describe an event that cuts across the distinction between confessional beliefs and unbelief, this life and the next life, and goes to the heart of a life worth living, a life of passion, which is structured like a religion without religion. The unsalted life, as we say in Socratico-Danish deconstruction, is not worth examining.

AN EXPERIENCE OF
THE IMPOSSIBLE

The philosophers are not accustomed to events but rather to arranging things according to the logic of being, to the "principles" of reason, order, possibility, presence, sense, and meaning, an intimidating parade of luminaries enjoying pride of place in philosophy, sitting at the head of philosophy's table. That is why, beyond any Greek sense of wonder, the texts of the kingdom read—if we may adapt a suggestion coming from Gilles Deleuze[9]—like a veritable *Alice in Wonderland* of wedding feasts as mad as any hatters' party, of sinners getting preference over perfectly respectable fellows, of virgins giving birth, of eventualities that confound the economy of the world.

If the truth be told—back to the short circuit—what comes about when the kingdom comes looks and sounds a lot more like what we are calling an event. We could say of the kingdom what Deleuze says of *Alice:* to understand it requires "a category of very special things: events, pure events."[10] The coming of the kingdom is an out-coming, from *evenire* (Lat.), the coming-out, the *événement* or bursting out of something we did not see coming, something unforeseen, singular, irregular, even a bit odd. Alternatively, the event is also what Derrida calls *l'invention de l'autre,* the in-coming *(invenire)* of something "wholly other," the breaking into our familiar world of something completely amazing, completely unexpected, which breaks up our horizons of expectations. To get the sense of Derrida's "incoming" *(invention),* recall its military sense, where, when the soldiers hear someone shout that word, the sensible thing to do is head for cover, for they are about to be visited by something that could blow them all to kingdom come.

This outburst or outcoming, this coming of the impossible, of the gift, of the kingdom, shatters the horizons of economics, of balanced payments and carefully conducted cost analyses, coming in and as a form of time, a giving of time, *donner le temps,* a moment of madness that tears up the time of Husserl and the philosophical tradition generally. Otherwise, nothing is happening, nothing much, nothing new; creation is grinding to a stop, and the *yes* is losing the strength to repeat itself, to come again; life loses its salt. The "event" is something for which no horizon of possibility or foreseeability is able to prepare us, something that contradicts our mundane expectations, which is what we mean by *the* impossible. To wait for the event is to expect to be surprised and overtaken, to prepare for something for which you cannot be prepared, which is like knowing that the kingdom will come like a thief in the night. The event presupposes both a horizon of possibility and expectation *and* the possibility of shattering our horizons and expectations, the possibility of the impossible.

Here then is the short circuit I propose. In imitation of the Master who dined with sinners, I invite the theologians to sit down to table with deconstruction and other disreputable French sinners. To the great scandal of secularizing deconstructors and the Christian right alike, I contend that the way the kingdom contests the powers and principalities of the world, the powers that be *(exousiai)*, that pretend to be and to have presence, can be wired up with the notorious critique of the "metaphysics of presence" *(ousia)* in deconstruction. I run a line between the opposition of the "kingdom" to the "world" in the Scriptures and the opposition of the "gift," which is *the* impossible, to "economy," in deconstruction. I wire the coming of the kingdom together with the in-coming of the *tout autre* or the out-coming of the event in deconstruction. Then I run for cover to find a safe place from which to view the sparks this gives off.

I am contending that in a poetics of the impossible—which tracks the coming of the kingdom—things are, shall we say, highly deconstructible. Being "deconstructible" is not as bad as it sounds; in fact, my contention is that it is good news, and it arises in the wake of *the* good news. For something is deconstructible only if it has been constructed to begin with, which is why deconstruction comes along in the wake of a theology of creation, and why its critique of the metaphysics of presence springs from a frame of mind that keeps an eye out for the idols of presence. Accordingly, deconstructibility is the condition for the "event." Otherwise things would be nailed down too tightly, and *ousia* would cling too tightly to *ousia* to allow the event to happen. Ousiology is the musicology of strong forces, while in the kingdom the soft music of weak forces is always playing.

What made the heart of Parmenides skip a beat, the Eleatic idea of a good time, was an airtight, perfectly spherical solid, which is, if you let yourself think about it, an exceedingly odd ideal to hold close to your heart. For anything new or surprising to eventuate, for anything strange or amazing to happen, which is what we long for and desire, things must be deconstructible and loosely, weakly strung together. So far from being the enemy of faith and religion, far from announcing the death of God, the deconstructibility of things is one of the hallmarks of the poetics of the kingdom of God, one of the first things to happen when God rules, one of the things we are praying for when we pray for the kingdom to come, for the event to happen, when we pray and weep, *viens, oui, oui.* Deconstructibility is the principal thing we need for things to open up and be pliable to the rule of God, when time is God's rather than the timelessness of a rock-solid, well-rounded, tightly wound sphere, which was the first form *ousia* assumed when it came into the world.

It is a little curious to me that anyone who reads the Scriptures faithfully, and who is in love with the idea of the kingdom of God, would also fall in love with "ousiology" or with Neoplatonic hyperousiology, or with the essentialist and Roman "natural law" theories with which ousiology often keeps company. I should think, following Catherine Keller's example, that they would be more interested in chaos theory. True, nature has its laws, but in the New Testament the rule of God is frequently—I am tempted to say systematically—symbolized by the interruption of these laws. That interruptibility and deconstructibility of things by the event is essential to what we *mean* by the kingdom of God. In the kingdom, God's rule is indeed shown in the regular course that nature follows, like the lilies of the field and mustard seeds, but no less by the disruptions and interruptions of nature's regular course, of which it is the point of this poetics to keep track.

Frankly, in the kingdom of God things happen a lot more like the way things fall out in deconstruction—which has to do with events, and whose least bad definition, Derrida says, is an "experience of *the* impossible"—than they do in classical metaphysics or natural law theories, which are too much taken with the princes and principalities of necessity, order, presence, essence, regularity, and stability. I do not know how to cushion this blow, either for the learned despisers of religion or for the holy despisers of deconstruction, for whom this good news is exceedingly bad news indeed: deconstruction, on my view, is structured like a religion, and makes use of religious structures. *(Hier stehe ich. Ich kann nicht anders.)* For Derrida can say, no less than St. Augustine, *inquietum est cor nostrum,* our hearts are restless and driven by desire, a desire beyond desire, a desire for *the* impossible. For by *the* impossible Derrida does not mean just any wild or crazy eventuality, however bizarre, mean, or violent. The event begins *by* the impossible, as he puts it. By that he means that the event is moved and driven by the desire for the *gift* beyond economy, for the *justice* beyond the law, for the *hospitality* beyond proprietorship, for *forgiveness* beyond getting even, for the coming of the *tout autre* beyond the presence of the same, for what Levinas, picking up on an ancient tradition, called the excess of the *good* beyond being (a lovely idea that lovers of the kingdom can use, if you drop the hint of Neoplatonic metaphysics, which has next to nothing to do with the kingdom, and Levinas's excessively grim view of being itself). The event is driven by a desire for the Messiah to come, a Messiah who will contradict the smug complacency and the pomp of the present, a Messiah who will confront the world and confound the way things are done in the time of the world. So if, on the one hand, the kingdom is the sphere where the weak force of God rules, and if, on the other hand, deconstruction means the rule of the gift, of the good, of justice, of hospitality, and forgiveness, then it seems to me that the two of them, deconstruction and the kingdom of God, should get along famously. Even if they have their differences, and even if their respective adherents and campaign staff workers do not trust each other, they should take a united stand against the opposing party.

By this poetics of the impossible, I mean to steer the interpretation of the New Testament around the rocks of the metaphysics of omnipotence. But I am not proposing thereby to put the New Testament on the same footing as *Alice in Wonderland,* even though I think the lovers of the kingdom have something to learn from Deleuze's love of Lewis Carroll in the *Logic of Sense,* and even though the relationship between a literary and a religious imagination—they are alternate forms of a "poetics"—is an important topic, as the admirable works of Richard Kearney testify. I am not launching a campaign to win the Nobel Prize (or the Templeton Prize!) by discovering a new physics of permeable and wondrously transformable bodies that will put quantum physics to shame and perhaps supply the much-longed-for unified theory of everything, although recent work in chaos theory does not seem at all at odds with a biblical way of thinking about matter.[11] I am proposing neither a supernatural pseudo-physics (= God magically intervenes in nature), nor a metaphysics of omnipotence (= a supernatural suspension of physics), nor a strictly literary exercise (much as I love physics, metaphysics, and literature). I propose a poetics of the event, a para-logical poetics of the kingdom, a deconstructive or even quasi-phenomenological poetics of the impossible, where an *epoche* is put in place—about which more next—in order to release the structure of the event and to allow ourselves to be overtaken by its life-transforming force. In this way I am trying to keep an ear out for the wondrousness of God's kingdom and God's good time and the tune it plays, without descending into fantasy, magic, or thaumaturgy.

I turn now to what Heidegger would call the "hermeneutic situation" of this poetics, to the "pre-understanding" from which this work proceeds, which will, I hope, hoping against hope, explain once and for all how the possibility of the impossible, which goes to the heart of a sacred anarchy, fits together with the weak force of God, which goes to the heart of a theology of the event.

SIX

Hyper-Realism and the Hermeneutics of the Call

And Mary said,
My soul magnifies the Lord,
and my spirit rejoices in God, my Savior,
for he has looked with favor on
the lowliness of his servant. (Luke 1:46–48)

THE HERMENEUTICAL SITUATION
FROM WHICH WE START

The basic presupposition of this study is the experience of the promise or the call. As a matter of method, the call has the status in this investigation of what Heidegger describes as a "hermeneutic pre-understanding." By this Heidegger means the implicit fore-structure that guides all interpretation in advance, upon which all interpretation draws, by which every inquiry that is anything more than an "unphenomenological construction" is nourished. Fleshing out a pre-understanding is how to constitute what Heidegger would call the "hermeneutic situation" of any inquiry.[1] In virtue of such a pre-understanding, we take ourselves, we who are interpreting and trying to resonate with the event that is harbored by the name of God, to be always already on the receiving end of an address, overtaken by the event of a promise. Theology, any theology, weak or strong, is the explication of the event that is implicit in the name of God. Weak theology means that the call originates from the name of God, from God knows where, from something I know not what—from God, from some World-Soul, or from a dark corner of the unconscious—soliciting us from afar and calling us beyond ourselves. If you do not have the least idea of what that means, you would probably be better served to stop reading and check the stock market page to see how your portfolio is doing. This little treatise will not be of any further help to you. (That is how hermeneutical pre-understandings work.)

That we who have been wooed by a weak theology express some diffidence about the provenance of the call is not a temporary defect in our account that we hope to remove at a later date, perhaps in a new revised second edition, when we are feeling stronger and the System is complete. The hiddenness of the source is actually *constitutive* of the call, part of its positive phenomenal makeup, a positive function of its weak force, and a permanent feature of our anarchic and weakened theological condition. For if we could identify it further, or definitively, if we would get on top of it, master it, make it our own, then we would not be "called" upon, but would be simply musing over what we want to do. If God were a giant green bird, Kierkegaard once quipped, and regularly and conspicuously appeared thus in the town square, there would be much less skepticism about him, and of course a proportionately less passionate faith.[2] In the hermeneutic situation from which I set out, we are all constituted as the recipients of a call about whose origin we cannot comment with assurance, a call floating out over the abyss of the radical hermeneutical fix we are in. The call is itself constituted by being heard, and its being heard is in turn constituted by our responding, by our heeding and not simply hearing, or by our hearing as heeding.

That means that the question of the determinate identity of the one calling, the name of the being or power behind it, of its cause or source, of the entity or hyper-entity who calls, *s'il y en a,* lies beyond our ken or *Erkenntnis*—in that lies its "transcendence"—and so the question of causal origin may be suitably saved for evening conversations in the hotel bar after a day of conferencing. The operation of identifying the caller, if one is so minded, is sometimes a project of a confessional faith (and then it becomes the centerpiece of a strong theology), and sometimes of rationalizing knowledge (as when Kant says that if it is not the voice of "pure reason" it can only be the dangerous phantom of a spirit seer), or even of reductionistic critiques, like Nietzsche's (who thinks it is a bit of undigested meat disturbing our dreams) or Freud's (who thinks that what is really being called for is our mommy). Is it *really* God who calls, or is it some hidden power in my own mind? Is it *really* the call of conscience, of some Socratic daimon, or of a Cosmic Spirit? How am I to say? Who has authorized me to preside over that debate, to decide that undecidable? I do not know the name or address of this address. To pursue that question is to treat the call like a strong force with a definite place on the plane of being or power, not a weak one that solicits me from afar. Indeed, to pursue that question is a way to change the subject when the only subject is the calling of and for the kingdom, rather the way someone who has been caught cheating might respond by asking, "How did you find that out?"—which is, of course, not the point.

REDUCTION OF THE NAME OF GOD

From a strictly methodological point of view, by *suspending* the question of the name or status of the caller in its ontical or ontological identity, we are sticking strictly to the formal or phenomenological character of the call's being called and to what is being called for. As to the question of the "real" or entitative status of the caller, then, we practice a rigorous *epoche* or reduction. For after having pointed out its phenomenal indeterminacy, to persist in seeking out the identity of the caller is to persist in the equivalent of what Husserl would call the natural attitude, which is more concerned with the natural properties of the call and with a real-causal explanation of where this call is coming from than with the structure of its phenomenality or the phenomenal content of the event. It is a way to wiggle out of the call. Events happen—don't change the subject.

But why so much reticence or discretion about the caller? Is this not plainly *God's* call and *God's* kingdom? Is it not the kingdom that God calls for? Is it not the rule of God that is being called for? Is it not God who calls for God's rule in God's kingdom?

To be sure. That is as plain as the nose on your face. But what then do we mean by God?

The name of God is the name of what is called for in the kingdom, the one whose name should rule. But this name, and the event that is astir in this name, is like the name of every event exposed to endless translatability into other names of comparable excess, other names with comparably bottomless or overreaching powers of surprise and solicitation. The name of God is a name of an event, of I know not what, of a bottomless provocation, like the name of love or of justice, and I am in no position to stop the endless chain of substitutions in which it is caught up. That questionability and translatability and undecidability is constitutive of the name of God, which is also why I keep speaking of the event that is astir in this name. That is the postmodern version of saying that God is *id quo majus cogitari nequit.* The question is never *whether* there is a God, or *whether* we should love God, but, as Derrida says in quoting Augustine, *what do I love when I love my God?*[3] What is being loved in my bottomless love of God, in the bottomless God I love, in the bottomless name I call the love of God? I love the possibility of the impossible, which is what I mean by God. But then I must confess—this has always been the subject of endless confession and circumfession and confusion for me—that I do not know whether "the possibility of the impossible" is the best description I have for God or whether "God" is simply the best name I have for the possibility of the impossible, which might have other names.

This reduction or *epoche* is neither a gesture of skeptical despair nor an attempt to bring the endless drift of substitutions to a halt by anchoring it in one supreme transcendental subject or transcendental signified. I simply mean to suspend the question of ontic or ontological origin on the grounds that it is an attempt to change the subject, when the only subject is to let this call sound forth so that we can hear the call and respond. I suspend the question of the strong force of some entitative causal explanation in order to let the weak force of the call itself present itself from itself in its genuine phenomenal character and in that way to grow more salient. *The call is on its own; it has no entitative authority to enforce it,* which also means that we cannot call the police if someone ignores it. I entertain the call as such, and what is heard, as such, and what is called for, as such. This is all part of my anarchic sensibility. My idea is to let the kingdom that is called for stand or fall on its own merits, to allow the call to compel us on its own, apart from any archical authority—God's, for example, or the Pope's, or Billy Graham's. I am not saying that the kingdom is something to be heeded on the grounds that this kingdom is called for by God and all authority is from God. On the contrary, I treat the name of God as something to be heeded and reckoned with because the kingdom that is called for in the name of God is visited upon me in a provocative appeal. The kingdom of God is an event that commands us on its own merits, whoever is its ontic author, like a beautiful poem from centuries ago whose author is now completely unknown. In that sense, the death of the author, which here would mean the death of God, is the narrow gate through which we reach the kingdom of God. God is not the authority who enforces the kingdom of God. The kingdom of God is the phenomenal field in which the name of God gets filled in and acquires a phenomenal but weak force.

I treat the name of God as the name of something, I know not what, that calls for the kingdom, as a poor or weak—that is, a phenomenological—force. The name of God is possessed, not of ontological foundation, institutional support, a large bank account, Swiss guards, a television network, or ecclesiastical authority, but only of phenomenological appeal or solicitation. By the possibility of the impossible, then, I do not mean the doer or the doing of some unbelievable deed, evidence of whose name, status, and origin I must produce for the prosecutor, but the weak force of an unconditional appeal. I am referring to the structure of an event of solicitation that stirs within—here—the Jewish and Christian scriptures, which on my hypothesis should be true of any religious tradition, any one of which, being sustained by an event, sustains a concrete form of life and is the subject matter of a possible hermeneutic explication.[4]

THE REDUCTION OF THE
WORD OF GOD

What we have been saying has obvious implications for scriptural hermeneutics, where the Word of God, the Scriptures, undergo what we might entitle a *methodological transformation into an event.* That represents a leading-back *(reductio)* of the sacred text *from* its status as either (a) a document to be studied in a historical or comparative *Religionswissenschaft,* which does not as such engage my existence or passion, or (b) as a divine revelation to be meditated upon by a *scientia divina* (a strong scriptural theology), which engages me but also definitively identifies its provenance, *to* (c) its pure hermeneutic-phenomenological content, to the event of appeal or claim or call that issues from it.

A theology of the event is neither "religious studies" nor "strong theology" but (a certain) hermeneutic phenomenology, what I like to call a radical hermeneutic, which gives rise to a weak theology, by which I mean one that faces up to the radical task of discerning the spirit that stirs in texts of such an elemental, unconditional—but weak—force. The sacred texts are treated, not as the Divine Revelation that definitively props up the authority of some confessional faith or ecclesiastical office, nor as the record of some extraordinary empirical event from long ago that tells us *wie es eigentlich gewesen ist,* as if human history was literally launched approximately six thousand years ago by two painfully naked and parentless people who made the big mistake of being drawn into a conversation with a sneaky snake. Historical-critical studies (not to mention science and common sense) should have long ago doused the fires of fundamentalism and inerrantism, but that does not settle the question of the appeal or the claim that issues from such texts. For these texts are solicitations that call for a response, appeals coming from I know not where about a way to be, a style of existence, about a poetic possibility that we are invited to transform into existential actuality.

The sacred text thus undergoes a twofold transformation: first, into the event of the call; and then the call, in turn, is transformed into a response, converted into the coin of existence.[5] Texts make claims, but even when the claims made are unconditional, the claim as such, without an army or an institution or an authority to back it up, is a weak force. The reduction is thus twofold, from text to call, and from call to existence, and in the process of this double reduction, the whole thing undergoes not a diminution but a magnification, as we will shortly see.

In virtue of my governing hermeneutical assumption of this twofold transformation into the call, the Scriptures are treated as hermeneutically explicative or phenomenologically disclosive or revelatory about a mode of being-in-the-world, not real-representational. They disclose something about the structure of experience without pretending to represent facts of the matter. As a cognitive matter, their truth is symbolic and not the truth of correspondence or the correctness of propositions; the call is not primarily a cognitive matter but an existential one. The Scriptures are true, but their truth is poetic not propositional. A poetics is not true the way the propositional form "S is P" is true, if and only if there is an SP out there that this sentence picks out, as if SP were something that a reporter with a video camera who was on the spot at the supposed time and place would have recorded. A poetics is not true the way a scientific theory is true, as a covering law that is weakened, altered, or refuted by the accumulated weight of evidence and replaced by a competing scientific theory. A poetics is true with the truth of the event; it wants to *become true,* to *make itself true,* to *make itself come true,* to be transformed into truth, so that its truth is a species of truth as *facere veritatem.* A poetics is true the way a novel is true even if it is classified by the librarians as a "fiction," or the way a poem is true without picturing a fact, or the way a hymn, a ballad, or a song is true, which is completely consistent with not being historically factual, that is, with not being a representational account. A poetics does not record the strong force of hard facts; it describes the weak force of a call for the kingdom, or for justice, which is true even if the real world is truly unjust. That is why there can be more than one religious discourse, and why religions do not compete with one another in a zero-sum game in which the truth of one comes at the cost of the falsity of another. The idea of one true religion or religious discourse or body of religious narratives makes no more sense than the idea of one true poem or one true language or one true culture.[6]

Religious discourses are not "verified" like propositions, by finding a fact of the matter out there with which the proposition makes a snug fit, but rather the event they harbor is "testified" to in experience, by being borne out or confirmed in our lives. They give interpretive life and breath to an event, to something that is alive within our sacred names, something going on within us. The truth of a religious discourse is whether a living tradition forms around it; its reality testifies to its rationality. By their fruits you shall know them. A religious discourse discloses or illuminates something about the event, about being born and dying, making love and giving birth, having hope and being filled with despair, being lifted up with joy or weighed down by suffering. The crucifixion and the resurrection are deep and overarching symbols of the rhythmic birth and death and rebirth that we call our lives, and the deeper such symbols sink their stakes into our conscious and unconscious life, the more enduring and compelling the narratives that embody them.[7]

In virtue of the transformation into the event, we stop thinking of the Scriptures as handing over a string of supernatural assertions whose truth lies in their correspondence to supernatural facts too far off or too high up for us to see with our unaided natural eyes, as disclosing super-facts that would otherwise be withheld from humankind, and we start thinking of them as invitations to transform our lives. The idea is to put a stop to the war between "reason" and "revelation" by adopting a more sensible idea of both, one that understands that "reason" (uncapitalized) makes abundant use of faith and interpretation, and that "revelation" is at bottom the disclosive power of a weak force. Contemporary astrophysics and the book of Genesis are not sets of competing claims engaged in a battle to the death,[8] in which one side takes its assertions to occupy the topside while looking down upon the poverty of the other side, whether that means disparaging the darkness of unbelief in the light of revelation or disparaging the darkness of religious superstition in the light of reason.

By taking the Scriptures as the site of an event, we find a way to read the remarkable texts of the Scriptures, to take seriously texts that describe the most impossible things, while avoiding the Scylla of the fiery faithful, who literalize them into facts, and the Charybdis of cold-hearted unbelievers, who dismiss them out of hand as fiction. The transformation into the event provides an alternative to the either/or of literalism or logic, fact or fiction, of Spirit-seers or *Aufklärer,* a way to call off both the dogs of fundamentalism and the hounds of reductionism. The idea is to avoid turning the poetics of the kingdom into thaumaturgy or magic, which is what happens if you take these narratives to be ontical accounts of facts of the matter, and also, for that matter, to avoid allowing the kingdom to fuel a too-powerful phenomenology of supersaturated phenomena.[9] The other side of the idea is to avoid explaining away the kingdom by means of old modernist reductionistic metanarratives inherited from Freud, Marx, or Nietzsche. In general, a poetics avoids grinding up these texts in a ready-made reading machine—of pure reason or supernatural revelation or hyper-phenomenology.

This poetics of the event begins with an *epoche,* for the *epoche* provides the entrance-door to phenomenology, as Husserl put it,[10] the uncircumventable *sine qua non,* which alone opens up the phenomenal field. Accordingly, my *epoche,* which opens the field of a poetics of the impossible, lies in bracketing the causal question of the caller. As long as you allow the question of the caller to be active, you will have to settle it by a particular confessional faith (if you want it to have a Divine Warrant), or by metaphysics (if you want to rationalize it), or by psychoanalysis (if you suspect it desires its mommy!). I turn off the switch that powers that question, which remains in the natural attitude, amidst the strong forces—either of believers, who rely upon faith to give them supernatural guidance through the worst, or of nonbelievers who think the Scriptures so much fantasy and superstition. By cutting off the power supply to this question, our reduction opens up the "eventiveness" or "phenomenality" of the kingdom, the structure of appearance of the poetico-biblical field, making it possible for us to safely tour the holy land without fear of being caught in the crossfire between the two warring parties. By this means we can call for a cease-fire, a cessation of hostilities, not just between the Jews and the Palestinians, although that is devoutly to be wished for, but also between the confessional faiths of the Bible thumpers and the reason of the *Aufklärer*. This epoche disarms both armies, bilaterally, allowing the phenomenal field of the poetics of the kingdom to show its head once again, once all the shooting has stopped.

Thus our poetics is not forced to prescind from the miracle stories like the resuscitation of Lazarus or the Easter narratives on the grounds that these are matters of divine revelation not philosophy. These narratives are there to be read; they are the stuff of texts that repay reading, and they bear the imprint of a certain understanding of space and time, of life and death, of God and human being. To debate the historicity of the post-Easter appearances; to question the realistic possibility of Paul's idea in the letter to the Thessalonians that in the second coming Jesus would come down to earth on a cloud, open the graves, and take both the living and the risen dead back up into heaven on that same cloud; or to doubt the scientific value of the opening creation narrative in Genesis about God dividing the waters from the land, as if these were so many propositional assertions of fact, could only inflict a fatal wound on this poetics and on reading. Are these stories scientifically plausible? Of course not! Among many other things, they belong to the limited imaginations of a pre-Copernican world. If the body of Jesus rose up on Ascension Thursday, it would be somewhere in orbit around the earth right now (and just what direction "up" would be would have been a function of what time of the day it was when he took off). But taking all that to be a serious objection to these narratives would be like excising the ghost from future editions of Hamlet on the grounds that modern readers do not believe in ghosts (actually, all the polls taken of Americans say they do, or at least that they believe in angels!) or that we have no critical-historical evidence to back up the real existence of these ghosts. But neither should we be stampeded by our debt to historical-critical studies, which lays literalism and creationism and fundamentalism to rest, *requiescat in pace,* into an Enlightenment blindness to these narratives or a rationalist insensitivity to the claim they make upon us.

The eyes, or rather the *ears*, of this poetics are firmly fixed on the call, on the way of life that is called for, on the event of the kingdom, the style of the rule of God, that is embedded in these sayings and stories. The ears of this poetics are firmly cocked to hear the call that emanates from them, to respond to the weak force of their strong appeal. Rather than debating their scientific plausibility and historical credibility, we plunge straight ahead into their implausibility and incredibility in order to take stock of the wondrous world they both inhabit and awaken, and the marvelous solicitation or provocation by which they are disturbed.

A *MAGNIFICAT* OF HYPER-REALISM

My talk of a "reduction" of God's being, or of the Word of God, to a call does not signify any sort of diminution but an emancipation of God from being that exposes being to its own beyond, that releases the event that stirs within being and passes beyond being. Weak theology does not preclude strong faith. In that sense, my ontological reduction is an existential magnification, weak theology's poor excuse for a rich *Magnificat;* and "realism" is the really reductive force that reduces the name of God to magic. The *logos* in this weak theo*logy* is phenomenological, not metaphysical; and in that sense, this weak theology is also a certain existential or radically hermeneutical phenomenology. So I do not thereby mean, in orthodox Huserlian fashion, to abandon the overwrought plane of existence in order to make a headlong retreat into the pacific calm of cool essences. As Kierkegaard complained long ago, we have had enough of philosophers taking a leap beyond existence while leaving the rest of us to face the worst, those of us who are still existing and have not gotten as far as to surpass existence.

The reduction lodges me more deeply than ever in the heated rush of existence, the booming, buzzing confusion of everyday life, by exposing me to being's restless heart, attuned to life's expectant, open-ended momentum. For by the reduction of the being of God I do not undertake a reduction that passes from concrete existence to a detached essence, but I make a movement that rises up from presence to provocation, ascending from being at present to the promise that insinuates itself into being and makes being restless. This is a reduction *from* any present determination or determinate form of the name of God, *from* what is happening or being named in the name of God at present, which contracts God to the order of being, *to* whatever event the name of God is promising, thereby freeing the name of God and letting it rise up to the order of expectation, so that the name of God is a way to hail the incoming of an event. That means that this is a reduction made in order to release the event of the future that this name harbors. So my reduction is a kind of *promissory reduction,* from presence to promise, suspending the oppressive presence of the present and taking up the name of God as a promissory note, as a promise of things to come, while whatever the name of God has signified up to the present is considered strictly reducible, provisional, and tentative, a temporary contraction, an interregnum, an interim placeholder for something coming.

I have fasted and abstained with all the ascetic rigor of a desert father from taking the name of God entitatively or ontologically in order to take it as an event, to let it vent, to release it, to let it loose in its vocative—invocative and provocative—force as the name of an event, as the name of a calling, of what we continually call for and call upon, what we invoke with this name or some other. That means this weak theology is never far removed from prayer, in particular a prayer of invocation, of calling *(viens)* for the incoming (in-vention) of the event. But by calling I also mean what always and already calls upon us, comes over us, in an advent that invokes and provokes us, continually calling up what is best in us, calling us out beyond ourselves. God calls us before we call upon God, calling up what is best or highest in us. In that sense, God pursues us, preys upon us, or even prays to us, inasmuch as God calls upon, provokes, and invokes us. The name of God is the name of what we desire, of everything that we desire, but it is also the name of what desires us, of what desires everything of us. I meditate upon, stir under the impulse of, what is calling "in the name of God." Something is calling *within* that name, something is astir in or within it, something in that name provokes us. Something calls *under* that name, on its behalf, the way a ship sails under the flag or banner of a given name. Something far off hails us under the name of God, something, I know not what, something we desire, that desires us, something coming to take hold of us, and we hail each other like ships at sea, or like travelers in the night, each calling to the other "come," *viens, oui, oui.* We are called by God, which is our vocation, even as we call upon God, which is our invocation. We subsist in the space between these calls.

Whether there is some entity answering to the vocative force of the name of God is a debate that transpires among those who have pitched their tent among strong forces, not weak ones, something to be puzzled over by the big players, by those who trade in powerful and prestigious entities in the power corridors of being, by dealers in higher beings or higher authorities, *hyperousiai* or *exousiai,* or who speculate about the cosmological principle that puts the bang in the Big Bang, people competing for the Big Money of the Templeton Prize. As for me, I am not talking about a Big Bang or a Big Being, a Big Bully or a Big Boaster—"Where were you when I created the world?"—who delights in intimidating his own creation. I am but a humble *Extraskriver,* a supplementary clerk of promises, who suffers from an advanced asthenia, a pale and scrawny sun-starved bookkeeper of promissory notes, like Johannes de Silentio, practiced not in dealing with such big semantic events and prestigious beings but only with promissory non-beings who have not yet managed to be. I pass my days in silence and obscurity, lending an ear not to the noise of what is, a domain I leave to the more qualified, but to what silently calls, for which I try to cultivate an ear while collecting the scribblings of a weak theology. For me, God is not the uncaused cause but the call without causality. For the call calls quietly and is easily lost to all but the most patient and attentive ear, one tuned to the silent peal of its appeal.

To summarize the hermeneutico-deconstructive issue, then, let us say that the position I am defending may certainly not be described as theo-logical realism, because I am methodologically abstaining from treating God or God's kingdom as a *res* or a *realissimum* inasmuch as I am refrain-ing from making any entitative or ontological claims about God-the-being or the Being of God. But neither is this a case of theological anti-realism, because my hermeneutical phenomenological reduction does not have the slightest thing to do with any form of reductionism, with reducing God to a metaphor or a projection of human wishes or any sort of fiction. On the contrary, by my reduction I raise God up beyond entity to the event, the hyper-event, the inner heart or driving force in things. My reduction is a magnification; my method is a *Magnificat.* I have no interest in diminish-ing this name, making it something less than it is, but in unfolding and magnifying its event—*magnificat anima mea dominum*—in saving it, in re-leasing everything that is at work or astir in it, everything that is happening in it, everything vocative, evocative, provocative, or promised when we use this name. An event comes over us, overtakes us, imposes itself upon us, lays claim to us—"from on high" as Levinas likes to say—by rising up from below, from within the bowels of Paul's *ta me onta,* in the name of God.

What I am doing should be described as a magnifying *hyper-realism of the event,* of the event stirring in the name of God with all the hyperbolic action of the beyond, of the force that commands my attention and de-mands that I collaborate in its realization, in transforming it into exis-tence.[11] The name of God is the name of an event neither inside nor out-side, above or below, but up ahead, neither real nor unreal, but not yet real. My assumption, my hypothesis, my faith, my *Magnificat,* and my method, is that the name of God is the name of an event that is unforeseeable, unimaginable, uncontainable, undeconstructible. The world cannot con-tain it, and so it makes the world restless until it is brought forth, which never quite happens. That is why the name of God occupies a considerable place in our conscious thoughts even as it settles deeply into our uncon-scious. I do not take the name of God to pick out an entity, as in realism, or an illusion, as in anti-realism, but an event, an advent, a future and a promise, a call and a claim, a hope and an aspiration, which is why I speak of a hyper-realism, which hopes in a being beyond or below being with a desire beyond desire and a hope against hope.

All that being said, let the event begin! *Viens, oui, oui!*

May your kingdom come!

Part Two

THE KINGDOM OF GOD: SKETCHES OF A SACRED ANARCHY

SEVEN

Metanoetics: The Seventh Day, or Making All Things New

> Abba of ours in heaven,
> let your name be hallowed,
> let your rule come,
> let your will be brought about,

We might, as a kind of artistic ruse or authorial conceit, think of Part One of this book as having devoted its time to the first week of creation, while Part Two turns its attention to our everyday life in the world God made, to the "eventiveness" of all the days that follow after that very eventful and famous first week. We might also think that while the first half commented on the book of Genesis, the second part is dedicated to a kind of commentary on the Lord's Prayer, which is a venerable theological tradition to which I will make a peculiarly deconstructive contribution. To carry this conceit to an extreme, the "Interlude" may be seen as a commentary on the "Angelus" (the impossible) and the "Magnificat" (hyper-realism). To be sure, my contributions are of such irregular and modest proportions that they may very well be returned to me in the mail by the authorities, who might on the whole think themselves better served without them, a judgment for which I cannot entirely fault them.

SEVENTH-DAY EVENTISM

Elohim, it turns out, was something of an optimist, a little too upbeat and idealistic. He—or rather the priestly author who was feeding him all those uplifting lines—gave us the impression that the world, having once been made, and having been declared good, would do very well for itself, thank you very much, and that we might all take a break and enjoy the weekend. But nothing is simple and, as the Yahwist pointed out, things soon get complicated. The created world remains permanently unstable, having a built-in indeterminacy about it, an element that provides an opening both for errancy and for creaturely creativity, for what Catherine Keller calls an "unformed future,"[1] while God's creative action has the character, *pace* Einstein, of a gigantic roll of the dice. There is an element in things that is not precisely God's image but is what God is trying to fashion in his image, which makes the work of creation an ongoing process, an around-the-clock job. Thus, far from constituting a day of rest, the seventh day will emblematize for us the unforeseen toils of time, the shifting fortunes of tide, and the unintended turns of history. On the grimmest assessment, history is hell, a nightmare from which we are all trying to wake up, as James Joyce said, or an accumulating pile of ruins, according to Benjamin, shortly before his suicide. But it is also an opening to the future, to the possibility of the impossible. The "kingdom of God," then, represents the infinite task of making good on Elohim's "good," of repeating his "good" from day to day, which means letting God's rule obtain.

I take my lead in this chapter from one of my favorite New Testament stories. One day the people brought a man with a withered hand to Jesus, and the keepers of the law watched him carefully to see if he would heal the man, even though it was the Sabbath (Mark 3:1–6). Jesus healed this withered hand, because hands were made to be used, and the Sabbath was made for the man, not the man for the Sabbath. The figure of Jesus crafted here is a perfect combination of the upbeat Elohist imagination and the more realistic Yahwist. Jesus embodies P's narrative emphasizing the goodness of things, the value of the Sabbath rest, and the need for an occasional party and good wine—"good soup," says Levinas—but like the Yahwist, he was also keenly sensitive to the way things keep going wrong. So for Jesus—this is my take on this lovely story—the seventh day is a day dedicated to healing and mending what has gone astray in creation, for reforming things first formed in creation. Creation is an unfinished work, and there can be no weariness in well-doing. The Sabbath is to be a day of recreation, of *re*-creation, of continually renewing the ongoing work of creation, of mending the broken and healing the sick, of straightening the crooked and making the lame to walk, of inscribing Elohim's "good" on the bodies and the minds of those whose lives he touched. So Jesus wants to keep the Sabbath holy; that is the law, and he has not come to destroy the law but to make it full of life. But he thinks that an important way to observe the day of rest is not to rest from the work he has to do of restoring the image of God on things. The seventh day emblematizes an unfinished task, and Jesus is the agent, or perhaps the instrument, or at least the locus of this endless but no less urgent work. Jesus, I will maintain, is a kind of Seventh-Day Eventist, a prophetic teacher and enactor of the "event" that breaks open the horizons that hem us in or bind us up, a parabolic figure of breaking with the dead works that kill, thereby letting something new, unforeseen, and unanticipated break in.

This new turn of heart, this renewal of heart and mind and body, is captured in the capstone word of Jesus' preaching, *metanoia,* the transformation and reformation of the heart, which continues the original work of forming things from fluid and plastic elements like the deep and the earth. That is the stuff of what I call a general "metanoetics," which takes the form of an ongoing and marvelous metamorphosis, giving the impression of a general—but sacred—anarchy. Metanoetics is the name of the general parabolic operation surrounding Jesus, both of the parables that Jesus tells and the parables that are told about Jesus. Elohim's "good" is both a proclamation and a promise—remember, this narrative was written for a people in exile—both a promise and a provocation, a call to us to make good on this "good," to repeat this good, and not to be faint of heart in the midst of our distress. Creation depends upon the supplement of recreation; the beginning depends upon the repetition; the origin depends upon the dangerous but necessary supplement of this "good," which is what is called history.

METANOIA

Toward the beginning of Matthew (4:23–25), shortly after the baptism of Jesus, when Jesus is just beginning his ministry, Matthew says that Jesus went about Galilee teaching *(didaskon)* and preaching *(kai kerysoon)* the good news and healing *(kai therapeuon)* the sick. Jesus begins his work by preaching the word that will change people's hearts and transform their minds *(metanoein),* and also, at the same time, not as afterthought or merely as a secondary or symbolic operation, heal their bodies. The Jewish notion of "sin," as Bruce Chilton shows, has to do with a shackle, a bond, or a debt, something that paralyzes us, so that the "forgiveness of sin" means "releasing"—*aphiemi* (Gr.), *shebaq* (Hebrew and Aramaic), *dimittere* (Latin)—us from sin. The closest natural analogy to sin is physical paralysis. To be pure of heart is to be released from sin, which means to break the shackles of sin, quite the way a crippled man is healed and thereafter able to move about freely.[2] These shackles are self-imposed, and God releases us from them. So when Jesus taught "your sins are released," he meant, you are made healthy again, no longer crippled or impaired. The English "forgive" turns on a different image, to which Chilton objects because it sounds like something weaker, "forgive and forget," overlook this fault. While we love this word "release," it being our entire aim to release the event, we are hardly ready to give up on the English word "forgive" because it is inscribed within the horizon of economy and the gift, which is no less important than that of being shackled and then set free. Besides, if we take "forgive" to mean "giving away" what we "have" on someone else, giving away the debt we could collect, then it means releasing the other from their debt to us, as we would like to be released from our debts, and then I think we capture this sense well enough.[3] Accordingly, Jesus was a healer of souls and a mender of bodies, of the two together, offering freedom from the shackles both of the mind and the body, proffering both a teaching, a didactics or kerygmatics, and a therapeutics.

News about such a remarkable man spread quickly, Matthew says, and soon they started bringing people to him from all around, people who needed help: all those who were ill, afflicted with various diseases and pains; those possessed by demons, epileptics, paralytics—"and he cured them." In the subsequent chapters of Matthew, one meets with a remarkable succession of similarly afflicted folks, a parade of the most distressed and unfortunate people: the needy, a leper, the centurion's paralyzed servant, Peter's feverish mother-in-law, two men possessed by demons, several more paralytics, a dead girl, the blind and mute, the poor, sinners—and let us not forget to mention the tax collectors, the ugliness of whose profession (they were collaborators with Rome) has always headed the lists of the servants of ignominy from time immemorial. All these men and women and children are fit subjects—fitted precisely by their unfitness, according to the paralogic of the impossible—indeed, privileged subjects in the kingdom of the unfit, where metamorphosis is the rule. In the kingdom, the general rule is that the unfit are fit and the outsiders are in.

There are several things about this early passage in the gospel, which is but one among many similar texts in the New Testament, that deserve our attention. The kingdom (basileia), much as Nietzsche says, albeit very much to the displeasure of Nietzsche's patrician nose, is aswarm with the most singularly afflicted people. There is indeed a pervasive preoccupation with bodies in the New Testament that amounts to what Levinas and Adorno do not hesitate to call a "materialism," although they are speaking of the Hebrew scriptures.[4] This is also something that Žižek today approves of in Christianity,[5] and it is completely consonant with the image of biblical life that was presented to us by James Kugel.[6] It is nothing like the *Phaedo,* which begins with the body just in order to tell us to learn to quit material matters, to learn to leave off a concern with sensation and feeling, and to take up the practice of death, of dying to the body. Philosophers from Plato to Heidegger have—perhaps realistically, perhaps fatalistically—sought ways to make a gift of death, to find a gift in death, to see what dealing with death can give us in return, as Derrida shows,[7] either by over-coming it ascetically or staring it down existentially. But in the New Testa-ment the idea is to heal disease and *raise the dead.* The evangelical idea is also quite unlike the *Critique of Practical Reason,* where the essence of the ethical lay in the triumph on the part of pure practical reason over what Kant called the "pathological," the sphere of sensibility and passion. In the New Testament, the kingdom is a kingdom of bodies, a realm or sphere of everything flesh-like and corporeal; the body is very much the business of the kingdom, its "concern" *(Sache).* Jesus is a very earthy fellow: two of his miracles involve spitting: once he makes mud with his spittle and cures a blind man (John 9:6); once he cures a speech impediment by spitting on his hand and touching the man's tongue. This concern with the body goes hand in hand, if I may say so, with preaching and teaching, *kerygma* and *didaskein.* The two together, teaching and healing, as two transformative powers, two powers of release, belong coequally to the "kingdom" he is an-nouncing.

The bodies we meet with in the kingdom are a singularly sorry lot: bod-ies laid low, afflicted with disease, bent by paralysis, racked with fever, with-ering away with leprosy, struck blind and dumb, or even lifeless. These are certainly not the bodies spotlighted by Greek philosophy or existential phe-nomenology, which are hale and healthy organisms, upright, agile, agential bodies that move with ease and alacrity through the *Lebenswelt;* sure-handed, swift-footed bodily intentionalities or concernful beings-in-the-world, which spend their weekends skiing or skydiving. Philosophy's bod-ies are active and well, every one a *corpus sanum* cut to fit a *mens sana,* a fit organ of the soul or a suitable seat from which to launch intentional acts. Let us, by way of a certain shorthand, call this New Testament body not a body but "flesh," and by flesh let us signify everything that is both vulnera-ble or able to be wounded, which means bent, cut, lacerated, ulcerated, withered, inflamed, paralyzed, numbed, or finally killed, but also healed, bound up, made comfortable and fed, and able to enjoy *jouissance.* These bodies of flesh are attracted to Jesus by an almost natural gravitational pull, and he seems literally to be swarmed by them: they brought to him every-body like that. "[A]nd he cured them." Surely this is a case of like attracting like, because in the end Jesus ends up as one of these bodies. The one who has become flesh becomes the most famous case of vulnerable, crucified flesh (which is also transformed and transfigured) ever to seize the Western world and imagination, which is why Mel Gibson's film *The Passion of the Christ* made so much money. While he lived, Jesus transformed their flesh, metamorphosized their bodies, just as he wanted to change their hearts, *metanoein.* Then they killed him, and from that deed, just before dying, he also released them.

The kingdom *(basileia)* is a kingdom of metamorphosis, of *metanoein* and *therapeuein*. If flesh is defined by its vulnerability, it is also for the same reason mendable, healable, transformable; and Jesus is a charismatic place of divine transformation. When these bodies grow hungry, they are brought to Jesus and he feeds them. It is of no small interest to observe that where the Greek philosophers tended to save the word "divine" *(theios)* to mark the unchanging, impassive, eternal stability in things, in the New Testament the divine powers that are at work in Jesus are forces of change and transformation. Whenever Jesus swings into action, things are transformed; whenever he touches others or others touch him, they are transformed. If flesh means everything that is laid low and vulnerable, it also means, by the same token, inseparably and correlatively, everything that can be healed. If Greek philosophy begins in wonder, the wonder *(thaumazo)* in which the poetics of the impossible begins is the "miracle" *(mirandum)* of transformation, the wondrous transformation stories that make up the narratives of the kingdom of God, which is a kingdom of transformability, reformability, metamorphosis, which abide by a logic of the impossible. The kingdom of God is a land of wondrous change, a marvelous sphere of *kinesis*—"one not dreamt of, Horatio, in our philosophies," says Hamlet (I.v.166–67), by which he undoubtedly meant Greek ontotheologies, a region more wild in its way than the *tohu wa-bohu* or than anything Alice ever encountered, the remarkable makings of a sacred anarchy.

It is not difficult to hear the echo of the ancient creation narratives here, to feel the flow of the deep and the breath of the spirit sweeping across it. The creation narrative describes a scene of the most amazing transformations of *tehom* and *tohu wa-bohu* into spaces swarming with living creatures, the metamorphosis of barrenness into life. Is not the figure of Jesus, as the place where the crooked are made straight and the lame are made to walk, very clearly a repetition of this opening scene of Genesis or of the long account of the marvels of creation in the book of Job, the place of re-creation, and thus a faithful echo of Elohim's "good"?

It is important to see how closely the work of bodily metamorphosis is juxtaposed in Matthew and the Synoptics with *metanoia,* which is the message of the Baptist *(metanoeite),* who first announced that the kingdom is coming near, which is mentioned two chapters earlier. In Mark, the metanoetic effect is even sharper. Mark knows nothing of the infancy narratives, so his gospel starts out abruptly with the shock of *metanoia,* even as it ends abruptly, starkly, with the empty tomb. Jesus takes over John's withering wilderness message, John's khoral and ankhoral call for *metanoia,* but only by first submitting it to a crucial re-orchestration from a dirge to a dance. The music of the event is not the blues—the Baptist wails, but the people do not mourn—but the dance: Jesus pipes, but they do not dance. Jesus takes up John's prophetic tune of *metanoia,* which is more in tune with the Yahwist narrative, but only after giving it a new score; Jesus wants us to re-tune, to undergo a change of tuning, of *nous* or *Stimmung. Metanoeite:* change your tune, adjust your tuning, change your mind and heart, transform your whole disposition, your *Stimmung,* your moodedness, your whole way of being in the world and being with one another. Immerse *(baptezein)* your old heart, your old mind, and wash away the meanness that is centered solely on itself so that you can be transformed. Here is a healing water, a *tehom* that washes clean. *Baptezein:* that represents a quite literal confluence, a flowing together, of *metanoia* and *therapeia,* of changing one's heart and healing one's flesh, a rushing together of the waters that cleanse the heart and the waters that wash and heal the flesh. In this kingdom, all things flow, as Heraclitus said, but this flow has a healing, not a Heraclitean drift, Heraclitus having argued that all such flowing streams abide within the same shores. Here the waters overflow and all things are transformed and washed clean, waters that wash up something new and clean, so that all things are *not* the same, *pace* Parmenides (and Heraclitus).[8]

AN ANARCHIC AN-ETHICS

These Christian waters are not quite Heraclitean on another count; they are not the waters of a private beach reserved for snooty old Greeks who, like Parmenides and Plato, looked with disdain upon the many, the *hoi polloi.* On the contrary, they are public beaches, waters that are especially reserved for the great unwashed, that is, for precisely the ones who need water and cleansing. The kingdom belongs to the unwashed, not to aristocratic Greeks or to the healthy, well-fed bourgeoisie of modern Christianity, those mainstream Christians whom Kierkegaard mercilessly attacked under the name of "Christendom." One of the most interesting events, or laws of the event, in the New Testament is that the out are in and the in are out. The characters in the kingdom are a cast of outcasts, of outsiders: sinners, lost sheep, lost coins, lost and prodigal sons, tax collectors, prostitutes, Samaritans, lepers, the lame, the possessed, the children. A list that we today could easily update: gays and lesbians, illegal immigrants, unwed mothers, the HIV-positive, drug addicts, prisoners, and, after 9/11, Arabs. Everyone who is outside, outlawed, outclassed—in short, everyone who is just plain out and should stay out of sight. Just the sort of folks who would send "For Sale" signs shooting up all over Christendom and who would send the Christian right scrambling for the exit signs at their next assembly (which schedules at least one session on their annual programs to denounce just about everybody to whom Jesus extended the kingdom).[9] These are the very ones whom Paul called the *me onta* of the world, the nobodies, the nullities, the nothings, as Crossan puts it; those without a dime's worth of *ousia* to their name, if I may add my own two cents. They are the ones with whom God has sided, the ones to whom the kingdom belongs, the poor ones who enjoy God's special favor, the passersby whom the host of that famous wedding party had literally dragged into the feast, one of the great surprise parties in the history of the West, where the surprise is on everyone who shows up. The farther "out" you are, the stronger the trace of God; the richer and more powerful you are, the tougher it will be for you to find a place in the kingdom. So the logic of the event is, the more you are out, the more you are in; the more you are in, the more you are out. That perversity is paradigmatic of the poetics of the impossible, the *fundamentum concussum* (very!) of the kingdom, its anarchic *arche*. These reversals are all "strategic," of course, as we say in deconstruction, which means that they are meant to counterbalance an effect that is currently tilted in the opposite direction, because in the kingdom God is not against anyone. At least, we would like to think that God is not partial (Eph. 6:9).

While the New Testament shows little interest in either the word or the concept of "ethics," Kant and philosophers like Kant think that beneath the mad stories of the New Testament there lies a reasonably sensible "ethics" book—which is also what Levinas thought about the Tanach—if only someone sober and clearheaded enough comes along to demythologize the superstitious stories and distill the purely rational ethical essence into the small jar of a learned journal article or treatise. Without following Kant in reducing God to the Moral God, I suggest that the prolegomenon to any such possible ethics would be to get ready for a surprise. For any such possible ethics would assume quite a different and startling form than the ethics of Kant's second *Critique*. *Pace* Alain Badiou, it would be organized, not around the principle of "universality"—except in the sense that it openly extended to everyone—but rather around the "un-principle" of difference and singularity. Badiou is perfectly right to say that the "event" was not a sectarian one, not to be restricted to the circumcised, and in that sense Paul's preaching is a "universalism." But the event itself that was being universally preached was the sacredness of each singular one, each one in his or her an-archic singularity, precisely insofar as they tend to drop out from universal schemata. So if, with Badiou, we speak of "universalism," we would have to distinguish between application and content: the scope or the application of the kingdom is universal; but the content or the meaning of the kingdom is singularity. The eye of the kingdom is not on the watch for the universal but for the singular. The event does not settle upon the ninety-nine but upon the one lost sheep, the one lost coin, the lost brother.

The universal principle is the principle not of the universal but of the singular; the *arche* is one that values the anarchic; the *principium* is one that singles out what is very unprincely, which is only a "kingdom" *ironice,* tongue in cheek, one in which royalty is at a disadvantage, like the dinner party or royal wedding banquet that ends up dragging in every passerby to its table (Luke 14).

The closest thing to this in Kant is the "Kingdom of Ends," which treats each person as an end in itself. In the kingdom of God, one valorizes difference, alterity, being out, being nothing in the eyes of the world; the most account is taken of those who are of no account whatsoever. You get nowhere in the kingdom by being well-born, well-bred, and well-to-do. You get nowhere by loving your friends and family, those with whom you share kin and kind, those who are like you, of like kind. Such people already have their reward, Matthew has Jesus say. The only true reward—if rewards are what you are after—comes of loving your enemies, those who are quite *unlike* you and who indeed actually *dislike* you, and hating your kindred kind, your father and mother, brother and sister, hating those who love you. The possibility of love turns on loving those whom it is impossible to love. "Family values" in the kingdom suffer rather a different and anarchic fate in the New Testament, according to the logic of the event, than the one portrayed to us by the Christian right today. Anybody can love the same; even the mafia has "family values." It is the unforeseeable event of hating the same and loving difference that counts in the kingdom. Who would not want to be a friend of the rich and famous? But standing by the least among us, the little ones, the powerless, the odiferous, the ones you must wear gloves to touch—that is what counts among the friends of God.

One gets nowhere in the kingdom of God by gaining the favor of the powers that be *(dynatoi)*. The idea behind the kingdom, its an-archic *arche,* is to take the side of everyone who is out of power, the *asthena,* which from the point of view of worldly advancement is a recipe for disaster. In the kingdom, the powers that be are regularly denounced as vipers and white-washed tombs whose fathers have killed the prophets, rather like the sort of thing we find in Kierkegaard's *Attack Upon Christendom.* The career diplomats in the churches who have made a profitable business out of the crucifixion and who know all the best restaurants seem to be exactly the sort of folks to whom Jesus opposes the kingdom, precisely the insiders who end up out at the wedding banquet. As both Kierkegaard's *Attack Upon Christendom* and Dostoyevsky's legend of the Grand Inquisitor pretty much agree, Jesus and the churches will find a lot to criticize in each other if Jesus ever does come again, which would inconvenience the churches enormously.

The whole idea of the "ethics" of the kingdom, if there is such a thing—ethics being a Greco-philosophical idea, a theory of action that gets no play at all in the New Testament, which is not concerned with theories[10]—seems to be organized around what we today call "difference" or "alterity," an idea whose day has come, chiefly under the influence of Levinas, who is going back to, and transcribing into Greek, the biblical concern with the widow, the orphan, and the stranger. From the point of view of what is usually called ethics, it would perhaps be better to speak of an an-ethics, or para-ethics, or hyper-ethics, to describe what is going on in the New Testament, a kind of eccentric ethics where the trace of God is inscribed on the "other one," the neighbor or the stranger or the outsider. If there are "virtues" in this an-ethics, they are the virtues of difference, of alterity, which turn on things like hospitality to the stranger, to those who are "out" rather than "in."

Virtue, suggesting manly power, translating *arete,* "excellence," is not quite the right word for the qualities of the prophetic heart that associates with everything that lacks excellence and power. It is quite fascinating to me to see how this paradoxical ethics of alterity, so powerfully and prophetically promoted by Levinas, has made its way into "secular" and "atheistic" writers (I will come back to "atheism" in my concluding chapters) like Derrida and Lyotard, who have each in his own way come under Levinas's sway and whose discourses, under his impress, also bear a biblical mark. Levinas himself is a kind of postmodern prophet, a certain Amos of the *rive gauche,* who desires not burnt offerings but justice, not ontology but ethics, not identity but alterity. So here we find ourselves setting up another short circuit, caused by crossing two different wires. For if there is a religious or even a biblical "philosophy" today, perhaps an important element of it is to be found among these mostly Jewish and Parisian, sometimes atheistic, postmodernists (if that is what they are). Given the Jewishness of Jesus, given the deeply Hebraic roots of his *Abba* spirituality, this would not be an outlandish result. As a Jew who made trouble for the authorities at the temple in Jerusalem, Jesus is a little un-Jewish, something of a "marginal Jew,"[11] but having never heard of Christianity, and having never had it in mind, he is also not quite Christian either. Jesus is in between, on the slash of undecidability between Jewish and Christian, which is the strategic place upon whose resources I would draw in order to nourish my little poetics of the impossible, the place I look to find the un-laws of the logic of the anarchic event. I cannot think of a better figure than Jesus upon whom to model a sacred anarchy, which is for me the desired upshot of an *imitatio Christi* with a twist of deconstruction.

The ethics or anarchic ethics of alterity which, I claim, articulates the ethical categories of the kingdom is likewise an ethics of "responsibility."

Unlike the garden-variety philosophical views of ethics, which are organized around the autonomous subject, where the self is an agent, an *arche*, in which responsibility means primarily being responsible for oneself, the kingdom is organized around what the philosophers call "heteronomy," where responsibility means responding to the other; so the self is not an agent but a patient, an-archic, not autarchic (whence an-ethics). One takes oneself to be always already on the receiving end of the call of the other, always already solicited by the one who comes to me from on high just because he or she is laid low, like the man lying in the road whom the Samaritan encounters. Remember the Genesis paradigm and the centrality of the structure of call and response. God speaks, and the world is the answer; God calls, and the people of God are the answer; God says "Abraham!" and Abraham says *hineni, me voici:* here I am, see me standing here. The call that goes out to creation and to the people of Israel likewise provides the model for "ethics," according to which the other one, the least among us, calls, and we respond *"hineni."* That is also why hospitality is such an important virtue in the kingdom, and why Derrida is being very biblical when he singles out the need for hospitality today, an important point (especially as regards who gets into the kingdom) to which we shall return in the concluding chapter.

The "other one" is not a purely formal or merely numerical conception that abstracts from substantive considerations about who or what is different. Ruthless billionaires, pederasts, and homicidal rapists are numerical minorities, thanks be to God, and they are certainly different from the common run, even in one sense the "others" whose alterity lays claim to us in the sense that they too need help and healing. We are responsible to and for them, but this responsibility does not consist in accommodating and affirming their actions but in restraining their violence and changing their hearts. The kingdom is for sinners, the lost sheep, but that does not mean affirming and encouraging sin. But the biblical and the deconstructionist notion of "alterity" is focused on the *qualitatively* other, which is not the same as the *quantitatively* other. It picks out the out-of-power and dispossessed, the out-of-luck and unfortunate, the hungry and the homeless, the *me onta* who suffer from their otherness (not advantaged by it), who are diminished by exclusion and apartness *(apartheid),* to those whose diminution of worldly being raises them up in majesty in the kingdom; alterity refers to the victims not the victimizers. That is precisely the power of powerlessness, the weak force of an unconditional claim, upon which the idea of a sacred anarchy is based. It refers to those who are ground under by the system, crushed by their alterity, as Isaiah said:

> What do you mean by crushing my people,
> by grinding the face of the poor? says the Lord God of Hosts. (Isa. 3:15)

Alterity means the power of powerlessness, not the power to buy your way out of the system and receive special treatment and privileged access to power by reason of your wealth. Responsibility in this anarchic sense means to be always already claimed by precisely that other one, the lame and the leper, to be always already responsible for such unseemly and suffering otherness. In a sacred anarchy, it is precisely by being "out," being "far" from the centers of power or wealth or kinship, that nearness and neighborliness is defined; my neighbor is not my own kind but the stranger, the other one lying on the road. As to my own family, those nearest to me, I must be prepared to hate them, that is, not to put their interests above the interests of justice and hospitality. That is the poetics of neighborliness that should govern the relations of Protestant and Catholic in Northern Ireland, of Palestinian and Jew in the Middle East, of all the parties in what once was Yugoslavia, and so on and on around the globe.

In the kingdom, responsibility implies heteronomy not autonomy, anarchy not autarchy, being held captive by the needs of the other, not the freedom to fill oneself up and satisfy one's needs. Not to fill one's pockets but to give what I need for myself to the other, not to fill one's plate but to take the food out of my mouth. To give, not from excess but of one's substance. When the widow gives two copper coins, she gives, not from her overflow but from what she needs for her own life *(bios)* (Mark 12:42–43), and she gives more than the rich who give thousands out of their excess. "What a wonderful arithmetic problem, or rather what a wonderful kind of arithmetic; it is not to be found in any arithmetic textbook," says Kierkegaard in the *Works of Love.* The greatness of the gift is proportionate to the greatness of the poverty, which is the opposite of how the world judges gifts![12]

Autonomy and freedom belong to the most classical assumptions of Greco-philosophical ethics, of onto-theo-logical ethical theory. In an anarchic an-ethics of alterity, I worry that my freedom and autonomy pose a danger to the other, to those who are defenseless; for it is my freedom that keeps them out, that keeps them down, that threatens to kill them. One needs, of course, the good sense not to let this heteronomic turn devolve into self-hatred and an ethics of guilt, which is what can come of emphasizing the second creation narrative over the first, and also to recognize that is not always a recipe for everyone, because some people have been systematically deprived of autonomy and subjectivity. Only those who have been overstuffed with subjectivity, not the famished, need to go on a diet in this regard. The idea is always, while conceding our self-love, to maintain what Derrida calls the most open-ended and hospitable narcissism. To develop this theme, Levinas makes use of the particularly felicitous translation of Abraham's *hineni* into the French *"me voici,"* literally, "see me here."[13] Me, in the accusative, standing under accusation, accused and responsible for the address that comes to me from on high, like the voice that overtook Abraham and called him out to Moriah. If Heidegger has undertaken a systematic critique of the Cartesian epistemological subject, in the sense of the *ego cogito,* and Levinas of the ethical subject, in the sense of the autonomous *ego volo,* this has not left us altogether without a subject in any sense. On the contrary, "after" the subject, after these subjects, Levinas reintroduces the subject in the accusative, the "me" not the "I," the subject that is responsible for the other, for the neighbor and especially the stranger. Thus, the first principle *(arche)* that rules in this anarchic kingdom is the *an-arche* of the one who never puts himself first, who always comes second, anarchically, in response to the word that comes to him from the other. To put it another way, subjects are constituted, galvanized, and radicalized by the event that overtakes them, a point on which Kierkegaard and the New Testament, on the one hand, and Badiou and Žižek, on the other hand, are agreed, the middle term between them being St. Paul. The common denominator between the Levinasian and the Kierkegaardian subject, then, is that the subject of responsibility is constituted by a response.

The rule is, more generally, to watch out for rules, to watch out for the killing power of the law, and to keep watch for everything that is ground under by the law. To come back to the story of the man with a withered hand, Mark says that the Pharisees watched Jesus carefully to see if he would heal the man, because that day it happened to be the Sabbath (Mark 3:1–6). The Sabbath here is the law, but "Pharisees" should be taken with a grain of salt; the New Testament authors were engaged in a polemic with the Jews from whom, by the end of the first century, they were splitting off, and in their efforts to give the Jews a black eye, their target of choice was the Pharisees. So to get the point of these stories, for the "Pharisees" read the "religious authorities," the lovers of legalism, among whom we would certainly include long-robed ecclesiastical apparatchiks, both Catholic and Protestant, and their strong dislike for dissent, homosexuals, feminists, and other devilish deconstructors (like Jesus). By Pharisees I recommend we understand in general the powers that be *(exousiai),* who hypocritically preach sexual morality (to the neglect of issues of social justice) while systematically covering up their own sexual misconduct in order to protect the "company"; or who try to ride herd over the people of God and to run the kingdom like a cost-conscious corporation, which is why they close down inner-city churches in order to build new wings on prosperous suburban parish halls, abandoning the kingdom of the *ta me onta* in order to join in the headlong flight to the *ousia*-rich suburbs. So the authorities wanted to see whether the work of healing, *therapeuein,* would triumph over the law of the Sabbath, whether in this kingdom healing or the law held sway. Suspecting a trap, Jesus turned the tables on them by asking them whether the

Sabbath was for doing good or doing evil, for saving life or killing. What-ever their other shortcomings, the authorities were not foolish enough to answer that question, but their silence was even more damning. So Jesus, who was grieved by their hardness of heart—when it comes to healing, we can also think of these so-called Pharisees as the New Testament version of the HMOs—lifted the law of the Sabbath from the man with a withered hand, suspending the law, and thereby gave the man a lift (or authorized payment to his hospital for his treatment). For the Sabbath was made for the man, not the man for the Sabbath. The Sabbath, the seventh day, to pursue our trope, is the day of healing and mending, of re-creating and re-fashioning the original work of creation.

Thus it was that the law of the Sabbath was deconstructed in the name of justice. With this remark, you will notice, I have wired up this familiar biblical story with a line from deconstruction.[14] But is not the transgres-siveness of Jesus, his reputation for being an outlaw, a lawbreaker, once again something that is articulated by a post-metaphysical understanding of justice, law, and judgment, by its affection for transgression? The story corresponds quite nicely to Derrida's principle, or quasi-principle, or un-principle, or principle without principle, that the law is deconstructible, but justice in itself, if there is a such a thing, is not deconstructible. The law is something written, a bit of *écriture,* a socio-historical construction that, if it is *not* revisable, reformable, rewritable, amendable—that is, de-constructible—would represent the worst form of terror. The justice that the law delivers always limps along lamely, while justice in itself, if there is such a thing, wings its way overhead, making gorgeous circles in the sky. The law is always a wooden and imperfect likeness of the supple spirit of justice. But that is not to say that we can do without the law, God forbid![15]

Justice in itself is not an overarching eternal Platonic form but the unique and particular justice that is cut to fit the *Augenblick,* the particular needs of the individual, that is subtly suited and sculpted to the most secret singularity of each individual. That is why the idea of mandatory mini-mum sentences, which takes away judicial discretion, so often produces ex-traordinary injustice. (Of course, it never was justice but the re-election of lawmakers pandering to public fears that inspired this law.) When it comes to justice, every hair on our head is numbered, every tear is counted, and so every secret and most singular need is respected. The knowledge of such se-crets is what is signified by the name of God, whether or not one rightly passes for an atheist. Singularity is nothing to deconstruct; singularity is that in virtue of which there is deconstruction, if there is such a thing.[16] Deconstruction is always undertaken *in the name of something,* which is its point, its stylus tip; deconstruction does not have a center or a univocal transcendental signified, but it has a point, a constantly shifting tip that probes here and there, that feels about for openings. But the law, which must be impartial, is universal; it must in principle blind itself to singularity. That is what the law is, and we should not criticize the law for being what the law is supposed to be.

Still the law should be just; the law is meant to deliver justice. That means it is intended to give an event a worldly form, to give the call a worldly body and incarnation, so justice in itself, if there is such a thing, needs laws if it is to be materially effective. Justice is a weak force, a specter that continually haunts the law with its soft sighs, but the law is a strong force that can be enforced against the violent. The idea is not to denounce the woodenness of the law while singing hymns to sainted justice with our eyes lifted to heaven like beautiful souls. The idea is to situate oneself in the space between justice and the law, to "negotiate the difference,"[17] in the irreducible gap or distance that opens up between them. This is a structural matter, for to make justice and the law converge absolutely is absolutely impossible. It will never happen. The Messiah is always to come, with the result that this anarchic ethics is also highly messianic. In the meantime— and *it is always the meantime,* messianic ethics is always an interim ethics, while we wait for him to come—we want to close that gap, which cannot be closed. Justice is urgently needed today, in the meantime. That is one of the impossible things that deconstruction loves, one of its impossible aspirations, part of its aspiration for *the impossible.* Deconstruction keeps watch over the singularities lest they be ground under by the law, and it calls for lifting the law in order to heal on the Sabbath. The act of healing a man with a withered hand on the Sabbath is an act of deconstruction, part and parcel of our sacred anarchy. Once again, and I insist on this in the interests of avoiding supersessionism, the historical Pharisees would have been the first to advocate such compassion, while their so-called legalism is an insult that the early Christians hurled at them to portray them otherwise in the fateful war that was breaking out between them, as a result of which the blood of many of Jesus' people, the Jews, would be spilled.

There is, of course, a price to be paid for deconstructing the law. The word goes forth that such deconstructors are dangerous, that they are the enemies of the law, that they mean to destroy the law and raze the temple (or at least ruin the university and the core curriculum and destroy the good name of Cambridge University!). That is of course a bad rap, a misunderstanding, a slightly panicked reaction to a certain kind of ethics, if you insist on that word, or an an-ethics that puts singularity first, that subordinates the law to the singular, an ethics that has a heart, an ever-so-slightly anarchic ethics of unexpected events.

KARDIA AND PHRONESIS

Notice that the biblical story says that Jesus grieved over the hardness of heart of these high-ranking authorities. He did not disagree with their argument and come back with a counterexample or a more comprehensive covering theory. He did not think that this was a dispute to be settled by the weight of "good reasons" one way or the other. He did not think it was a matter of reason, of *logos* or *nous,* at all, but of the "heart," that it came down to whether or not one is "hard of heart." That is one of the categories of the poetics of the impossible that I want to single out, one to which the philosophers have been blind or systematically insensitive (to which, one is tempted to say, they have hardened their hearts). For the poetics of the impossible might just as well be called a poetics of the heart. The heart is how things happen in the kingdom, where things turn around.

Kardia is not what Aristotle called practical reason *(phronesis),* even as the *nous* in *metanoia* is not Aristotelian *nous.* Metanoetics, which trades in weak forces, is a matter of *kardia,* not *logos,* which trades in hard arguments, and if it is a matter of *nous* it is of *nous* as *kardia,* not a primarily noetic and cognitive *nous.*[18] But among the philosophers it is Aristotle who has seen the most clearly that "judgment" must be addressed to the needs of the particular situation, responsive to the demands of singularity, and that is the essence of what he meant by *phronesis. Phronesis* is a certain ethical adroitness that sees into the complexities of the situation, that shifts with the shifting, for ethics has to do with changing things, with the continually shifting sands of circumstances. *Phronesis* is the capacity to see how the general schema can be brought to bear upon the singular situation. *Phronesis* does not mean a descent into particulars but an ascent from the vacuousness of the abstract to the lush and sensuous concreteness of the singular, the *tode ti.* Aristotle's ethics reflects a lesson we also learned from Genesis: creation is not a fall from the One into multiplicity, but the ascent from indifference to the multiplication of differences, the differentiation of sky and earth and sea, and filling them with a multiplicity of living things; creation does not move from the one to the many, but from the undifferentiated to the differentiated. The production of differences, of singularities, is not a loss or a fall but an enriching. *Phronesis* refers to the way the empty and schematic knowledge of the ethical universal can be raised up to the reality of concrete knowledge, of what is to be done, here and now.

But still, with all of that, *phronesis* is not *kardia. Phronesis* is a kind of *nous,* a practical *nous,* to be sure, but always a matter of insight and seeing. It is the sight that comes from the acquisition of training, experience, time, and a certain expertise; it is in some ways comparable to craftsmanship, to

the skill acquired by the handicraftsman who has completed an apprentice-
ship *(techne)*. *Phronesis* and *techne* are forms of practical *nous,* and the opposite of this *nous* is stupidity, inflexibility, wooden and blind application of
rules. But *kardia* is not insight or the agility of practical knowledge; it is not
application or the skill of seeing how the general schema can be fleshed out
in the concrete situation. The opposite of *kardia* is not stupidity but hardness of heart, not the inflexibility of mindlessness but the insensitivity of
uncaring indifference. It was just because of the tendency of the Greeks to
consider evil as a form of stupidity that Augustine had to invent his idea of
will, of ill will, which corresponds to the idea of hardness of heart in the
kingdom. That is also why Johannes Climacus thought the Greeks were too
beautiful. *Kardia* represents a certain "succumbing," a surrendering, a *"se
rendre,"* giving into, giving oneself over to, the claims of singularity, a melt-
ing down, a surrender to the needs of this other one—this poor one, this
lame or leper, this withered hand, this justice—over and against and sometimes even in opposition to what is required by the law, which is universal.

When Jesus heals the man with the withered hand, he does not bring
the universal schema to bear upon the particular situation, but he lifts or
suspends the universal in the face of the demands of the singularity before
him. The weight, the demand, the claim, the call of the singular one outweighs and trumps the requirements of the law. This is suspension, not application, choosing in the face of conflicting demands, not a smooth im-
plementation; mercifulness, not *nous.* In metanoetics, the rule of a strictly
cognitive *nous* is broken and replaced by a heart-based *nous,* a *nous* that in
terms of the old physiology would have its seat, not in the head but in the
breast, for indeed the word *phronesis* itself refers to the *phren,* the chest and
heart.

Metanoia thus tells us to change our heart, to become merciful to a
fault, to lift the strictures of the law and to let ourselves be laid claim to, to
be besieged by the other one, by those who suffer from their alterity, to let
ourselves be touched and besieged by those who are under siege, to be overcome by the power of their powerlessness. *Metanoia* is how one is touched
by a weak force. *Metanoia* means to grieve over mercilessness and to suc-
cumb to the demands of mercy, to let oneself be touched, be affected by the
claims of flesh laid low. *Metanoia* means to be vulnerable to the vulnerability of the other, to become weak at their weakness, to be wounded by their
wounds, to be affected by their affliction, all of which are rigorous axioms
in the poetics of the impossible. If I break the law, which is a strong force, I
may end up in jail and "do time," which is another strong force, but that
has nothing to do with experiencing *metanoia.* Nor is *metanoia* insight in
the manner of Aristotle's practical reason; still less does it have anything to
do with the purity of Kant's pure practical reason that triumphs over the

pathological impulses of sensibility. On the contrary, *kardia* is precisely *pathos* and sensibility, a communication of flesh with flesh; it is a sensibility that triumphs over the universalizing impulses of reason, a matter of sensibility in the Levinasian sense, which is a deep and sensitive *pathos* that suffers with the suffering of the other, that enters into a community and communication of suffering, the paradigm of which—if I may miscegenate Levinas and the New Testament—is the communication of withered hands and healing hands.[19]

One of the most important events, perhaps the central event, in the teaching of Jesus is the event of forgiveness, a point to which I will return in more detail below. But I want at least to delineate here how *metanoia* is always and already implicated in forgiveness. The other one is not only someone whose neediness lays claim to me from on high, who needs me, but she is also the one who offends me and then claims my forgiveness, even as I require to be forgiven. If the other one goes wrong—and who does not?—but then has a change of heart *(kai ean metanoese),* then you should forgive her or him *(aphes auto): aphienai; dimittere:* to dismiss, send away, let go, discharge what the other owes you. If the other offends you seven times over, then you should forgive him or her seven times over. Luke 17:1–4 puts this in terms that Levinas would appreciate. After offending you seven times in the course of one day, "he turns to you" *(epistrepse pros se).* The phrase suggests that the offense was perhaps done behind your back or to your side, but now the other is face to face. He turns to you, Luke says, speaking *(logon):* that is what Levinas would call the mode of *le dire,* of saying, of the human proximity of speakers, as opposed to the cold content of what they say (which could be sent by e-mail). *Le dire/le dit:* contact/content.[20] Now the man or woman, your brother or your sister, turns to you and looks you in the eye and speaks to you. This transaction does not take place in the sphere of *le dit,* where the point is the content of what is said, its cogency or its elegance. The man does not bring up the nature of the offense, the circumstances, the mitigating considerations, the witnesses, if any; he does not mention that his wife has been ill and he has been out of sorts of late. In the kingdom, that is not what matters. He just asks for an event! The language of the kingdom is not the language of the said, of contents, reasons, justifications, circumstances, rationalizations, but a language of saying, of the event. The kingdom is a kingdom of saying *(logon).*

The man who has turned to you, saying, simply says, *"Metanoo,"* "I have had a change of heart." *"Metanoo":* I have been transformed and turned around; my heart has been made over; I am of a new mind and heart; my whole disposition and attunement *(Stimmung)* has undergone a change; I am now playing a new tune, I have been retuned. "Repent," the traditional translation of *metanoia,* which means, I visit pain *(poena)* my-self, again *(re),* I give myself (and everybody else) a pain, misses the upbeat turn of this very beautiful word. To be sure, that is not false; but it is, at best, a Baptist translation, John the Baptist (and perhaps Southern Baptist). "Repent" is the wrong tune, or not the whole tune; it is the Baptist's tune; it is the dirge, and in the background is the Yahwist "guilty," not Elohim's "good." That is, at best, a prelude preparing the way for the kingdom, a voice out in the desert announcing the coming of the kingdom, but not the kingdom itself, not quite the language of the kingdom; it is the wrong talk and the wrong tune. "I have a new heart"—that is Hannah Arendt's translation, Jesus' tune, the dance, not the dirge.[21] The man turns to you, saying, I am ready to dance, my heart is light, I have a new *nous,* as when the author of the letter to the Hebrews speaks of turning away from dead works *(metanoia apo nekron ergon)* (Heb. 6:1). You notice that he does not make an excuse, give a *logos* in his defense, an *apologia,* of himself, because in the kingdom it is not the *logos* but the *legein,* the pure saying, that counts. He does not give an account, or get mixed up with the *ratio red-denda,*[22] offering reasons and explanations that should compel you to con-clude that he reasonably warrants forgiveness; he does not get into a ratio-nal settling of accounts *(le dit).* On the contrary, the other man has done you in seven times today, and he is your brother, and the day is not over yet. So if you follow the dictates of reason, the strong force of reason will point you elsewhere.

The use of numbers in the story has the distressing effect of stressing that it is reasonable to forgive someone up to a point, it makes sense, but that after a certain point it is madness. That is when the accounting of the kingdom, the poetics of the impossible, kicks in. The chap just turns to you, face to face—this is the Levinasian staging—saying *metanoo,* I have been transformed. He does not go into the particulars; this is a case of pure *dire.* And you, and we, what are we to do? We should melt, soften, weaken, change our heart, be transformed; you, we, should just have a heart and for-give him *(apheseis auto).* Our heart should be reformed by this word like the *tohu wa-bohu* responding to the words of Elohim. As a being of *kardia,* we are vulnerable, sensitive, sensible of and to the other, responsive to the heart of the other, and our hearts should be changed by the change of heart of the other. So Jesus says, Let it go, let the past be, let it go by, and forgo the debt you could collect here. Be of a new mind yourself; be renewed; change your tune. Let the event happen. Do not, as Nietzsche would have said, bear any ill will to the past (sometimes Nietzsche, despite his very great dili-gence in this regard, lapsed into very Christian sentiments).

Twelve centuries later, Peter Damian would raise the question as to whether this change of mind could be so radical, this change of heart so utterly transforming, that God would, by an exercise of compassion reserved exclusively for the divine goodness, see to it that the offense that was committed was remitted to the point of being revoked, undone, made into something that was *not* committed. Talk about an event! An event to end all events! I will explore the details of that heady suggestion, which goes to the heart of the para-logic of the kingdom, in a later chapter. Suffice it say for the moment that Damian had hit upon something crucial about the kingdom, something of the evangelical spirit of forgiveness, of its amazing grace, but—misled by the idea of *creatio ex nihilo*—he mystified the whole idea by turning the power of powerlessness into a laser show of divine omnipotence, a dizzying display of Disneyesque proportions, which ultimately undermined the idea of forgiveness. Forgiveness is not an exercise of power but a forgoing of the exercise of power, giving up the power one has over the other.

THE EVENTFUL TIME
OF THE KINGDOM

In the kingdom, the best way to raise the question of *time* is to begin with the time of *forgiveness,* which brings out the event-ful character of time that is quite different from the steady beat of now-points that Greeks from Aristotle to Husserl have put forward.[23] What is this moment, this *Augenblick,* this blink of the eye, the time of this transforming change of heart? What is the eventful temporality of forgiveness? Even without embracing Damian's extreme and misguided hypothesis, we can agree that forgiveness somehow involves a readiness to wipe away the past in some way, a willingness not to hold on to it, to dismiss it. The time of forgiveness is a kind of double time, involving as it does both the painful past, the time of the *skandalon,* the time of the offense or the sin *(amarte),* and the wiping away of the past. The "past" of forgiveness is not accounted for in the classical phenomenology of time, although it assumes this phenomenology, upon which it introduces an evangelical variation. The forgiven past is minimally but not *merely* time gone by, something over that remains in the past, where it assumes an "irremissible" place, where such a past is "retained," held onto so it can always be recalled, as Husserl would say. If that is all it is, then you and I always know it is there. I may not mention it or ever advert to it, but we both know that this is something that in retaining (holding) I hold over you, that I have the power to call back if I want. But in forgiveness, the retained and irremissible past must somehow become remissible and I must abdicate that power. I must give up the power, forgo repayment, or give away *(fort-geben)* the advantage I have over you. I wipe the ledger clean so that the offense is gone, actively wiped away, wiped out, and you are released. But just as creation is *transformation* and not *ex nihilo,* the wonder here, the amazing grace, is not *annihilation,* for what is in the past is still there, but *re-formation* or *transformation,* where the offense is transformed in the moment of forgiveness into something that is no longer hanging over us, no longer between us, not anymore.

Forgiveness is the opposite of repression. In repression, something that is there keeps recurring just because I deny it; in forgiveness, something that is there is dismissed just because I affirm it and forgive it. In an important sense, it is there *without* being there, readable only *sour rature,* so that we look upon someone who is forgiven in a new light; the other has been given a new life, just the way Elohim filled the desert spaces with life. In the as-if time of forgiveness, we proceed *as if* it never happened. Of course it did happen, and it is retained, otherwise there would be nothing to forgive, but it is retained as forgiven, as struck out, under erasure, the object of an active forgetting (Nietzsche again!). The eventful character of the forgiven past is that the past is not simply retained or sustained or simply wiped away— nothing is simple—but retained *as* wiped away. To treat what has happened *as if* it never happened is different both from its never having happened at all and from constantly recalling that it happened. Still, this is not a completely imaginary event because the forgiving is real, and the past is in some way disarmed or struck out. Forgiven time is a kind of as-if time in which we willingly suspend our disbelief that the past never happened. Put in the most straightforward phenomenological terms, the past is neither annihilated nor forgotten, but it is given a new meaning, the meaning of the "as if it never happened," which presupposes that it did, which constitutes the temporality of forgiveness as an event.

The kingdom thus runs on a very odd time indeed, a nonstandard time, an eventful and metanoetic time that is not dreamt of in all our philosophies, Horatio. Medieval theology, however onto-theo-logical its tendencies, remained, to its credit, quite inwardly haunted by its biblical sources. The possibility of this impossibility, of changing past time, that Peter Damian posed, is exactly the opposite of the puzzle that the past posed to the Greeks, who were moved to ask whether, once a thing was past, it did not become necessary, even though it may have started out as contingent at the time that it happened, as Aristotle wondered in *De Interpretatione.*[24] The past, by its very nature, seemed to the Greeks to suffer from a kind of *sclerosis,* that is, the longer an event sits on the shelf of the past, the more it seemed to them to harden over into necessity. But the Christian theologians were provoked into musing over the opposite and very metanoetic possibility, and this because the horizon of their thinking was shaped by the opening pages of Genesis. They viewed things as contingent all the way down, having come forth in the first place from a beneficent and transforming word that made the barren spaces alive and made the waters swarm with life. When it comes to human life, they sought to avoid letting action harden over, to avoid the hardness of heart *(sclerosis tes kardias)* that turned things to stone, that petrified and froze them over. As Hannah Arendt says, resentment and revenge pull the strings of the past ever tighter and tie us up into knots, but forgiveness cuts things loose, sets them free of the past.[25] Resentment resolves to "get even," to settle accounts, to balance the books in a rigorous "economy" of exchange, to hold on tight to the past, never to let it go unless and until it is paid back. "Don't get mad, get even": that is as vicious, as deeply unbiblical a sentiment as one can imagine. But forgiving lets go.

To have a creational frame of mind is to think, not in terms of an absolute movement between being and absolute non-being, but of a transformation from barrenness to life; creation is like birth and re-creation is like rebirth. Thus to be forgiven, on a biblical model, is to be reborn, to come back to life where you were once as good as dead. For what has been created can and must be re-created, even as what has been constructed is deconstructible, for in this sacred anarchy, creation, re-creation, and deconstruction hang together like the steps of a dance. Right from the opening pages of Genesis, things are made good but then turn bad. That is the logic of creation, which requires that there be some way to mend what has gone wrong, the emblematic role we are assigning to the seventh day. Can you restore this flesh, these withered and distorted arms and legs, can you make them straight again the way God made them? And this leprous ulcerated flesh, can you make it whole and wholesome again? And even this dead girl, can you make her live again? Even so, can you restore this wounded heart? The only way that the Yahwist author thought that Yahweh could deal with good-turned-bad was to wipe the whole thing out in a flood and start all over again. He seems not to have thought of the more peaceful solution of forgiveness, but for that he may be forgiven, since he was still new at this thing called creating—and besides, he had his own agenda, to sound an alarm about hubris in the Davidic kingdom. In any case, we owe thanks to the Yahwist for bringing us back to the earth. The dreamy priestly author thought that we, like God, could all take a rest on the seventh day, but the Yahwist knew better, that things were going to go wrong and that we could never take a break. The seventh day is for recreating the mess that was soon made of creation. (P and J, the priest and the Yahwist, were the first in a long line of spiritual bulls and bears.)

The psalmist said, *renovabitis faciem terrae:* "When you send forth your spirit, they are created; you keep on renewing the face of the earth" (Ps. 104:30). "Keep on renewing"—that is the rest of which Elohim is deprived on the seventh day, the discovery that there is no day off. Creation is an unfinished work, an ongoing process. So the work of healing the man with the withered hand, or healing the lame and the leper, or the heart of the man who turns to you saying, *I have had a change of heart,* belongs to an ongoing supplementary operation of the Spirit. Elizabeth Johnson puts this all very nicely in *She Who Is,* her compelling feminist rewriting of our discourse about God. She speaks of the figure of the Spirit as a feminine Spirit-Sophia, and she argues that the Holy Spirit is the Cinderella, the poor relation in the traditional Trinity, who, no matter how much you stress the perichoresis, always comes third and is generated by two male figures. The Spirit, she says, is marked by this sense of transformability, which is linked to the notion of creation as an ongoing process.[26]

This transformation happens, Johnson argues, when the natural world is renewed in the spring, when the social and political world is renewed by reform, hence in green fields and fields of justice (Isa. 32:15–17), and in personal renewal, when a heart of stone is turned into flesh (Ezek. 36:26), bathed in the waters of forgiveness. In the closing chapters of the book of Revelation, the Lord says "See, I am making all things new" (21:5), just as Genesis opens with Elohim making all things good to begin with. What else then is this "metanoetics" than the continuation of creation under another name, at another time, in time—indeed, time itself? What else are time and creation than the ongoing and incessant process of giving life and habitation to the wild, the extended seventh and longest day reaching out across time, as time, in which time fills up what is lacking, or what has gone wrong with the good things made by Elohim? What else is time than a certain rhythm of creation marred by destruction and renewed by recreation, like the opening chapters of Genesis?

Now I ask, by way of bringing this introduction to metanoetics, this propaedeutic to a poetics of the impossible, to a philosophical conclusion, what then is the "time of the kingdom"? What is metanoetic time? What is the time of *metanoia,* of forgiveness, the time of spreading the healing word, *kerysoon,* and of healing *(therapeuon)* itself, of recreating and renewing? If we were to give in to an almost irresistible urge implanted in us by the Greeks, we who are their phenomenological offspring, we would ask, What is the being of this time and the time of this being, this being made new, this metanoetic way to be and to temporalize?

Metanoetic time is a time of rebirth, renewal, and transformation, of radical metamorphosis and alterability. It is not a Hegelian time in which a deep historical momentum makes a steady advance by way of a progressive, self-correcting, upwardly moving dialectic. Far more challenging than that, it is time of incessant rise and fall, gain and loss, suffering sometimes unsettling setbacks that leave us hopeless, which summon up a hope against hope, the time that is captured so poignantly by Benjamin's "angel of history." Far more immediate and instantaneous than any *Aufhebung*, this is a time of the instant, of the *Augenblick*,[27] in which a man or a woman undergoes a transforming change of heart, putting off the old and putting on the new. There is no recourse to mediation, no passage through a mediating state, no dialectically guided passage through opposites. It is all more sudden, more unmediated and direct than that, coming as it does like a thief in the night. The flesh of the leper and of the man with the withered hand are changed, made new, made whole, by the power of God that is with Jesus, in a moment of therapeutic transformation. "Then he said to the man, 'Stretch out your hand.' He stretched it out, and it was restored as sound as the other" (Matt. 12:13). In a flash. Like Elohim in the opening chapters of Genesis: God speaks, and the world is made; God calls, and Abraham packs his bags; Jesus speaks, and it is done. Elohim fashioned life out of a wilderness, and Jesus mends and amends living things, refashions what has become ill-shaped, leprous, or hard of heart. So when a man offends you seven times in one day and seven times asks to be forgiven, then seven times you must dismiss his fault, for that is the work of the seventh day, the work of a seventh-day eventist. Seven times, that is to say, time and time again, over and over, countlessly, repeatedly falling and repeatedly being lifted up again, until the heart is healed. You are to make him new again, the way Elohim made all things new to begin with. Re-create in the image and likeness of that first act of creation.

This is not an Aristotelian time, which glides smoothly across the surface of substances whose potencies pass over into acts for which they were all along being made ready. It is not a time of continuity, of smooth transitions, of potencies passing into act by first passing through the intermediate state, of acts that simply realize the potentialities that have all along been present, that have slowly and patiently waiting their turn in the gentle circular rhythms of genesis and corruption. Metanoetic time is more discontinuous and abrupt, more shocking and surprising; this is a metamorphic not a hylomorphic world. Metanoetic time is the time of the surprise, a time in which one is struck by the amazing changes that take place before one's eyes or in one's own heart. It is not a time that rides smoothly along the grooves of the potential and the possible, but one that is continually disturbed by the shock of the impossible, by acts for which no potency prepared the way, acts that far outstrip the potencies that they actualize. It is a world that Aristotle would have thought was quite mad, quite impossible; and we freely admit that it is, which is why we love it so.

The time of the kingdom is not the time of *ousia,* of the steady beat of presence that rides out every change, that persists and perdures, that presides over the transience of particular changes. It is rather the time of thoroughgoing upheaval, of a totally transforming renewal that is possible only in a thoroughly creationist world. In the kingdom, the assumption is not that things have always been and will ever be thus; rather, the presumption is that things have come to be by being drawn from the deep by Elohim's formative word, so that things are shot through with *createdness.* That means in Genesis not exactly that they are permeated by "contingency," where God is "necessary," which is a very Hellenic way to put it, but that they are defined through and through by their formability and reformability. So the world does not have a rigid inner structure, a kind of ontological hard-wiring that makes it highly stable and resistant, for of itself it is a desolate wild, a *tohu wa-bohu,* that has been filled with life by Elohim, and that means that there is nothing about it to suggest that it is going to hold up under the press of the future, under the force of alteration and change. In terms of our personal time, the time of our own lives, one knows neither the day nor the hour, one can never be sure whether the next moment will not be the one in which we abjure what we believe, or whether it will be the last, whether the end will come and that will be that. Let the kingdom come! Let it happen! Let it arrive! Let the Spirit come. *Veni creator spiritus.* Let it come even though we are not able to see it coming, to predict it, to observe natural signs, the way a red moon predicts a hot summer day. We can only be ready for a moment that could be any moment now.[28] Come, Derrida says, *viens, oui, oui,* repeating the lines of the Psalms and the book of Revelation without even knowing it.

In the kingdom time lacks the steady beat of presence, the permanence and the perdurance of *ousia.* This is not an onto-theo-logical world in which the being of time is permanent presence, and in which the time of being is to be steadily present. It is a world in which both being and time defer to the formative power of God, to the press of a power of utter transformation. The world is not thought in substantial ousiological terms, where things tend to persist in virtue of their own inherent and autonomous qualities, which is the oldest and fondest faith of ontotheologic. The world is a world without *ousia* and *hypokeimenon,* without *essentia* and *substantia,* without essences following their essential natures that preclude interruption or disruption. On the contrary, the kingdom belongs to a world in which the regularities of *ousia, substantia,* and *essentia* are regularly suspended, a world that is peculiarly prone to interruption and disruption. The being of time and the time of being are defined by their utter transformability, their thoroughgoing vulnerability and susceptibility to transformation; being and time are radically re-creatable, repeatable, reformable, reworkable, remakable, remarkable.

(Deconstructible!)

Contrary to the most cherished beliefs of onto-theo-logic, such a world is largely *nominalistic;* things do not have deep essences whose essential laws dictate their future destinies. That anti-essentialism, we will see, shows up in Peter Damian, who misconceived it in terms of divine omnipotence. Even the principle of noncontradiction was for him something that offered no resistance to the power of God. It too was not an essence but a non-essence, a mutable creature. Natural things have life, but the Spirit is the life of their life, as Hildegard of Bingen said; the Spirit is what Derrida would call the law of the law![29] Withered arms and paralyzed limbs, eyes that cannot see, ears that cannot hear, feverish and even dead bodies—that is the stuff that the kingdom is made of; and in the kingdom they are capable of being transformed in a flash, in the blink of an eye, as is the human heart. No abiding *ousia* dictates the terms under which things transpire in this Wonderland; no essential nature lays down the law by which all things abide. In the kingdom, things reflect the original operation of creation: they are forged from a formless, fragile, slippery, and supple stuff that is stiffened neither by essence nor by nature, that does not obey a natural law or inherent necessity, which means that they are capable of undoing what has been done even as they are capable of being made whole and new. In the kingdom, things lack good Germanic *Selbstständigkeit,* the ability to stand on their own and to persist in their own subsistence, to subsist by their own persistence. Things lack standing, self-standing, sub-standing, substance, and substantiveness. Things are marked rather by their mutability and readiness for change, so that they can be struck down with death and disease, with paralysis and pain, and also by their responsiveness to the word that makes them new, restoring and resuscitating them, calling the world itself out of a great void, calling bodies back out from their graves— calling to Lazarus, Step forth—in graveyard scenes that would make Stephen King's hair stand on end.

Metanoetic time does not operate according to a rule of recall, a principle in virtue of which whatever happens is a repetition or recollection or retrieval of something that has been there all along. Metanoetic time is not dominated by philosophy's love of the circle or of Parmenidean spheres that dictate that we always come back to our point of departure, that becoming is coming back to where we were, that *Wesen* is always *Gewesen.*

Metanoetics does not operate by a law of Platonic *anamnesis,* according to which to learn is to remember or to recall something that must have already been known, on the grounds that knowledge must arise from knowledge and there cannot be such utter transformation. Plato says in the *Republic* that learning is not a matter of giving the soul something that it does not have, of inserting sight into a blind eye (*Republic,* 518). Yet that is exactly what it is in the kingdom: giving us what we do not have, putting sight into blind eyes. Much as we love Plato for coming up with the Good beyond being, and for doing the best he could under the circumstances to save the appearances, the Platonic conception is still a bit scandalized by change, by novelty, and by the emergence of something new, and it keeps looking for a way to save time from the strictures laid down by father Parmenides without simply killing off the old man. So Plato looks for a way to contain the *renovatio,* the transformation from ignorance to knowledge, without simply defying father Parmenides and embracing the possibility that what the father said was impossible. But in the kingdom, novelty is not a paradox or aporia to be explained away, not a symptom of a world that is not really real; it is the rule of the day, of the new day, of the renewal of our works and days.

Metanoetics has nothing to do with Hegelian *Erinnerung,* with an interiorizing memorialization by which the in-itself labors and strains, tested by the powers of negativity, to become itself, to become what it already is, to be what it all along has been, to be what it already is. In metanoetics, one becomes what one is not, and one ceases to be what one was. I have had a change of heart, I have been transformed. I have not become what I am but I have become something else, something new. Metanoetics is not Heideggerian *Andenken,* according to which thinking forward *(Vordenken)* means thinking back upon or being devoted to what has been, to the oldest of the old, so that what is coming to us from the future comes to us from what has been. In metanoetics the future has not yet been and we cannot foresee it (even as the past can be undone); we know neither the day nor the hour, and when it comes we will be transformed into something new.

In the kingdom things do not look much like the prevailing conception of being and time in the history of Western metaphysics to which Christian theology has lent its considerable institutional weight, sitting all rouged and powdered in the window, as Johannes de Silentio says.[30] Things have a less substantial, less essential, more nominalistic, more contingent look. There is little in the kingdom to suggest the hegemonic rule of being, essence, natural law, intellectualism, the primacy of the universal and generic, the rule of law, the primacy of the same over the different, for which philosophy—ontophilosophy, ontotheological philosophy, metaphysical theology—shows such an ineradicable predilection. The kingdom does not seem to be made up of substances running their natural course in time, following up the inner tendencies of their nature according to natural laws, which is a more Greco-Roman and ontotheological way to think about things, for which we do not need and cannot use the New Testament. The kingdom is considerably more "eventualistic," made up of happenings, events, singular constellations; and living in the kingdom means being more sensitive to the singularity of the situation and to the novelty of what is to come. In the kingdom, things seem to "happen," to break out, so that the best way to describe an event is not to say "it *is*" but it happens, *es geschieht, il arrive,* and try to avoid the substantialistic, ousiological over-tones of *is* and being and essence.

A final word of caution: remember that because this metanoetics belongs to a *poetics* of the impossible, it has to do with the event, not entity. Remember that we have pronounced the epoche, taken an oath against the natural attitude, sworn our allegiance to a certain hermeneutic phenomenology, one intent on describing the style of life in the kingdom. And remember that we have renounced power. We are not reading these stories as exhibitions of *divine power,* the miraculous power to alter the course of nature, or to intervene in nature or history, but as narratives that betoken the rhythm of life in the kingdom, what sober philosophers like Husserl and Wittgenstein would have called its *Lebenswelt* or its "form of life." Setting aside the war between fact and fiction, what is the "meaning" of these narratives, the lived, experiential, eventful sense of life? What is their *poetics?*[31] When we say, when we pray, "Come, creator spirit," *"viens, oui, oui,"* what are we praying for?

EIGHT

Quotidianism: Every Day, or Keeping Time Holy

> Give us today the bread we need from day to day.
> (Matt. 6:11, my translation)

Having reflected on the first days of creation, and having given a somewhat symbolic interpretation of the seventh day as a supplementary day of re-creation needed to mend what goes amiss in creation, we turn to the nature of the "day" itself, the way we pass the day in the kingdom, from morning to night, each day of our lives.

KEEPING TIME HOLY

The event that is harbored in the name of God is an event of time, signifying a thoroughly temporal sense of life. The structure of that event is captured quite nicely by John Dominic Crossan, who wrote some years ago that the basic idea that Jesus had was to keep time holy and to ward off the idolatry of time:

> [T]he basic attack of Jesus is on an idolatry of time. . . . The one who plans, projects, and programs a future, even and especially if one covers the denial of finitude by calling it God's future disclosed or disclosable to oneself, is in idolatry against the sovereign freedom of God's advent to create one's time and establish one's historicity. This is the central challenge of Jesus. . . . It is the view of time as man's future that Jesus opposed in the name of time as God's present, not as eternity beyond us but as advent within us. Jesus simply took the commandment seriously: keep time holy![1]

The "event" of God's advent lies at the heart of the intertwining of the time of the kingdom with a deconstructive or eventualistic concept of time. To keep time "holy" means to recognize its non-programmability and open-endedness and to see that time is in God's hands not ours, that in time, be it personal or historical, it is not we who rule but God. It would be idolatry to forge a god out of *chronos* itself and to give it the force of necessity. An idolatrous time would run on its own, according to its own immanent rules, with its own necessities and density, its own chronology, equipped with its own *logos* and *arche*. But to keep time holy is to lighten the weight of time, to thin it out, *to make it transparent to the event,* which means here to the event of God's rule, to turn it over to God and *to ask God to give us time.* Then time takes on a more kairological, eventualistic, grace-like, gratuitous, anarchical quality, not chrono-logical but kairo-logical—or rather, kairo-poetic.

To adhere to the anarchical character of the things in the kingdom is to say that the rule of God in time, the holding sway of God over time, is event-ful, alive to the moment, turned toward the surprise, tuned to the absolute future. To ask God to give us the gift of time is to ask for the most eye-opening moments and to expose us to the most impossible, unforeseeable things. There is no clock that can keep or keep up with the time of the kingdom, where who knows what is going to happen next! In the kingdom, time is given not kept.

Not only must we keep the Sabbath holy, which is commanded explicitly in the Law, but we are further enjoined by Jesus, according to Crossan, to keep time itself holy. Jesus calls us, in the only prayer he handed down to us, to keep every day holy, each day, this day, today, *quotidie*. In the kingdom, we leave time to God, who gives time, who gives us each day, which is what Jesus taught us to pray each day. *Abba,* give us today. To live from day to day is to take each day as God's gift, to feel the pulse of God in time, to move with God's rhythm, with God's rule. *Abba* gives us each day the gift of the day, from day to day, so that when we pray we press our ear against the chest of time, press our finger on God's pulse in time. In that sense, every prayer is a morning prayer, a prayer for the coming and the giving of the day, for the rising of the light. Thanks be to you, *Abba,* for the gift of the day and for this day of gifts.

That brings us to another stratum of the poetics of the impossible, to a certain para-logical time, or a certain para-ousiological time that I call "quotidianism" (or "epi-ousiology") where God's rule is over "each day" *(quotidie, epiousios).* In the kingdom we trust what time gives because God gives time, whereas to give ourselves over to time's own necessity (destiny), or to try to give ourselves time, to assume sovereign command of our life and freedom (autonomy), is to so dominate time as to crowd God out and give up what God gives in and through and as time, to suppress the event of time that transpires in the name of God. Time is the string on which God is playing, and we may either heed its gentle rhythms or drown God out. We pray each day for God to provide what we need "for that day" *(epiousios),* the "quotidian," the *panis quotidianus,* which is what we mean by speaking of the time of the kingdom as a quotidianism.² We must learn to let God be God in us, as Meister Eckhart said, to let God be God each day, day by day, as Jesus is saying.

In the kingdom—here comes the short circuit—things turn on giving time *(donner le temps),* on how time is given. In the kingdom time turns *by* the impossible. In the kingdom time too, perhaps time above all, is *the* impossible.

> Don't worry.
> Must we not work and plan and provide for tomorrow?
> Yes, indeed, you must, but God will provide, each day, day by day;
>   don't worry.
> Must we not worry about our daily bread?
> Yes, indeed, you must, but you must also not worry.
> Must we not sow lest there is nothing to reap?
> Yes, indeed, but you must sow without worry.
> Must we not worry about the future, our children's future?
> Yes, indeed, but you must worry without worry.
> That is impossible.
> Yes, indeed, *the* impossible.

There is no simple exterior to economy, no pure outside, no pure gift. You reap what you sow and God is not mocked (Gal. 6:7), but on the other hand you must be like the birds of the air who neither sow nor reap and are clothed by God. You must sow quite energetically and be like the birds quite completely. It is not a question of choosing between the two or of striking a middle position midway between the two. That is the grip of *the* impossible. Economy is inescapable, but it must be continually interrupted, its grip broken, even as it is set in motion *by* the impossible, by *the* impossible, by a prayer for the impossible. The poetics of the "give us this day" is a poetics of the gift, of the gift of the day: *Abba,* give us today as we give everything to today without thought of the morrow; *Abba,* give us what we need from day to day even as we do not worry about the return tomorrow.

So, once again, let us reinstate our *epoche,* reset its dials, tighten its tensions, and prepare ourselves to be shocked by the blow of a slightly mad Aramaic imagination, to be shaken by the foolishness of the kingdom. Let us be prepared for the odd reversals and even slightly mad things that happen, all along listening to God's beat in time and the prayer to the *Abba* for time.³ What is the gift of the day, of the today, of the day to day? What does it mean to keep time holy, to keep bread holy? Let the event begin.

BELLUM QUOTIDIANUM: HEIDEGGER'S
HERMENEUTICS OF TROUBLING
OVER OUR DAILY BREAD

First a propaedeutic. One of the prototypes of this poetics of the impossible is found in the work of the young Heidegger in his first Freiburg lectures (1920–21). My project is modeled very closely on Heidegger's but with this difference: it is aimed at producing almost exactly opposite results. Heidegger's earliest work took the form of a "hermeneutics of facticity," that is, a retrieval of the factical "experience of life" that he found embedded in Aristotle's ethics. He read Aristotle's *Metaphysics* in the light of the concrete life-experiences from which Aristotle's metaphysical categories arose, which he located in the *Nicomachean Ethics* (even as, in 1916, he had proposed reading scholastic metaphysics in the light of its mystical and moral theology). This was the first form taken by his famous *Destruktion* of the tradition, which did not mean to raze or level it but to shake it loose from its sedimented forms in order to return it to its life-giving sources.

But this was in fact a dual project, the other leg of which was a parallel retrieval or *Destruktion* of Christian theology down into its founding life-experiences.[4] This took the form of a hermeneutics of the life-world of the earliest Christian communities, a hermeneutic phenomenology of early Christian historicality, as this is recorded for us in the New Testament. Heidegger was in those days much impressed by the work of Franz Overbeck, who had claimed that by the time of the writing of the New Testament the earliest Christian experience had already begun to sediment and be layered over, and this because the earliest Christians expected the second coming to be so imminent as not to allow for the building of any permanent institutions or founding texts.[5] They were not worried about—because they did not think there would be—any subsequent generations. By the time things started to get written down, the Christians were beginning to settle in for the long term, to unpack their bags, and to exercise a little messianic patience about the second coming.

Heidegger's attention was drawn, not to the Synoptics, but to the letters of Paul that address the apocalyptic expectations of the early Christians, their belief that, having warned "this generation" about the imminent end of the world, Jesus would soon come again on a cloud down from heaven to judge the living and the dead. In a course entitled "Introduction to the Phenomenology of Religion," given in 1920–21, Heidegger comments on the letter to the Galatians and the two letters to the Thessalonians, seeking to explicate the factical experience of time and history among the early New Testament communities. In Paul's first letter to the Thessalonians, the oldest document in the New Testament, antedating the earliest gospels, Paul answers two questions put to him by the community at Thessalonica on the coming of the Lord, the first concerning those who die before Christ comes again, and the second concerning the timing of the *parousia,* or second coming of the Lord.

In answer to the first question, Paul assures the Thessalonians that those who have died before the parousia do not suffer a disadvantage compared to those who will still be alive. For when the trumpet sounds and an archangel announces in a loud voice that the Lord is coming, all will be made equal. First the dead will rise, and then those who are still alive will be lifted up to a cloud to join them, and together they will all meet the Lord in the air (Thess. 4:13–18). This cloudy scene is a good example of how things get clouded if you think that, in accordance with a representational theory of truth, these texts pick out real objects; this scene provides as good a case as any to illustrate our need for a certain *epoche* if we are going to understand what is going on.

Heidegger is—understandably—more interested in the second question, about the "when?" He singles out the structure of their being-and-becoming-Christian, what he calls their "having become" *(genesthai, Gewordensein)* Christian.[6] He emphasizes the fact that for Paul Christian life, "having become Christian," is never a finished fact but always an ongoing struggle, a matter of fighting the good fight, of running a good race toward the prize that is ahead (Gal. 5:7), of forgetting what is behind and straining toward what is ahead, pressing on toward the goal and winning the prize (Phil. 3:13–14). Becoming Christian is a battle waged in fear and trembling (Phil. 2:12), a war with legalistic religious authorities who look for signs and with unbelieving Greeks who want arguments, which is repaid with distress and persecution, scars and imprisonment, tribulation and suffering. Christian life is a matter of "standing firm" in the faith, of the special "knowing" that comes with firm faith and steadfast hope, of enduring everything, holding up and holding out, until the parousia happens and we are lifted up on a cloud and the church militant—Heidegger always had a flare for the militaristic!—is transmuted into the church triumphant.

For Heidegger, the "when?" of the parousia is not a matter of an objectifying calculation, of spreading a calendar out on the table and making one's best assessment about the length of time between now and then. It is not a matter of determining a datable *when* in objective time, but of a transforming and transfiguring *how,* of how to live until then, an existential-phenomenological "when" in virtue of which the Thessalonians are not to worry about "times and seasons" *(chronoi kai kairoi),* that is, not to try to predict the parousia as if one were forecasting the weather. It belongs to the very essence of the parousia:

that the day of the Lord will come like a thief in the night. When they say, "There is peace and security," then sudden destruction will come upon them. (1 Thess. 5:1–3)[7]

Those who are lulled into a false sense of security by the distractions and comforts of everydayness will be taken by surprise. "But you, beloved, are not in the darkness, for that day to surprise you like a thief" (1 Thess. 5:4). The eyes of the Thessalonians are open; they are in the light, and they understand the incessant vigilance that Christian life requires, to stay always awake, always sober, always ready. So Paul tells them to put on the breastplate of faith and the helmet of hope and be ready (5:8). The question of the "when?" is not a chronological question of making a good estimate in terms of days, months, or years, but the existential question of being ready. Never mind when; be ready, "battle-ready,"[8] vigilant, on the alert. Do not try to calculate calendar time but stand ready all the time, "all alone before God."

Heidegger comments, "Christian experience lives time itself ('to live' understood as *verbum transitivum*)."[9] The factical sense of life of the Thessalonians is shot through, from beginning to end, with a sense of the radical contingency and facticity of time and the trembling of history. They stand ready for the trumpet's call whenever it sounds, day or night. Time and history are transfixed with urgency, pushed to an extreme of tension, radically energized by an apocalyptic sense that demands complete existential vigilance. The future is God's doing, not theirs; the day of the Lord's coming is the Lord's business, not theirs; and they are to keep time holy by respecting God's incalculable initiative in this matter. They are not to try to seize control of time or to make its *arche* or *logos* their own, for time is God's business. Their business is to make themselves ready.[10]

Heidegger has formulated the rule of God in terms of "anticipatory resoluteness," keeping constantly ready for an unforeseeable future, battle-ready, *Angstbereit*. Like Kierkegaard, Heidegger was very much taken with the tempestuous and volatile figure of Paul and with the Pauline thematics of anxiety and the kairotic moment of transforming conversion in faith that knocks us off our horse and blinds us, leaving us to wonder what in heaven's name just happened to us. For Heidegger and Kierkegaard, the kingdom is full of manly Christian warriors and knights of faith. They were both taken with the militant Pauline figure that forges ahead, pressing toward the goal, free for the future in fear and trembling. In Paul and Luther, Augustine and Pascal, Kierkegaard and Heidegger, the existential individual looks into the abyss of freedom and possibility and swoons with anxiety. The structure of Christian "factical life" is toiling and troubling, *Bekümmerung* and *Sorge,* worrying about one's daily bread *(sorgen um das* '*tägliche Brot*'),[11] fighting the good fight for bread and faith—in short, the very Pauline-Augustinian claim that the Being of Dasein is *Sorge,* dodging the bullets and boulders *(molestias)* of existence.

Augustine called this the *bellum quotidianum,* the daily war we have with concupiscence, the battle with the world to keep our mind's inner eye on God. Time is a day, and the day is a war. Quotidianism is militarism.

The upshot of Heidegger's analysis is a twofold emphasis on the priority of battle, struggle, difficulty, toil, disturbance, and anxious care *(Sorge),* on the one hand, and the privileging of the future as the prize up ahead, the goal to be won, the coming parousia as the *vita ventura,* the *vita futura,* on the other hand. For the church militant, eternity is up ahead and must be earned, unlike the eternity of the Greeks, which is back behind us and must be recollected, to use the categories of Constantine Constantius. So what Heidegger found when he sought nourishment in the New Testament was a phenomenology of temporality and historicity tuned to war, struggle, anxiety, and an uncertain future.[12]

Heidegger himself points out that while Paul's letters proclaim Jesus as the Messiah, the Synoptics are concerned with Jesus' own proclamation of the kingdom of God.[13] But the question that I want to pursue is what the result would be of shifting our attention from Paul to the Synoptics, from Paul's missionary preaching to the sayings of Jesus. What would result if we turned from the early Christian expectation of the day of the second coming of Jesus, to Jesus' own instructions about living each day, switching from the time of the coming parousia of which Paul spoke to the day-to-day quality of the *basileia tou theou* in the preaching of Jesus? By shifting from the evolving faith-situation of the later Christian communities to the sayings and the figure of Jesus himself, we break with the apocalypticism that Heidegger interprets—brilliantly and existentially—but that he simply assumes. Although it is clear that the later Christian communities held apocalyptic beliefs, it is not clear that this was the case for Jesus himself, for in Jesus' own sayings the kingdom of God is upon us, within us, here and now, and the kingdom begins today.[14] Jesus was not alarming us about something that was approaching that we cannot foresee and that may strike like a thief in the night. Rather, he was calming us with something that had already happened to us but that we do not appreciate. Jesus was not encouraging us to launch a daily battle for our bread, *sorgen um das tägliche Brot,* but calling upon us to ask God to give us the bread we need for the day. Jesus did not take the daily, the day to day, the quotidian, to be a sphere of fallenness from God, of what Luther called "God-forsakenness," but to be precisely a delicate sensor of God's rhythm, of the beat of God in time, the way that God gives time from day to day. If all this is so, it throws the time and day, the time of the day, of the kingdom into a different light.

It will certainly still be true that "Christian experience lives time itself," but we will find a rather different sense of living time and keeping time holy in the sayings of Jesus.

The world's time has been faithfully recorded by the philosophers, where time is said to keep a steady beat, to maintain the steady ticktock of "now" succeeding "now" in a succession so regular that Husserl called it a "form" and was even able to draw a diagram of it. The razor-thin source point of the now-phase is thickened by the now that has just lapsed and the now just about to come. Now-phases flow smoothly from the future into the present, enjoying their fleeting moment in the sun of the present, only to flow off just as smoothly into the past where they assume their inalterable place. Everything is tightly organized and regularized around the rule of retention and protention, memory and expectation, which is the basis of all the prudent long-range planning and careful record-keeping that goes on in the world. The time of the world is the sort of time that you can count, the time that you can count on, the sort that economics depends upon; it is regular and reliable enough for us to calculate equivalences and fair exchanges and to do a close cost analysis. Ticktock, ticktock.

But the beat of time in the kingdom is different. The steady beat and strong force of *ousia,* of its permanent presence in the world, fades before a more "ephemeral" openness to, and dependence upon, God's daily provision. Behold the lilies of the field, the weak force of daylilies, which are only strong enough to last for a day: they are not worrying about anything, for "today" is God's day, today is in God's hands, and God will provide. Give us this day our daily *(epiousios)* bread, the bread we need for today, for the cares of today are enough to worry about, and I am not even worrying about them. The strong force of "ousiology" gives way to the weak force of "epiousiology" *(epiousios),* which means the "quotidian" *(quotidie)* day-to-day time of the fragile, fleeting daylily. The strong, steady reliability of substance and the power of people of substance, the *ousia* and *exousia* of this world, give way to a more fragile, lily-like, insubstantial, transient, weak *un*-self-sufficiency. The "world" stands there on its own, in all its pomp and worldly adornment, boasting of its *Selbstständigkeit,* self-standing, self-sufficiency; it is as if the world thinks itself able to put up a kind of ousiological resistance to God or to declare its independence of God. But the towering lordship of the world, the awesome and ominous power of the world, is laid low, not by a great thunderous explosion of divine power from on high, like bolts of lightning from Zeus, in a war between the Lord of hosts and the powers of this world that would make Hollywood envious, but rather by the "weak force" of the lilies of the field, who neither sow nor reap, while God keeps watch over their every need. When Dostoevsky's Grand Inquisitor yields to the Messiah, whom he had imprisoned and planned to execute, he yields to the weak force of the Messiah's kiss, not to the power of Jesus' sword, for Jesus has none. When God rules, time yields to the weak force of God's sway, becoming entirely transparent to God, alive to God, responsive to God, who watches over each day, each moment, from moment to moment, making every moment precious. For God has counted every moment, just as God has counted every tear and every hair on our head (Luke 12:7; Matt. 10:30), and the price God puts on each is to make it priceless, which means it is not for sale.

Let us turn now to the gift of the day in the kingdom sayings, where once again the categories of post-metaphysical thought will be of more help than the classical "ousiological" categories of metaphysics or onto-theo-logic to which traditional theology has grown attached because, according to my unorthodox hypothesis, something of the kingdom of God has turned up in deconstruction and other like-minded and infamous frames of mind. In a final section, I will wonder out loud about how living like the lilies of the field communicates with the weak force of God.

DONUM QUOTIDIANUM:
THE GIFT OF THE DAY

The "kingdom of God" does not refer to a physical place, locale, or region that we might pick up on a powerful enough satellite or travel to one day on a sufficiently powerful space vehicle, but to a way of reigning or ruling, a way of being in time when God holds sway rather than the human will or even Satan. The kingdom is a certain "how" of time, as Heidegger said. Far from referring to some heavenly hinter-world or "world behind the scenes" or future locale, the kingdom of God refers to human life here and now, to a human life over which God rules. The kingdom of God is not a far-off place but the rhythm of God in time, the way God gives us each day, from day to day, the way God rules in each day, like a melody that God is playing. Let us listen to the beat.

Against Anxiety. I begin with the famous discourse *against* anxiety, *pace* Heidegger, who bends his efforts on being ready for anxiety:

> Therefore I tell you, do not be anxious *(merimnate)* about your life, what you shall eat or what you shall drink, nor about your body, what you put on. Is not life more than food, and the body more than clothing? Look at the birds of the air: they neither sow nor reap nor gather into barns, and yet your heavenly Father feeds them. Are you not of more value than they? And which of you by being anxious can add one cubit to his span of life? (Matt. 6:25–27)

If Heidegger (following Paul) cultivated a sense of temporality precisely out of anxiety about the future, there is an interesting, quite contrary temporality in Jesus' discourse *against* anxiety, which was, however, something that, as a religious author, Kierkegaard did not miss, even though he also wrote a book about the concept of anxiety.[15] Do not *waste time* worrying about tomorrow. The day is always time enough. The future is not our doing, not under our control, nothing we can master or provide for, and there is no fail-safe way to shore ourselves up and make provisions against the future. The future is God's; it is under his sway *(basileia),* not ours. Trust God. If a man gathers a great harvest and thinks himself secure for the future, he is a fool, for this night God will require his soul of him (Luke 12:16–20). Live without anxiety for the future, live with freedom from concern; trust the future to take care of itself because the future is God's business and God will provide: "Therefore, do not be anxious for tomorrow *(aurion),* for tomorrow will be anxious for itself. Let the day's own trouble be sufficient for the day" (Luke 6:34).

Let the day's own time be sufficient for itself, let its troubles and its gifts suffice. Let the day be time enough, all the time one needs, all the time one needs to be concerned with. When tomorrow comes, then tomorrow will be today and will absorb all our attention; in the meantime, let tomorrow worry about itself. Today is the day of the Lord.

Do not be anxious about tomorrow or today; do not be anxious at all, but trust God's rule. Anxiety frets about what is coming next, about how we will get through tomorrow. Anxiety is like a leak in time, a seepage, which drains the day of its time, which saps its sufficiency, which robs us of the day, which exposes us to ghosts and specters. (That is why, as Kierkegaard points out, when the object of anxiety is finally realized, we are always relieved, because what we were worried about turns out not to be as bad as the anxiety itself; just so, the worst things that happen to us are unforeseen.)

Let time be; let it be without a care for what time brings. For the measure of time is life. The merit of today is that today gives life, and life is all we need. Anxiety, on the other hand, turns us away from life and toward other needs. Anxiety is anxious about this or that, but life is always greater than this or that. What we have—bodily life—is greater than what we are anxious about not having, which we think we need for life and the body. Let your time and your life and your bodily being in time be like the birds of the air, who neither sow nor reap nor make stores for the future, for whom the day is always time enough.

Anxiety does not expand life or lengthen life or enrich life. Anxiety cannot add an inch to our stature or a day to our time. On the contrary, it takes time away, drains the life out of time, and makes life a day shorter, worries life away. Rather than giving time, anxiety is lost time; it takes time and life

away; it de-temporalizes and de-vitalizes. Anxiety causes a man to fret foolishly about what he will wear, while humorously forgetting that he is already alive. We must tell such a man to stop and remember that life is here
already, now, a life and time that is being squandered by anxiety. Such a
man has much to learn about life and time from the lilies of the field, which
take no care about what they wear:

> And why are you anxious about clothing? Consider the lilies of the field,
> how they grow; they neither toil nor spin; yet I tell you, even Solomon in all
> his glory was not arrayed like one of these. But if God so clothes the grass of
> the field, which today is alive and tomorrow is thrown into the oven, will he
> not much more clothe you? (Matt. 6:22–30)

This all sounds a little mad, like a "mad economics," without foresight,
long-term investments, or long-range planning. It invests everything in
today and makes no provisions for the future. It takes the gift of today to be
all in all without prudently planning for tomorrow.[16] However, a time without anxiety, a time ruled by God, not by human care, is not a time without
a future, not a time that is only present, for that would not be time at all,
but eternity. In time, the present is always a future that has become present,
whereas eternity is a present that never was a future. It is not a time without
a future, but a time without anxiety over the future, where the future is
tremendously important, but it is not approached anxiously. What has been
lifted in the kingdom is not the future, but anxiety; what has been lifted is
not the future, but the weight of the future, or responsibility for mastering
the unknown, as if the *arche* of the future lay within us. What has been
lifted is not our cares, but our caring for our cares, which we cast upon
God. The future is God's domain, God's rule. The future and its cares remain, but without anxiety—open and free. We are never without our worries, but we must worry without worry. Let the future come.

What time and life ask of us, which looks a little mad, is to let go. Do
not be an "oligopistologist" (Matt. 6:30), one of little faith who takes nothing for granted, who has little trust in the future, who wants a method to
master the future and subdue its uncertainty, who will not let go, who does
not have enough faith and hope and trust to let God rule.

> And do not keep striving for what you are to eat and what you are to drink,
> and do not keep worrying. For it is the nations of the world that strive after
> all these things; and your Father knows that you need them. Instead, strive for
> his kingdom, and these things will be given to you as well. (Luke 12:29–31)

Let God rule within you, for God knows what you need and these things
will be added on to you *(prostethesetai),* given to you as an addition, so long

as you do not treat them as matters coming under your rule instead of God's. Do not try anxiously to provide for yourself, to foresee what is coming and to begin to make provisions. The Father sees what you need; there is nothing for you to foresee. Today is all the time there is and all the time you need worry about, and do not worry about even that, because worrying about it will not get anything done. Do what you have to do and don't worry.

Instructions to the Disciples. We find the same sense of temporality in the instructions that Jesus gave his disciples concerning their conduct when they travel, texts that belong to the oldest and most authentic sayings of Jesus. If you go on a journey to preach the word, he said, take nothing with you. Do not bring along heavy stores for the journey; accept no wages for your labors; take no bread or money with you; wear sandals but do not bring along an extra tunic (Mark 6:8–9). Once again, this looks a little mad. But each day is its own time, and God will provide for his children, who must be itinerants and mendicants, like birds and lilies. Do not try to foresee; God will do the seeing and see to your needs. Do not worry about your needs, even when you do not fare as well as the birds or the foxes: "Foxes have holes, and birds of the air have nests; but the son of man has nowhere to lay his head" (Matt. 18:20). Still, do not worry.

A line of recent scholarship has compared these instructions to like practices among contemporary Hellenistic Cynics.[17] Despite the pejorative connotation of their name today, the Cynics bear a striking resemblance to the style of life prescribed in these instructions to the disciples: they were itinerants who lived like the birds of the air, who scolded society for its falsity, who said outrageous things to shock the establishment, and who set out on journeys with the barest of provisions. But the singular difference between the Cynics and the followers of Jesus was that the Cynics went nowhere without their knapsacks, which contained a little food and the few things necessary for life. The Cynics stressed their independence, their self-sufficiency, which they achieved by reducing their needs to the minimal point at which they could provide for themselves; they needed nothing because they wanted nothing that they could not provide for themselves. The followers of Jesus, on the other hand, took nothing with them, not even a knapsack for the day's food. But they did this, not in order to show their independence, but because they trusted that their needs would be provided for by those who would receive them in the next town, by the hospitality of the brethren, which means by God's rule:

> Whenever you enter a town and they receive you, eat what is set before you; heal the sick in it and say to them, "The kingdom of God has come near to you." (Luke 10:9)

For the very hospitality, the very kindness with which the brethren receive one another, means that there God's rule holds sway; the hospitality is the holding sway of God's rule. The kingdom has drawn near *(enggiken);* it is not off in a distant place. It reigns here, now, in this hospitality.

The Lord is the shepherd of time. Time is God's. We are not our own but God's, and time is God's, and God's time is today. God: time: today.

Nearness. The same temporality is encountered again in those sayings that tell us the kingdom of God is near at hand, not off at some distant point in time. The coming of the kingdom is not a matter of prediction or prophesying some coming event off in a dark and unknown future. The coming of the kingdom has nothing to do with reading signs:

> The kingdom of God is not coming with signs to be observed; nor will they say, "Lo, here it is!" or "There!" for behold, the kingdom of God is in the midst of you. (Luke 17:20–21)

Entos humon: inside you, within you, already, now, and you are in the midst of it. The kingdom is already in us and something we are already in. The time of the kingdom is today, now, already. We should live, not by looking for signs, which are outward and exterior, but from within, from the presence within us of God's rule and God's power.

> But if it is by the finger of God that I cast out devils, then the kingdom of God has come upon you. (Luke 11:20)

Here, already, in Jesus, who heals tormented minds, God rules now, in Jesus, who says that the kingdom is upon us. The finger of God, God's rule, has come over us *(ephthasen eph humas),* overtaken us, come upon us.

At this point we need to be careful. Jesus does not say that the kingdom is "always already" within us, that it has always and already been there, and that we need to simply awaken to what we have all along possessed. Were that the case, then the kingdom would be a matter of "recollection," of *anamnesis,* and the *metanoia* would amount to nothing more than a kind of Platonic conversion, a turning in that recovers what we have always possessed but have lately forgotten. Then the Teacher would only be the "occasion," as Johannes Climacus says, which is, as Climacus rightly insisted, the Greek view of things and essentially at odds with the temporality and historicity of biblical experience. Jesus says that the kingdom has come upon us, not that it has always been within us. The temporality of the kingdom is not the temporality of the always already *(immer schon),* but of something that is happening now, that has begun to happen today, with the advent of God's rule that Jesus announces. It is a prophetic conception that God's rule has come over us *(ephthasen),* and therefore an essentially historical conception—and not a Greco-ontological theory about the makeup of the human soul that has driven off the highway of eternity into the ditch of time. The proclamation of "God's rule" is not a theory about human *ousia,* about the being of the soul, but the announcement of a historical event, that the time of God's rule has begun. Now, today. Not *ousia,* but *parousia,* and *parousia* now.[18]

Daily Bread. The ancient words of the Lord's Prayer, upon which this part of our study in general and this chapter in particular is a commentary, ring with the same sense of temporality. When we pray, what should we say? Say *Abba,* father, in the most familiar sense, not a severe and distant father, a forbidding, unconscious law that prohibits and says no, but *abba,* a near and loving, gift-giving father, providing, sustaining, close at hand, here, now, supplying whatever we need and ready to forgive if we go astray. Say *abba,* may your rule, your *basileia,* come; and provide us each day *(epiousion)* with the bread that we need for today *(semeron)* (Matt. 6:11). Today's bread is all the bread we need and ask for, for when tomorrow comes, it will be today, and that will suffice. Let your rule come each day, day by day, for that is what the kingdom is, the rule of the day, the rule that holds sway today. The time of the kingdom is today. The kingdom lasts but a day, but that day is every day, and it starts today. The kingdom is "hemeral" *(hemera),* for the day, ephemeral *(ephemera)* even, for the day only, where each day is enough, a great deal really, for it always is today *(semera).* The kingdom is emeral, ephemeral, semeral. Do not pray for enough bread to last well into the future, for enough capital to live securely on the interest. Pray to be like the daylilies *(hemeracostis)* that blossom for a day, for that day only, for today. (The interest of the Christian right in cutting the capital gains tax so that they can increase their wealth and capitalization is uniquely, profoundly un-Jesus-like.) Do not build great barns in order to store up great reserves of bread against the future, for if tonight our soul is required of us, what good will all that bread be? The father, who knows what you need before you ask, will give you whatever you need. Say father *(Abba),* give *(dos)* us today, give us the gift of the day. May your rule come to pass today. May the rule of the day be given. *Abba,* may you keep time holy, may you sanctify today.

Forgiveness. That brings us back to forgiveness once again and to its link with the kingdom sayings on time. Give us the bread we need today and we will not fret over tomorrow and *(kai),* the prayer goes on, forgive us the debts we owe, as indeed we forgive the debts that are owed to us (Matt. 6:12). Dismiss *(aphes)* them, send them off *(dimittere),* send them packing. That introduces an important temporal shift. Forgiveness is the complementary operation to the alleviation of anxiety. So far the kingdom sayings have had to do with dismissing the future as an object of concern: forget to-morrow, forget what you have no memory of yet. But the prayer continues: forgive—which means in the New Testament "dismiss"—the debts we owe as indeed *(hos kai),* since and to the extent that, we have forgiven/dismissed the debts that are owed to us. That signifies a reciprocal dismissing. For-giveness is aimed at dismissing the past. Dismiss our past just insofar as we have dismissed the past of others. Just as we give up providing for the future on our own and let God's providential rule do the providing, so do we give up holding on to the past. We ask the Father to forget our past as we forget the past of others. Forget the past; forget the future; the kingdom's rule is now, today. For just as the future, which we cannot master or program or plan, is unpredictable, so the past is irreversible. If our redemption from the future is to live without anxiety, the only redemption from the past is for-giveness. Jesus, according to Hannah Arendt, saw the need for:

> forgiving, dismissing, in order to make it possible for life to go on by con-stantly releasing men from what they have done unknowingly. Only through this constant mutual release from what they do can men remain free agents, only by constant willingness to change their minds and start again can they be trusted with so great a power as that to begin something new.[19]

Forgiveness keeps the net of social relationships open and makes possible what Arendt calls "natality," the fresh, natal, initiating power of a new ac-tion, a new beginning or a new start. Each day is a new day, a renewal of the day, a new gift. Today is always new. Today you can begin again.

When God holds sway, the past is dismissed. Where God rules, the past does not rule. If we are slaves to the past, we can expect the future to look like the past. But the work of forgiveness always comes as a surprise and hence makes possible an open future. When God rules, our responses are startling and unpredicted, amazingly free from the past and, one might be tempted to say, a little mad:

> To him who strikes you on the cheek, offer the other also; and from him who takes away your coat, do not withhold even your shirt. Give to every one who begs from you; and if anyone takes away your goods, do not ask for them again. (Luke 6:29–30)

And just as you do not react in the expected way, by the same token, do things without expecting the usual, predictable, results:

> And if you lend to those from whom you hope to receive, what credit is that to you? . . . lend, expecting nothing in return. (Luke 6:34–35)

If you expect a return, that is a sane and sound *quid pro quo* economy, not the mad economy of the kingdom, where you must expect nothing in return, where the circle of giving in order to get back must be torn up.[20] Break the cycle of injuring and getting even, do not try to balance the books of the past, to even accounts with the past, to get even with your debtors, which perpetuates the destructive cycle of debt. Dismiss your debtors, forget the past, and forgive the man who offends you. Today is the day that a man may change his mind, may undergo a change of heart *(metanoia),* may make a new start. And if that happens, do not block it off, do not stop it. Must not the past itself bend before God's rule? Is it not an idolatry of time to ascribe to it such inexorable necessity, such irreversibility? Even if it cannot be changed or annihilated, cannot the past be transformed by acquiring a new meaning? Cannot God clear away the debris of the past to make for a fresh start and a new beginning, to clear away the space of today? Is not forgiveness a more benign way than the great flood that the Yahwist championed to clear away the past and start anew? Is not today the day that the Lord has made?

The kingdom sayings tell us that the kingdom is an open space, free from anxiety about tomorrow, on the one hand, and free from recrimination against the past, on the other hand. Today is a gift. Let the kingdom come today. Today is a gift to be received freely, graciously. For if you, who are not all that good, "know how to give good gifts to your children, how much more will your Father who is in heaven give good things to those who ask him!" (Matt. 7:11). Do not let today be a way of being bound to the past, or an occasion of being anxious over the future. That would destroy the good gift from the Father, the gift of today; it would drain the day out of today, take the time back from the time that is given.[21] That would drive us out of the kingdom and drive the kingdom out of us, for the kingdom has already come, and it is within us, here, now, as we are within it. Time is not ours, but God's.

WORRY WITHOUT WORRY

What, then, does it mean to keep time holy in the kingdom? What is the temporal sense in the kingdom sayings of Jesus?

In contrast to the temporality that Heidegger derived from Pauline apocalypticism, it has a very different futuricity, for the future is approached with faith not anxiety about what is coming next, with trust not fear and trembling at the uncertainty of the time. The coming of the kingdom lays anxiety to rest, for the rule of God, which is in the midst of us, sustains us. The man or woman who is anxious is of little faith. The kingdom has a *presential* quality, as a time of presencing, which lets today be today. By trusting oneself to God's rule, the day is not drained of its time. Today is not sacrificed to tomorrow, exchanged, invested, traded off, or spent in making oneself safe and secure against tomorrow, for tomorrow never comes. It is a temporality of trust, of trusting oneself to God's rule, which in no uncertain terms means trusting ourselves to time and the day. God, who is the Lord of the day, is revealed in the structure of time, which is touched by the finger of God. Faith takes the gift of the day, today, and gives itself entirely to it.

But if this is not the temporality of anticipatory resoluteness in *Being and Time,* it is rather like the later Heidegger's more meditative—even more Japanese—moments in dialogue with the mystical poet Angelus Silesius, the versifier of the mystical writings of Meister Eckhart, who wrote:

> The rose is without why, it blooms because it blooms,
> It pays no attention to itself, asks not whether it is seen.

Angelus Silesius's mystical rose should be added to the botany of the kingdom, along with the lilies of the field. Upon this rose Heidegger comments that we too are to live without why, learning something from the temporality of the rose, which he called its "whiling," its *weil* and *dieweilen.*[22] By this, Heidegger meant to recommend a life in which one suspends calculative thought, for calculation is bent on justification, on rendering a reason for a being, which is always sought in some other being farther up or down the causal chain. But in the experience of "whiling," this discursive, ratiocinating thinking is kept in check, and thinking comes to rest in an experience of things "in themselves," in their own "presencing" or presential emergence or upsurge, their rising up and falling back, in and out of presence. Unfortunately, Heidegger does not follow the mystical poet all the way through. For when Heidegger tells us to be like the rose, he is not telling us to trust to God's loving care, which is what Angelus Silesius was saying, the way the lilies of the field do, which is what Jesus said, but to trust ourselves to *physis* and to the child-play of *aion. Physis* is the worlding of the world, the world's own energy and life, not God's. Heidegger is concerned with the divine playing, but this he takes to be an exercise in *phainesthai,* the world's shining beauty, which is why Levinas said that Heidegger is a pagan, for he makes a god out of time and even hopes this god will save us.

Levinas is right, but still there is something going on to interest us here. In the sapiential eschatology of the kingdom sayings, the experience of the kingdom lies in suspending or lifting projective planning for the future, disarming our human anxiety about what is coming next, on the one hand, and a recriminatory, vengeful cleaving to the past, on the other hand. The result is to experience the day in its own "whiling" or "day-ing," if I may say so, its own "hemerality" or diurnalness, its own coming to be and passing away, letting the day "while" for awhile. This letting-be *(Gelassenheit),* an expression first found in Meister Eckhart and then taken up by Angelus Silesius and finally by Heidegger, is essentially a letting go of human self-sufficiency, of human *Selbstständigkeit,* of what Levinas and Marion call Dasein's "autarky," which would deny the very meaning of the time of the kingdom as the time of God's rule, not ours. In the kingdom time can be experienced authentically only by taking time as God's gift and trusting ourselves to time's granting, which is God's giving. We trust what time gives because God gives time. If time gives being in these texts, it is God who gives time, in a divine *donner le temps.*

By letting go of our own self-possession, by opening ourselves to God's rule, we release the day from its chains. The temporality that is opposed to the kingdom is a bound time, a time in which today is dragged back into the past by recrimination or wrenched forward into the future by worry, planning, and calculation. The temporality of the kingdom, on the other hand, is free, open, unbound, unchained, a day or time that is savored one day at a time, experienced, lived for itself, in its own upsurge, instant by instant, day by day.

Then and only then will we be able to *work.* For what is more obvious than that we who have been summarily marched out of Eden by a furious Yahweh must work for our bread by the sweat of our brow? Must we not save for a rainy day, work for our daily bread, plan for the future, make regular payments into our pension plan, provide for our children's college education, take risks that expose us to an uncertain future? To be sure. Behold the squirrels of the trees and bears of the forest, who forage and make provisions for the future! God is not mocked; we reap what we sow. True enough. Who would deny it? That is the tension of *the* impossible, the creative difficulty we are in *both* to sow and reap and gather into barns *and* to be like the birds of the air who do *not,* to understand fully that life is a risk and not to be overwhelmed by that fact. That is the impossible situation we are in, the dynamics of this poetics of *the* impossible. The idea is not that we have no cares at all, which is the more Elohistic vision of life, for that will never happen, as the Yahwist was quick to remind us, but that we cast the cares that we most certainly have upon God. The idea is not that we are without worries, which will never happen, but that we must worry without worry. Go gather a harvest, but do not think yourself secure, for the future is God's and it is quite unforeseeable, and do not fail to be mindful of those who have no harvest, for what have you that you have not received? And if you yourself have no harvest, remember likewise that the future is God's and do not place any confidence in your forecast of doom. Benjamin should have waited one more day.

We require economy, and there is no simple standing outside economy, no simple exterior to economy. We are enjoined both to work for our bread and to trust God to give us our bread, to plan for the future and to realize that the future is in God's hands. Both together, not one without the other. But *God* first. We trust God *first*. Seek *first* the kingdom of God and then these daily supplements will be added to you. Get up and go to work in the morning, but thank God for the gift of the day, put your work in the context of the gift, and trust that in the kingdom God holds us in the palm of his hands. Just the way the Redactor put the Yahwist's story second, after Elohim's opening and majestic claim that everything he made is good. Work and do not worry. Trust but do not stop working. Worry without worry. We all have lots of worries, but don't worry. Do all that you can, but know that God does the rest, which is everything. To slightly adapt the paradox of Madame de Maintenon's sentence that serves as the epigraph to Derrida's "The Time of the King," let us say that in "The Time of the Kingdom," "Our cares take all our time, but we give the rest to God, to whom we would like to give all."[23]

BREAD AND TIME

Such a presential time, then, has nothing to do with the famous "metaphysics of presence" of which Heidegger and Derrida are expressly critical. For the presencing in question is transitory and fragile, like the daylilies and grasses of which Jesus speaks that today are here and tomorrow are thrown into the oven. The presential time of the kingdom is not *ousiological* time, the time of *ousia,* in which things have their own substantiality and essentiality, their own resistance and *Selbstständigkeit,* but epiousiological or "hemeral" *(hemera).* In ousiology, presence means a kind of subsistence that offers resistance to God, that stands on its own, that is opposed to the radical createdness of things, of a world that arises as an answer to God's call. Ousiology is foundationalism, a philosophy of self-security. Ousiology is the philosophy of "people of substance," who build up stores against the future, whereas in the kingdom, populated by "people of God" (the people of the day!), there is no self-certainty or self-securing, and the rule is the rule of the day to day. One falls back, not upon one's own resources, but upon God's rule. The presential or sapiential time of the kingdom is not ousiological but "epiousiological" or quotidian, granted from day to day, like a gift, fleeting, fragile, diurnal, epihemeral. Not *ousia,* which proclaims the subsistence of being, of one's own being, but *epi-*

ousia, that strange word in the New Testament that means having to do with what we need in order to survive today, what is addressed to life's needs, where *ousia* means not a metaphysical substance but the things of daily life, like the bread one bakes each day to meet the day's needs.

In the kingdom, things do not have their own independent subsistence, their own ability to fend for themselves, but they remain deeply created, fashioned fresh from the *tohu wa-bohu.* Both human and nonhuman beings can be what they are only by ceasing to assert their own self-subsistence and self-reliance and letting God rule. Their being and time are from God, a trace of which is perhaps detectable in St. Thomas's notion of a *potentia obedientialis* in his otherwise highly ousiological account of things.[24] Far from asserting the primacy of ousiological presence, far from asserting a kingdom or rule of *ousia,* sapiential time can only be experienced by letting go of human rule and letting go of the self-sufficiency of the natural order, by letting God rule, entrusting oneself to the quotidian rule of God. If it is the law of *nature* that feeds the birds of the air or clothes the lilies of the field, then God is the law of that law. God rules in nature as he rules in human life. God rules over *physis* and *polis,* over bread and time, over *ousia* and *epiousios.* If I had the time and the wit to match wits with Heidegger, which I do not, I would entitle my rival treatise *Bread and Time,* and on his advice forget Being, since he himself said Being does not belong in theology.

So however attached philosophical theology has been to the classical onto-theo-logical tradition, the New Testament shows little interest in the metaphysics of *ousia* or in the time that measures the motions of *ousia.* The kingdom runs on nonstandard time, a time that departs from the standard conceptions of time that have dominated Western philosophy from Aristotle to Husserl. The time of the kingdom is neither a line nor a circle, but a new beginning, a fresh start—now. It is not a sequence of now-points that measure motion in terms of before and after, as in Aristotle. It is not a progressively accumulating self-completing time, as in Hegel's philosophy of history. It inverts Husserl's protentional-retentional schema, which is organized around the attempt to stretch the now out into the future and to hold on to what has lapsed. It is not the *agida,* the agitated time of ecstatic existential temporality in *Being and Time.* It does not turn on a conception of *Erinerrung,* in which one gathers together what has all along been in travail, groaning for birth over a gradual process of inner development and growth, as in Hegel. It does not invoke a Heideggerian notion of *Andenken,* in which the task is to recall the archi-beginning which has fallen into a gradually escalating history of oblivion, as in the later Heidegger.

The time of the kingdom is a more profoundly simple time, a free time, a time of freedom that has been disconnected from the chain of nows, disengaged from anxiety and recrimination, interrupting protention and retention, suspending anticipation and recollection. By trusting God's rule, one breaks the chain of time and frees up the day, letting the day come to presence, tearing up the chain of time, freeing it from the circulation of debts and anxieties, letting the day be a "gift." Forget what is owed to you in the past; forget about insuring yourself against the future; tear up the chain of time and take today as a gift, a free gift, a free as opposed to a bound time, an open or released time.[25] In it, something new and freeing has begun now and is now with us and frees us from the debt of the past and weight of the future.

That is the event, not of the exceptional and extraordinary, but of the day, of the day to day, the marvel of the rising and setting of the sun, the gift of time. So at once we are led back to our pesky hypothesis, that such a time is better thought in terms of the categories of "event" and "gift," both of which characterize the work of recent French thinkers, whether they are Christian (Jean-Luc Marion[26]), Jewish (Levinas), or rightly passing for atheists (Derrida, Deleuze, and Lyotard). An event *(événement)* is a certain "happening" that is "linked" but not bound causally to antecedent and consequence, not bound by efficient causality to the past or by teleological causality to the future, but is taken for itself, in its own singularity. The event has a certain free-floatingness, an innocence and gift likeness; it is a happening over which we have no mastery, in which things happen to us, overtake and overcome us, as when we say that the rule of God has come over us. Events have the quality of a "gift" that is given us—give *(dos)* us this day—where the grace of being human is to be gracious, to take time without anxiety or revenge, with a kind of sapiential grace, with a letting be that is grateful, with a gratitude that lets be. A gift is a gift for Derrida when it is removed from the circle or circulation of giving in return or paying back (remuneration, retribution), of action and proportionate reaction, when we let the gift be.

That is also why I think something of an old biblical idea, something of the spirit of keeping time holy, has turned up in Derrida's idea of an absolute future, of something absolutely to come *(à venir)*. The future is not a future present, whose coming can be foreseen, but the surprise of a future that, as it were, comes out of nowhere, that is not our doing, not within our ken and control, a future *sans voir, sans avoir, sans savoir.* The future for Derrida is the issue neither of a linear progression nor a circular repetition, but comes rather as an unforeseeable surprise, a promise and a threat, but about which Jesus would tell us not to be afraid, not to be of little faith, but to trust in God's rule.

LIVING LIKE THE LILIES OF THE FIELD
AND THE BREEZE BLOWING OUT OF PARADISE

What, then, does it mean to live like the lilies of the field?

Benjamin said that history is a storm blowing out of Paradise, a destructive wind that wreaks havoc across the epochs, piling ruin upon ruin. That is true enough, and it has evidently always been true, right from the start, true enough to cause Yahweh—Benjamin sounds like he is referring to Yahweh's outburst (Gen. 3:14–19)—to throw up his hands in despair and wash the whole thing out and start history over again (with no noticeable improvement the second time around). But that is only half the story, only the second of two narratives, which the Redactor has placed second for a very good reason. There is good news and there is bad news; but first the good news, then the bad. There is another wind, the breath of another breeze blowing out of Paradise, the breath of another Spirit, gentler and weaker, though powerful in its own way. That is the context for my final take on the lilies of the field, which is as follows.

If one approaches God as a weak force, an unconditionality without sovereignty, the powerless power of a call, and not the Lord God of hosts who raises an army against his enemies, then what can the "rule of God" in time and history[27] possibly mean? If Benjamin is right, that time and history run their bloody course, to the consternation of moralists and the embarrassment of theologians, then in what possible sense does God "rule" over anything? And what can living like the lilies of the field possibly mean if we do not think that God will intervene in our affairs and turn the tide against the wicked and lift up the righteous? What would it mean to trust in God? If the believer trusts in God, what can God do that a trust can do that proceeds without God? Would there be trust anyway, with or without God? If, as I have insisted, creation is a dicey business and the elements are signifiers of life's irreducible risk, what can we learn from the lilies of the field?

In arguing against an interpretation of God as the archical center of power and cosmic energy, which vests the sacredness of God in the power of the *arche,* I am essentially arguing against a thaumaturgical conception of God. In the more sober assessment of God's creative act that I have been offering, which allows for a certain powerlessness in God, I am saying that the creation narratives tell of the "inscription"—by word of mouth, *avant la lettre*—of a fundamental goodness in things. The divine word calls things to life in P's narrative and calls life good, but in short order Cain murders Abel, directly reversing the divine life-giving action. So the word must keep on calling, *re*-calling, again and again, what things are called to be—alive and not dead, fruitful not barren, filled not empty. Creation is not a finished deed but an ongoing process of re-creation. The originary act inserts things within the call, within the word "good," letting the word *good* embrace and encompass them, but it does not hold things absolutely fast.

On my account, *"creation" gives the world significance and promise, not a cause.* The work of a word (a "speech act" to end all speech acts, or to start them!), it gives the world meaning. The creation narratives do not offer physical information about, or a metaphysical explanation of, the origin of the universe, one that competes with astrophysics and of which science must take account. The creation narratives are a brilliant poetics, not a questionable metaphysics or a completely imaginary physics. They describe a *poiesis* in the sense of a poem, of a work of religious imagination, not in the sense of a physical or metaphysical production.

The world is there—*il y a, es gibt*—like it or not, with or without God, with or without an explanation; it always was. To turn Gertrude Stein around a bit, there is a there, there. God is not responsible for *that,* that things are *there.* God supplies an interpretation. The name of God harbors an event of interpretation. In the narratives, the elements are just there, a given, pre-given, presupposed, an everlasting companion of Elohim, who was never consulted about that. That is not up for discussion; it is never mentioned or negotiated. That is what the preexistence of the elements in the narratives signify, what the elements are "saying" in their silence and wordlessness, what they say by saying nothing, what the narrative is saying by means of the fact that the elements do not say a thing. The elements are dumb in a literal sense: not stupid, mean, and meaningless, just silent. They are not absurd or chaotic, just silent and wordless, innocent and "before" good and evil, in a word, uninterpreted. They are not *de trop* or an anonymous rumbling—all of which would constitute an anachrony, a retrospective illusion; they are just "there," like it or not.

Elohim, on the other hand, does all the talking. Elohim is the "word," the one who speaks, who introduces meaning, articulation, intelligibility. In a rigid monotheism, Elohim is technically speaking to himself, speaking a divinely private language (something that philosophers will tell you is technically impossible, for several perfectly good reasons, which is an objection only if you think that that matters when you are reading poetry!). In fact, historico-critically, there is some evidence of a residual polytheism, in which Elohim is consulting with a divine council, and they all agree to create something in "our" image. Be that as it may, God is responsible for the "word," the work of language, meaning, *sens* in the dual sense of both sense and direction. Elohim pronounces a judgment, a word, a verdict, *vere dictum,* a benediction, *bene dictum,* upon things; he pronounces them "good." Elohim draws vast and sprawling expanses of sky and air and sea, that is good, and then he fills them with living things, and living things are good, and he hangs lights like lanterns in the sky-dome, and light is good. And he makes human living things and makes them fruitful just like him, and human fruitfulness is good.

Good, good, good, good, good—very good. Yes, yes. That's the word. That's the world. That's the interpretation, the hermeneutics. (Another interpretation would be Nietzsche's, that the elements are innocent of good or evil.)

Elohim thus is the reason that things are *good.* Creation is not a movement from non-being to being, which makes the heart of the metaphysician skip a beat, but from being to the good, beyond the muteness of being to the speaking of the good, which is the heart of the Hebrew poetry.

Then Cain murders Abel and the bloody course of history is launched. A mighty storm blows humankind out of Paradise across the stretches of history, to use Benjamin's image. God's work has just begun; Elohim's word is at best a fore-word, his verdict representing a certain premature rush to judgment. The call must be re-called, again and again. For history has blurred and distorted and at times nearly erased that inscription. The screams of history's endless violence have nearly silenced that word. Think of the creation narratives as a vast map of the world where the word "good" is etched in such enormous letters, sprawled across such an infinite expanse, that we can barely read them. The closer you look at things, the less you see them, and the more you see the disasters.

God says "yes," calls "yes" to us from afar, from across an infinite distance. To say "yes" in turn, to countersign the signature that God has sprawled across the surface of the world, is not to count upon some kind of divine intervention from on high to straighten out things here below. It is to affirm, or re-affirm, P's majestic declaration that what God made was very good, while taking into account the bloody course that history takes, which tests that faith by piling disaster upon disaster in an accumulating history of ruins. To say "yes" to God, to invoke the name of God—and here we come to the nub of the issue—is not to sign on to a belief in a magical suspension of natural laws in order to allow for a divine averting of natural disasters, or the divine advocacy of particular historical causes, of a particular nation, political party, religion, race, or gender in order to see that in the end one historical cause will win out over another. God does not steer hurricanes away from the mainland and out to sea, any more than God has a favorite in the Super Bowl, the NCAA Final Four, or the World Soccer Cup tournaments. God is not a powerful but invisible hand who magically bends natural or historical forces to divine purposes so that in the end things turn out just the way God has planned, just so long as we are patient and willing to take a long view. That is, on the one hand, an essentially thaumaturgical idea of God that nourishes the New Age book industry and

Hollywood movies about angels; and, on the other hand, it is a metaphysical idea that in the end this is the best of all worlds, or at least as good as you could hope for. But it does not withstand cold reflection upon the actual and brutal course of things, not if you look upon the historical record with a certain impartiality and set aside an unfalsifiable belief that proceeds on the indefeasible assumption that the good news is good news, proof that God is watching out for us, and the bad news is also good news, proof that God writes straight with crooked lines or has some mysterious purpose up his divine sleeve. The truth is, the bad news is bad news.

But what then, on this colder cosmo-hermeneutical scheme, do the lilies of the field have to say to us? The lilies are remnants of the work of Elohim, flowers first planted by Yahweh in the garden, places where Elohim's "good" emerges into view, points of contact with the original plan, like bits of sunlight breaking through the clouds, or water bubbling up to the surface from hidden springs in a desert oasis. Coming across the lilies is like finding Elohim's ancient inscription on the earth, which whipping winds had buried long ago.

The lilies of the field are the traces or echoes or remnants of the first "yes," uttered by the word. They bear witness to the agreement Elohim made with the world, and they assure us that it has not been broken. They ask us to countersign Elohim's *yes* and to trust that the world is not finally a hostile place, of which we should take leave like the ascetics or the old gnostics who thought that a transcendent God could not be the author of such an immanent mess. The lilies of the field assure us that the surpassing beauty of the world and the joy life holds are not drowned by senseless and tragic suffering. They bear witness to the "good." Behold the lilies of the field, behold the "good" that Elohim has fashioned, and do not let hope die. Life goes on amidst the ruins and the devastation. Trust in the momentum of life, for Elohim has breathed life into the lifeless elements, and wherever there is life, there the Spirit breathes. The fundamental contract we have with life—"and Elohim saw everything that he had made and indeed it was very good"—which was signed in advance on our behalf by Elohim, is not broken, and we are simply asked to countersign, to say "yes" to the lilies of the field.

Even though that is risky business.

Take one day at a time and let the breath of life flow through you and do not let the storm of evil overwhelm you. Say yes to today and let tomorrow take care of itself. Tomorrow we will say yes again, come what may. Today is the day the Lord has made, the day to say yes, and tomorrow, which will be the time for another *yes,* will come in all due course. For each day, its own yes. To each day, its own good and its own evil, but always in a measured, apportioned way. Do not take on the burden of every day, or worry about having the strength for every yes. If you try to take the measure of the totality, of all of history, of the whole future, or of the whole past, you will be overcome. Life as whole is a repetition, yes, yes, day by day, each day. Come, Creator Spirit, yes. Today is the day that the Lord has made, and to say yes to today is to keep the future open. Keep the future open—and release the burden of the past. Trust in the momentum of the day, keep the future from closing in, dismiss the past that ties us in knots and locks us in.

Listen to the word spoken by the lilies of the field, listen to their "yes," the *parole soufflée* that breathes the breath of "good" through things. The winds that blow across the stretches of time are not only the fierce and raging winds of Benjamin's disasters, but the gentle breezes of Elohim's "good" that lists across the epochs, that inspires us, lifting our hearts. "Good" is the word that Elohim calls out in the beginning, which, in a great acoustical shift, also calls us forward, luring us ahead.

The rule of God is the rule of God's *word,* which is the *call* of God, the call of the "good," the word Elohim breathes into creation, the uplifting call beyond the muteness of being, which threatens to oppress our spirit. The power of God is the weak force of a word, a meaning, a sense, a solicitation, an invitation, a hermeneutical rather than a physical or metaphysical rule, a call that calls us beyond ourselves and our self-concern, that assures us that the "world" is not all in all. For the rule of the world, the economy of the "world," where everything has a price and everyone is made to pay, is inwardly disturbed by the lilies of the field. The lilies of the field are the foolishness of not seeking one's own interests first, the power of powerlessness, the weak force of something of unconditional beauty.

The lilies of the field live for free, gratuitously, almost by chance, like a gift, an-economically; and behold how gloriously they are arrayed. They do not go to work and earn a wage by the sweat of their brow. *They boldly and baldly defy the Yahwist verdict,* the curse on work (Gen. 3:14–19), the outburst which is the wind that Benjamin felt. They live for free, without labor, and God blesses them (it must be Elohim) more abundantly than Solomon and David. The lilies of the field are an event, the event-fulness and graciousness of existence.

Be like the lilies, without why and without care. They bend and bow under the gentle listing of the breeze, which is the *ruach Elohim,* the soft winds of the spirit blowing across the epochs from creation that caress us. Be open to the gratuitousness, the grace, the chance, or perhaps just the "perhaps" in life, which keeps life open, in motion. Say yes to the grace of the day, dismiss the shackles of the past, and keep the future open, because today is astir with life, with grace, with the spirit, with the gratuitous gift that the lilies enjoy.

Life is a risky business, and we worry constantly about the future, about what is coming, for ourselves and for others—and so we must, but we should worry without worry, and do so in the name of Elohim, who said that everything he made is good. Tomorrow it may be better or *perhaps* it will be worse, but that is another day. Today is the day to say yes. Life is a beautiful risk, and the lilies are the beautiful part.

For the believer, Auschwitz—every Auschwitz, every murder, and every ethnic cleansing, the death of every innocent child—is an inexplicable and unjustifiable violence against life, against Elohim's creation, like Cain and Abel, which invites the same wrath that Yahweh displayed, calls up the same nihilistic impulse to curse the day the world was ever made. Auschwitz, every Auschwitz, is irreducible and irredeemable loss, and not even God can undo that. And if sometimes some good somewhere comes out of it, it would be an obscenity to suggest that that is either an explanation or a justification. As Moltmann says, Auschwitz spelled the end of "theodicy." Besides, such good would in any case be no good to the dead, having arrived on the scene too late. God does not prevent evil in advance, nor can God, *pace* Peter Damian, retroactively remove evil after the fact. The name of God occurs, not on the plane of being, but of the event; it is the name of a signification or an interpretation, not a substance. The name of God gives evil a different meaning because it gives us a faith in the face of evil, a faith that is stronger than death and mightier than the sword. But if that is so, and I think it is, the strength of this weak force must never be confused with a sword, or an army, or with thaumaturgical remedies.

Think of faith, like creation, as an acoustical event. It gives us the ears to hear an ancient voice, with a slightly Jewish accent, resonating rhythmically across the epochs: "Good, good, good, good, good—in sum, very good." Think of faith as a meteorological event, carried by a breeze blowing out of Paradise: behold the lilies of the field, blowing in the wind. Behold the *ruach Elohim.*

NINE

Back to the Future: Peter Damian on the Remission of Sin and Changing the Past

. . . and send away our debts . . .
(Matt. 6:12, my translation)

WITH GOD ALL THINGS ARE POSSIBLE

Axiom 1: What's done is done.

Axiom 2: With God, everything is possible, even the impossible.

Aporia: Can God make it to be that what's done is undone? That, of course, is impossible, the doing of which, however, in a way of speaking, is God's very job description, or what we mean by the name of God, and something that touches close to the nerve of the "event" that stirs in the name of God.

That is the aporia posed by the theology of the event as it was framed back in the eleventh century by Peter Damian (1007–1072). Damian wants to know how hard a hard fact is, whether time is hard, fast, and un-yielding, or whether God, for whom nothing is impossible, can make time yield and release the event, whether God can change the past, making it to be that what was done was never done. This was not simply a bit of specu-lation for Peter Damian, but a question about forgiveness and the healing of wounded souls. Damian represents a telling case study in this poetics of the impossible, both a hero and an anti-hero. For Peter Damian was one of Christianity's first gay-bashers, who coined the word *sodomy,* and he was also a most unforgiving ecclesiastical authoritarian, who had no compunc-tion about torching heretics. But even here the situation is complicated. It cannot be forgotten that his critique of sodomy occurred in the context of an outspoken and courageous campaign for clerical reform on his part. While we today on the left cannot countenance his homophobia, that should not prevent us from seeing that Damian was out to put an end to the sexual abuse of women and children by the clergy, and of junior clergy by senior clergy, in a time when clerics were not subject to civil law. He forthrightly pinned a lot of the blame for this problem on the hierarchy of the day, on the bishops and the pope himself, for looking the other way and for refusing to root out the offenders by strictly enforcing church discipline. Indeed, he looked to women and the laity for help in setting things straight. Is there nothing new under the sun?[1]

Damian raised a perfectly fascinating hypothesis about the time or event of forgiveness that is an important ingredient in a weak theology and this by way of an obsessive and unforgiving stress on divine *power.* Here we see, all too predictably, a metaphysics of omnipotence converge with a symptomatic love of ecclesiastical power. Damian criticized human power, not in order to displace the primacy of power itself or to open the way to the power of powerlessness or to the weak force of God, but precisely in order to clear the way for an unprecedented display of divine omnipotence, of which he proposed perhaps the most extravagant account in the history of Western metaphysical theology. To put it politely, Damian had a tin ear for poetics. He thought that the only alternative to logic was a magico-metaphysical and onto-theological omnipotence. He never thought of countering logic with poetics or of opposing the power of this world with a weak force. He never chose a weak force when he thought a strong one was available. So Damian will be as important to us for his failings as for his success, and we can offer him only tertiary membership as a remote predecessor in the select circle of sacred anarchists.

A HIGHLY HIERARCHICAL ANARCHY

Peter Damian defended a perfectly good idea—the anarchy of the event—in exactly the wrong way. Second-century theologians like Irenaeus could not resist the temptation to carry the idea of creation and divine power to its metaphysical completion by creating the idea of *creatio ex nihilo.* Peter Damian rounded out this argument by paying God's power a complementary compliment, by attributing the opposite capacity to the omnipotence of God, namely, annihilation, *reductio ad nihilum.* God's power was so absolute that God could make it to be that what was done in the past—for example, that Rome was founded—was not done or could come undone. Were God so minded, God could change the past. God can do *anything*—that is almost what Damian means by God—the only limit being whether it was good to do so, which tended to make God look like Zeus, but with better intentions. So Damian is a fascinating case study of what happens when the idea of God is completely taken over by the fantasy of power, when the idea of divine power races wildly out of control. Even so, it was God's power to forgive sin that led Damian to claim that, were it good to do so, God could make it to be that the sinner did not sin, that the sinner was not only forgiven but actually rendered innocent, thus striking a provocatively anarchical pose on the time of forgiveness that repays our study.

Damian represents something of a *reductio ad absurdum* of divine omnipotence. He is a perfect example of Catherine Keller's idea of "(te)homophobia," in which the exaltation of the power of the father goes hand in hand with a fear of femininity and a fear of homosexuality.[2] But if by the "kingdom" we mean to emphasize the astonishing anarchical alterability, unpredictability, reversibility, revisability, and contingency of the event, we will find no better champion than Damian. In Damian we find the *pièce de résistance* of the reversals of which the kingdom is capable, for not even the past is safe from change! What could be more anarchical and kingdom-like than to turn time on its head—even if Damian is also the perfect example of how *not* to make this argument?

So I have mixed feelings about Damian.[3] Like Angelus Silesius, he dares to go where you cannot go, pushing us in the direction of an idea of time that would have added a whole new dimension to Alice's confusion in Wonderland. Indeed, at the end of this chapter, I will propose a seemingly unseemly short circuit—of the New Testament with *Alice in Wonderland*— the point of which is not blasphemy but finding a way of rereading or rewriting Damian that brings us back to the poetics of the event that takes place in the New Testament.

Like Kierkegaard (and like Levinas later on), Damian is a philosopher with an ear for biblical time, however authoritarian his hand.[4] Beyond the contingency of the future, Damian affirmed *the contingency of the past. Mirabile dictu!* Amazing grace! The density of past time was hollowed out for Damian by the goodness and omnipotence of God, who just might be of a mind and a heart to alter it. For the Greeks, in contrast, the very idea of the divine meant the rule of the unchanging and immortal, so any mention of the divine for them injects necessity and immobility into things. The Greeks divided everything up into unchanging and changing being, immortals up above and mortals down below, and they bent their knee above all to the things that could not be otherwise, about which they said there was alone true *episteme,* which was alone truly "divine."

So the effect of the Greeks' love of things "divine" was to prize the necessary, immobile, and universal over the contingent, changing, and singular, which is exactly the opposite of the way things work in the kingdom of God. The Greeks would have preferred the ninety-nine to the one, the general rule to the unruly oddity, which should be cast away, while their gods traveled in circles thinking endlessly and only of themselves, quite heedless of and impassive about us bleeding mortals down below. In the kingdom, on the other hand, we think of God as having counted every tear and every hair on our head and as grieving and suffering with us through our every crisis. The Greeks wanted to subordinate *(pros hen)* the changing things that just happen to a thing *(symbebekos)* to what that thing steadily and permanently is *(ousia)*. In general, they wanted to see to it that necessity ruled in all things, which is what they would have meant by the "kingdom" of what they called *theos,* had anyone among the Greek philosophers coined such an expression. Which nobody did.

Peter Damian, on the other hand, was, however ham-fistedly, touching upon a metanoetic view of time in terms of a *new creation* in which the past lapses in order to let life begin anew, which means to make all things new. This evangelical or metanoetic time is exemplarily realized in the time of forgiving, which requires the giving of a new time, a second chance, a "gift" of time and of a new birth, in which all things are made new, which is what it means to be "saved."[5] Who among us, upon making a grievous mistake, has not wished to have that time *back*? Is that not our desire beyond desire, our hope against hope (Rom. 4:18)? And if that were not possible, if the impossible were not possible, if we could not repair the irreparable, "how then can we live?" as the great prophet of turning around *(teshuvah)* asks (Ezek. 33:10).

Does not forgiveness require the remission of the irremissible past? Do we not, in forgiving, reach back into the past in order to remedy what has been done, in order to undo the harm done? *Dimitte nobis debita nostra:* please, *abba,* dismiss our debts, even as we dismiss the debts of others. Yet on the other hand, we all know very well that the real is irremissible and that, much as God would like to help, what is done is done. The answer to this aporia, I think, depends on sorting out power from love, the power of love from the love of power.

THE TIME OF THE VIRGIN

Here is the aporia Peter Damian poses to the Palace Theologians: Could sorrow for sin be so perfect that beyond crying out to heaven for forgiveness it pleads with God to annul the sin itself? Could God make it to be that this sin was never committed so that the sinner would come "back to the future" free of sin? The God of Jeremiah proclaims, "I will forgive their iniquity, and remember their sins no more" (Jer. 31:34). But could God strike the sin from the annals of time, expunge the record—not just the official archives and accounting books kept by ethics, which demands payment for every offense—but revise the very work of history itself (*Geschichte,* not just *Historie*), altering the very movement of the past? Could sinners, beyond being forgiven, have their actual innocence restored? This would be something of a high-water mark in the sacred anarchy we advocate, a kind of "holy historical revisionism," all for the good, of course.

The aporia is the perfectly logical metaphysical counterpart to *creatio ex nihilo,* that is, *annihilatio* or a *reductio ad nihilum,* the complementary power entailed by the extravagance of the thesis of omnipotence, here pushed to its (il)logical limits. (To put it all in plain English, the *reductio ad nihilum* is the *reductio ad absurdum* of *creatio ex nihilo.*) God, who made space and time, can traverse either in a flash, and neither the one nor the other can offer God any true resistance. The omnipotent God is omnipresent to every point of space and time over which he rules with sovereign power.

If the first figure of innocence is sexual innocence, and if, as both Levinas and Luce Irigaray agree, the first form in which alterity presents itself is sexual difference,[6] then the first form that knowledge of alterity takes is the form of "carnal knowledge." The nakedness of Adam and Eve was modestly clothed in ignorance, their nudity covered more completely by their nescience than by opaque garments. Without lapsing into a self-destructive identification of sin and sexuality, we can very well speak of a "loss" of childish innocence (despite Augustine's doubts about the matter, *Conf.* I, 19). In the passage into the adult world of the knowledge of good and evil, we feel the weight of decision and responsibility tugging at our every move. (The Yahwist, we recall, preferred childish innocence to a full measure of maturity.)

The "virgin" is a figure of an absolute "before" or "not yet," like a morning field after a night's snowfall, a figure deeply implanted in our unconscious, the paradigm of every possible form innocence can take. Virginity departs forever if it departs at all. A single moment lasts forever in its effects. Can the undisturbed surface of this "first" be *repeated* in a repetition that does not really repeat or reactivate, for every repetition comes second, but rather returns us to the first time before the loss, the virginal time when all things were new? Can God turn the past into a past that was never present? Is that not impossible? But is not the impossible God's business, and is that not why we desire it all the more? That is the impossible question, the question of *the* impossible posed by Peter Damian almost a thousand years ago, not in the course of an abstract academic dispute, but in a missive to his brother monks about the power of God to forgive sin.

CAN GOD DO WHATEVER
IT IS GOOD TO DO?

In Damian, both power and the good are beyond being. God can will and can do *whatever* it is *good* to do (B3, 348/L4, 351: *Quod vero bonum est, velle potest, et facere*), which means that the only limit on God's will is his unlimited goodness and bounty *(bonitas)*.[7] Thus, in a debate over the divine omnipotence, Damian pushed the point that God is good beyond being further than anything we find in Levinas or Jean-Luc Marion. But if he is one of several champions of the good, he is the undisputed champion of the metaphysical power of the Creator God. There is nothing in heaven or on earth, in logic or in physics, in time or space, that can resist the sway of God's almighty will, for without God nothing is made (John 1:3). He who has brought forth being from nothing has not tied his own hands in so doing. God has not in creating set before himself an obstacle that thereafter impedes his will, limits his freedom, or constrains his power. If the author of nature is revealed by the regularities of nature, how much more so by its irregularities, by those exceptional moments—shall we say the "events"—in which the course of nature given by its author is also interrupted by that same author—in order to make a point? The world is like a drama in which the author steps on stage from time to time to make a point or two just in case the audience has missed it in the dialogue. There is nothing to stop the God revealed in the Scriptures from making the sun stop in its track at Joshua's command or to make it move backwards across the sky for Hezekiah (B3, 367/L4, 368–69), even as Jesus walks on water, heals the lepers, raises the dead, and changes water into wine in the New Testament. But beyond even these natural marvels recorded in the Bible, Damian goes on to affirm something that stretches thought to the limit and beyond—beyond being and beyond thinking—so that if it is true that being *(estin)* and thinking *(noein)* are the same, as the philosophers boast, then so much the worse for the philosophers, because by being beyond both, the good is also beyond the philosophers.

God has the power to annul the past just so long as that would be *good*. For the good is the measure of what is and is not, assigning to each entity its appointed time to be. The good is the *and* inserted between being and time: it is the good that gives time to being, and being to time, that gives and forgives both being and time. The good alone checks God's power from running wild, for of itself it is infinite and unchecked.

No doctrine of the Christian faith seems to have captured Damian's religious imagination more completely, no image touched his religious sensibilities more deeply, than his faith that by the power of the Holy Spirit a woman conceived a child and gave birth to him with her virginal integrity intact. One of the marks of divine power that fascinates Damian is the permeable body, and his work includes what we might call a phenomenology of such permeable, porous, pregnable bodies. Like the locked doors of the upper chambers in which the apostles closeted themselves after the crucifixion and through which the body of the risen Jesus passed effortlessly, the Holy Spirit entered the locked chambers of the virgin's body without disturbing the closed quarters of her womb, which is a sacred vestibule, a holy of holies. Here is the "physics" or hyper-physics of virginity: a woman's body entered divinely without disturbance, like a mystical snow that allows the foot to fall without leaving an impression. Here is a world of substances without substance, an insubstantial *ousia* calculated to confound the philosophers, which enriches our idea of "epiousiology" discussed above. Indeed, the letter *(epistola)* on divine omnipotence that we are about to study concludes—this is its epistolary conclusion *(clausula)*—with the story of the angel in Acts 5:9–20, who passed through the locked doors of the prison and freed the apostles.[8]

The occasion of the letter *On the Divine Omnipotence in the Restoration of What is Destroyed and in Rendering what is Done Undone* (its title in Migne) is to challenge Jerome's opinion that while God may do all things, and may forgive a sinner for his sins, God "cannot cause a virgin to be restored after she has fallen *(suscitare virginem non potest post ruinam)*." Although Damian thought Jerome always spoke with great piety (B3, 350/ L4, 353), a sentiment not shared by St. Augustine, he said we should not lightly ascribe impotence to the One who can do everything *(qui omnia potest)* (B3, 343/L4, 346). Furthermore, the opinion seemed even to endanger the center of Damian's spirituality, for if God could not do this, how would a kindred miracle like the virgin birth be possible?[9] The feat of restoring both the honor and the flesh of a fallen maid, of closing her opened doors, pales before the feat of the Spirit passing through the virgin's body and the newborn Jesus passing from her womb without hymenal rupture. But if God can do the greater, God can do the lesser.

Contemporary feminists would rightly raise a howl about all this. But we must take a deep breath at this point and realize that something very important is at stake here, despite the fact that the whole thing offends our contemporary gender sensitivities. Damian is an eleventh-century Benedictine monk, living in a very patriarchal world, writing to his fellow monks in an effort to effect monastic reform—not a member of the Modern Language Association putting together a panel on French feminism. One can understand without trying to justify the distorted patriarchal terms of the exchange. The sin of choice is the loss of virginity (variously referred to as *corruptio, lapsus,* and *ruina*) by a woman. Sometimes he means a woman who has been raped, so that what was done was an evil done to her, not committed, and then the question is whether God could then restore what she was innocently robbed of. But he seems able to switch, almost in the same sentence, to speaking of a "fallen woman," and to show little or no appreciation of the well-established metaphysical principle that it takes two to tango, that sex inside or outside marriage is the doing of a couple, not of a woman alone, and that men, too, fall with a complementary symmetry (charging through closed doors), and also "lose their virginity," both their physical and moral innocence, albeit sometimes with a more enthusiastic sense of gain and a lesser sense of loss. Damian offers an insensitive treatment of the distinction between the loving consummation of the sacrament of holy matrimony and extramarital sex (B3, 349/L4, 352), not to mention rape.[10] But this is a letter and not a book (B3, 378/L4, 380), and what is uppermost on his mind in this regard was clerical celibacy. His condemnation of homosexuality came in the context of denouncing homosexual activity among the clergy. That is why he runs together the question of whether a sin against chastity can be annulled with that of whether a widow or widower can, later on in life, take a vow of celibacy and still win the *corona* or moral crown of "virgin," closing the doors of carnal knowledge after they were left open.

But our justifiable desire for sensitivity to gender issues should not insulate us against learning something from the past. It should not obscure the point that lost virginity can be taken as a placeholder here for the loss of innocence generally. Damian enters this abstract debate in the context of a consideration of God's power to forgive sin, to heal the past, to wipe away our tears. The larger point that Damian is making applies just as well to the murderer or the thief:

> How, therefore, is a murderer restored so that after a fitting penance he should no longer be a murderer? How can a thief, or a perjurer, or a robber, how indeed can those who are guilty of all crimes, after they have truly reformed themselves, be no longer what they were? (B3, 367/L4, 370)

For Damian, to be forgiven, *teshuvah,* turning around, putting on a new being, means that the sinners who are forgiven would "no longer be what they were *(jam non sunt, quod fuerunt)."* Forgiveness restores the time of innocence, the virginal time, and he poses an absolutely remarkable hypothesis about recovering or recuperating lost innocence, raising a question that reaches far into our unconscious.

If God wants us to put off the old being and replace it with something better, then what is to stop God from making that happen? Would it not be better? So not only does the good rule over being, but so also does God's power. Put no philosopher's impoverished logic in the path of the divine omnipotence! Cannot God remove not only the debt and penalty for the sin (the mainstream position taken by Aquinas) but the sin itself, so that the sinner would not only be forgiven but rendered innocent of the deed?

THE DEATH OF DEATH

We do well to remember that for all of his love of the good and of forgiveness, Damian has a very sharp tongue, and he would make even the most conservative churchmen of today look tolerant. In the *Book of Gomorrah* (*Liber Gomorrhianus*), written in 1049, sixteen years before the letter on divine omnipotence, Damian launched an uncompromising attack on clerical homosexuality (there is nothing new under the sun).[11] *The Book of Gomorrah,* while it does not make for pleasant reading, is interesting to the present study because of its extraordinarily unforgiving treatment of homosexuality and sin. In it Damian declares the loss of virginity *"irrecuperabilis,"* and beyond that, he verges on formulations that leave us with the impression that sodomy—he coined the word *sodomia*—is an unpardonable sin that represents a kind of spiritual death. This contrasts sharply with the argument about virginity in *De divina omnipotentia,* with the ideal of *teshuvah* and sorrow for sin that characterizes the biblical tradition generally, and most certainly with the teachings of Jesus on forgiveness that Damian can be seen to be radicalizing in the later work on divine omnipotence. Indeed, the way his later views undermine his earlier views on this point is particularly worth watching.[12]

The *Liber Gomorrhianus* breathes the air of unpardonable vice and irremediable ruin. Whether Damian mellowed a bit in later years I leave to his biographers to decide. But the argument and the climate of the *De divina omnipotentia* are strikingly different, even if Damian still retains his polemical manner and still enjoys a good story about eternal damnation. In the letter on omnipotence he is addressing the evangelical council of chastity, whose model is Mary Immaculate, not the extermination of what he regards as filth and infestation, which he never mentions in the letter. If the *Book of Gomorrah* is a book of death, of inexpungible evil, everything in this letter is oriented around the *death of death,* around undoing evil deeds, restoring fallen sinners, extending the work of creation by giving a new being to those who wallow in the non-being of evil. His emphasis falls not on punishing the sinner but on the annihilation of the sin, not eternal torment but the contingency and insubstantial character of the moment in the past when sin was committed. Where in the *Book of Gomorrah* he was horrified by unnatural penetration, the letter on divine omnipotence celebrates the penetrability of preternaturally permeable substances. Where he was in-

sistent on natural necessity in the *Book of Gomorrah,* he is a virtual nominalist here, arguing that the only necessity is found in God.

His purpose is to champion the glory and power of God and to defend
the honor of the faith against those whom he takes to be its detractors, once
again in a "letter" (like medieval *cartes postales,* which by the conventions of
the day became public documents). His opponents—"dialecticians,"
"philosophers," "heretics" (terms used fairly interchangeably)—are treated
with abuse. Two issues are thematically analyzed in the letter. The first and
guiding problem is whether God can restore virginity after it has been lost.
But the first question draws us into a deeper, harder, more radical question:
If God is omnipotent, "can he so act that things that were made become
things that were not made *(ut quae facta sunt, non sunt fuerint)*?" (B3,
350/L4, 353). Could God make it to be that the couple that lost their virginity did *not* lose their virginity at all?

THE FIRST QUESTION

In a human manner of speaking *(modus significandi),* the only thing that
God "cannot" do is evil, not because of a real lack of power but because of
a real excess of goodness. There is nothing good—nothing that truly is and
is truly good—that God cannot do. If virginity is lost by sin, God may
allow the stain of this sin to remain as a reminder to sin no more, or as a
just punishment, the way God allows death to remain as a just punishment
for sin, even though he desires the death of death (Hos. 13:14: *mors mortis;*
B3, 348/L4, 350). There are certain good things that God does not actually
do for reasons of his own providential "secrets." But granted that God
might not always will to do it, one should be on guard against saying that
God *cannot* do it, for example that God cannot restore virginity—if God is
good and omnipotent and this would be a good thing (B3, 348/L4, 350).
Absit: take care, let it be far from our mind, "God forbid" that we should ascribe impotence to God's almighty majesty (B3, 368/L4, 370)![13] Damian's
reflections are typically driven more by fear than by love (cf. B3,
374–75/L4, 376–77) despite the beautiful character of the thought of annulling the sinner's sin.

Damian distinguishes the restoration of virginity in the moral order
(juxta meritorum plenitudinem) from the restoration of virginity in the
order of physical integrity *(juxta carnis integritatem:* B3, 349/L4, 351).
Now since a physical transformation is more easily brought about than a
moral one, then if God can effect the moral transformation, which is
harder, he can certainly effect the easier. But the Scriptures are full of
proclamations of God's ability to forgive sin, to wipe away the tears of the
sinner, including the famous text on *teshuvah* from Jeremiah that Damian

does not fail to cite, "I will no longer remember any of your sins" (Jer. 31:34). But the forgiveness of sins is a far mightier deed than moving a mountain. As a physical feat, the restoration of virginity is in one sense not difficult to imagine. Who can doubt that the God who can heal the infirm, free the imprisoned, cure every ill, who can make a complex organism from just a little sperm (Damian did not know too much about the ovum) would be able to repair or refashion the virginal hymen *(reparare clausulam virgineam)* after it was breached (B3, 350/L4, 352)? How much of a challenge would this be to the God who created heaven and earth and who, by his divine power, effected the miraculous impregnation of the Blessed Virgin by the Holy Spirit and then allowed the infant Jesus to pass miraculously through the virginal membrane without rupturing it?

However, such physical restoration clearly does not satisfy Damian's demands. For even if his sin is forgiven and her hymen is restored, the couple who had carnal knowledge have still *had* it, which is really what it means to "lose one's virginity" when you come right down to it. The deed was done, what is done is done, and that is that. So the real question is, more radically taken, can God, who can do all things, so long as they are good, do—or undo—*that*? Can that deed that the couple did be undone? Is that *not* that? The first question, about restoring lost virginity, implicates us in a second and more radical question. While we can imagine the author of nature seeing to it that impermeable substances would be made miraculously permeable, or that a ruptured hymen would be resealed, it would be a much stiffer challenge, perhaps flatly contradictory, to cause something that was done in the past *not* to have been done at all. In this stronger sense, God must reach back into past time and alter or annul a past deed or event *(factum)* so that these two who had carnal knowledge would *not* have had carnal knowledge. Husserl said that it is an eidetic law that each now-point flows off in a chain of retentions where it assumes its place irremissibly in the past. But if God can restore lost virginity in this more robust sense, Husserlian phenomenology will have met its match in a new logic of the kingdom, of the impossible, before which his own formal ontology pales in comparison. Or has Peter Damian run up against the limits of phenomenology, ontology, thinkability, dialectics—in short, against all the vainglorious disciplines that he treats with such disdain in the *Letter* that will earn philosophers a place in the sulphurous fire?

THE SECOND QUESTION

The first, more pastorally oriented question, about whether God can restore the standing of the sinner (B3, 343–50/L4, 345–353), gives way to a harder question that pushes farther into the realm of *the* impossible (B3,

350, 361/L4, 353, 363). The question is not whether something that was made could subsequently be destroyed, which happens all the time, but rather, to put a fine point on it, whether God could make it to be, for example, that Rome, which *was* founded in antiquity (*p*), was *not* founded (*~p*). The question he is putting is not whether God could have created another possible world, one in which Rome would not have been founded, but rather whether it is possible, *after* Rome *was* founded in *this* world, for God to reach back and pull a metaphysical lever in the past that brings it about that Rome was *not* founded. Damian is concerned with appeasing the majesty of God, the logicians or philosophers be damned (literally).

To this bolder question, Damian gives two answers, which seem to contradict each other, a kind of *sic et non.* First he *denies* that this is possible and denounces the question as idle speculation and literally perverse, while warning those who pose it that they are putting their eternal salvation in jeopardy. For the divine goodness is expended not in making nothing of something but in making something from nothing (B3, 361/L4, 363–64). God is *pantakrator* (B3, 349–50/L4, 353–54), and his power is productive, not reductive; to reduce being to non-being would introduce a kind of perversity into the divine omnipotence. "What God makes is something, what God does not make is nothing" (B3, 349/L4, 353). Nothing, he says, playing with the phrase from John's Prologue, is something that is made without God. Indeed, the question has a ring of blasphemy about it, suggesting as it does a contradiction or alterability, not only in the world God has created, but in God himself, implying that God could change. To the authors of this idle *(supervacua)* question, Damian recommends an emetic, so that they may disgorge all the humors of this illness that makes them ask such a question.

However, things are seldom so settled in Damian's turbulent world. What drives this analysis is not a cold logic but the praise of God, and things will be settled in the end on the basis of whether the goodness of God is served or not. If this question reflects badly on God, it deserves the flames. But to the extent that it does not impugn God's power but actually affirms God's majesty, it is after all worthy of response *(responsione dignus).* In this regard it makes all the difference as to whether what was done in the past was good or evil. Evil is a certain non-being or lack of being, as we learn from Augustine. Damian describes evil as an appearance rather than as a *privatio.* A privation would mean lack of being where it ought to be (as blindness is a physical evil, a lack of sight in an organ capable of sight; stones are not blind). Damian's position is stronger and more Neoplatonic: evil is the mere appearance of being. What truly is, what God has made, is good, for everything that God has made is good and exists in a genuine or robust sense. The good, God's *bonitas,* apportions the measure of being, deciding whether something has true being or not. Evil things, even if they appear to be, do not exist in truth *(etiam cum videntur esse, non sunt)*. Evil is beset by ambiguity *(alternitas)* and a confusing fluctuation or undecidability—like Derrida's "cinders"—wavering between being and nothing. The more Neoplatonic account of evil, while less satisfying philosophically than the more realist Aristotelian theory of *privatio,* nonetheless serves Damian's purposes. For it provides him with an even stronger way of striking the classical chord that God is the cause of what is good and real about a deed, while washing God's hands of any responsibility for what is evil (B3, 365/L4, 367–68).

The first and immediate result of introducing this consideration of the distinction between good and evil is to reinforce the *non.* For this means that if what happened in the past was evil, then God did not make it and it is *already* non-being:

> Consequently, when the question is asked in these words "How can God bring it about that something that has happened will not have happened?" a brother endowed with a sound faith should reply that if whatever happened was evil, it was not something but nothing. (B3, 378/L4, 380)

In that case, God would not reduce the evil done *(factum)* in the past to nothing *(infactum)* because God *does not need* to reduce it to non-being, since it already wallows there by reason of its own nullity. "However, if whatever happened was good, it was surely made by God" (B3, 378/L4, 380). If what was done in the past was good, then it would be deeply contradictory to the divine will to reduce it to non-being. That godless thought would mean, for example, that God could make the innocent guilty, turn virtuous deeds into vice, love into hate, and condemn people to punishment for a deed that they did not do (the first time around, anyway). Anyone who breathes such blasphemy, who thinks such an abomination, is a contemptible scoundrel who should be "sentenced to branding" *(ad cauterium)* (B3, 378/L4, 380). (More fire!) The question is idle *(supervacua),* and it deserves to be committed to the flames *(execrationi)* rather than to paper *(stilo)* (B3, 361–62/L4, 364).

But there is another way of looking at this response and another possible impiety floating about in this question. For the relative non-being of evil implies that the question is impious and blasphemous *only if* it concerns undoing something good, something whose existence is protected by the divine goodness. The question is still on the table if what was done is evil, where undoing the past means undoing something that does not have true being. For in that case, undoing what was done in the past *continues the work of creation,* of drawing being out of nothing, of converting non-being into being, which is the proper work of the divine power and entirely consonant with the divine dynamism. The will of God is not only what causes things to be in the first place but also the cause "whereby those things that have been lost might return to the integrity of their state" (B3, 347/L4, 350). In the kingdom, what is lost—lost coins, lost sheep, the lost son—is found, and then we have a party. Like the sinner in Ezekiel and Jeremiah who turns around, undoing the evil done in the past is undoing non-being and part of the "death of death," part of the business of *amending creation, of continuing the work of creation, creating followed by re-creating.* Almighty God is not destructive of being, but its creator. The idea that God would cause something that was made *not* to have been at all is out of the question—first answer *(non)*—*unless* we are talking about something that already consorts with non-being—second answer *(sic).* For then God is making non-being not to be, undoing something done that is marked by its nullity, filling up what is missing in the body of creation, which is to say continuing the work of creating. All those negations would be strictly grammatical fictions, creatures devised by our human way of speaking, which when viewed from the reality of God's power, and thus from God's point of view, are utterly positive operations of the divine omnipotence, part of the "energy for existing" (*vis existentiae:* B3, 363/L4, 365) that he communicates to things. Restoring *(reparare, restoratio)* is the follow-up to creating, the continuation of creation by another means—whether that be spiritually (forgiveness), physically (restoring the *clausula virginea,* healing the sick, raising the dead), or even, God be praised, annulling what was done in the past. The two answers do not contradict each other, as Resnick and Cantin allege, but represent two different stages of one argument.[14]

That is why instead of concluding, the letter continues: "nevertheless" (*tamen,* B3, 378/L4, 380) we must now take into account something else. The nullity of evil cannot be the end of the story. The simple truth is that evil, whether it is called seeming or privation, sticks in our craw. One need only recall the *Book of Gomorrah* to see what an enormous distress and agitation clerical sodomy represents to Damian; evil, whether as seeming or privation, disturbs and haunts us. Cannot almighty God, who heals and repairs our broken bodies, reach back down into the inner chambers of the past, which, for all the world's wisdom, is frozen in place, and heal our shattered past? Does not the power of the divine goodness, the goodness of the divine power, repair time itself? Cannot God Almighty restore the lost innocence of sinners by making them innocent *again,* or rather, since you can't be innocent *twice,* cannot God undo the loss of innocence in the first place by altering the past, by making the past into a past that was never present? To deny that is to risk another impiety coming from another direction from which Damian must now protect himself.

Damian is arguing that to undo a good deed done in the past—to turn a virtuous person into a sinner, say, by undoing the good the person has done—is a contradiction of the very tendency of the divine will, of the goodness of the divine will. But he is not arguing that it is a *contradictio in adjecto*. Two centuries later, in the High Middle Ages, Thomas Aquinas would treat the suggestion that God could alter the past, good or bad, as a flat-out contradiction in terms (ST, I, 25, 4, ad 2) and would deny, on those grounds, that it was possible. But Damian thinks that the good precedes being, that the consideration of what is good or bad precedes the consideration of the principle of noncontradiction. He belongs to the older tradition where the good lies beyond the distinction between being and non-being, where the horizon of our understanding is not saturated by being, where the first thing that enters our head, or falls under our understanding, is not being, as Aristotle and Aquinas thought, but the Good, as Plato and the Neoplatonists thought. The Good is not bound by Being's demands, including, for Damian, the demand to be and not to be at the same time. Damian thus gives a metaphysically reifying expression to a phenomenological insight into a "sacred anarchy" by way of a frontal assault on the most sacred *arche* or principle that ontology has to offer. For Damian, the only true *arche* is God, and the world is a kind of insubstantial, nominalistic, and anarchical conglomerate of contingencies. At the bottom of things there lies a sovereign freedom, a sovereign goodness, which is also a *sovereign power.* That is the reason why there is something rather than not, and sometimes, as for him, why there is something that is *and* is not. (In chapter 10 below, we will follow Levinas, who shows the way to alter the past without having to embrace the boldness of Damian, without driving under the influence of the idea of divine omnipotence.)

But Damian fears God, not logic, and he does not fear to put God's goodness before the laws of logic. In the language of Paul Tillich, Damian is a "non-correlationist"—indeed, of a most extreme sort, a kind of medieval metaphysical version of Karl Barth. Damian does not proceed by first determining whether something is logically contradictory and then on that basis denying that it is possible for God Almighty, for that is the procedure of dialecticians (logicians, philosophers, heretics) (B3, 367/L4, 369), the kindling wood for the fires of righteousness. He does not let the logicians pre-set the terms for the exercise of divine power, which must be unconditional. On the contrary, he first determines what is possible for God from the point of view of what or who God is, that is, from the study of the God revealed in the sacred Scriptures, in order to determine what is or is not impossible, which is the procedure proper to sacred science. It would be an abomination for the divine will and power to undo the good that is done in the past, and the question of whether it is a "self-contradiction" never arises. That is why the question of undoing an evil deed in the past remains on the table, the objections of the logicians to the contrary notwithstanding.

Damian has argued the *non* thus: if God made something good, he is not going to unmake it; if it is evil, God did not make it, it does not really exist, and so it does not need to and cannot really be unmade. However, Damian continues, in order to "refute the insolence of these impudent opponents for whom the above solution to this question is still not satisfactory" (B3, 379/L4, 381), we must add a further argument. The hard case, which he has been ducking, comes into play if what was done in the past was evil, since even the apparent being of evil is a thorn in the flesh. This argument, which has to do with the distinction between time and eternity, is the knockout punch he saves for refuting the wicked *(improbos)* and the sharp-tongued *(dicaces)*. The ability to do everything *(omnia posse)* is co-eternal to God, as is his knowledge, so that "he contains, determines, and forever confirms within the compass of his wisdom all times past, present and future in such a way that nothing new at all can happen to him, nor can anything pass away through forgetfulness" (B3, 379/L4, 381).

The flow of things for us human beings, which is described very nicely in Husserl's phenomenology of the time-flow, from the future, through the present, off into the past, is present as a whole to God, in the twinkling of an eye, in a moment without distension or passage of time. God surveys the movement of time from beyond time, from on high, without being contained by it. Time passes before God, but God does not pass away in time. What has passed away for us, who are situated within time, does not pass from God, who is present *to* every moment in time, for God lives in an "eternal today" *(aeternum hodie),* an "eternal present" *(sempiternam praesens).*

Accordingly, if we are to speak properly of God, we should always speak in what, from the point of view of human language, we call the present tense, which is the least imperfect way to speak of God. We should always say God is or is not such and such, and not that God was or will be such and such, for the tenses of verbs reflect the temporal limitations of our human way of speaking. Again, we should say that God can do *(potest)* such and such, not that he could have once, some time ago, or perhaps will, some time in the future. Whatever God can do, God always can; whatever God could do, he still can; whatever God will be able to do, he already can. When it comes to God's omnipotence, *potest* is the word that rules. That means that if (humanly speaking), some time ago in the past God could have done *(potuit)* something, say, seen to it that Rome was not founded, then, in virtue of what we have just said, God can still do it *(potest)* now. God sempiternally can do whatever he could have done or will be able to do. He does not lose a capacity he once had or acquire a capacity he does not have yet. These temporal qualifiers, expressed by adverbs and verb tenses, have to do strictly with the limits of our temporal being and language (our *modus significandi*), not any limits on God's power, which is a *modus sine modo*. God is not constrained by the modal limits under which we labor. "Whatever God could do, he also can do, because his present never turns into the past, his today does not change into tomorrow" (B3, 379–80/L4, 381–82). Damian does not simply mean that God will have always had the power to create another possible world, one in which Rome would never have been founded, although that is true enough. He means that as God was able to see to it that Rome was not founded and still retains that power, *even after it was founded,* so God could (can) reach back into the past and alter it:[15]

> Wherefore, as we may rightly say that God *could* cause Rome before it was established to be non-established, so no less rightly may we also say that: God has that power after Rome was founded that it be non-founded. (B3, 379/L4, 382)

So what is true for us, *secundum nos,* "He could have caused Rome not to be founded," means for God, relative to himself, *secundum se,* "He can cause Rome not to be founded." He could have before and he still can now, even after it was founded, because before and after are differences that make a difference only for us, who pass through time one moment at a time, not for God who is present to every moment in time all at once in an eternal today. God has the same power now to see to it that Rome would not have existed as he had before it existed. That power "remains forever immutable and intransigent in the eternity of God" (B3, 379/L4, 382). The power to do all things never passes away from God. So God can now reach back into the past (from our point of view) and alter the past. This means that if what happened was evil, God can reach back and drain it of its nullity and non-being, leaving only its being to stand.

What will settle the issue of annulling the past, in the end, is whether it is *better* for Rome to have existed. For once it would be *better* for an entity not to have been—for a man not to have been born, as the Greek satyr Silenus lamented, or for a city not to have been founded—that entity is in serious danger of being swept away by the divine hand so completely as never to have been there in the first place. Silenus uttered his famous lament, that it would be best not to have been born at all, in the secret comfort of not believing that such a thing was possible. He might have thought better about giving voice to such a complaint in the presence of the God of Peter Damian, who just might have been willing to accommodate him in this regard. If it is better in God's providential design, such a fate might be visited, on the one hand, upon a place as evil as Gomorrah, so that it would be better for that generation not to have been born, or, on the other hand, upon a sinner who has repented so purely and perfectly that it would be a sin to leave the sin on the record. Not only is the sin forgiven, it is forgotten, and not only is it forgotten, it is annulled. The perfection of the sorrow cries out to heaven to annul the deed—and God responds in perfect love.

That would also imply, although Damian does not draw this out, that the more debased and evil the sin, the more closely it consorts with non-being, and hence the more inviting it is to God to annul it. That would make the sodomite, on Damian's account, a prime candidate for an "annulment," for wiping his sin from the face of the earth. On the other hand, Damian could be interpreted as representing a kind of Christian Silenus, arguing that it would be better for clerical sodomites never to have been born in the first place, something that in the present treatise he thinks possible. I choose the more benign reading! Needless to say, there is no mention of sodomy in this text, which might have been a real test case in this letter, not for God, but for Damian.

Damian offers something close to a Husserlian analogy to imagine the possibility of annulling the past. Imagine the following: in speaking the small word *caelum,* while we utter the first syllable in that little point in time (the "now-point"), the second is yet to be spoken, but while we say the second, the first has already passed; whereas God is able to see and say it all, the whole sweep of the ages, in one eternal now, in one stroke *(ictus),* in the twinkling of an eye, in a divine *Augenblick* (B3, 357–58/L4, 360). In fact, however, as Husserl has shown, and as Damian might have remembered from the *Confessions* (XI, 28), if one word is to be heard, the two syllables must be held together for us, by protention and retention, in a "living present" that is compounded of the expected now, the immediate punctual now, and the just-lapsed now. So we too, by a very limited power of retention and protention, can hold the flow of time together in a composite intuition of the living present, or, as William James called it, the "specious present." Now imagine, by an extraordinary extension of the Husserlian doctrine of protention and retention, an intuition that would hold together the flow of time in its entirety, a living present that, furthermore, would not be specious because it would embrace the "the infinite spaces of all the ages," and this not by retention and protention, but in an eternally intuitive now without lapse into the just now and without projective expectation.[16]

Damian's literal logic of the impossible—Damian is one reason we have spoken of a poetics, not a logic, of the impossible—is meant to trump the garden-variety logic of the logicians, because logical rules articulate only the rule of the human mind. Damian treats the laws of logic and mathe-

matics with a ruthless "psychologism" that would have set the teeth of
Husserl on edge. In the first volume of the *Logical Investigations,* Husserl
complained that by naturalizing or psychologizing the laws of logic, one
makes them a kind of physics of the soul, imputing to the law of contradiction a force that is qualitatively the same as the law of gravity. Husserl
mocked "psychologism" for treating the logical impossibility of thinking
the simultaneous truth of contradictories as if it were a physical impossibility, like a boulder that we cannot lift. But that seems to be exactly the status
of logical necessity for Damian. He does not divide the sciences into *phys-
ica, logica,* and *ethica,* allowing each its own domain with its own eidetic
laws, which would be for him a thoroughly pagan or idolatrous frame of
mind. For him, a "non-correlationist" to the end, the operative distinction
is between sacred science and the secular sciences, and the way he understands this distinction gives us an insight into the older medieval tradition,
in which good preceded being, before the thirteenth century when Aristotelian logic and science ruled the theological and philosophical roost. Sacred science means the study of Scripture and of God's will as it is manifested in what God has done in the sacred stories, to which all things are
subject, that is, the kingdom of God. The *artes liberales,* which Damian had
studied and mastered at Parma (B2, 320–21/L3, 109–110; B3, 75–76/L4,
377–78), are the domain of the secular masters, and these disciplines are
concerned with the alterable order of words and logic, and hence with
things that are other than and utterly dependent upon God. There is no
true, independent, eidetic necessity in either logic or nature, both of which
are consequent upon God, and as such are effects of the divine will and the
divine goodness. Outside of the ontological necessity in God and the
purely verbal necessities woven by language, there is no necessity in the
physical world. *But ethics would be an exception to this rule,* because ethics is
ruled by the necessity to do the *good.* So Damian's critics are mistaken when
they criticize him for allowing a world in which God would make the just
unjust, or murder virtuous; that is the *last* thing that would be permitted in
a world ruled by God's goodness, and those who suggest such a thing had
better take care lest the spirit of Damian track them down and hand them
over to the Inquisition.

For Damian there is a kind of blasphemy or idolatry involved in affirming any irremovable necessity outside of God, any rock against which
the divine will could bump. Damian thus submits the laws of both logic
and nature to divine intervention—something surely, he thinks, that any
reader of the sacred Scriptures must have observed happens all the time. So
in an odd way, the psychologizing of logic denounced by Husserl opens the
door to divine intervention in nature and logic (of course, even if the door
were closed, that would not stop God). That was hardly the intention of

the naturalists, but it fits very nicely into Damian's plan. God has the power to cause both (p and $\sim p$), *if indeed that is what is good,* but not if it would be bad (or too confusing) for us creatures (B3, 365/L4, 367).[17]

Damian might have had a moral objection to *sodomia.* He might reasonably have concluded that it was condemned in the Scriptures, and he was in any case right to say that sexual intimacy of any kind, straight or gay, is a violation of priestly celibacy. But it is extremely difficult to see how the author of *De divina omnipotentia* could condemn *sodomia* or anything else by saying that it went against nature. In *De divina omnipotentia* the idea that something is *contra naturam* or an irregularity in nature is a recommendation of its excellence, an occasion for God to make his presence felt, a mark of divine intervention, not of perversity or of a degraded status. For if God is manifested in nature's regularities (the logic of the possible), he has found it fitting to manifest himself all the more poignantly in nature's irregularities (the para-logic of the impossible). On the basis of the letter on divine omnipotence, we are tempted to add an addendum to First Corinthians 1, to say that, in addition to having chosen the weak things of the world to confound the strong, and the foolish things of the world to confound the wise, God has chosen the queer things of this earth to confound the straight and manifest his glory! Of course, if Damian overheard us say such a thing, we would have to head for cover, for the flames would not be far behind.

HOLY HUMEANISM

In Damian, a powerful insight into the hermeneutics of the event, here the event of forgiveness, is given a literal and reified expression, a discursive confusion in which the poetics of the impossible, the poetics of the kingdom, suffers a dangerous distortion. A discourse whose standards are set by the needs of a monastic faith and prayer, above all the Lord's Prayer, the prayer to *Abba,* is pressed into the service of a difficult metaphysical argument.

Elohim's "good" echoes across the pages of Damian's letter, not as a "call" but as raw power, not as praise but as pure will. If God is unable to cause the evils of the past, present, and future to be undone, then how could we pray to God? Such a God, who would have succumbed to the arguments of the dialecticians, would not be the God revealed in the Scriptures. When Aristotle debated the several senses of *ousia,* he never imagined a world whose own substance offers no resistance to the divine will, a world of permeable substances and resurrected bodies, as if the substances had no substance at all, no interior makeup, as if they were a completely pliable surface without interior structure. Damian thought and wrote with a great fear of attributing too little to God and too much to the world, of ascribing too little to the good and too much to being. He was fearful of what we have been calling ousiology, of allowing the world too much "*Selbst-ständigkeit,*" independent self-standing, something that could only come at the expense of God and the Good. That seemed to him a heresy and blasphemy, a kind of idolatry or atheism, the only alternative to which was an extreme theory of divine omnipotence. He never considered the option of a poetics; he never chose a weak force if he thought a strong one was available.

Damian proposes a strictly relative or provisional anarchy entirely oriented in the most hierarchical way to the absolute power and *arche* of God. The work of the theologian is to proclaim the marvelous power of the divine *arche* while safeguarding the divine power from its detractors, namely, the heretics and dialecticians (philosophers). The natural world is shot through and through by the wondrous power of God, filled with wonders like the burning bush that is not consumed, even with holy water that works as a divine pesticide.[18] It is as if nature—which was fashioned against nature (from nothing)—lacks a deep substantiality, as if it were a substance without substance, as if its own natural stuff is so thin and pliable that it easily gives way to God's power. Too robust a theory of substance will block the path to faith in transubstantiation, or too robust a theory of natural laws will block the way to faith in miracles like the Virgin Birth. If the past is indestructible and the course of events in the past irreversible, the doctrine of forgiveness will be undermined. In a theory that can be described as a kind of Christian nominalism, it is not so much the patterned regularity of nature that leads us to God as it is its irregularity and mutability. Following the usual course of things leads us to the laws of nature, but the exceptions lead us beyond nature to its *author.* While it is true that God's power is manifested by the usual course of nature *(cursus rerum consuetus),* his genuine majesty is revealed all the more perfectly by the exceptional interventions.[19] Neither logic nor nature can offer God real rebellion or resistance *(obsistat);* both serve their author like faithful servants (B3, 368/L4, 371). As the lights of logical principles are liable to suspension by the author of light (B3, 354–55/L4, 357), so the empirical regularities of nature are only probable sequences which are liable to interruption upon the intervention of the author of nature. That amounts to a kind of Holy Humeanism. It is as if logic were nothing but a string of signifiers without purchase on natural things, and as if nature had no interior constitution or makeup, as if its laws regulated only the superficial shapes that nature assumes, which leaves it vulnerable to irregular configurations and interventions.

Above all, Damian pushed his thought so far as to think the unthinkable, the possibility of *the* impossible. But his sense for what I have been calling a sacred anarchy remains imprisoned within a reifying onto-theo-logical thaumaturgical realism. His thought is marked by a religious aspiration, a hope of transformation, that tries to describe the contingency of religious time. He holds up before his fellow monks the horizon of the possibility of an impossible forgiveness, for which they must pray and weep, sigh and dream, for with almighty God all things are possible, including the impossible.

In all of this, Peter Damian was perversely, or rather inversely, right—right in such a way that this metaphysical reification needed to be inverted and converted into the coin of a poetics of the impossible event, of which it was an alienated expression. His logic of unlimited power needs to become a hermeneutics of the power of powerlessness, in which Elohim's "good" is transformed from a sovereign power into an unconditional call. Peter Damian had an ear for the madness of the kingdom, but he allowed it to stay steadily tuned to an onto-theology of omnipotence in which the dance and the rhythms of the kingdom—which he could hear as plain as day—became the background music for a performance of metaphysical prestidigitation.

CONCLUSION: AN EXISTENTIAL AXIOMATICS OF THE IMPOSSIBLE

With Damian, it is as if someone tried to supply the metaphysics that would explain all the odd things that Alice experiences, on the premise that even Alice's wildest adventures would be small potatoes for a creator God creating *ex nihilo*. So our anarchic idea would be to transcribe what Damian has written with the perfectly straight face of an onto-theo-logical exposition of divine omnipotence into an ironic hermeneutics of the space and time of the kingdom, to transcribe his metaphysics into the poetics—the imaginative field or space—of the event. The result will be a whimsical but existential "axiomatics" of the kingdom, which will provide us with an irreverent conclusion to our discussion of this formidable thinker, a slightly (divinely) mad or impossible axiomatics that contains the quasi-principles of a sacred anarchy.

So, once again, I cross the wires of the kingdom with a minor voice, here crossing the venerable lines of the New Testament with Lewis Carroll's *Alice in Wonderland*. If Radical Orthodoxy makes a base in Cambridge, I will choose Oxford for my international headquarters! Following my constant if irreverent contention that there is an interesting communication between the Scriptures and current post-metaphysical currents, I will maintain that one finds a comparable contemporary axiomatics, a comparably dissident view of nature, space, and time in Gilles Deleuze's *Logic of Sense*.[20]

(To be sure, we can only smile when we imagine Peter Damian reading *Anti-Oedipus* or Lyotard's *Libidinal Economy* or Derrida's *Glas*!) For Deleuze, the "event" is a surface without interiority or inner depth that offers no resistance to the most amazing transformations. Making use of the resources of Stoic logic, Deleuze illustrates this logic by the marvelous kinetics and dynamics of *Alice in Wonderland*. On my telling, however, one could, were one so minded, develop an analogous axiomatics of what I have been calling "metanoetics." In biblical space and time, the focus is not on the reversibility of simulacrum and original, but on the miraculous transformability of things in the kingdom of God, where the workaday logic of being, sense, and possibility is given a rest in order to allow the holiday logic of the impossible its place in the sun.

This holy poetics holds sway when space and time are affirmed as God's domain, when the horizons of space and time are taken to be radically permeable and porous to the grace of God. It would constitute a "series of paradoxes" something like those that Deleuze develops that turn on what might be called a *bonum*-factor or agency, since all of these paradoxical effects would be charged or triggered as effects of the good. These paradoxical events result from exposing the world to the name of God, to all the disturbances that are harbored in the event of that name. Such disturbances in the regularities of being have been set off by a certain epiousiological intervention of the good beyond or outside being upon the regular workings of spatio-temporal being (ousiology). I propose, programmatically, at least three such series: a spatial series, a temporal series, and a modal series.

(1) The "first series of kingdom paradoxes" in Damian's world—which I am maintaining is poetically faithful to a central theme in the Scriptures—have to do with *spatial paradoxes* and would include such phenomena as the permeability of bodies. Damian's "bodies" are "events" that suspend the resistance that bodies ordinarily offer one another, according to which the presence of one body displaces the other, precisely so as to allow bodies to be permeated by other bodies that are bearers of the good. That would allow for all sorts of intramural penetrations, permitting bodies to pass through the locked doors of prisons and upper chambers; and it would, above all, provide for virginal conceptions and virginal births that do not permeate the hymen. A related phenomenon in this series might be called suspended gravitation, in which bodies that are marked by the good can walk on water without sinking or be lifted up on a cloud without falling to the earth. One thing that would emerge in such an analysis, let us say it would be the first theorem derivable in this series, is that for Damian a body is less an extended mass ruled by laws of gravity and displacement than a field of happenings in which one event can overtake another. This series would have to include the metanoetic paradoxes of transformability, which

have to do with a "becoming" that is very astonishing indeed, one that allows bodily substances to be converted into each other, when that is good (or better, or best)—like water into wine—or that would allow bodies to glow with a holy whiteness. That would also encompass those becomings in which the blind come to see, the lame to be straightened, the leprous and ulcerated to be clean, and then, most remarkably, the dead to live, to emerge from their tombs and walk around.

As a second theorem of this series, we would posit the idea that a body appears to be a substance without substance, a me-ousiological *ousia,* all surface without an interiority that would offer inner resistance to these spatial effects, like a drawing or a painting in which visible surfaces can be transformed without limit. As a third and final theorem in this series, closely related to the second, we would affirm the "virtual" character of this world, which means that in the kingdom "real" bodies behave like bodies in virtual space that can be summoned up from great distances or superimposed upon one another or instantly reconfigured, all with a click. That is why, in the "postmodern" world, there is so much interest in angels, where even major philosophers like Michel Serres have written about the phenomenology of angelology, the remarkable flights and feats of angelic beings who can "move through space at the speed of their own thoughts."[21]

(2) After that groundless ground was covered, we would need a series of *paradoxes of time,* first and foremost among which would be that of the "undoability" of what has been done, or the reversibility or remission of the past, which would announce that what is done is not necessarily done, but may come undone if it was bad and its undoing is better. That would be part of a temporal discontinuity paradox, which would break with the dual logics of the line and the circle that dominate philosophical thinking about time and would instead undertake to think of time in terms of events, which neither melt into a continuous flow of now-times nor circle around and meet each other in a theory of recurrence. Events have a unique discontinuity, for example, the epiousiological quotidian quality of the "today" of our "daily bread," or the unforeseeable quality of the day of the Lord, of the absolute future, as opposed to the plannable and programmable future present that is based upon and extends the present.

(3) Finally, as a logic of the impossible, one would certainly need to constitute a series of *modal paradoxes.* One of these is surely the axiom of "past contingents" established by Slattery and McArthur, according to which, in Damian's world, there would be, in addition to a logic of "future contingents," like the contingent possibility that the Dow Jones average will someday reach 20,000, another logic of past contingents. According to the Slattery-McArthur axiom, we would no longer say that Rome was founded, but that Rome *may have been* founded, but then again it may *not*

have been, and this not because we just do not know, or not because all the facts are not in yet, but because facts are always liable to become *infactum,* because the pressure of the good may not allow what was done to stay done.[22] Secondly, we would need a line of modal axioms surrounding the possible, which would be divided into the standard-form sense of the possible and the impossible, which has already been adequately studied in common modal logic, and the para-logical possibility of the impossible, the paradoxical sense of the impossible, which would always look a little non-sensical to garden-variety logicians, and would open up a brand new field of investigation ripe for doctoral dissertations to explore. The logic of the possibility of the possible and impossible would hold sway in the humdrum world of pedestrian life, where being, sense, and possibility are all in all and current logic books will do just fine; while the latter series would apply to the world of *the* impossible, for in the kingdom, in which God rules, all things are possible, even *the* impossible, so long as the impossible is good.

My idea in proposing these imaginary axioms is neither to reduce the New Testament to fantasy nor to literalize its scenes, but rather, by means of the *reduction to the event* or to the call, to release the event from the stricture of beings, to exhibit the hyper-real hyper-possibilities of the event of the kingdom. I am proposing a way to read these scenes without reifying them, the way one would not reify *Alice in Wonderland* or the ghosts in *Hamlet,* a way to avoid fantasy and magic, alchemy and thaumaturgy, just in order to release the event. To a great extent, modern technology, including medical technology, has begun to perform just the tricks that fascinated the ancient imagination and to relieve us to that extent of fantasizing such transformations. The virtual world displays a great deal of the virtuosity of these miraculous changes, and modern medicine and modern means of transportation have begun to actually do the sort of rapid transporting and wonder-healing of which humankind in the past could only dream. So miracles of these sorts have become somewhat less necessary and less fantastic.

If the world had been high-tech from the very start, perhaps the energy of our religious imaginations would have been directed elsewhere, maybe to imagining unimaginable justice rather than to imagining walking on water or healing lepers or dividing the seas or flying through the air. But more importantly, if—and we have this on the highest authority—the kingdom of God is within us and we within it, then the event of which I have been speaking plays out not on the plane of being but on the plane of the existential. The kingdom is not describing physical transformations of entities but the *existential transformability of our lives,* having to do with the most powerful and transfiguring figures of self-transformation, in which we and all things are made new. It has to do with the *call* that the kingdom issues, the call to be of a new mind, a new heart, *metanoia,* which is itself a repetition of the opening pages of Genesis, which describes a scene of astonishing transformation. The preaching of the kingdom of God does not have anything to do with advocating the advancement of wizardry, as I have tried repeatedly to make plain, but with a hermeneutics of the call, a transforming event on the level of meaning and existential significance. The kingdom belongs to the order of the event, to the eventive dynamics of a metanoetics, of making all things new, of transforming the face of the earth. In the biblical view, everything goes back to the beginning, when things got started by a breathtaking transformation, not *ex nihilo,* to be sure, but one in which the void and barren earth and the empty sky and sea are made to swarm with living things.

That is, if you think about it, still quite an amazing feat even if it departs—at its own risk!—from Damian's view of divine omnipotence. And all this at the drop, not of a hat but of a word, which was not a cosmic explosion or the Really Big Bang behind the big bang, but, true to its word as a word, a call that sweeps across the epochs, ever soft and low, like cosmic background music, calling to us from a time out of mind, even as it beckons us toward an unforeseeable future, breathing rhythmically "good, good . . . very good."

TEN

Forgiven Time: The Pharisee and the Tax Collector

> . . . as we send away our debtors.
> (Matt. 6:12, my translation)

> Two men went up to the temple to pray,
> one a Pharisee and the other a tax collector.
> The Pharisee, standing by himself, was praying thus,
> "God, I thank you that I am not like other people:
> thieves, rogues, adulterers, or even like this tax collector.
> I fast twice a week; I give a tenth of all my income."
> But the tax collector, standing far off,
> would not even look up to heaven,
> but was beating his breast and saying,
> "God, be merciful to me a sinner." (Luke 18:10–13)

In the kingdom of God, we have been arguing, strange, incalculable, un-accountable, impossible things happen (which is also why we love it so). Among the most impossible of these, the most resistant to calculation, the most unaccountable, is forgiveness. Forgiveness, in many ways the most amazing grace (gift) in the kingdom, disturbs our sense of law and order, disrupts our sense of economic equilibrium, undermines our desire to "set-tle the score" or "get even," blocks our instinct to see to it that the offenders are made to "pay for" what they did. Hence, it is the decentering center-piece of a poetics of the impossible (if there is a center), the heart of the kingdom, the heart of a heartless world, and the principal un-principle of our sacred and eventful anarchy.

There is something perversely right about Peter Damian on the alter-ability of the past, *not* in the baldly reifying and metaphysical terms in which he has cast his views, but rather in terms of the poetics of the event that nourishes his audacious argument. In forgiven time, the past must be repaired and the wrongdoing wiped away. *Somehow.* But even if it were good for God to annul the past offense, it would be, alas, as regards forgiveness at least, too much of a good thing, if that is possible, for God actually to do so. In doing so, God would also annul forgiveness, for if the offense is annulled, there would be nothing left to forgive. So even if the idea of annulling the past is coherent, *concedo, non dato,* and even if it might sometimes be better for God to annul a past offense than to leave it standing, that would not be a better account of *forgiveness.* For along with the offense would go the forgiving. To annul the offense is to render the subject innocent, not forgiven, and innocence does not as such require forgiveness. Forgiveness requires something to forgive, the way healing requires a wound to heal. The offense must be left standing and never quite forgotten, *and* it must be annulled, dismissed, wiped away, forgiven. It must survive, live on, *sous rature,* still there but under erasure, becoming somehow an offense without offense. We must somehow be able to reach back across the temporal distance and alter the past, but do so without annihilating it.

Driven by the fantasy of power by which he was possessed, Damian imagined forgiveness on the same scale as the remaking of history and time itself when a good theory of the *hermeneutics of the event* would do just fine. Had Damian devoted more time to a theory of meaning than to a theory of omnipotence, he would have avoided the emperor-God for whom the forgiveness of sins amounts to a challenge to the divine testosterone. For it would be enough to say that in forgiven time the past is given a new meaning, another interpretation, one that removes its sting and puts it behind us. Even so, from another point of view (more hermeneutics), the past remains standing, inalterably there, as something we cannot, and indeed *should not,* forget.

So the experience of forgiveness is an experience of *the* impossible—as is everything really interesting, everything for which we pray and weep!— suspended as it is by the tensions of a confounding *double* temporality. Forgiveness requires something of both the "forget it, it never happened" that captivated Damian, and the "never forget" that attaches itself to an implacable past. For even as the offended party must be as magnanimous as possible and waive off the debt with a "forget it," so the offenders must come to grips in sorrow with the darkness within their hearts, with a past that needs forgiving, that will not go away, that must not be forgotten. For this unusual temporality the sober dynamics of Husserl's phenomenology of retention and protention is necessary but not sufficient. Husserl's phenomenology is a start—because we need a theory of retention of the past offense—but as Jean-Luc Marion rightly points out, it is too much taken with "poor phenomena" and does not show enough interest in the strange and implausible.[1] Thus, to trace the dynamics of forgiven time, the poetics of the event of forgiven time, we require stronger stuff than standard-form phenomenology. This we hope to produce by crossing the lines of the stranger, more para-logical aporetics of the gift in Derrida with the ancient story of the Pharisee and the tax collector.

THE APORIA OF FORGIVENESS

Forgiveness reproduces perfectly the paradox of the gift, where the very conditions that make forgiveness possible also make it impossible. Forgiveness is the gift in which I *give away* the debt you owe me, the *for* in "forgive" having the sense of "away" or "forth." That is why, when someone owes us something, we say we "have something on them," which means that in forgiveness, I give up what I *have* on the other. I release them, dismiss their debt, and let them go. As a gift, the giving in forgiveness must be unconditional. As that famous deconstructionist Thomas Aquinas said of a gift:

> A gift is literally a giving that can have no return, i.e., it is not given with the intention that one be repaid and it thus connotes a gratuitous donation. Now the basis of such free giving is love; the reason we give something to others freely is that we will good to them. Therefore what we give first to others is the love itself with which we love them. And so it is manifest that love has the quality of a first gift, through which all other free gifts are given. (*Summa Theologica*, P. I, Q. 38, a. 2, c.)

So if the other is to be forgiven only after measuring up to certain conditions, if the other must earn or deserve forgiveness, then to forgive him is to give him just what he has earned, to give him his just wages. But that would not be to give a gift, but to give the other his due, to repay the labor of his repentance with the wages of forgiveness; it would be not a gift, but the economy of retributive justice. As Derrida asks:

> And does one have to deserve forgiveness? One may deserve an excuse, but ought not forgiveness be accorded without regard to worthiness? Ought not a true forgiveness (a forgiveness in authentic money) absolve the fault or the crime even as the fault and the crime remain what they are?[2]

But in the great religious traditions, in both Jewish and Christian theology, forgiveness always functions as an economy, where it is regulated by a certain calculus, by a balance of payments that accords with a rigorous set of conditions: (1) the offender must confess the wrong that was done, (2) feel contrite and sad about it, (3) make every effort at restitution that circum-

stances permit, and, finally, (4) resolve to offend no more. But if the other
has met all four conditions, then the other deserves and is owed forgiveness, and we no longer "have" anything on the other, for the other has paid
it off. If, on the other hand, only three of these conditions have been met,
then the other is, to be perfectly logical, only three-quarters worthy of forgiveness (or perhaps worthy of only three-quarters' worth of forgiveness).
The repentant person deserves forgiveness the way a person who has paid
off a mortgage deserves the title to the property: if the purchasers of forgiveness have never missed a payment of repentance, the merchants of forgiveness must meet their part of the bargain at settlement. Such forgiveness
is governed by the laws of fair trade. That means that conditional forgiveness is not a gift but is offered in exchange for full repentance. That is the
economy of *reconciliation,* and it makes sense, but it is not the event of forgiveness.

Reconciliation is not a bad economy and certainly not a bad thing, and
it is much to be preferred to vindictiveness and endless cycles of retribution.
But it is not the gift of the event or the event of the gift, which is not an
economy but an excess. Reconciliation remains within the realm of economy, being, sense, possibility, presence, and the principle of sufficient reason; it runs on the time of the world. Reconciliation, which is the form forgiveness takes in its ordinary mundane existence, belongs to the economy
of the world, taking place on the plane of being. Forgiveness, on the other
hand, belongs not to the entitative order of checks and balances but to the
order of the event, which is here the order of the gift, of the grace and gratuitousness of the event beyond being's transactions. The gift belongs to another realm, another plane, another more unaccountable kingdom, one
governed by the axioms of the event, of the para-logic of the impossible,
where the accounting system is extremely odd (for example, "1 > 99," the
lost one is greater than the ninety-nine who are safe). The gift is bound only
by the bounty of *bonitas,* not the bonds of being; the gift wants only to be
as good as it can be, and it need not have a sufficient reason for being, let
alone add up. The gift of forgiveness would go beyond the law, in the direction of a certain saintly excess that forgoes power and the returns that
being promises.

The gift of forgiveness is another, indeed, an exemplary instance of
something unconditional but without force or power. If forgiveness is to be
anything more than economics, if it is to be a gift, then it must be an unconditional expenditure. Yet unconditional forgiveness looks like madness,
implying that one could only forgive someone who is still offending, who
does not deserve it, who has not earned it, but upon whom it is bestowed
"graciously"—or should we say, gratuitously. We would forgive those who
are guilty and unrepentant and who have no intention, now or in the fu-

ture, of making restitution or of sinning no more. The aporia of unconditional forgiveness would come down to the madness of *forgiving sinners,* to forgiving sinners *qua* sinners, just insofar as they *are* sinners, while they are *still sinning.* It would come down to the mad axiom that the only thing that is truly forgivable is the unforgivable, while the more pedestrian and forgivable offenses fall beneath the scope of real forgiving and represent cases of reconciliation.[3]

Thus, by wiring up deconstruction to the New Testament, "forgiving sinners" emerges as one of the most fascinating short circuits of all. To be sure, forgiveness is a well-known and quite venerable idea that enjoys an excellent theological reputation, but it appears, upon closer examination, to be utterly mad and, in the anarchical sense we are describing here, actually to have been more or less *rejected* by both the theological and philosophical traditions, despite the favorable press it is regularly given there. We all agree that forgiveness is for sinners, but when we speak of forgiving sinners, we usually mean those who are not sinners anymore, former and reformed sinners, or sinners who at least *intend* to sin no more. But if by sinners you mean people who *are* sinners and are *still sinning,* with little or no intention of ceasing their sin, then it appears unreasonable or mad to forgive them, because they do not deserve it and common sense tells us we might not be doing them any favors in forgiving them when they have no intention of reform.

Is forgiveness for those who are no longer sinners, or is it for sinners in the sense of one who *is* a sinner? As a famous moralist, or extra-moralist, once said, and quite rightly, I think, it all depends on what the meaning of "is" is, a point that Heidegger tried repeatedly to make for many years before President Bill Clinton vividly impressed it upon the public mind. It would be nothing more than a fair exchange to forgive those who deserve forgiveness, and it would be mad to forgive those who do not. But if we are not simply giving back to repentant sinners what they have earned and deserve, then it is the sinner *qua* sinner, the sinner who is still sinning, whom we must forgive, who, in a certain sense, is the *only* one we *can* "forgive" if forgiveness is a gift and not an economic exchange.

Unconditional forgiveness would institute a kind of special alliance between God and sinners, which makes religion, although it *says* it is for sinners, very nervous, even as it also makes the philosophers nervous, for they drag their feet when it comes to doing things without a sufficient reason. In actual practice, forgiveness is reserved for *non*-sinners, while the sinners can go to the devil unless and until they shape up and stop sinning. We forgive non-sinners, who have earned it, for whom it is a supplement or a complement (or compliment), but not sinners, who really need it. Matthew has Jesus say, very astutely I think, that just as physicians are for the sick, not the healthy, forgiveness is for the sinners, not the righteous (Matt. 2:17). But in actual practice, the logic of forgiveness works less like the para-logic of the impossible and a lot more like the logic of banking, which tries to keep risk to a minimum. The bankers make loans only to those who have good credit and can offer the bank a security, whereas the truly destitute, who really need a loan, can never get one because they are a "credit risk." Bankers lend money to people who have money, not to people who do not. That is because bankers do not make gifts, and when a bank offers to give you a gift, be on guard, for that is pure economics, and they are only after your business, the proof of which is that if you later on miss a payment, they will not easily forgive you. True gifts and radical forgiveness are not good business. Giving and forgiving, if there are any, do not make for either good banking or good ecclesiology. Thus, to ask whether there is a giving in forgiving is also to ask whether the one who gives forgiveness is more like a healer who treats the sick or a banker who lends to the creditworthy.

We might try to dodge this bullet by saying—and this is a famous axiom of the econo-logic of forgiveness—that we forgive the sinner but not the sin. Now while that very careful calculation is better than not forgiving either one, it is too conditional, calculated, and well-crafted, and it represents something less than the full gift of forgiveness. We are letting ourselves off easy. I forgive you but not what you have done. But what is a *sin*? It is a sinner sinning—didn't anyone do it?—a concrete, factical deed, datable in time, locatable in space. It is not some abstract, ethics-book definition of something evil, of murder or theft, say, which politicians and other people in love with their own rhetoric but with no taste for action can sanctimoniously denounce. It is a concrete murder, which requires a concrete murderer, who is built right into the definition. And what are *sinners*? Sinners are in an important sense the sum of their deeds. You cannot separate the doer and the deed, as a famous anti-moralist once said. In the moment of sinning, the sinner and the sin are one. So to forgive the sinner and not the sin is to forgive the sinner up to a point but no further. It is to forgive that part of the sinner that did not sin in the past and will not sin in the future, but not that part of the sinner that has been sinning and so needs forgiveness. I do not forgive you in those moments of your life where you were or are still sinning or are planning to sin some more. So once again, I am not forgiving sinning, which needs forgiveness, but non-sinning, which does not. I do not forgive that part of you that has done this, and if you do it again, if you revisit me again with this part of you that I don't forgive, then I may call the whole deal off. If I forgive the doer but not the deed, the offender but not the offense, then I am inserting an important condition into my forgiveness, which gives every appearance of being a very tentative and conditional arrangement.

THE PHARISEE AND
THE TAX COLLECTOR

The "forgiveness of sins" is a central part of the kingdom of God and precisely the sort of thing that happens when the mundane transactions of the world are exposed to the event that is harbored in the name of God, that is, when impossible things happen. So we now turn to the scriptural account of forgiveness to find out how forgiveness functions according to the rule of God, who acts unconditionally, not of human beings, who are always up to something and looking for a return. How does God—as opposed to bankers—forgive his debtors? Let us turn to the well-known story in the gospel of Luke (18:9–14) in which a Pharisee and a tax collector go up to the temple to pray. Let us recall that a tax collector is not like a perfectly respectable employee of the Internal Revenue Service, a family man who coaches in the Little League and faithfully mows his lawn every weekend, but a fellow who earns an unsavory living collaborating with the Romans who occupy his land by collecting Roman taxes from his fellow Jews. The Pharisee thanks God that he is not like everybody else, like the adulterers and thieves, and especially not like this tax collector. The tax collector, on the other hand, cannot so much as lift his head, but simply says "God have mercy on me, sinner that I am." We can hardly fail to grasp the conventional point of this story about vaulting moral pride and a lowly, touching humility.

But one suspects that there is something more simmering in this story, not a self-evident piece of the economics of pride and humility, but something more eventful, more gift-like. Let us consider a more radical rendering of this parable suggested by A. N. Wilson, who claims that the story goes back to an older pre-Lucan source, and that Luke has misunderstood the story.[4] That is possible, unless the story is of Luke's own devising, which is also possible.[5] We get a better picture of the supposed original story by taking two crucial steps: (1) We should remember that by the end of the first century the figure of the Pharisee had become a focal point of the Christian struggle against the Jewish establishment, while the historical Pharisees themselves represented an honorable line of men who were zealous in their observance and knowledge of the law, not the hypocrites and bigots trumped up in Christian propaganda. (2) We can expose a core story by removing the prefatory and concluding verses (18:9 and 18:14), which Wilson regards as Lucan redactions that function as a frame that recasts the core story as a parable of stiff-necked pride and humble repentance. The remaining core story itself goes back to an older tradition (and perhaps to Jesus himself), which is both more radical and more revolutionary than

Luke's Christian polemic against the Pharisees, namely, that in the kingdom, where there is no calculating, there is no difference that makes a difference between these two men. *That* would be an event, and *that* smacks of the kingdom! On this older version, the Pharisee is a good man, who meets his obligations, does what is expected of him, gives to the poor, and avoids what is forbidden him, while the tax collector is indeed a collaborator and a sinner. But the point of this version of the story is that God's gracious mercy is so bountiful that the difference between the men is leveled; the good deeds of the Pharisee hold no real weight before God, the sun of whose love and forgiveness rises upon both the good and the bad. Indeed, the sinful tax collector even has a preferred access to God, while the Pharisee, having nothing to forgive, "cannot get in touch with God." That version of the story has the ring of an event, of a paradox, of *the* impossible, of incalculability, which means that it has the ring of truth, both in the sense of the sort of incendiary sayings truly associated with Jesus, and in the sense of our pursuit of the hypothesis of a truly sacred anarchy.

On Wilson's more radical telling, the focus of the story shifts away from the Pharisee and the tax collector and shifts toward God. It is a parable about God as the giver of an unconditional or radical forgiveness, about God as the author of forgiveness. God forgives us without regard to our merits, thereby radically leveling the difference between the Pharisee, who does well, and the tax collector, who does not. In the kingdom of God, where God rules rather than the calculations of human reason, God does not submit to the "logical conditions" under which forgiveness functions for human beings. Unlike human beings, God—the idea of God is the idea of some other way of doing things than our human, all too human way—dispenses forgiveness unconditionally, not according to the conditions imposed by the principle of sufficient reason, let us say, the conditions *human beings* require to forgive one another. Told in this way, the story of the Pharisee and the tax collector sounds a little bit like the parable of the Prodigal Son, which is also to be read as a parable not about the sons but about the father. That parable, on the anarchical reading, should be called the parable of the *Prodigal Father,* who is himself, like God, prodigal with love and forgiveness, and who does not calculate and weigh against each other the respective merits (or lack thereof) of his two sons, but who loves them both unconditionally.

It is as if we could turn that famous line from Augustine's *Confessions* around and say that God has made us for himself and *God* cannot rest until God holds us in his embrace, for there is nothing we can do that God cannot forgive. God is the God of unconditional gifts, of giving and forgiving. Anselm said that God is "that than which no greater can be conceived," that God's being is unconditioned, unrestricted by any conditions that would limit God to this finite and conceivable order or that. Just so, God's giving is that than which no greater can be conceived, and as such it is not conditioned by any conditions that would constrict God's giving under this or that finite measure or constraint, this or that finite demand of reason and human calculation. God is not constrained by the finite conditions of an economy of exchange, by the principle of reason.

Our whole idea has been to liberate the event that is harbored in the name of God, to set it free from the plane of being, which prevents that event. For the uncontainable giving contained in the name of God is "constrained" only by goodness, so it is marked by excess, by exceeding whatever finite constraints are imposed upon it by conceptual thinking. The event that is harbored in the story thus is not an economic equation about the pride of the Pharisee and the humility of the tax collector, which is part of a later Christian polemic, but a kingdom story about the surpassing and paradoxical greatness of God, which levels the calculable and measurable difference between human deeds and misdeeds. In just the way God leveled the tower of Babel, he levels the difference between the moral heights and valleys of human action. Furthermore, beyond leveling the difference, the story even suggests a certain *priority* of the sinner, which implies a radical moral anarchy, a certain perversion and inversion of the order of moral rank, in which sinners, who have more to be forgiven, get a larger share of the kingdom, and perhaps even priority seating, rather the way in an emergency-room triage the more seriously wounded are preferred to the less seriously wounded.

Is not Wilson's rendering a scandal? Does not such a rendering suggest outright anarchy, an ethical reason gone on holiday, an "anything-goes relativism," a sacred anarchy become a holy relativism, to be sure, in which God forgives all and makes the sun of forgiveness to rise equally upon the good and the bad (Matt. 5:45), but a relativism just the same? Is it not a terrifying thought to anyone who thinks that we must be held responsible for what we do—and who does not?—and that whether we do well or do ill, justice or injustice, makes all the difference? That is what makes Wilson's reading interesting to those of us who harbor furtive thoughts of a sacred anarchy, who dream of an event, whose last waking thought before we nod off is of an event.

JESUS AND THE SINNERS

Wilson, however, is not a New Testament scholar, and as brilliantly suggestive as this suggestion is, he offers no documentation or evidence for his reading, nor does he address the very real possibility that Luke has not misunderstood the story but invented it himself. But Wilson's point is not without scholarly merit.[6] One of the more unassailable things we know about Jesus, if there are any, is that forgiveness was a central part of his teachings. The historical Jesus was—Hannah Arendt put this very nicely[7]—the master of forgiveness, and that may have played some role in the trouble that Jesus brought down on himself. One has to be very careful in dealing with this matter because it is very much steeped in Christian apologetics and a testamentary supersessionism that goes all the way back to Marcion. The gift—the graciousness, the loving excess of God—tends to be the way Christians lay out the case for the superiority of the "New" Covenant over the "Old." That is why I turn for guidance in these matters to E. P. Sanders, a scholar who is acutely sensitive to Jesus' Jewish sources and to the excesses of Christian polemics against the Jews. According to the standpoint adopted by Christian apologetes, Sanders says, "we [Christian New Testament scholars] have love, mercy, repentance, forgiveness, and even simple decency on our side, and that is why our religion is superior to its parent" (*JJ*, 199). As Derrida says, the scene of Christian apologetics is usually staged as a war against the Jews in which the Christian is opposed to the Jew as the living word to the dead letter, the word of honor to the written contract, forgiveness and mercy to commerce, the love of the poor to the wealthy banker.[8] For Sanders, as for Derrida, Christianity defines itself as eventive, in terms of love, grace, and the gift, while defining Judaism in terms of the eye-for-an-eye economy of legalism and externalism. The poetics of the gift and the distinction between gift and economy are not an abstract debate in French postmodernism, but it insinuates itself into every crevice of Jewish-Christian dialogue.

With that in mind, let us follow Sanders's more scholarly and documented inquiry into the place of "sinners" in Jesus' preaching about the kingdom and just what was so disturbing about it. If Jesus had simply been repeating the classical doctrine of *Teshuvah*, if he had simply been elaborating the traditional conditions under which atonement may be attained, he would not have attracted any attention to himself. To have brought down so much trouble upon his head, he must have introduced an innovation on the classical teaching that caused a collision with the religious establishment of the day. In Sanders's view, the one distinctive thing that "we may be certain marked Jesus' teaching about the Kingdom is that it would include the 'sinners'," that the kingdom had in a special way to do with the lost sheep (*JJ*, 174). By sinners *(hamertoloi)*, Sanders insists, we do not mean the righteous who have repented of their sin, but those who are still sinning, even "professional" sinners, those who earn their living by sin (e.g., usurers, tax collectors, prostitutes), by associating with whom Jesus earned a great deal of criticism for himself. The kingdom has to do with those who are "lost" *(apololos)*—the lost sheep, the lost coin, the lost son (Luke 15:4, 6, 9,

32). Even if we concede that the expression that "there is more joy in heaven over one sinner who repents" is a bit of Luke's editorializing, still Luke is on the right track (*JJ*, 179).

The sinners, Sanders insists, are not to be confused with the "common people" *(am ha-aretz)*. As Jesus would not have caused a stir by ministering to the righteous who sin no more, so he would not have caused a stir by ministering to the poor, to common and uneducated people, who were certainly not irreligious. To have fallen afoul of the powers that be, he must have mingled with, and offered the kingdom to, the wicked, those who flagrantly disobey the law (*JJ*, 187). The challenge Jesus posed does not lie in letting the common people into the kingdom, for they were not excluded in the first place. The only ones who think they were excluded are those who hold the cynical view of the Pharisees cultivated in Christian polemics, in which the Pharisees are portrayed as a small purity group who excluded everyone but themselves from the kingdom, which, Sanders argues, has more to do with Christian apologetics than with historical truth. The common people were uneducated, which may have diminished their responsibility about the fine points of the law, and they did not observe priestly purity laws, which is something that they would need to remedy if and when they wanted to enter the temple. But neither of these things would make them wicked or "sinners." Although it is certainly true that Jesus was inclusive, that he was a "champion of plain folk" (*JJ*, 198), no right-minded observer of the Jewish law would have objected to someone ministering to the poor and uneducated. Rather, what must have brought so much trouble down upon Jesus was that he offered the kingdom to the wicked, to sinners who are still sinning.

Once again, caution is required. As Sanders points out, that sinners could be forgiven, that forgiveness is always available to those who have a change of heart, both on an individual basis and to Israel as a nation, is a standard part of Jewish theology and would have been well known to Jesus the Jew (*JJ*, 106–108). In Ezekiel's famous discourse on *teshuvah* (33:10–20), the Lord God says "I have no pleasure in the death of the wicked, but that the wicked turn from their ways and live; turn back, turn back from your evil ways . . . and as for the wickedness of the wicked, it will not make them stumble when they turn from their wickedness." The Lord God desires the death of death *(mors mortis)*, Peter Damian commented. If they turn from their sins, restore what they have stolen, and sin no more, "they shall surely live. None of the sins that they have committed shall be remembered against them." *Teshuvah*, which we tend to translate into English as "repentance," derives from the verb "to turn" or "return" *(shuv)*—"Return, O Israel, to the Lord, your God, for you have stumbled because of your iniquity" (Hos. 14:1). This was translated in the LXX as *apostrepho*, to turn away from, to turn back from, wickedness, which would also link up with *metanoia* in the New Testament, to be transformed into and to take on a new mind. If Jesus taught a doctrine of the need for sinners to repent or "return," he would have just been saying something very Jewish, something already to be found in Ezekiel and Hosea, and that would hardly have attracted any unfavorable attention to him. Repentance was also the salient motif of the preaching of John the Baptist, although, unlike the Baptist, who was concerned with national repentance, Jesus seems to have had individual transgressions in mind.

We ought not to imagine that the Pharisees were offended by love, mercy, and grace, by the graciousness of the forgiving God preached by Jesus, while they themselves, being hard of heart, demanded punishment, an eye for an eye, a merciless retribution for every transgression; indeed, the evangelists portray the Pharisees not only as unforgiving but also as willing to kill anyone who taught forgiveness (*JJ*, 201–202). As Sanders says, the standard Christian renderings of the Jews are so cynical that they deprive Jesus of "a living context in Judaism" (*JJ*, 18) because they make it difficult to understand how Jesus could have been a Jew himself and lived as a Jew. In fact, as Sanders argues, repentance and forgiveness were staples of Jewish theology, and had Jesus been able to turn the tax collectors and thieves around, to effect a change of heart in them and bring them back into the fold, he would have been hailed as a national hero.

What, then—if anything—was Jesus saying about forgiveness to give offense?

Might it have concerned *the time of forgiveness*? Might it be that Jesus offered forgiveness to sinners who were still sinning and this *in advance* of their having repented? Then the line that divides Jesus from his critics is this: traditional Judaism offers "conditional forgiveness," forgiveness only to those who have repented, who have become righteous, whereas Jesus offers what might be called "unconditional forgiveness," forgiveness in advance to those who are still sinning. On this telling, the Pharisees said, God forgives you *if* you repent, and Jesus said, God forgives you, *so* go repent and mend your ways. "[T]he gift," Sanders says, "should precede the demand" (*JJ*, 204). The gift of grace would precede repentance. That is a difference that makes a difference, but however interesting and provocative a theological point it may be, it hardly seems likely that it would have caused much of an offense, or that Jesus would have been led to the cross by this distinction. On the whole, it seems that the Jewish people would have been delighted if, after Jesus dined with the usurers and tax collectors and told them that God forgives them, the usurers would actually have been led to give up their usury, or the tax collectors to give up their collaboration with Rome. Such an offer of forgiveness, moreover, would hardly have been unconditional, for Jesus would have simply been offering them forgiveness "on credit." The timing would have been different—it would have been given in advance—but he would have expected follow-through; if he were thinking like a banker, he would have expected them to keep up with the payments.

Sanders's own proposal is this: while the Jewish law—Ezekiel is very clear about this (Ezek. 33:15)—required repentance and restitution, Jesus may have earned the wrath of the religious—the temple—authorities of the day by offering forgiveness to sinners, not only while they were still sinners, and not only in advance on condition that they subsequently give up sinning, but rather *without requiring restitution and repentance,* which would have represented a sharp departure from Ezekiel. That would also sharpen the difference between Jesus and the Baptist, who most certainly required repentance and, as we have seen, on a national scale. It is not that Jesus did not *desire* that sinners repent, but that he did not *insist* on it, perhaps because John the Baptist was doing a good job of making the need for repentance clear, and his particular mission was to address the outsiders, the sinners who were still sinning (*JJ,* 227). In the story of Levi the tax collector (Matt. 9:9–13; Mark 2:13–17; Luke 5:27–32), there is no mention in any of its versions that the tax collector gave up his profession, but only that Jesus "called" him and he "followed." It may be that this means that Jesus had tax collectors who remained tax collectors among his followers, which is what drew down the fire of the authorities upon him. If Jesus was saying that the kingdom is ours if we follow *him,* not if we repent and make restitution, that would have put him at odds, not with hypocrites and bigots, but with Ezekiel, Hosea, and the mainstream teachings of Judaism. When Levinas remarks in *Nine Talmudic Lectures* that "there is no forgiveness that has not been requested by the guilty,"[9] that is, by those who have had a change of heart, he is commenting on a passage of Mishnah that is a classical element in Jewish theology of forgiveness. Suppose, in addition, Jesus said that the sinners would get *priority* seating in the kingdom, that there was some kind of preferential priority, not just for the poor, which in a way is "fair," but for the wicked, which is not fair. If he did indeed say "the tax collectors and the prostitutes are going into the kingdom of God ahead of you" (Matt. 21:31), that would have added fuel to the fires.

That would indeed constitute a certain madness, as Derrida would say, an act of forgiving that utterly jettisons the demand for a *reason* for forgiveness, which inserts forgiveness into the poetics of the impossible, and it would have redirected the focal point of Jesus' teaching about forgiveness to the God of forgiveness and away from the sinners themselves or the human differences between the good and wicked. That would frustrate a certain need or impulse we all feel to use the strictly economic terms to which we have recourse on these occasions, to get even, or to settle the score, a point that would lead us back to Nietzsche's *Genealogy of Morals.* For it is just maddening that someone would get off scot-free, without having to pay for what they did. It offends all economy, our economic reason, which cannot tolerate this sort of disequilibrium.

Jesus' views on sinners and repentance invite a comparison with the command given to the young man who wanted to follow him but who wanted first to bury his father. When Jesus told the young man to follow him at once and unconditionally and to let the dead bury the dead (Matt. 8:21 ff., Luke 9:59 ff.), he was suspending a precept that was sacred in both the Jewish and the Greco-Roman world (that, of course, reminds us of what Creon told Antigone). Jesus thereby indicated, if not outright opposition to the law, as a good many New Testament scholars think, at least the willingness to claim that the law is not enough, not the last word, not final (*JJ,* 267), and this, not because he opposed it, but because he thought we were in transition to the coming of a new age, of the kingdom. Thus, if one follows him and heeds his call about the coming of the kingdom, then certain provisions of the law—like burying the dead and doing repentance—may on occasion be suspended or superseded (*JJ,* 255). That sort of thing, which "challenged the adequacy of the law," would attract the attention of the priests, who "were the administrators of the law, and also those who were authorized to say whether or not atonement had been made or purity achieved" (*JJ,* 300). Eventually that is the sort of thing that would make the Romans nervous.

That, Sanders argues, casts the Christian-Jewish polemic in a clearer light. This was not a debate between the lovers of the gift and coldhearted legalists. There was no disagreement between Jesus and his contemporaries, his fellow Jews, about whether God was loving, gracious, and forgiving. Everyone was agreed on the beauty and the value of the "gift" so long as it is taken abstractly. What they disagreed about was whether the gift of forgiving occurred under the concrete conditions of repentance and restitution traditionally required by the law and set forth explicitly in Ezekiel, or whether God granted forgiveness unconditionally and without repentance or restitution to those who followed Jesus. Jesus was being opposed, not by bigots and hypocrites, the unworthy opponents whom Matthew has devised (Matt. 6, 23)—and this is the text that Derrida seizes upon in *The Gift of Death*[10]—but by earnest and responsible religious people who were understandably offended by his views on forgiveness. They were also offended by the importance he attached to himself and to those disciples who followed him, from whom the demands of the law could on occasion be lifted, and by his claim to be God's spokesman and to know what God was going to do next (*JJ,* 280, 293). But all these things are theological fine points, it should be insisted, compared with Jesus' attack on the temple and his prediction of its fall, which, in Sanders's view, is the main thing that led him to the cross (*JJ,* 300).

There is another dimension to the question of the time of forgiveness. It may be, Sanders notes, that Jesus *desired* the repentance of the sinners but did not *demand* it because he thought that the sinners did not have the time to remake their lives (*JJ,* 207–208). It may be that he was convinced that the end time was at hand, and that at this eschatological moment sinners would not be given the time that is required for the lifelong work of making themselves into new beings and of making restitution, of undoing the damage they have caused. In the urgent moment of the end time, God issues a blanket amnesty. If, however, Jesus' notion of forgiveness was forged under the peculiar circumstance of the end time, that would mean that it was not absolutely unconditional but was subject to the peculiar condition that the end was at hand. It may be a peculiarly eschatological notion, where there was time for *metanoia* only if that meant to be of a new mind, but no time for *metanoia* if that meant the more elaborate work of restitution and striking out on a new course in life. If one thinks that time is up, then the future takes on a rather different sense and it cannot be made a necessary condition. Forgiveness, like justice, cannot wait. Like justice, forgiveness deferred would be forgiveness denied. Forgiveness cannot depend on the future reform of one's life if there is no future. Forgiveness cannot depend on sinning no more if there will be no "more." If you think the end is at hand, that time is all but over, then everything is changed.

That puts the eventually institutionalized church that survived Jesus in a tough spot. For when the end time did not come about and the church began, as it were, to unpack its bags and to prepare for a longer stay on earth, it faced a difficult decision. Should it stay with this radical teaching of unconditional forgiveness, or reinstate the traditional conditions? Bite the bullet of this more radically anarchical stance, or accommodate itself to the world and to the way institutions conduct their business, which is always hierarchical? Should it attenuate the trauma of the event, the blow of the impossible struck by the teachings of Jesus, or abide in their paradox? The gospels of the last quarter of the first century leave no doubt about the course that the church followed. The choice to get back in line with the mainstream tradition is plainly in evidence throughout the gospel of Luke, in his insistence on meeting the conditions, on the need for repentance and sinning no more. That would also explain why Luke would have been motivated to supply a *revised* version of a pre-Lucan story about a Pharisee and a tax collector in the way that A. N. Wilson suggests, if that indeed is what happened.

It is impossible to tell if that is what Jesus had in mind. Would he have settled for the more traditional doctrine if he concluded that he had been jumping the gun about the end time? Was his offer of unconditional forgiveness subject to the eschatological condition, so that Jesus too would have required a follow-up repentance and restitution if he had come to see that there was indeed time enough to undertake it? Or was the forgiveness of which he spoke indeed absolutely unconditional, offered to someone without regard to repentance, as a pure gift, for the unrepentant sinner who is still sinning is the one who most needs forgiveness, the repentant having already put their lives back in order? Unconditional forgiveness would have constituted the greater paradox and the greater scandal, which, on the criteria set forth by Johannes Climacus, would require the greater passion, intensity, and faith, all of which are marks of greater subjective truth, of an objective uncertainty held fast in passionate inwardness, which is one of the "un-principles" of a sacred anarchy. On the criteria set forth by Sanders, that he must have taught something that had a particularly scandalous force to have been brought to the cross by the temple and Roman authorities by it, the notion of an absolutely unconditional forgiveness seems like a more likely candidate. That, in turn, would lend some support to the radical reading of the story of the Pharisee and tax collector who went up to the temple to pray.

FORGETTING THE PAST: IT NEVER HAPPENED

Forgiving is not forgetting, because it is both stronger than forgetting, requiring as it does a kind of absolute forgetting, and also weaker than forgetting, since it also requires remembering. Let us examine each of these lemmas in turn.

"None of the sins that they have committed shall be remembered against them," Ezekiel says in his famous hymn to repentance (Ezek. 33:16). "For I will forgive their iniquity, and remember their sin no more," says the Lord in Jeremiah (31:37). The one who is offended must forget the offense, even as the offender must be able to put the offense behind him and move on, beyond the offense but also beyond the forgiveness, lest he incur a lifelong and incapacitating debt. For otherwise, "how then can we live?" (Ezek. 33:10). The offended must forget the offense even as the offender must forget the forgiveness. Forgiveness requires absolute forgetting. The trespass is over, I dismiss what you owe me, we should both forget it.

Derrida, in *Given Time,* and in evident agreement with the prophets (whom he does not cite), tells us that the gift requires forgetting, but an absolute forgetting, stronger than any mere psychological lapse of memory. Indeed, when we give the gift of forgiveness, one of the things we say to the debtor or trespasser is, "Forget it. It never happened." The *time* of the gift on this account is most amazing, for it requires a past that ceases to be: in forgiveness, it is to be as if it never happened. Forgiven time is not to be confused with a revisionist history in which a propaganda machine wipes out our *knowledge* of the past. Forgiveness must somehow strike a blow against the *past itself,* which is what seduced the petulant Peter Damian. The past would be *somehow* wiped out, annulled, or erased, so that, were it possible, it really would be the case that "it never happened."

That absolute *amnesia,* I contend, is the event, the beautiful dream of the undoable past, that lay behind the reifying ontology in Peter Damian that we discussed in the preceding chapter. From the standpoint of Husserlian phenomenology of retention, the present flows off into the past where it assumes a fixed and inalterable place. But Damian's speculative argument about the divine power addresses the amazing grace at work in the amazing case of being forgiven, in which what was true *then,* that the sinner sinned, is (somehow) not true *now,* now that the sinner has been forgiven, and the Pharisee and the tax collector are on an equal footing. The bountiful goodness of God has somehow seen to it that the sin has been wiped away. If that is not *somehow* true—without leaping off the ontological cliff like Damian to establish this position—if we cannot somehow reach back and wipe away the past, then we have no future and we cannot live.

I propose to convert the coin of Damian's metaphysical excess into the currency of saintly excess, as a contribution to a theory of the event, of a sacred anarchy, as a hyperbolic theory of forgiveness that can help us understand the radical reading of the story of the tax collector and the Pharisee proposed by A. N. Wilson.[11] On this reading, the tax collector has indeed sinned, but he has been forgiven by the bountiful mercy of God. His sin has been wiped away so that he now enjoys equal status with the Pharisee, because the only thing the Pharisee has on him is in the past, is passed, is "gone." He has been made new and is of a new mind and new heart, *metanoia;* he has turned around, *teshuvah.* Thanks be to the God of mercy who says to the tax collector, Forget it, it never happened. The event of the rule of God is a radical leveling of the human difference between the Pharisee and the tax collector, which persists so long as one is lodged on the level of being. Inasmuch as they are both turned toward God, they are both pure and thank God for lifting them up, and hence they are both Pharisees. But insofar as even the Pharisee too has sometimes fallen, they have both been forgiven, and hence they are both sinners asking God for his mercy. Are we not all Pharisees and tax collectors, and do we not show both sides, and are we not in continual unrest because the one side of us is continually disturbing the other? Is there not a holy undecidability between them?

Moreover, we have seen that, according to Sanders, the peculiar scandal given by Jesus lies in offering forgiveness to sinners who are *still sinning,* in consorting with sinners, not those who have repented of their sins and been forgiven, but those who, like the tax collectors, earn a dubious living by their sin, who have sinned in the past and whose sins, far from having ceased, still persist. That smacks of the *event.* But we must, following Damian, distinguish God's point of view and ours. Jesus was inviting us to see the sinner from God's point of view; from the point of view of the kingdom, where God rules; from the point of view of the event, where there is an absolute remissibility of sin, for it is only God who can forgive sin. That is the point of view from which Damian wanted to see things. There is nothing in the story of the Pharisee and the tax collector to say that the tax collector went out from the temple and tendered his resignation from his job. That is why Jesus both preached about the forgiveness of sins and consorted with sinners. From the point of view of the kingdom, the sinner who has sinned also sins again. Sinning is a lifelong state of affairs, and sinners are those who have had their sins lifted by God as many times as they sin, even if they sin seven times a day, or seventy times seven. In the kingdom, there is no sin that can overtake God's love, no sin that can best the Good, no sin that God could not wipe away. For the kingdom is where God's love rules, where nothing can resist his love, which is beyond seventy times seven, that is, beyond calculation, which is what we mean by an event.

NEVER FORGET: THE TIME OF CONFESSION

But if forgiveness requires a kind of absolute forgetting, one that touches the past itself and is not merely a psychological act of forgetting, it is also *not* forgetting, or less than forgetting. That is because, as we have seen, if the past offense were by some mysterious act of divine power/goodness annihilated, so would the forgiveness be eradicated, for there would be nothing then to forgive. In forgiveness, there is always something to be forgiven, something that remains standing, something *irremovable* although not *irreparable.*

Up to now we have approached the gift of forgiveness from the standpoint of God, who forgives sin, that is, of the one who is offended, the one who must give this gift (for we cannot give it to ourselves), and that is where we have located the time of forgiving as one of absolute forgetting. But if we shift our focus to the standpoint of the offender, of the one who confesses sin, then time takes the very different form of a work of memory, where we must not forget, where there is always something to forgive and the past remains standing. Let us approach this question by way of a valuable discussion in Rosenzweig and Levinas, brought to our attention by Robert Gibbs. What *tense,* Gibbs asks, following Rosenzweig, is the sinner supposed to use to describe his state? Should he say "I *am* a sinner" or "I *was* a sinner"?[12]

We know that in Alcoholics Anonymous, experience teaches us that the members should begin by giving their name and confessing that I *am* an alcoholic, and this on the well-founded belief that if I say my alcoholism is behind me, I will fail to see it lying in wait for me up ahead. According to Rosenzweig, however, the first word we hear from the sinner is "I have been a sinner" up to now, but from here on it is over, past and gone. I have put it behind me and made it go away. At this moment, as Gibbs says, "the 'I' that speaks is not the sinning one." However, "with this confession of having sinned," Rosenzweig says, "the soul clears the way for the confession: 'I am a sinner'." Even with these other sins behind me, I have not become a pure will. I continue to fall, and I have no illusions about my weakness and imperfection. After all, even Peter Damian, who was extremely optimistic about the ability to heal the past, signed his name "monk and sinner," as if the two go naturally together, for he became a monk just because he was a sinner.

From the standpoint of the *gift,* which always involves an excess beyond economy, we might say that, in confessing that I am still and will ever be a sinner, I am aiming at the excess of unconditional responsibility. In a discussion of marriage in *Either/Or,* the author of the letters of "B" tells us that in a marriage that has been reduced to an economy—we will use Derrida's language—each partner will seek to justify his or her actions before the other, to prove that he or she is in the right. But in a marriage built on love, that is, the gift, the two partners will eagerly seek to put themselves in the wrong for the sake of the love, each attempting to assume all blame and all responsibility—without a calculation, without an objective adjudication of who is right and who is wrong, the very thought of such a calculation representing a kind of violation of the love. Each will compete with the other in a veritable potlatch of confession, each seeking to outdo the other in assuming blame, each seeking to assume all the responsibility and to leave the other blameless so that the love may flourish. As the country parson reminds Judge Wilhelm, who exhibits all the self-righteousness of ethics vis-à-vis the aesthete, love trumps the economy of right and wrong by saying, "It is all my fault, all my doing," in order to preserve the love, whereas ethics judiciously weighs both sides according to the principle of sufficient reason.[13]

Hence, in just the way we speak of the surpassing generosity of a God who forgives unconditionally, we can in a parallel way speak of the surpassing responsibility of the offender. If God's excess is one of unconditional generosity, the sinner's excess is one of unconditional responsibility. What moves us most about the tax collector is that he puts up no defense:

> But the tax collector, standing far off, would not even look up to heaven, but was beating his breast and saying, "God, be merciful to me a sinner."

He stands far off and does not make a display of himself; he divests himself of all *ousia* and *exousia*. He approaches God with bowed head and without a word in his own defense. He does not say that while he concedes that he is on the whole a sinner, still we should also take into account that he has done a lot of good things in his life and that it is not commonly known that he supports a number of local charities. He does not point out that he has been having a particularly bad time of late—he has lost his job and his wife has left him—and that is why he is a sinner, or that while it is true enough that he is a bit of a sinner, still, who is not? And every bloke deserves a break once in a while. He just lays down every defense in advance. His gift is to *give up* every defense that would excuse his conduct. Even if there were a defense to be made, it is for God, or for the other, to make it on his behalf. Putting up a defense is not the business of the sinner but of the one who has been sinned against. The sinner holds himself irrecusably responsible, makes himself wholly responsible, without availing himself of excuse or exoneration. As Rosenzweig says, the soul "is freed of its burden at the very moment of daring to assume all of it on its shoulders."[14] The onus is lifted if and only if I do not exonerate myself (which is a vintage sample of how the poetics of the impossible works). That is why, in addition to saying that this sin is behind me, I then confess that I am and continue to be a sinner.

Forgiveness must ultimately come from the other, while confession is my business. Although it is also true that I must forgive myself and not allow the past to destroy the present and the future, as a sinner I must also not allow myself even to entertain the thought that I can unilaterally undo what I have done, unilaterally balance the accounts. In this beautifully mad and impossible kingdom, just as the one who is offended gives away every claim to recompense that he has on the offender, so the offender *gives up, gives away* any possible claim to a defense, any claim that he can earn or deserve forgiveness. Hence, the sinner would always *remember* a certain unforgivability in the offense, so that if the one who is offended, in the idealized magnanimity of forgiveness, urged the sinner to "forget it, it was (it must become as if it were) nothing," then for the idealized sorrow of the offender it was *everything,* and therefore quite *unforgettable.* From the perspective of the sinner, the past is to be *conserved,* not lost, lest it revisit me in the future, so that the offender's duty is to remember the harm done to the other. So if, from the point of view of the giver of forgiveness, the temporality of forgiveness lies in "Forget it, it never happened," then from the point of view of the sinner, the one who gives not a gift but an offense, the temporality of forgiveness lies in the "never forget." Forgiving is not forgetting, is weaker than forgetting, because confession cannot forget.

That brings us to the double bind embedded in the temporality of forgiveness. Forgiveness means that we are not to be held forever a prisoner of the past, that the weight of the past must be lifted. Confession means that we can never forget. The two temporalities—forget it/never forget, it was nothing/it is everything—contradict each other, are at odds with each other, but not as simple logical contradiction, a simple or absolute impossibility, which is the ham-fisted way things are handled in a logic of being, but in such a way as to constitute the tension that is an ingredient in the experience of *the* impossible, which is what it means to think the event. The two temporalities constitute the terms of *the* impossible, co-axioms in the poetics of the impossible, constitutive of the aporetic experience of the no-way-to-go that is a condition of the true experience of motion and of really getting somewhere. For on this poetics, we are not really getting somewhere unless we experience the no-way-to-turn.

At this point we must, at the high risk of incurring the wrath of Peter Damian, recall the counterbalancing experience of the event, which arises from the standpoint of the sinner, not of God, of the offender, not of the offended, that is, of the inalterability of the past, an inalterability that is not simply metaphysical or logical (what is done is done—otherwise there is nothing to forgive) but phenomenological, and this because of its *singularity.* That is why this phenomenology of time is a modification of Husserl, not a simple rejection, for the past offense must also be retained. A murdered child can never be replaced even though parents may have another child; the memories, the family keepsakes, the photographs, the atmospherics of a home destroyed by an arsonist can never be replaced, even though a house with the same market value can be constructed on the same lot; the grief caused by disloyalty to a friend or a spouse in the past lasts a lifetime even though one may never be disloyal again.

Still, as Levinas says in a powerful text on forgiveness *(pardon),* we can "give the past a new meaning,"[15] "repair the past," by retelling the story of the past in a new narrative. We can put the past in a new perspective, which *frees* or opens up the future. Here is where we think it enough to call upon hermeneutics and leave Rome standing. In this text Levinas has in mind what he calls "the discontinuous time of absolute youth"—a time to which

I will return in the next chapter—that is, the discretely different existence of the parent and the child in which the child represents a new beginning, a new and separate life that does not bear the sins of the parent. But the discontinuity of time can be applied as well to the lifetime of a single individual. If I am forgiven, I am given a new life and become like a child because my past is given a new interpretation, which is the phenomenological truth behind the extraordinary metaphysical claim made by Damian. The rush of the past into the present made possible by retention is interrupted, and I am sufficiently separated from the past as to be allowed to breathe again. Forgiveness gives us time to breathe by effecting a kind of sacred discontinuity with myself. As Levinas says: "This recommencement of the instant, this triumph of the time of fecundity over the moral and aging being's becoming, is a forgiveness, the very work of time."[16]

The time of Husserlian phenomenology proves to be necessary but not sufficient as regards both forgiveness and confession: the irremissible retention of the past is necessary to forgiveness, lest we fall into the embrace of Damian's alluring hypothesis, but if the past is not somehow altered, it becomes an obstacle to *forgiving,* where the deed should be somehow wiped away by the one forgiving, even as the continuous flow of the present into the past proves to be an obstacle to *being forgiven,* where some kind of discontinuity or breach with the past is required in order for the offender to get a second chance. Levinas, like Kierkegaard—both biblical thinkers—introduces a Cartesian theme into his thinking of time as an event by treating each moment as a *new creation,* which allows the past to lapse and life to begin anew. The time of forgiving is metanoetic time, the giving of a new time, a gift of time, of a new beginning, like the dream of restoring a virginal time. Forgiveness is a giving of time—*pardonner: donner le temps*—a metanoetic time, in which all things are made new. Otherwise "how then can we live?" (Ezek. 33:10).

Unlike his medieval antecedent, Levinas gives the undoing of the past, the reversibility of time, a purely ethico-phenomenological rather than a metaphysical sense. Levinas would think that Damian's hyperbolic heart was in the right place, that he rightly loved the Good beyond being, but he does not share Damian's appetite for speculative argumentation or his love of power. Still, Levinas would hold that what Damian was getting at should be approached in terms of a rigorously *ethical* event:

> The paradox of forgiveness lies in its retroaction; from the point of view of common time it represents an inversion of the natural order of things, the reversibility of time . . . it permits the subject who had committed himself in a past instant to be *as though* that instant had not passed on, to be *as though* he had not committed himself. Active in a stronger sense than forgetting,

which does not concern the reality of the thing forgotten, forgiveness acts upon the past, *somehow* repeats the event, purifying it.[17]

Forgiveness reverses the past, not because it changes it "physically," as it were, but because it transforms the past in and through an event. Forgiveness alters the significance of the past by a kind of holy hermeneutics (which looks a little devilish to the philosophers) that gives it a new meaning and thereby repairs the past. Forgiveness does not alter the past *itself,* as in Damian—which would undermine the very need for forgiveness—but the *meaning* of the past, the *event* of the past, while preserving the past offense. That is why forgiving differs not only from annulling the past but also from forgetting: the past *itself* must be *conserved* ("retention") and given a new sense:

> But in addition, forgetting nullifies the relations with the past, whereas forgiveness conserves the past forgiven in the purified present. The forgiven being is not the innocent being.[18]

The past undergoes a change of sign, as Husserl might say, into the mode of the *as if,* as Levinas says, which allows us to put the "neutrality modification" to work in a more heartfelt way than it is employed in *Ideas I.* It is henceforth *as if* it never happened. Hence, from the perspective of the sinner, the past is not *forgotten,* which would simply annul our relation with the past and destroy our responsibility, nor is it *distorted* and manipulated, which is what happens in revisionist history, which is always written by the oppressor, nor is it *undone,* as in Damian, which is a beautiful thought for God, for the One who gives forgiveness unconditionally, but does not quite do for one who has given up every defense and assumed unconditional responsibility. Rather, the past is conserved and "cleansed," which means reinterpreted and taken up into the event. On Damian's account, the deed itself would have been washed away *(munditia),* while on Levinas's account, the deed has been cleansed, but not washed away. The past has been repaired by being re-understood. Beyond merely re-describing the past, but short of physically undoing it, forgiveness "cleanses the event" or repairs it by "repeating" the past *as forgiven.* While the past is not actually altered, forgiveness permits the sinner "to be *as if* that instant had not elapsed, to be *as if* the subject had not committed himself." Forgiveness releases us from being and sets us free for the event. What Damian would permit in an unqualified sense as part of the unlimited power of God, Levinas casts in the mode of the *as if,* which marks the past with a new sign. But, as Gibbs points out, for Levinas the power to alter the past is not invested in the sinner—who would thereby retain all the powers of an autonomous agency—

but in the one who is sinned against: "It is FORGIVENESS that changes the past, *not* repentance."[19] Now since, as Levinas argues in *Time and the Other,* time is not my doing, not the achievement of the ticktock of internal time-consciousness, but the accomplishment in me on the part of the other who represents an absolutely unforeseeable future, then the gift of forgiveness from the other belongs to the way the other, in forgiving me, gives me time. By releasing me from my past, the other gives me a new past and hence a new future.

O FELIX CULPA

This analysis also enables us to understand another part of the paradox of forgiven time: the privilege of the sinner over the righteous, which is the more radical—and more anarchical—reason for preferring the tax collector to the Pharisee (as opposed to prizing him for his humility, for his *not* sinning, which is how the story comes out in Luke). For in this same text from *Totality and Infinity,* Levinas goes on to grant a certain "distinction" or eminence to the sinner, a certain "surplus of happiness, the strange happiness of reconciliation, the *felix culpa,*"[20] which renders being forgiven a higher state than that of having remained innocent all along. What Levinas says reminds us of the three parables in the New Testament, according to which there is more joy in heaven over the lost sheep who is found than over the ones who never strayed, or over the lost coin that is found, or over the lost son who returns home with his tail between his legs. Indeed, in describing the forgiven falling as a *felix culpa,* Levinas is citing the Latin expression in the Easter vigil liturgy which refers to the happy fault of Adam's fall that was worthy to have been given such and so great a Redeemer: *O felix culpa, quae talem et tantum meruit habere Redemptorem.* The human race is better off *"post ruinam,"* having sinned and been redeemed and thus lifted up by the grace brought by Christ than it would have been in remaining all along in the state of nature, *integritas naturae,* in which case Christ's coming would not have been precipitated.[21] "O truly necessary sin of Adam," the liturgy says, "that is wiped out by the death of Christ" *(O certe necessarium Adae peccatum, quod Christi morte deletum est).* Levinas does not hesitate to invoke this central Christian narrative—and there is none more central—as a model for forgiveness, in virtue of which there is a higher grace in redeemed humanity than in the innocence of Eden, in the forgiven misdeed than in steady loyalty to the law, even as a scarred tissue is stronger than the unwounded flesh, which is also why converted sinners make passionate saints.[22] In the same way, I would add, adults who have come to grips with their finitude are to be preferred to the childish innocence of Eden before they ate forbidden fruit.

THE KINGDOM'S STROKE
OF GENIUS

At the end of *The Gift of Death,* Derrida cites the passage from the second essay in Nietzsche's *Genealogy of Morals* in which Nietzsche is explaining the genesis of what the West calls justice from a fairly bloodthirsty sense of economics, of the balance of payments, of an eye-for-an-eye accounting.[23] Nietzsche, who has an eye out for the system of payments in which the offended gets "retribution" (payback) from seeing the offender suffer, sees this at work in the Christian logic of sacrifice or "economy of salvation." Because the offense given God by sin is infinite and thus far exceeds any means of repayment at our disposal, it has thrown humankind into the bonds of an unpayable debt. God must be repaid, preferably with a blood sacrifice, but we do not have the funds on hand to repay him. Accordingly, God sends his Son among us as a scapegoat to supply the missing payment, Nietzsche says, "paying himself personally out of a pound of his own flesh." In the crucifixion, God repays God. The debt is discharged in the only way possible: someone must suffer—that is the coin of the realm in the economy of salvation—and suffer infinitely, given the measurelessness of the offense. Seeing the Son, his own Son, suffering on the cross, seeing the agony and the blood, witnessing this spectacle of divine suffering, satisfies the Father's need to be repaid. And this, Nietzsche says, "from love (can you believe it?), from love of his debtor." That, Nietzsche says, is "Christianity's stroke of genius."

I think Nietzsche is right about this. This story—which probably gets its most extreme formulations in Anselmian economics, in *Cur deus homo?* and in various "penal atonement" theologies—runs throughout the Christian tradition in varying versions, some tougher and some more ameliorated, as its central narrative, from St. Paul to the present. If it fits in with Paul's sacrificial frame of mind, I do not see how it fits into the frame of mind of the kingdom. For the coin of the realm in the kingdom is forgiveness, not suffering, where the event of the gift is distinguished from an economy of exchange; or rather, the only coins with any currency in the kingdom are lost coins, and the only economics are usually quite mad expenditures without reserve. In the kingdom, the sons we meet are lost sons over whose return the father rejoices. In the story of the Prodigal Son, the father does not sit down and calculate just how much suffering he should inflict on his errant son for his prodigality but is prodigal with forgiveness; indeed, the idea that seeing the son the suffer would in some way constitute a payback to the father would clearly be abhorrent to the sort of father portrayed in this story. It would be abhorrent to any father or mother worthy of the name, which is why it is unworthy of the name of God. It is a priestly story that turns on priestly sacrifice, and it stands at odds with the radicality of forgiveness in the kingdom sayings.

The story got its start in a brilliant leap of the Pauline imagination, and it captured the fancy of the Christians at Antioch and then gradually spread around the ancient world, obliterating alternate interpretations of the death of Jesus along the way, getting incorporated into the gospels that got to be chosen for the canon, conquering the older church at Jerusalem, and gradually conquering Rome itself. Paul was a religious genius—Kierkegaard would hate my saying this—but his reading of the death of Jesus as a sacrifice contradicts the figure of the "father" in the kingdom as the father of all good gifts, as a person of loving care, of rejoicing in the son who returns, who gives us daily bread and tells us not to be anxious for the morrow.[24] When the prodigal son returns and says, *metanoo,* I have turned around, the father throws a party. That is how events work. He does not send his son to be crucified as a just repayment of his outraged sense of justice.

The sinners we meet in the kingdom are forgiven, even as Jesus forgave his Roman executioners—which is the sort of reversal we have come to expect in the kingdom. Sinners are protected from stoning, even preferred, not crucified, and the preference shown them leaves the noses of the righteous out of joint. Paul's sacrificial narrative, which is more of a Yahwist tale of retaliation than a story of Elohim's benign design in creation, does not sound much like a kingdom saying. It is too bent on a balance of payments, on a retribution that approaches revenge; it takes too much pleasure in pain, is far too un-gift-like, too unforgiving (too "priestly," Nietzsche would say). It may be mainstream Christianity's stroke of genius, but it does not belong to the stroke of genius of the "Way," of the kingdom, which is, as Hannah Arendt says, the genius of forgiveness, what we call the genius of the event.

It may be the story that caught on and gained the upper hand in the tradition, but it was not the only Christology to be found in primitive Christianity; the "sacrificial" death of Jesus was not the only story that was being told.[25] His death was also interpreted in the early church as a *prophetic* death, not a sacrificial one, that is, the death of a just man who took a hit for telling the truth, for speaking the prophetic word, for contradicting the world and interdicting its hardness of heart with his parabolic stories of the kingdom. It was the "world" that made Jesus pay—not God—for contradicting the world. It is the world that thinks in terms of paybacks. In this sense Jesus died because of the sinfulness of the world, not in sacrificial exchange for wiping out the debt of sin or to offer the devil a ransom. Jesus came into the world and brought to the world the paradoxical word of the *Abba* and the kingdom, and so the world received him not. In fact, the world positively hated what it heard, hated this madness of the gift and this kingdom of forgiveness. He came into the world and contradicted its ways, and the world made him pay for that. The system of payments belongs to the world; it is one of the defining marks of the world, one of the defining features of the rule of the world, even as priestcraft, thinking in terms of rigorous sacrificial exchange, is sheer and utter worldliness (economics), even though it is engaged in celestial commerce in the exchange of heavenly wares. But the rule of God, of the *Abba,* is an event, is marked by the gift and forgiveness.[26] In the next chapter we will also discuss the obscenity of treating suffering as a coin, because deep and radical suffering is an ir-reparable loss, a purely ruined time that, as an event, does not belong to the time of the world.

Abba, forgive them, for they do not know what they are doing. Forgive these unrepentant Roman soldiers, who mock and torture and kill, and who are not the least bit sorry. Now *that* sounds like the kingdom. *That* has the ring of paradox of an event, of the weak force of God, of the power of powerlessness, of a sacred anarchy, of the parabolic excess of the kingdom. That is the way things work in the mad economics, the an-economics of a sacred anarchy, where abuse is returned by love, where offense is met with forgiveness, where Jesus completely disarms the Grand Inquisitor with a kiss, where the strict accounting system in the economy of exchange is thrown into confusion and disarray by unaccountable, impossible gifts.

I leave it to the professional (strong) theologians to sort these things out about the "theology of the atonement" in their annual meetings, and to the theological powers-that-be to convene their councils and administrative boards to excommunicate the dissidents and outsiders for their heterodox views, for the latter would surely weaken the power base of the *exousiai* and endanger their income. That is how the powers-that-be earn a profitable living off the crucifixion. As for myself, I am content to be a humble *Extraskriver,* a supplementary clerk, as Johannes de Silentio said, making notes on the theo-poetics of *the* impossible and collecting fragments of a weak theology for a possible concluding unscientific postscript to a lengthy but, I fear, disorganized treatise on a sacred anarchy over which, in fear and trembling, I constantly pray and weep.

THE PHARISEE AND THE TAX COLLECTOR

Let us now revisit this wonderful story one more time, which indeed we will never tire of retelling. Two men go up to the temple and stand before God, the one, by any human reckoning, an honorable man who honors the law, who could, if anyone could, withstand the scrutiny of good and evil, the calculus that weighs them against each other, and the other, by anyone's reckoning, a sinner. But by going up to the temple, they stand before God, *coram deo,* as Augustine would say, the undeconstructible giver of all good gifts, and not before the bar of the law, *coram lege, Vor dem Gesetz,* which calculates and weighs merits. By going up to the temple, they submit themselves to the rule of the gift, the realm in which giving is not the giving of reasons *(ratio reddenda),* not a weighing or reckoning of comparative merits and demerits. In the kingdom of the gift, every human measure, every economy, is suspended, and the only rule is God's rule, which is the rule of justice, not of the law, which means the rule of the gift. Before the law, there is all the difference in the world between these two men. But before the Gift, where God rules, the God who makes the sun of his love rise upon the righteous and the sinner, the distance between them is leveled. For the father loves the son who has been loyal to him all the days of his life even as he rejoices in the son who has come home. This also goes for mothers and daughters, who also get to go up to the temple and tell their versions of the story. The Pharisee gives God praise for the sins he has escaped, not by his own resources but by the bottomless grace of God, while the tax collector, who gives up every defense of his past, casts himself upon God's bountiful mercy.

Now in a final, farcical twist, allow me to insert two more figures into this famous evangelical scene, which I have already disturbed by admitting women into the temple. The first is Peter Damian, *monachus peccator,* taking numerous notes in Latin on what unfolds before him, in which he speculates on just what God could do to heal this tax collector if he took it into his divine mind and divine goodness and divine omnipotence to do something for the man, which, Peter thinks, he just might include in a letter he is writing at the moment to the monks at Monte Cassino. The second is Rabbi Augustinus Franco-Judaeus, the author of *Circonfession,* variously known as Reb Rida or as Saint Jacques,[27] in a dark, distant corner of the temple, taking illegible notes in Christian Latin French, who is struck by the undecidability of the scene, by the madness that has leveled the difference between the tax collector and the Pharisee, by the incalculable effects of the gift in this scene, which he thinks he may use in a book he is currently working on to be entitled *Pardonner le temps,* which his American friends suggest be translated *Forgiven Time.*

ELEVEN

"Lazarus, Come Out":
Rebirth and Resurrection

And do not bring us to the time of trial
and deliver us from the evil one. (Mt. 6:13)

DEAD MAN WALKING

Once, during the time that Jesus was using Bethany as a base of operations, staying with his close friends Mary and Martha, he had left
town for a short spell when Lazarus, the brother of Mary and Martha, became ill. The two sisters, whom Jesus loved, sent him a message to return at
once. By the time Jesus got back, however, he found that Lazarus had been
dead for four days. At his approach to Bethany, Martha had gone out to
meet him on the road into town and as much as rebuked him for having
been away at this critical time: "Lord I know that if you had been here, my
brother would not have died." Mary, it seems, would not even meet him
and came out only after being entreated by Martha and Jesus. Together the
three went to the tomb where Lazarus was laid and, as the gospel says very
movingly, "Jesus began to weep." He was touched to his heart by the loss of
his friend, by the inescapability of death, by the grief that engulfed them
all. Then he cried to the tomb, "Lazarus, come out." And in one of the
New Testament's most famous scenes, out came the dead man, walking—
reborn to a new life by the words of Jesus.

To be sure, the author of the gospel of John, writing many years later
and from an ultra-high Christological perspective, one that tries to make
the Jews look bad and the new religion look good, has orchestrated this
story into a messianic message to the Jews who rejected Jesus. It was not, according to John, that Jesus was unable to get back in time. Rather, he in-
tentionally stayed away from Bethany for two more days, during which
time Lazarus died. In John's redaction, then, Jesus is not subject to the lim-

itations of time and space but purposely manipulates them. As Ernst Kase-mann says, "He permits Lazarus to lie in the grave for four days in order that the miracle of his resurrection may be more impressive."[1] Jesus took this delaying action in order to give Lazarus time to die so that he could use this death as a way that the Son of God could be glorified. If so, that was a particularly tough way to treat his dear friends Mary and Martha, not to mention poor Lazarus lying moldering in his grave, and all in order to glorify himself. One can only imagine that Lazarus must have grown exceedingly anxious the next time Jesus left town.

What event stirs within this story? What event is harbored there and kept safe, sheltered but also concealed?

Exactly what original historical core lies behind this narrative is impossible to say.[2] As we have had occasion to mention more than once, in a theology of the event, we have to make do with archives, not the *arche*. Perhaps Jesus revived the flagging spirits of a man at death's door and was able by the magnetism of his person to persuade Lazarus not to pass through that door but to come back, to "come out." Perhaps Lazarus died in the flesh, but the return of Jesus healed the spirit of Mary and Martha and gave them the strength to go forward, to "come out" of the dark abyss of grief. Jesus and other spiritual masters over the ages undoubtedly move about in the ambiguous ambiance of the psychosomatic and, without being expected to magically "cure diseases" or magically resuscitate corpses, they are indeed able to "heal" whole persons.

The tears of Jesus, his weeping in the face of death and loss, is the most human-and-divine component in the story. He weeps because he is too late, because his friend died before he was able to help. This story takes us back, not to divine omnipotence, but to the powerlessness of God that we identified in the original Genesis creation myths, to the limitations with which God him- and herself is confronted, to the inoriginate and formless void, the *anarche,* that seeps into the very bones and interstices of creation and causes everyone, human and divine, so much trouble. The Genesis myths provide for the limits under which all action, divine and human, takes place.

But if it is hard to say what historical core lay behind stories like this, it is not as difficult to discern the event that they harbor, that they visit upon us. We have said from the start that the kingdom is marked by amazing metamorphoses, stunning reversals and transformations, the radical capacity for reinvention. Now among all such anarchic events in a world that is defined by its unforeseeable irregularities there is none more amazing than the raising of the dead, the transformation from death to life. Rebirth and resurrection—that is what the kingdom is all about. The stories of Jesus are stories of exorcizing evil spirits, healing the lame and leprous, transforming water into wine, and, most amazing of all, of one who raises the dead. Then above even that, he is himself raised.

This singular transformation from death to life contains in a preeminent and paradigmatic figure the very substance of what Jesus is always doing in all of his works and deeds; it describes, in a word, what he is always teaching in all of his sayings. Even as the creative act of Genesis is a movement from a lifeless wild to a world teeming with life, the work of Jesus is to assist in the reversal of death into life. That is what he has been sent by his *Abba* to do; that is what constitutes the coming of the kingdom. Jesus is the locus of divine transformation, the prophetic center of the transformative energy of the kingdom, by coming in contact with which all things are made new, which is what the kingdom means. Thus, in the person of Jesus, the work of the two creation myths is continued and extended—for through him things are remade, refashioned in accord with their original and congenital goodness. Where there is sorrow, he brings joy; where there is illness, health; where there is death, life. "I am the resurrection and the life. Those who believe in me, even though they die, will live." Even as Elohim brought forth life from the lifeless void, Jesus restores life where there is death. He is always about his *Abba's* work.

What is the event harbored inside the literal narrative? Once again we come back to the difference between religion and magic. In keeping with the distinction I am maintaining between name and event, I do not understand this story to reveal the *arche* of divine super-power that intervenes on natural processes and stands them on their head, reversing the decomposition of a rotting body, which is the literal narrative. Rather, it lays bare, first, the powerlessness of God before grief and sorrow—and "Jesus began to weep"—and our impotence before pain and death and suffering; accordingly, it reveals the finitude, the *an-arche* in which we are all steeped, always and already. Still, it is not a story of death and defeat but of life and rebirth—those who believe in him shall live—in the face of inescapable death, even though they really do die. So this literal story of resuscitation contains the uncontainable miracle of rebirth.

Miracles belong to the sphere of a theology of the event, not to a mythology of magical occurrences. The miracle narratives should not be read as exercises in magic. The whole idea of my poetics of the event is to provide an interpretation of these miracle stories that neither reduces them to supernaturalism nor inflates them into a metaphysical tour de force. They are not magic, but they do disclose something miraculous, the event of the impossible, which can be explicated in terms of a poetics of the impossible. A "miracle" harbors an event of a deeply incarnate kind. A miracle is constituted by its head-turning and astonishing power to make things new, to transform our lives, to give us hope where there was despair, love where there was hate, companionship where there was only solitude. Miracles are figures belonging to the wondrous stories of the Scriptures, but the Scriptures belong to the poetics of the event. They are to be read for their imaginative power to portray the life-transforming character of the kingdom, not literalized as if they were giving eyewitness reports of supernatural occurrences.

The gospels sing songs of the legendary charism of Jesus. Magic, on the other hand, involves being really released from the limits of space and time, being effectively *disincarnated,* actually exempted from bodily constraints and suspending the laws of nature, allowing us to dream away the constraints imposed by finitude. Magic relieves us of our finitude and even of our mortality. A magician can resuscitate corpses or be himself physically resuscitated; he can shrink cancerous tumors, cause physical wounds to mend, pass through solid walls, walk on water, and calm stormy seas. A miracle is an element in a narrative, a component of a poetics of the event, but belief in magic results from the mistake of *not* suspending your narratival disbelief, of taking miraculous narratives literally. A miracle requires the hard work of hoping in the impossible; magic simply waves a wand or a word. Miracles are narratival elements that are crudely mimed by magic, which is a psychical and religious fantasy. In magic, we take a striking narrative that captures our fancy, like the story of Lazarus, and fantastically transcribe it from imaginative to real space, from an event to an entity. Belief in magic results from failing to understand a literary genre, from locking the meaning of a miracle narrative inside its literal content, which would be like investigating whether the sorts of things Stephen King writes about actually occur, or whether there really was someone named "Jane Eyre" who really could have heard someone named Mr. Rochester call the name "Jane" from miles away across the moors, which ruins the story.

A miracle has hermeneutical authenticity on the plane of the event by figuring in a purely narratival and imaginative space a transforming experience in our lives, whereas magic is the superstitious transference of narrativity to reality. Miracle stories teach us something about our real life, even while they occur in poetic space, on stage and screen, in literature and art; whereas magic distorts real life and leaves us holding the straw of illusions when we come back to the prose of our senses. Resurrection is miraculous, but resuscitation is magic. Healing is a miracle, curing real diseases by the wave of a hand or a word is magic. The opposite of a belief in the miraculous is despair and despondency, the tragic sense that we are trapped and everything is hopeless; the opposite of belief in magic is good sense. The miraculous has the structure of what is called in deconstruction *the* impossible; magic is a cruel trick that is simply impossible. Magic is an illusory strong force; a miracle is the genuine but weak force of God.

I am trying to quash the idea of an intellectual somersault in which a metaphysical argument is mounted that shows that there is no trick too great for an omniscient, omnipotent, and beneficent being, not even resuscitating a corpse, since such a super-being who can create *ex nihilo* can do pretty much anything whatsoever that it comes into his or her super-head to do, a notion I rejected earlier on in this book. Just as miracle stories stir the souls of plain folk, such metaphysical demonstrations stir the souls of archi-theologians of divine omnipotence like Peter Damian. Such proofs at once prove too much—they make light of the *tehom* and the *tohu wa-bohu,* the formless void with which we must all cope, starting with Elohim himself, to whom we have attributed a certain limit on his power—even as they prove too little, because they are themselves abstract, unpersuasive, and, if I may say so, impotent arguments, metaphysical paralogisms, logically problematic from top to bottom, a point that Kant demonstrated over two centuries ago.

My purpose is to put the epoche (as in putting the kibosh) on all such magic and mental metaphysical leaps and to pursue a low-flying path that clings closely to the phenomenological surface of the event. My purpose is to release the event by finding the phenomenological "form of life" that stirs in these stories, to identify the sense of time and space, of embodiment, affectivity, and lived meaning that give them such enormous significance for us. Their significance is their head-turning, life-transforming power to make all things new, what I have been calling their "metanoetic" power, which is, I propose, the phenomenological core of what theology calls a miracle, which I am wiring up with what Derrida calls "*the* impossible." So the question I am posing in the present chapter is this: If we are unwilling to reduce Jesus to a divinely sponsored magician, if "rebirth" and "resurrection" do not mean magical resuscitation, what do they mean? What event is sheltered there and kept safe? What does it mean to speak of living even if you die? What is the phenomenological cash value of this transformation? What is the saving power of the kingdom? The question, in short, is not, How is such magic physically or metaphysically possible? but rather, What event do these stories harbor? What do these stories *mean?* Hermeneutics is all. All things flow in a river of meaning.

SALARIES VERSUS SALVATION

Lazarus was gone, irreparably swallowed up by death and irreversible time, or so it seemed. Having arrived back in Bethany too late, Jesus wept. But Mary and Martha had come to expect the impossible. They expected Jesus to turn things around, to reach back, deep into time's clenched jaws, and restore the life of Lazarus, not just on the last day along with everyone else

(John 11:24), but that day, that very day in time, in Bethany. They wanted Jesus to save Lazarus from death, from the dreadful days of the last week, which had been a nightmare for the sisters. They wanted, not eternity beyond time, but a new time, one in which Lazarus lived again.

What then is the phenomenal structure of the event of new time that is portrayed in the story, a time cast as a phenomenon of rebirth and resurrection? Clearly, this event is intimately linked with the preceding discussion of the event of forgiveness, which also seeks a new time, a "forgiven" time, in which we are also released from the sting of the past. The new time is to be distinguished from ruined time, from which we seek to be released, "pardoned" in a more comprehensive and sweeping sense from the past even if we are not guilty of wrongdoing, issued a kind of "general pardon" in which we are released, not from sin but from the destructive power of pain and death, in order to be able to go on. Just as sin requires forgiveness and release, suffering requires relief. Ruined time is evil, and we need some way to be delivered from evil, not just when evil is the evil we have done, but when evil is visited upon us from without and through no fault of our own. Lord, rescue us from the forces of the evil one, release us from the ruins of evil, from evil's ruined time.

In order to analyze ruined time, I will re-enlist the aid of Levinas, who makes a critical distinction between the "time of the world" and the "time of salvation," which corresponds to our distinction between the time of being and the time of the event. So in the spirit of improving Christian and Jewish relations, I propose to read the story of Lazarus by way of Levinas, to use Levinas to read a story from a gospel of love that does not much love the Jews. The "world," Levinas says, is "the possibility of wages," of a salary *(salaire),* whereas the exigency of suffering and ruined time is for salvation *(salut).* In the time of the world, which is the time of economic calculations and market exchanges, we can be compensated for our time or for the losses we suffer. But in the time of *salvation,* or "messianic" time, there is no question of any counterbalancing economic consideration, but rather of being redeemed or reborn. That is because ruined time is irreparable, and when the loss is incalculable or irreparable, the only repair is rebirth and a new time, which in religious discourse we call *salvation.* In the time they keep in the kingdom, there is no table of equivalences, no scale of compensation, nothing that can repay a loss. In the kingdom every loss is infinite, so something else must be done. Incalculable suffering is an event of another sort that overflows any possible measure, not an event that bears good news, but an evil that exceeds any measure.[3]

Thus, in the order of the event, what is required—indeed, the only thing that is possible—is "salvation," being saved *from* ruined time *for* a new time. Salvation, rebirth, renewal are events of time, time's most treasured events. They do not mean to be saved *from time* in order to pass one's time in eternity—Lord, we know Lazarus will rise on the last day, but that is not what we need now—but to be given a new time. Rebirth does not mean to escape from time into eternity but to transform *time,* to make time new. Not salvation *from* time, but a time of salvation, time as rebirth and salvation, time as an event. Salvation means a new beginning, a new life, a new influx and incoming of God's own good time, a new day, a future, the coming of the Messiah who saves us and gives us hope, today. So in keeping with the book of days that we have been writing, we are dedicating a chapter here to the new day. Like a death followed by resurrection, which is the figure of a new time.

The need for rebirth holds true for both sin and suffering, for both the evil that we do, which requires forgiveness, and for the evil that is done to us, which requires salvation. In either case, what we want is to be saved from the time of the world, which makes us "do time" for the evil we perpetrate, or which "robs us" of time in sickness, suffering, and "untimely" death. Forgive us our trespasses and deliver us from evil. That is what we pray daily. Deliver us from evil, from the evil one who stalks us, from evil itself, if it has a self, from the evil that we cause and from the evil that befalls us. Levinas is addressing phenomenologically the same problem, *mutatis mutandis,* that concerned Peter Damian in a high-flying metaphysical way: how to reach back across the temporal distance into the past and repair what has gone irreparably wrong.

IRREPARABLE LOSS

By ruined time I mean irreparable loss, and by that I mean irredeemable suffering, suffering lodged irremissibly in the past, suffering and loss beyond repair. The irremissible past is a time of ruin, *mal-heure,* a bad time that seared and scorched the souls of the dead—in Auschwitz or Belfast, in Kosovo or the West Bank, in all the Auschwitzes, Kosovos, and Belfasts recorded in history and unrecorded, from time out of mind—and then slipped away forever, without repeal or compensation, without redemption or any possible remuneration. The time of irreparable loss cannot be worked into an economy or a balance of payments. The sufferings of the irrecuperable past were not undertaken voluntarily in exchange for the reward that follows, like a long period of punishing, grueling physical training in preparation for an athletic event, or of prolonged study for an examination in order to win a degree. This is not the pain of "sacrifice" willingly undertaken in exchange for a higher good, part of the economy of no pain, no gain. Irreparable loss is not even the suffering, involuntarily suffered, that finally issues in an unforeseen and unintended reward, like a childhood passed in stinging poverty that forges strength of character in adulthood. Of this irreparably ruined and irrecuperable time we will never be able to take a long view and say, "It was all worth it." There is nothing that makes it worth it, nothing with which it can be "compensated." This is not the pain that pays off, but the misery of pure loss, of disaster. A child born with AIDS, whose life is short and painful, which no one can justify or compensate, which one can only try to comfort or ameliorate. The innocent victim of a crime, like a child inadvertently caught in a crossfire between warring drug lords on an inner-city street. The child, who is a special emblem of new life, is a special victim of death and the sort of loss that makes theodicy an obscenity. Or the years of confinement, abuse, and humiliation suffered by people who are unjustly imprisoned, which cannot be returned or restored, for which there cannot be any compensation, whatever monetary considerations the government may later offer, whatever honors their advocates might later bestow on them for their courage. Indeed, is not the strongest argument against capital punishment the irreversibility of the state's action when the accused is innocent, which unhappily happens all too often and has occasioned more and more caution among state legislatures in recent years? The lost time, the ruined life, is gone forever, without return, without remuneration. The misery and grief descend upon us with impunity and then vanish like thieves in the night. The damage is done, the forces of destruction make their escape, and we are left without recourse, defenseless against the destruction, abandoned to wanton violence. Lazarus lies cold in his grave, and Jesus, too late, weeps.

We pray to be kept safe from such evil, to be guided around the fiery pits of the evil one who stalks us. For there is no good face to put on the face of faceless evil, of irreparable loss, no theodicy to explain ruined time that is not an obscenity. As Lyotard has said, the Holocaust is pure death, not a "sacrifice" of the Jews in exchange for something higher. The very attempt to offer some sort of rationale or explanation for the Holocaust, to fit it into some larger account or Providential design in which it is but a moment, is an obscenity that defiles the very names of each of its victims, of each one, taken singly, one by one.[4] The decision to name the dead, one by one, by their proper names, on the Vietnam War Memorial, is a powerful way to recognize the infinite loss of each one where the death toll is quantitatively staggering, a way to accommodate both the large numbers and the qualitative infinity of each of these little ones. Imagine, then, a memorial that would contain the names of every victim on both sides of every war, of every evil, of every natural disaster, in every place and every time. Imagine a record of all such evils, recorded and unrecorded. Imagine as a counterpart to the Book of Life, a Book of Death.

Irreparable loss escapes the order of economy in a way that is precisely contrary to the gift: rather than an expenditure without return, an unlimited giving, we suffer an uncontainable destruction without repair, unlimited taking away, without compensation, remedy, or redress.

At the end of these remarks, I will point out the implications of this analysis for the possibility of another style of doing history, which is the record of evils done and suffered, a history other than the one that Levinas denounces as totalizing in the Preface to *Totality and Infinity*, a messianic or eschatological history of radical historians, or of what Edith Wyschogrod calls the "heterological" historian.[5] Such a history, which allows itself to be haunted by the voices of the dead, whose unrequited misery and persecution cry out for justice, would be the record of the unrecorded, the archive of the anarchivable and anarchical, the treasury of irreparable loss. It proceeds from the recognition that history and justice come too late for the dead and persecuted. Justice, however swift, is not swift enough to return to the moment of their misery and redress it. History, however sweeping and radical, cannot erase the misery of their lives. That impossibility is what drives the radical historian who would, were it possible, reach back into the past like Damian's God—whose metaphysical madness is always a limit case and an odd inspiration for me in these investigations—and undo the evil done to the dead, bringing them back to life, like Jesus raising Lazarus or the widow's son in the Gospels. But radical history is not God (and even God is not up to what metaphysics calls God). All that history has to offer is fragile memory and meek mourning, a poor substitute for omnipotence, but the only one available, and that is what Benjamin means by a weak messianic force, which is not far from what I am calling the weak force of God.[6]

How, then, are we to console the dead who are long since dead? How console the survivors who live on in inconsolable grief? How are we to repair irreparable loss? That is the impossible demand that is placed upon us, the demand for a time of salvation that would be no less a salvation of time, a remedy or renewal that time builds into itself. Lord, if you had been here, our brother would not have died. Those words of Martha describe a fundamental quality of time ruined and of time forgiven, and hence of time itself.

SOLITUDE AND SUFFERING

The point of maximum intensity is only reached at *the* impossible. How to forgive the unforgivable? How to hope when all is hopeless? How to repair the irreparable? To pursue this impossible question, I invoke Levinas's analysis of suffering in *Existence and Existents*.[7] To be something existent, to be a subject, is to be fashioned from the abyss of *il y a* but then, starting out from there, to be held captive there *(y),* in being, where it has *(il a)* us, from which we need to escape or be saved. That is why Derrida says, commenting on this text, that the existent requires "forgiveness" and this "from the threshold of existence,"[8] a pardoning of our being, not of our deeds, from the prison of being and the solitude of the present. The existent is "fatigued" by the exertion of the act of existing, its fatigued movement being made up of stops *(arrêts)* lurching discontinuously from instant to instant, punctuating the "anonymous flow of existence" (*DEE,* 48/ *EE,* 34), tearing or ripping out little commencements or beginnings from the flow without beginning (*TA,* 32/ *TO,* 52). The time of suffering is fractured, each instant starting out from itself *(à partir de soi)* all over again, a new beginning, a momentary triumph in constant need of renewal, as in the Cartesian and Malebranchian conceptions of time (*DEE,* 126–29/ *EE,* 73–75). Each instant is a stop *(arrêt),* but this stop does not threaten annihilation, but rather an "irremissible," inescapable bonding to being or existence, so that one cannot escape the steady beat, the ticktock, of existence in which the existent is established.

The discontinuity of time is intensified in suffering. The passing of Lazarus is the presence of pain, which causes Jesus to weep and Mary and Martha to cry out for relief. We are caught up in an "event of irremissible engagement, without the possibility of being redeemed" *(sans pouvoir de rachat)* from it (*DEE,* 49/ *EE,* 34), which is revealed in a "state of purity" in pain:

> In pain [*peine*], sorrow [*douleur*], and suffering [*souffrance*], we once again find, in a state of purity, the definitiveness [*definitive*] that constitutes the tragedy of solitude. (*TA,* 55/ *TO,* 68–69)

Physical pain represents "in a state of purity" the bond of the subject to itself, the tragedy of solitude, and this because:

> [P]hysical suffering in all its degrees entails the impossibility of detaching oneself from the instant of existence. It is the very irremissibility of being. The content of suffering merges with the impossibility of detaching oneself from suffering. . . . In suffering there is an absence of all refuge. It is the fact of being directly exposed to being. It is made of the impossibility of fleeing or retreating. . . . In this sense suffering is the impossibility of nothingness. (*TA,* 55–56/ *TO,* 69)

In physical suffering I am riveted to being, panicked by the absence of refuge, haunted, not by death but by the impossibility of death, which would be an escape, forced to live on. The painfulness of pain lies in a sense of unremitting assault, of being pinned to existence, backed against the wall of being (*TA,* 59–60/ *TO,* 72). It is one thing to stand tall against overwhelming forces and take a beating, like a virile Heideggerian being smashed to pieces (they all love it!). But it is quite another thing to be beaten senseless, reduced to "crying and sobbing" *(le pleur et le sanglot),* turned inside out, reduced from a subject to subjection, my activity thrown in reverse into passivity, which is what happens when suffering "attains its purity."[9]

PARDONING OUR BEING

Enter *l'autrui.* Or, Jesus returns to Bethany.

Death does not relieve the tragedy or "curse" of solitude because it cannot truly "give" *(donne)* the future; death cannot give time (*TA,* 68/ *TO,* 79). It shatters the solitude by shattering the subject (*TA,* 63/ *TO,* 74), by crushing this solitary being (*TA,* 65/ *TO,* 77). There is nothing that death or I can do to transcend my solitude. I cannot give transcendence to myself. I must instead be *for-given* my solitude by the other. The radical breakup of my solitude, the release from solitude—that means to be pardoned *(c'est être pardonné)* (*DEE,* 144/ *EE,* 85), particularly in the biblical sense of *released.* The givenness of my being, in which I am steeped, can only be *forgiven by the other,* not forgiven for a wrongdoing, but released from metaphysical solipsism—like the coming of the other in Husserl's *Fifth Cartesian Meditation* (of which this is a transcription), like Jesus coming down the road to Bethany (for which this provides a phenomenology).[10] The other comes and forgives me, not by forgiving my trespasses but by releasing my existence, unchaining not my doing but my being, even as the arrival of Jesus in Bethany releases Mary, Martha, and Lazarus. *The coming of the other is time and forgiveness.* Jesus comes too late to avert physical death, but the event he visits upon them, the comfort he gives them, gives them time, and maybe it also gave Lazarus time, if it rallied his spirits, giving them all a new time, a new birth. In Greek metaphysics, time is a mark of our insufficiency and limitation, a changing image of the plenitude of eternal being. But in Levinas's biblical view, our being is all too sufficient and self-sufficient, all too saturated with presence and replete with itself, and time is "a remedy for the excess of the definitive contact [with being] which the instant effects." Time is salvation *(salut)* from the present, welcoming the other.

The more gravely I am weighed down by the present and the more I am pressed in upon by the present, the sharper and livelier the hope. Hope flourishes most when the situation is most hopeless:

> The irreparable is its natural atmosphere. Hope is hope only when it is not permitted. Now what is irreparable in the instant of hope, is that this instant is itself a present [*c'est son présent même*]. (*DEE,* 153/ *EE,* 89)

What is more "irreparable" than the bond of the present to itself in suffering, when the subject is riveted to itself in pain and loss? Even if the future, the subsequent course of moments, brings relief, consolation, or even "compensation," still "the suffering of the present remains like a cry whose echo will resound forever in the eternity of spaces" (*DEE,* 153–54/ *EE,* 89–90).

The moment of suffering cannot be entered into a system of exchange; or, when it is—you can always sue a person or an institution that causes you pain and injury—that occurs only in what Levinas is calling the time of the "world," the "time of economy" (*DEE,* 154/ *EE,* 90), the time of the lawyers. That transaction is marked by the breezy lightness of an "I" that presides over our conscious acts and barters with them. The ego is on hand at a *later* moment to collect its "compensation" for the misery of an earlier moment that has, by then, acquired a certain cash value, deciding what it will take "for its trouble." In that way suffering is indemnified instead of "releasing *(détendent)* the torsion of the instant upon itself," letting the intensity of pain be what it is, insisting on or standing in the pain of the *instans,* in order to pass over into a new time. The "profound exigencies" of the pain are nullified because they are bought off by economics. When pain is taken in its irreparability, the ego is contracted to the instant, arrested, mired in the misery, the *malheure,*[11] of the moment, and only then experiences the hopelessness, the no way out, which is really the *only* way out, if the Messiah arrives in time.

"The world is the possibility of wages," Levinas says, the ego willing to strike a bargain. The time of the world dries all our tears, and it enables us to forget "the unforgiven instant and the pain for which nothing can compensate" (*DEE,* 154/ *EE,* 90)—by putting them in the bank! But it is precisely this unforgiven, uncompensated quality of suffering that strips away the mask of the ego with which it masquerades in the world and exposes the fraudulent lightness of its mundane transactions. It is just this suffering for which nothing can compensate that constitutes the "torsion" and "exigency" of the moment—what pain and sorrow and suffering of the moment truly demand—which gives it the force or energy to "unleash the future," to open up the future and make a new beginning possible. In the time of the world, Levinas says, the "engagement in existence which is effort is repressed, compensated and amortized"—like a "mortgage"—"instead of being repaired in its very present" (*DEE,* 154/ *EE,* 90).

In the kingdom, we require salvation *(exigence du salut),* an an-archic an-economy in which living through irreparable loss releases the event of a new birth. The "world" is through and through "secular" *(laïque);* that is, the world is the place where everything is for sale and everything has a price, where everything is done for a salary or a wage. That is a corruption from which religion itself is hardly immune. Religion is not religious when it is reduced to rewards gained for expenditures made, which is made plain by Derrida's critique of the "celestial economy" that is invoked in the gospel of Matthew against the Pharisees.[12] There the light that illumines the children of the light simply makes for more enlightened investors, buying stocks in goods that will not rust or perish.

Hope transpires in—or unleashes—another time, a time of rebirth, resurrection, and salvation. In this time, it does not suffice to wipe away a tear (Rev. 21:4), or to avenge a death, or to make things "even." Instead, Levinas says, "no tear should be lost" *(DEE,* 155/ *EE,* 91). We do not want to wipe away these tears but to preserve them, for they have a saving power, and they are precious beyond any price. Likewise, he says, "no death should take place without resurrection": it is not a question of avenging death, of putting a price on a priceless life in a wrongful death lawsuit, for example, or of counting ourselves even by exchanging death for death in war or capital punishment, say, or of exchanging eternal life for temporal death, but a question of following death with resurrection. The exigency of suffering is not for compensation but for salvation *(salut non salaire);* the exigency of ruined time is to be given a new time. What is required and demanded *(exigence)* is a double gesture in which the subject first undergoes irreparable loss and then, *without losing the loss,* in a precisely *non-indemnifying* movement, *demands repair,* not as a worker demands a wage, but as death demands resurrection or rebirth.[13]

Levinas makes contact with the poetics of the event, the poetics of the impossible that is at work in the time of the kingdom, with the phenomeno-logic of rebirth and resurrection, which requires a transformation that shifts us into another "messianic" time. Messianic time, the time of salvation, applies no less to sin, which requires forgiveness, than to suffering, which requires rebirth. Either way we get a new start, "pardoned" from evil suffered, from which we require release, and from evil committed, from which we require forgiveness. Salvation always means a new time, a new beginning, a fresh start, new life, rebirth, the continuation and multiplication of the original work of creation described by the priestly author where Elohim looked upon all the things he made and declared them good.

MESSIANIC TIME: THE TIME
OF SALVATION

My goal is a phenomenological transcription of Jesus' mighty deeds when he called Lazarus from his tomb or raised the widow's son and the daughter of Jairus—a transcription that resists the temptation to turn them into deeds of magic.

> [Jesus] cried with a loud voice, "Lazarus, come out!" The dead man came out, his hands and feet bound with strips of cloth, and his face wrapped in a cloth. Jesus said to them, "Unbind him, and let him go." (John 11:43–44)

How, then, are we to do the impossible, to repair the irreparable? How are we to change the past, according to the dream of Damian? How to resurrect the dead? How are we to hope if it is hopeless? What hope for life is there in death? But is that not what hope is? Is that not when hope really gets under way, really gets some traction, when all is hopeless? Still, small comfort that, to know that hope is *the* impossible, for how are we to do that? Hope, for Levinas, is not the market-wise ego trading in his most marketable moments precisely for the highest price. "The true object of hope is the Messiah, or salvation" (*DEE*, 156/ *EE*, 91), the coming of Jesus down the road to Bethany. I need the Messiah, a paraclete, a consoler, to console me. I need a healer, to lay hands on me and release me from myself. Like Lazarus in the grave, I need the Messiah to lift me up, to call me out of the grave. I need the miracle of the caress, which is the first form in which we can identify the saving event:

> The caress of a consoler, the lightness of his strokes in our pain, do not promise the end of suffering, do not announce any compensation, and in their very contact, are not concerned with what is to come *afterwards* in economic time. They concern the very instant of physical pain, which is then no longer condemned to itself, is transported "elsewhere" [*ailleurs*], by the movement of the caress, and is freed from the vice grip of "oneself" [*soi-même*], finds "fresh air," a dimension and a future. (*DEE*, 156/ *EE*, 91)

The "doctor," the healer, beyond being an empirical individual, "is an a priori principle of human mortality"[14]—that, at least, before the advent of HMOs, which reassimilate the healer back into economics—even as Jesus, beyond speaking prophetic words, speaks words of healing. A lot of people exercise this healing power without ever having seen the inside of a medical school, while a lot of medical school graduates know very little about healing. The alterity of death, the alien force that menaces the sufferer, far from stripping me down to my authentic *Selbstsein,* pries open my solitude, opening up an "appeal to the Other, to his friendship and medication."[15] The threat of death elicits hope in the Other, in the messianic coming of the Other.

Salvation requires the time of the consoler, who lifts the subject out of himself by way of the caress, whose soft and gentle stroke, whose light embrace, *effleurer,* opens up the self-enclosed subject to the other, allowing an even momentary escape. Blessed are those who mourn for they will be given comfort, and blessed are those who give comfort (Matt. 5:4). The time of the consoler is to divide the self-enclosed instant of mourning in half and share it. If I may be forgiven a repetition, a self-citation, I would put it thus:

> Therapists and clinical psychologists and counsellors of every stripe belong [to] . . . the paradigm of the "healer," people who "drive out devils," usually by "laying on hands." I imagine what is behind such old jewgreek stories is the power of a man or woman of compassion to calm a troubled heart, to take the hand of the troubled one in their hands, literally to lend them a hand, to be on hand. They did not have anything special to say to them or the miraculous power to suspend the laws of nature. They did not know anything special. Who does? But they talked with their troubled friends through long nights or lonely days, hand in hand, flesh in flesh. It is not what they said *(le dit)* that matters but the saying *(le dire)*—and the flesh of their hand. That was the miracle of what they did. . . . The hand heals of itself, because it is a hand, because it is flesh. We all have the hands of healers and we can all heal by laying on hands. . . . It is not a question of finding an answer to the night of truth but of sitting up with one another through the night, of dividing the abyss in half in a companionship that is its own meaning.[16]

To divide the abyss in half, to break open the tragic solitude, to divide the instant by sharing it between us, that is the time of the consoler, of the paraclete, of the Messiah, of the one who is to come.

Economic time moves along the circle of the same and so cannot effect a genuine release from the present. Only the Messiah can save us from our *malheure,* our miredness in the misery of the moment and open up another time. Salvation can be effected only from without, from a movement that is initiated *elsewhere,* by a laying on of hands by the other, by the coming of the Messiah who has come to save us, who is defined by, and is interchangeable with, salvation: "that is the Messiah or salvation," that is, the Other, and who thereby opens the ego to the future, to time and the future, which it cannot give itself. The voice that consoles, the hand that gently touches, the vow to be with you through this long night, to stay by your side, the promise, absolute and unconditional, to be there when you awake: *c'est le Messie ou salut.* That is the messianic time and the salvation, the coming of the Messiah for which we pray and weep, *viens, oui, oui,* as Derrida says (prays, weeps), the coming of Jesus for whom Mary and Martha prayed and wept. That is the weak force of God, not the strong force of magician.

The future that thereby opens up, the new time, is more than a "simple future," more than the foreseeable future that we can reasonably expect on the basis of present investments. For pain does not belong to secular time; it cannot be bought off or paid for *(ne rachète pas). Pace* the Utilitarians, you cannot justify the misery *(malheure)* of an individual by saying that it purchased the happiness *(bonheure)* of many. *Malheure* and *bonheure* do not constitute an economy; that is a category mistake. The rewards of the future do not wipe out the misfortune of the present. There is no justice—here Levinas means a "retributive" justice—wise enough or swift enough to "repair" the present, which has been irreparably ruined. Such "repair" of the irreparable as there is, is the effect of salvation, is the exigency of salvation. Salvation requires the reparation of the irreparable, beyond retributive justice. Reparation requires *the* impossible. "One should have to return to that instant, or be able to resurrect it" (*DEE,* 156/ *EE,* 91). Reparation requires time-travel, a miraculous return to the instant to repair the irreparable, to resuscitate the dead, the way Lazarus was resuscitated. Reparation requires something like the dream of Peter Damian, that Damian be *somehow* right about the alterability of the past, which is the time of *the* impossible! Beyond the wise but calculative justice of Solomon, who knew how to split the difference and was willing to roll the dice, reparation requires the caress of the Messiah himself, for whose appearance we can only hope against hope. Reparation requires messianic *hope.*

> To hope, then, is to hope for the reparation of the irreparable. It is to hope for the present. (*DEE,* 156/ *EE,* 91)

The hope is for *now.* Martha believes that Lazarus will rise on the last day, but that is not what she is asking of Jesus. It is not a question of hoping to escape time, but of hoping for a new time, for a new day and a new birth. Hope is not a hope in an afterlife, for gaining entrance to the "world behind the scenes," the *arrière-monde,* which would be no less worldly or secular for Levinas, for the very reasons pointed out by Derrida in *The Gift of Death.* World-time is any economic time whatever, which includes the "celestial economy." An after-world-time called eternity, "which does not seem to us indispensable," Levinas says (*DEE,* 156/ *EE,* 91), belongs to the calculations of the world, not the kingdom. Heavenly rewards are celestial salaries, not the event of salvation. Salvation is situated, not in a heavenly pleasure but in pain of the present, "the very instant of pain." It is effected when pain is not compensated but comforted, healed, released, caressed, in the balm of flesh softly stroking flesh, or simply with words of comfort, or more simply still with wordless companionship; and it transpires, not in eternity, but now, in an hour or two, or a long night of anguish and suffering, or many nights. Is that not the essence of time? "Is not the future above all the resurrection of the present?" (*DEE,* 157/*EE,* 91–92). To hope, is that not to hope in the coming of the Messiah, of the Other, *autrui,* in what Derrida calls the incoming of the other *(l'invention de l'autre)?*[17]

In *Totality and Infinity,* the miracle of resurrection is the miracle of the child, which is a new beginning, a new life—an "event"!—humanity's ongoing internal auto-resurrection. Life is passed on to life, thus enabling life to elude the snares of death, which arrives too late, for life has already moved on to the child and a new life begun with which death will never catch up.[18] The exigency of suffering is the subject's "very need [*besoin*] of time," what Levinas later called the "desire," as opposed to the need, of the time of the other. But it cannot "give itself" this alterity; it cannot give itself time. We require the Messiah to call us forth from the tomb. The subject cannot save itself, even as it cannot effect the movement of time by itself. Neither time nor salvation, neither rebirth nor resurrection, is possible in the solitary ego. Levinas means thus to overturn the Augustinian motif (which made its way into Kierkegaard and Heidegger), when Augustine said, do not go elsewhere *(nolite foras ire),* for God is here, within us. For Levinas, on the contrary, what is here *(ici)* is a prison from which we hope to be released by the coming of the Messiah, who does indeed come from elsewhere *(ailleurs),* from the other *(autrui),* like Jesus hastening back to Bethany.[19] The pardoning extends the saving hand of the healer who heals the subject trapped in the tension and intensity of suffering, of the consoler who gives the subject consolation.[20] And when it is we who are offended, then we occupy the messianic position; we are the ones who have been waited for to come and release the other.

Release us from our trespasses as we release the other. We must offer the dead salvation or resurrection, even as we require rebirth and resurrection. We stand alternately in the position of the trespasser who waits for the Messiah and in the position of the Messiah himself. As if *we* were the Messiah for whom the past was waiting, which is the Benjaminian idea to which we now turn: the present is the messianic time, and we are the ones for whom the past, the dead, were waiting, and we must offer them such salvation as memory provides. The para-logic, or the ethics, of the tear, the poetics of the impossible, does not call for wiping away every tear but for seeing that "no tear is to be lost, no death without resurrection."

HISTORY AND THE DANGEROUS
MEMORY OF SUFFERING

The idea of messianic time—of rebirth and salvation—in turn opens up the idea of a messianic history, of a salvation history, not in the sense of a history of salvation, but of history as offering a form of salvation and rebirth, providing another variation on the death of Lazarus, where the historian is cast in the role of the messianic healer.

History always runs the risk of romanticism and nostalgia, of a voyeuristic desire to revisit ancient sites, to observe, invisible and unnoticed, as bygone worlds unfold. That desire feeds the historical novel or film, seducing us into suspending our disbelief so that we may walk again the streets of medieval Europe, pray again in Gothic cathedrals, dine with the landed gentry of Austen's England, and slip unnoticed into vanished worlds. That knowing relation to the past, as Levinas would say, is too possessive, too much aimed at reappropriating or reconstituting the alterity of the past. A more radical history, one written with prayers and tears, in which justice precedes truth and ethics precedes *episteme,* is constituted by the impossible desire to repair the irreparable. That does not mean to wipe away every tear (Rev. 21:4) but to see to it that no tear is lost—like Benjamin's chronicler who records every event, however minor, or like the biblical God, who keeps watch over every hair on our head (Luke 21:18). A radical salvation history records every loss and remembers every forgotten death, proceeding in the belief that memories are dangerous.[21]

Damian's dream conceals a profound reflection upon history as a response to the sighs of prayers and tears now long gone. We are carried by the wings of historical desire above the constraints that time and being place upon us, to "brush history against the grain," as Benjamin says,[22] across the—alas irreversible—flow of moments, to a moment that is no longer there so as to undo the damage and destruction, to stay the hand of the oppressor. But, as we learn from Levinas, the past is not to be altered or annulled but to be "saved." The time of the consoler, I contend, enters—by an impossible gesture—into the structure of writing history with prayers and tears, driven by the desire to console the dead and grant them resurrection. Note well that we speak of "resurrection," which is miraculous and a weak force, not of "resuscitation," which is a magical trading in strong forces.

The historical act is to record the tears of the dead, to keep them in our heart *(re-cordare),* even and especially when their deaths are lost and unrecorded. The historian re-cords with the feeble tools of memory—not a passive, reproductive memory, but an active, heartfelt, searching and re-

searching memory, which understands that history is the archive of countless tears and untold deaths. Radical history is a weak messianic power, re-
flecting what we have been calling the weak force of God. Matthew says
that God has counted every hair our head (Matt. 10:30), an operation that
I would say very beautifully describes the biblical God, as opposed to the
impassive, apathetic, tearless *nous noetikos* of the Athenians, who thought
of God in terms of a self-thinking thought. I would assign that divine operation to the desire of the radical historian,[23] who would reach across the
uncrossable space of time and comfort those who weep and are persecuted,
to tell the stories of the untold dead and thereby to offer them resurrection
in the hope that the flames of hope would flare up from their ashes. Radical
history is the record of unjust and unrecorded deaths, the archive of those
without *arche,* who have vanished without a trace.

In "Diachrony and Representation," Levinas says that I am commanded by the "mortality" of the other, by his very weakness and vulnerability. That is what we are calling here a weak force. I am commanded, he
says, "not to remain indifferent to his death, to not let the Other die alone,
that is, to answer for the life of the other person"—lest I become an "ac-
complice" in that death (*TO,* 109). The authority of the Other is his pre-
cariousness, his strength is his weakness, his power is his powerlessness, in
perfect accord with the poetics of the impossible. But if I am commanded
by the "mortality" of the others, then I am no less commanded by their actual death, commanded *post mortem,* after their death, like Lazarus lying
cold in his grave for four days. The command that comes to me from the
living Other, "Thou shalt not kill," comes no less from the dead, comes no
less from those who have already been killed. The command of the dead
comes back to me from the grave and fixes me in its gaze. The blood of the
dead cries to us from their graves like the blood of Abel, making us all responsible, making us all the children of Cain.

Benjamin speaks of the "chronicler who narrates *(hererzählt)* events
without distinguishing between major and minor ones," who believes that
"nothing that has ever happened should be regarded as lost to history." For
a "redeemed mankind," Benjamin says, every moment in the past is deserv-
ing of memory and citation.[24] Every moment of the past is to be remembered, the way someone is remembered in our prayers. We must become
like saints who remember *everyone* in their prayers, the whole world, even
the least of God's creatures. The link between memory, recording, keeping
in your heart, devotion, and prayer is never stronger than in this moment of
remembering the injustices suffered by the dead. Prayer is not a way to ask
God to exert his mighty power to make things different; it is a way to draw
strength from our weakness by recalling in our hearts every slain and fallen
innocent.

That is why the memories of the historians are dangerous, which is what Johann Baptist Metz calls, in a magnificent expression, "the dangerous memories of suffering," the memories of countless tears and unaccountable untold deaths, the record of unrecorded evils.[25]

The historian has come to supply the voice of these mute dead, to sigh their sighs, to weep their tears, and to offer them the weak force of a resurrection that comes too late. *Sero te amavi.* If the dead constitute those whom Levinas calls the "subjectivity poorly heard in history,"[26] then the historian must make them better heard and amplify their cries. The historian of prayers and tears must in a certain sense rise to the revisionist historian's challenge that Lyotard denounces in *Heidegger and "the jews,"* to let those who were gassed to death step forward and register their complaints, to let the untold dead of nineteenth-century Ireland register their complaints against the English from the grave, to transform them from the *differend* to which the revisionist historian would confine them, into historical plaintiffs, with new voices and new life.

The history denounced in the Preface to *Totality and Infinity* was a totalizing or "teleological" history, an economic affair in which the countless deaths were cost-accounted as a good investment in the progress of the world spirit, the high but affordable toll the Spirit must pay for advancing from one *Gestaltung* to the next. The sufferings of the past would eventually bring a good return or "result," and Auschwitz would be but a challenging "example" of a deeper and more sweeping law. Teleological history is one in which many an innocent flower is trodden on the way to *savoir absolue,* very brilliantly explicated in "Result," the central chapter of *The Differend.*[27] Thus instead of opposing eschatology to historiology, one would speak instead of an eschatological history, a salvific or saving history of prayers and tears. This would be a history that goes beyond history, to that *eschaton* beyond or beneath the sweep of world history, in order to take heed of the innocent flowers, the tender shoots that are trampled under the boots of teleology.

Eschatological history deals in the bottomless infinities that are the stuff of a poetics of the impossible, the priceless ones who cannot be counted in quantitative terms, who are the concern of the odd para-logic of the countable and unaccountable that we encounter in the New Testament and with which we began these remarks. Eschatological history would attend to the secrets of the heart that are unknown to the "judgments of history," secrets that are revealed only in the "judgment of God,"[28] in the *kardiognostes,* the God who knows the human heart (Luke 16:15). Rather than entering irreparable loss into a long-term gain, eschatological history would let the loss be a loss and seek, by an impossible gesture, to comfort the dead. The historiographer, Levinas says in *Totality and Infinity,* is a survivor who cal-

culates the contributions of the dead to the living, a historical cost accountant who computes and recapitulates the investments of the past in terms of
the return they make in the present. In the time of the scientific historiog-
raphers, "particular existences are lost [*se perdent*],"[29] taking a position that
perfectly reproduces the one struck by Johannes Climacus against Hegelian
world history. But as long as I am alive, as long as I have breath enough to
protest, I take a "leave of absence" *(congé)* from world history, I postpone
the reckoning against which I will be defenseless in death, when I will not
be on hand to explain myself. To be alive is to safeguard the secret of the self
from the calculations of the historiographer, where no hair is uncounted,
no tear is lost, no grief allowed to dissipate in the economy of historiographical reckoning. After that, I depend upon salvation by the other.

This work of the radical historian is to offer the dead not compensation
but salvation, an impossible salvation, for its caress is not made of flesh but
of memory and re-cord, its gentle hand is stretched out to those who no
longer receive its touch. As an event, the act of radical historical memory
does not effect an entitative change but gives a new meaning. The historian
cannot, of course, caress and give hope *to* the dead, save them or release
them from the present of their suffering, now long gone. The radical historian can only offer hope and a future *for* the dead, on their behalf, pleading
on their behalf for the future, for a new birth, new life, for such resurrection as death allows. That means that historical desire is directed at an
opening on the future that would not be the "afterwards [*après*] of economic time," like returning the art stolen from the victims of the Holocaust, but the future of hope. That would come about *as if* we had assisted
at the sufferings of the past, *as if* we had been on hand to lend a hand to
their grief, like the consoler *"qui effleure dans la douleur,"* and to offer them
a word of consolation. What remains now is to *hope,* and to hope, Levinas
says, requires first to be driven into a state where, calculatively speaking, it
is hopeless, where the odds are hopelessly against us, to hope against hope,
as St. Paul says. Hope is not hope if you can see what you are hoping for on
the horizon. We need hope when we cannot see the way out. Hope requires
blindness. Hence, the work of the historian is the impossible one of giving
comfort to the dead by way of memory and hope for the coming of the
messianic time.

By memory we mean not a Hegelian memory that interiorizes, that
sucks up the interiority of the dead into the present and makes it our own,
but a memory like mourning, which preserves the distance of the dead,
their fallen tears, the irreducible loss, then offers hope for the future they
will never know. The historian sees to it that their lives are a gift without return, because they cannot return, a gift to the future, so that their memory
makes its impossible that the future would ever close, that we would ever

give up or give in to the odds against us. The irreparability of the past goes hand in hand with the open-endedness of the future, with the radicality of the *to come,* so that the more intensely we experience the tension and intensity of the past, the more radically we pray and weep, *"viens, oui, oui!"*

For as Walter Benjamin says, not even the dead are safe from the assaults of the antichrist, whom the Messiah must subdue.

The correlate of the irreparable past is the irrepressible future, the future of the "come," the *"viens"* of the *"à-venir,"* the unforeseeable, unprogrammable future, whose unforeseeability is directly proportionate to the irreparability of the past, which was at the least neglected by Benjamin. That is the new time, the time of hope, the time of the gift, beyond calculation and reparation, the future that converts the past into a gift without return, the new life that follows death, like a newborn child. Only the dead can give a gift without return. A genuine gift must be given beyond my death, for an absolute future that will never become present. That is possible for the dead alone. For the dead alone cannot be compensated, cannot draw some secret, unconscious payment for their expenditures. So they alone stand able, by the strange dynamics of the gift, to give a gift without return and reappropriation. Their gift alone outstrips all economy. The future of the gift alone provides for a "resurrection" that, beyond resuscitation, alone grants new life.

Levinas was early on thinking of the time of the other in terms of the *child,* the gift of fecundity. If, with a heart full of despair, one asks, What can come after Auschwitz, or after Kosovo? How is poetry or even life itself possible after Auschwitz or the Middle East? the answer is always the child. The child, who is a paradigm in the kingdom of God—for one must become like a child to enter the kingdom—is no less a paradigm for the historian, for the children are the ones to come in history no less than in the family. History is being written *for* the children, *to* the children; and it is to the children that we call "come," for whom we pray and weep, *viens, oui, oui.* History is written *in* prayers and tears, *with* prayers and tears, *about* prayers and tears, now long gone, praying and weeping over the coming of the Messiah, praying for the time of salvation, for the messianic time which will have recounted unaccountable death.

Suffer the little children—to come.

Come out, Lazarus. It is as if when Lazarus comes out, and they unwrap the strips of cloth by which he is bound, a child steps forth.

THE TEARS OF GOD

The figure upon which I seize in the story of Lazarus is that of Jesus weeping, which is the figure of the weakness of God. It is impossible to believe the Johannine contrivance that Jesus purposely stayed away for two days and also to believe that he would then weep. That is just bad storytelling. There is nothing divine about it, but a purely human, all too human love of displaying power. The only thing that explains Jesus' weeping is that he could not get there in time. The divinity is in the weakness, not the power. It is the weeping that is divine, not this high Christological sleight of hand, as if Jesus would be the source of immense human suffering in order to stage a display of divine might. But the weeping is the weakness of God, the tears of God, which is the compassion, the healing, the restoration of lost life. The divinity is the compassion he would have extended to Lazarus, the long night at his bedside, had he gotten there before his death, which is the weak force of God. The divinity is compassion he extended to Mary and Martha in the days after his death, the courage he gave them to go on, the joy he taught them to take in a brother well-loved, now lost, but always loved.

Behold the lilies of the field; how beautiful they are, but they only last for a day. How much more beautiful our days, which the Lord God, blessed be his name, has multiplied many times over. Over the next weeks and months, Jesus and the two sisters would have laughed over many a good story about the foibles of Lazarus, his good heart, his love for his sisters and his friends. Gradually they would gather the strength to come out from the dark grave of despair and go on, like the sun that rises every morning, like the new day that never fails to come, like the new tide, the new moon, the new spring—all figures of the new time. Jesus always had the gift, the grace, to see things that way, God's gift, God's grace. That was precisely who Jesus was, and that is what everyone remembered about him.

TWELVE

The Event of Hospitality: On Being Inside/Outside the Kingdom of God

[Jesus] said to her [the Syrophoenician woman],
"Let the children be fed first, for it is not fair
to take the children's food and throw it to the dogs."
But she answered him,
"Sir, even the dogs under the table
eat the children's crumbs." (Mark 7:27–28)

THE HATTER'S WEDDING FEAST

Who gets into the kingdom of God? If it is made up of the people of God, are some people God's and some people not? If it is a time of messianic peace and forgiveness, of rebirth and of making all things new, where do I apply? What are the admission requirements? Who decides who gets in and who is left out? Is there limited seating? Does it have borders, an inside and an outside, and are there border patrols? Do they have a problem there with illegal immigrants? Do I have to be Christian? Jewish? Islamic? Must I believe in God? Is there an official language that I must learn to speak?

When you look through the kingdom texts for guidance about the conditions of membership, the results are very surprising—which is, of course, not very surprising by now. Remember that in the kingdom God rules, not the world, which means that there the human, all too human rules of entrance requirements, etiquette, and human hospitality hold no sway. From a strictly human point of view, the whole place looks a little mad or anarchical, like all hell has broken loose—holy hell, of course.

"When you give a luncheon or a dinner," Jesus said, "do not invite your friends or your brothers or your relatives or rich neighbors, in case they may

invite you in return, and you would be repaid. But when you give a banquet, invite the poor, the crippled, the lame, and the blind" (Luke
14:12–14).[1] Can you actually imagine such a thing? That is just crazy, sheer
madness. The kingdom of God is a like a dinner party that is spurned by all
the invited guests, who make up all sorts of excuses and send their regrets to
the host. As a result of this rejection, the host orders the doors thrown open
to everyone: "Go out at once into the streets and lanes of the town and
bring in the poor, the crippled, the blind, and the lame." Then, finding
there is still room, the host orders—I would say almost comically—that
passersby be compelled to enter and share in the feast (Luke 14:15–24).
Think about that—being dragged off the street into a dinner party or, on
Matthew's version, a royal wedding reception (Matt. 22:1–14), made to eat
and drink and celebrate when I was only running an errand and just happened to be passing by! If I am to toast the bride and groom, should I not at
least know their names? Who can imagine such an absurd dinner party,
such an unimaginable wedding reception, such impossible hospitality? If
you let yourself visualize this scene, it is as anarchic, as mad as any hatter's
party attended by Alice.

Such hospitality has all the earmarks of the event, all the disequilibrium
and excess of the event that stirs within the name of God and that mobi-
lizes a kingdom exposed to God's rule. The kingdom of God is not a mundane circle, assembly, or club, and belonging to it is not a matter of membership in a worldly organization but a way to respond to the event. If the
event calls upon us, addresses and invites us, then we enter the kingdom by
responding to the invitation in spirit and in truth. Ask and it shall open to
you, or answer, because you have already been called. Membership in the
kingdom is the work of the event, not of human admission procedures.

The Gospels show that even Jesus evidently had to struggle with this
one.[2] He had told the story about the "good Samaritan," the implication
being that Samaritans belong in the kingdom just as much as Jews from
Galilee, even though they honored Yahweh on Mount Gerizim and not in
the temple in Jerusalem. He had healed the servant of the centurion, a
God-fearer sympathetic to the Jews but not a Jew, the implication being
that the kingdom could be even extended to Roman soldiers, provided they
loved God. But above all, he said, "Listen to me, all of you, and understand: there is nothing outside a person that by going in can defile, but the
things that come out are what defile" (Mark 7:14–15). That was an unconditional statement, a "principle" that there are no earthly rules of purity, no
outer, entitative circumstances, no mundane signs that mark one for the
kingdom. There is nothing about one's place in society, nationality, gender,
dress, or eating habits that makes one unclean; impurity proceeds only from
an impure heart. We defile ourselves by sin alone. Mark has Jesus say this

just after he had given the Pharisees a piece of his mind about their preoccupation with traditions, externals, and rites at the expense of the real meaning of the word of God. When the disciples, who are made out by Mark to look a little slow-witted in grasping the point of his sayings, ask him to explain what he means, Jesus repeats the point graphically: what goes into a person is digested and goes out into the sewer (no mistaking the meaning of that), but that is not what defiles anyone. "For it is from within, from the human heart, that evil intentions come," and that is what defiles us (Mark 7:17–23).

But then, in the very next verse of the same chapter, Jesus meets the Syrophoenician woman, who made him, shall we say, eat his words. She is not a "separated" Jew, like the Samaritan, nor a male Jewish-sympathizer like the centurion, but a woman and a Gentile; and her daughter is "unclean" (which might just mean she has an irregular menstrual cycle). But in Matthew's gospel, Jesus first puts her off: "I was sent only to the lost sheep of the house of Israel" (Matt. 15:24). And then, in both Matthew and Mark, Jesus puts her down in the harshest and most biting terms: "Let the children be fed first, for it is not fair to take the children's food and throw it to the dogs." A brutal insult comparing a Gentile woman and her daughter to dogs.

With a humble and deft stroke, the woman makes Jesus eat every word: "Sir, even the dogs under the table eat the children's crumbs" (Mark 7:28). Jesus is forced to back down from his exclusionary view of the kingdom and to understand for himself the implications of his own views about purity of heart which, he had just complained, the disciples were slow to understand. There is nothing about one's external situation that makes one unclean—or a "dog"—but only what proceeds from the heart—and the heart of this non-Jewish woman melts him down. Jesus is forced to put into practice what he has been saying about the kingdom, that it really is only the heart that matters—where, on my accounting, the "heart" means our response to the event, under whatever name. Even so, as with the centurion's servant, the healing takes place at a distance, and he does not deign to pay a house call to either the servant or the daughter.[3] But the implication is plain: whether one is a Jew or a non-Jew, master or slave, male or female, none of that makes any difference. The kingdom is everybody's, which is the point that has recently been made on behalf of St. Paul as the "founder of universalism" by Alain Badiou.[4] The kingdom is in the midst of all of us, and we are all in the midst of the kingdom—*all* of us—and it is just a question of saying yes to it. Let the kingdom come, *viens, oui, oui.*

Indeed, one can even go further: when it comes to getting into the kingdom, there is actually a certain privileging of the outsider, a strategic reversal meant to make a point about the kingdom. The conditions of admission to the kingdom are quite unaccountable: the ones who get *in* are the ones who are *out;* on the other hand, the ones who end up left *out* are the *insiders* who did not take the invitation to heart.[5] That is everything that one would hope for from an event, everything you would expect when you are counting on the unaccountable poetics of the event. In the kingdom, God's rule means the rule of "hospitality," where the rules of hospitality are rigorously faithful to the aporetics of the event, which here takes the form of the alogic of welcoming the other. For hospitality, as Derrida likes to point out—here is the short circuit between deconstruction and the kingdom that I am introducing into this discussion—means to make the *other* welcome, which is very much the opposite of what hospitality means in the world. Outside the kingdom, hospitality means welcoming the same, even though it pays lip service to welcoming the other. The world's hospitality, which is carefully calculated and practiced under strict conditions, is extended only to those who are on the list of invited guests, which is made up of selected friends and neighbors who can be counted on to reciprocate. But that is precisely not the coming or welcoming of the other, but rather staying precisely within the circle of the *same.*

In the world, one is always very flattered to be included on a guest list, to be part of the "inside crowd" who have gotten an invitation, whereas on the un-principles applied in the kingdom, such an invitation might not be quite so flattering. The kingdom of God sometimes sounds a little bit like the quip of that famous philosopher Marx (Groucho) that he would never join any club that would have him as a member. In the world, hospitality is constituted by a cozy circle of insiders, by the rules of the club, where all sorts of folks who are different need not apply. In the world, hospitality is a strong force—*hostis + potens,* having the power of the master of the house over the guest—in which one fortifies oneself against the unwelcome intrusion of the other.[6] But in the kingdom, hospitality is a weak force that leaves itself entirely unfortified. In the kingdom, it is the outsiders who are in, just the sort who would empty a room full of the respectable types, who would send realtors' sales signs shooting up all over what Kierkegaard called Christendom. In the world, hospitality moves within a strong chain of reciprocity; invitations circulate back and forth in a closed circle of the same, like a gift exchange, for which, of course, it is but another name. In the world, economy is always passing itself off as generosity, so that the very conditions under which hospitality is possible, the invitation of the other, make it impossible, for the other is precisely the one who is *not* invited. One of the senses of a "community," we should recall, is to build a fortified circle around oneself (*com + munis*) to protect against the coming of the other.

When we call for the kingdom to come, therefore, we are being called upon to push against these limits, to strain against these conditions, to practice a mad and unconditional hospitality, which is impossible. We are asked not just to welcome the stranger who comes knocking at our door, but to seek out casual passersby who had no intention of knocking—while exercising caution about kin and kind. We are pressed to put our own power at risk, our home and our community, to seek out the lame and lepers, outcasts and outsiders. But who would be so mad? Especially after September 11? The kingdom is a gathering of the un-gathered, who are gathered by the event, an assembly of the dispossessed who are possessed by the event, under the several names that the event comes calling.

THE GOD WHO LOVES
THE STRANGER

To be sure, there is reason for this madness, a good reason and a divine madness (in the kingdom the sane are at a disadvantage). In the kingdom, the mark of God is on the face of the stranger, on the "other," not the "same." In the biblical tradition, God is not the object of a speculative mysticism that sweeps us up into an eternal now where we are one with the One, but the one who comes knocking at our door dressed in rags in search of bread and a cup of cold water. This is a very ancient idea in the Semitic world, for after all, in a world of desert wanderers, what could be more important? What is more sacred than what Louis Massignon calls "sacred hospitality"?[7] What could be a more fundamental condition of life and survival? The duty owed the wanderer and the stranger is holy and inviolable, and without it the world of wanderers would perish under its own weight. To provide a place of respite and refuge, to offer bread and water, even to take the food out of one's own mouth in order to share it with the stranger—in short, to make the other welcome—that is the law of the land and the law of God.

Hospitality could very well be taken as the very emblem of morality in the biblical sense, as Thomas Ogletree argues.[8] The traveler who appears at our door bears the mark of God upon his brow. God has signed the face of the stranger and placed him under divine protection. The one who receives the stranger, receives God, "the God who loves the stranger." So when the stranger comes knocking at my door, it is not only the stranger who has come calling, but the event. That same idea shows up again in the beautiful story in the New Testament in which the disciples ask the master, when did we find you hungry and feed you, or find you in prison and visit you, and the master says, whatever you did to the least of mine, you did to me (Matt. 25:35–40).

Once again, Levinas, who keeps his ear cupped close to the music of these biblical scenes, has "transcribed" this idea into terms that philosophers can understand in his analysis of *"adieu,"* and Derrida uses this analysis as the basis of a discussion of hospitality. We, in turn, can make use of both Levinas and Derrida, these two jewgreeks who unfold the poetics of the event, to explore this anarchic site, which decides who gets in and who is left out of the kingdom, who counts as God's people.

For Levinas, *adieu,* from *ad deum,* "to God," has the sense of being turned to God. The *à* in *à-Dieu* represents a turn toward God, not a turn taken by the conscious freedom of an auto-turning autonomous self, but a *being-already-turned* to God, long before the conscious self steps in and takes one turn or another. Hence: here I am *(me voici)* always already turned *by* God *to* God: *à Dieu.* I am promised over to God from time immemorial, long before I would, by my own intentional act, seek or aspire for God, before I even know this name, his inscription on the face of the stranger being how this very idea first comes to mind, how this word first springs to my lips (*DVI,* 7–13/ *GWCM,* xi–xv).[9] No preposition, including this *à* to which we here have recourse, can transcribe or translate my being pre-positioned to and by God, my prepossession by God. No preposition can plumb the depths of the devotion by which I am always already vowed to God (*DVI,* 250/ *GWCM,* 165; *A,* 179/102–103).[10] This preposition *à* signifies a being prepossessed by God—by the event of the infinite—which is designated and proposed by it. When, in prayer and devotion, the subject turns to God, that turn comes as a turning back, as response to a prior address by God, who has already called us. Before I desire God I am already desired by God. The *à-Dieu* is the very diachrony of time, the disproportion of the finite and the infinite, the very being-vowed before any conscious act, which is "devotion to God" (*DVI,* 12/ *GWCM,* xiv; *A,* 180–81/ 103–104; cf. *TO,* 114–20).[11]

As Derrida says, "it is not unusual that at the moment of saying in what the *à-Dieu* consists, Levinas evokes God's love of the stranger. God will be first of all, as it is said, 'he who loves the stranger'" (*DVI,* 250/ *GWCM,* 165; *A,* 180/103). When the stranger is lost in darkness, God makes his face to shine upon the face of the stranger; when the stranger is endangered by the desert heat, God leads him into the shelter and shade of his loving care. The self is always already turned to God, who has in turn turned the self to the stranger, deflected it in a certain way, ordered and commanded the self to the stranger, who bears God's trace and seal. Being turned to the other means a devotion to God that responds without desire for reciprocity, in a love without eros, in a relation without correlation and reciprocity, like the nonreciprocity, the interruption of symmetry and commensurability that constitutes the gift, or death itself. *A-Dieu,* to-God, to-the-infinite, to-the-*tout autre,* who is a positive infinity, an infinite yes, an unlimited *oui,* an event. To respond to the event is to say yes to what separates itself, to welcome and greet what separates itself, whose departure is not different from its coming, and this "deference" is the breath of the *à-Dieu* (*A*, 113/61).

HOW CAN DERRIDA SAY "ADIEU"?

Hospitality is no less central to Derrida's thought, where it is pressed into the service not only of ethics but also of politics. Derrida is very much taken by the "crimes against hospitality that are endured by the wayfarers and hostages of our times, day after day incarcerated or expelled, from concentration camps to retention camps, from border to border, near to us or far" (*A*, 132/71). Politics today, and it seems this has always been the case, turns on the war waged by the same on the other, on the "rogues," the rogue states, and much depends upon the ancient people of Israel's capacity to make welcome the Palestinian other, or the capacity of the Christian West to welcome the Arab and to understand that there are more rogues than you think, where you yourself are the rogue.[12] So the biblical story of this mad wedding feast cannot be written off as an odd or extravagant biblical parable, for it touches upon a crucial political idea, arguably *the* crucial political problem of our times. Exiles and refugees wander constantly across the surface of Derrida's texts, periodically showing up at the door, illegal immigrants in need of help, their solicitous faces pressed against the window like the defenseless scapegoats of the right wing in France and the United States. This is something, Derrida says, that he has at least in part learned from Levinas.[13] These exiled and displaced people—very *biblical* figures, just the sort who are to be invited to the wedding banquet—who lack the wherewithal to lay down their heads, are a constant concern and preoccupation of Derrida's work.

Adieu is a touchstone word for a theology of the weakness of God, a holy word, harboring an event that audibly resounds with God's own name. One could hardly imagine a word that would be more a word of God, more a word from and to God. *Adieu:* (I commend you) "to God" *(à Dieu)*, may God be with you. This word is a beautiful prayer embedded in ordinary language,[14] and it is very precious for Levinas, for upon it, in a real sense, everything turns. But as scandalous as it may seem to Derrida's secularizing, Nietzscheanizing admirers, *adieu* is also very precious to Derrida, for whom it is also a kind of poem and even a prayer in French (*A*, 205), even though Derrida "rightly passes for an atheist" as he says in *Circonfession*.[15] But how can Derrida say *adieu*? How can he mean it? What does he mean? How can we imagine Derrida being always already turned *to God,* by God, if Derrida rightly passes for an atheist? By whom is he turned, and to whom? To whom is he praying?[16] How can this be a word of elemental importance and commanding holiness for Derrida? How can someone who rightly passes for an atheist rightly commend someone to God? Are we to believe that Derrida prays, that he keeps a secret *prie-Dieu* sheltered from the eyes of the world, that Jacques Derrida is a man of prayers and tears? Surely *"adieu"* is just an expression for him, a turn of phrase, a linguistic convention, a matter of semantics, a conventional way to bid farewell in French, especially to a dearly departed friend and sage, whatever it might mean *ad literam.*

The answer lies in the event. For the event that overtakes us in *"adieu"* slips across the border erected by the name of God. On the one hand, how can one say and pray *adieu,* practice the mad hospitality of the kingdom, and not be *in* the kingdom of God? But, on the other hand, how can one rightly pass for an atheist and not be *outside* the kingdom, since the kingdom is God's, which seems very theistic? But then again, is not the kingdom precisely for outsiders (while the insiders who take it for granted are out), and who could possibly be more outside the kingdom of God than one who rightly passes for an atheist? So by the mad para-logic of the impossible, rightly passing for an atheist is no obstacle, and might even be an advantage, while rightly passing for one of the inside crowd could spell trouble. That is possible because the kingdom is constituted by the event that simmers in the name of God, by our response to the event, under whatever name the event addresses us, whether or not it is to the name of God itself that one responds.

One way to put all this is to ask, Can *adieu* be "translated," carried outside or across the borders of the kingdom? Does the kingdom even *have* borders or a border patrol? Going by the story of the dinner party or wedding feast, does it not practice an open admissions or open doors policy? Is one inside the kingdom just by virtue of the very fact of commending someone to God? How can you be excluded from the kingdom of God if you commend someone to God? Is someone like Derrida an illegal immigrant in the kingdom, having been smuggled across its borders undetected? So the question of the dynamics of hospitality *in* the kingdom inevitably passes into and provokes the question of the dynamic hospitality *of* the kingdom. Who is in and who is out? That is one of humankind's most pointed, poignant, and painful questions.

Translation is downgraded by hierarchists (like Heidegger) who make a profitable living out of degrading the derivative vis-à-vis the original. But that is not the case with Derrida, who thinks that the origin is always deferred, that the *arche* has always already slipped away in favor of the archive, so that everything is a translation of an original that was never present and is possessed by no one. For Derrida, translation is an elemental demand of hospitality, requiring us to adopt a new idiom, to speak in a new tongue that can be understood by the stranger—by the *goyim,* the Gentiles. Unlike St. Thomas's famous treatise, Derrida, had he ever been minded to write any such sort of *Summa,* which I sincerely doubt, would rather have written a *Summa "pro" gentiles,* on behalf of the *goyim,* of the others, who need translation, ministering, inclusion. We cannot translate—something idiomatic is always lost—but still we must; and furthermore, it is no loss, because a translation is an expansion and the incoming of something new.[17]

So Derrida might be seen to be working all along on a translation of the word *adieu,* of the event astir in *adieu.* The event is what would be translated, both in the sense of getting it out of its biblical tongue, if you are not a card-carrying member of one of the religions of the Book, into a more universal, open-ended idiom. The translation Derrida seeks is not a question of a semantic transfer, of trading a name for name, but a matter of the event. On the plane of the event, translation is a question of translating *adieu* and hospitality into action, *facere veritatem,* of translating the event into the text of existence by responding to the event. The name of God is the name of a deed, Johannes Climacus says, which means that the name of God contains an uncontainable event that comes calling upon us and requires a response. That is what Derrida calls "an event of translation," the event "of *another translation,* of another thought of translation" (*A,* 205/119).

One of the claims of this theology of the *event* that stirs within the *name* of God, which seeks to release the event from that name, is that the name of an event, of something as elemental and indecipherable as the event, is endlessly translatable into other names. No name can be allowed to have a lock on the event, even the name of God itself, for the event that unfolds under that name comes and goes under many other names.

Levinas says that hospitality demands opening the Torah to all the nations, *translating the Torah,* letting the Torah cross the borders marked by Mount Sinai, opening the gates of Jerusalem to all the "nations." The nations look on this intimate relation of Israel and Yahweh and do not understand the language that these lovers whisper in each other's ear. Hence, this intimate relation, in which each is jealous of each other's affections, must be opened to the peoples, to the third one, so that translation is a requirement of justice and hospitality for the other others, for the third, for we are *all* the people of God. "Is God a God of the Jews only? Is he not the God of the Gentiles also?" (Rom. 3:29). God is not partial. Levinas wants to share the Torah like a gift with the *goyim,* to translate the Torah into Greek, to produce a kind of philosophical Septuagint, for Greek is a universal language for him in which he hopes to translate what he considers the universal, human message of the Torah.

But Derrida keeps pressing a further question on Levinas, how to *translate his ethics of the other into a politics of the other,* how to transport Levinas's biblical ethic of hospitality into a politics of hospitality. Here the anarchic paradox of hospitality becomes a risky business, as risky as raising the dagger over Isaac's outstretched limbs (cf. *A,* 201/117, 204/119), especially after September 11. After all, how can a nation-state, a civil society, which is concerned above all with national security, be hospitable to the other? How do we translate and transport our hope in messianic peace into the "peace process" in the Middle East? What import does it have for Israel's punishing and harsh military occupation of Palestinian lands, which has nothing to do with hospitality to the stranger and everything to do with national self-interest, with preserving the nation's sovereign place in the sun? Must not the ethics of substitution—of giving everything to the other, our jobs and our schools, even the bread out of our mouth, the ethics of being responsible to the other—must that not be strictly confined within the borders of private ethical life? How can a *sovereign nation-state* practice an absolute, unconditional hospitality to the other? Is not national hospitality always subject to conditions, to immigration laws, to security concerns? But then would such a conditional hospitality still be hospitality (any more than "conditional love" would still be love)? Would it not be a disaster to let hospitality out of its ethical confines and make it the basis of public policy? "Thou shalt not kill" sayeth the Lord God, blessed be his name, and that is the sum of the Torah. True enough, but it is also necessary to raise an army to defend oneself and discourage aggression against one's place in the sun. What is the way from the heavenly Jerusalem to the earthly one? Is there one?

That is the *radical* translation sought by Derrida, which requires a deed, a translation, shall we say, in truth and in deed, in the Augustinian sense of *facere veritatem,* doing and making truth happen, bringing it about as an "event." We do not "understand" the word *adieu* by thinking something, but by *doing* something, by letting the rationality of *Realpolitik* be disturbed by the madness of the impossible, thus preventing the political order from enclosing itself in a crust of inhospitable hostilities.

My hypothesis is that making the truth happen, *doing* hospitality, is what *constitutes* membership in the kingdom. Even—and maybe even especially—if one rightly passes for an atheist, so that the line dividing the kingdom and the world is not the line dividing theist and atheist; it is a matter of the event, not of nomination and denomination. That distinction, which is a distinction between names, is relativized in virtue of the endless semantic translatability and deconstructibility of names as opposed to the undeconstructibility of the event that is harbored by these names. That is how, according to the mad hatter's logic of the kingdom, it is precisely the *outsiders* who are *in,* while those who complacently take their membership for granted, who take their invitations to the banquet for granted, find themselves left *out.* Accordingly, and this is the point, the borders of the kingdom become porous, wavering in a kind of "holy undecidability" between theism and atheism, among Christian, Jew, and Muslim; between theology and a-theology, *Dieu* and *sans Dieu, à-dieu* and *a-Dieu* (in the privative sense, as in a-morphous), religion and "religion without religion," and this precisely in the name of the God who loves the stranger.

That is because *the name of God is the name of an event, of an event that comes calling at our door, which can and must be translated into the event of hospitality.* That is something that the beautiful French word *adieu,* this Franco-semitic poem and prayer, embodies *ad literam.* Otherwise, the name of God is a tinkling cymbal and sounding brass, a signifier emptied of the event. Derrida is not out to erase or wipe away the name of God— God forbid!—but to open it up to translation, and by translating it to keep it safe, *sauf le nom,* at least as safe as anything can be, since nothing is finally safe and insulated from risk. That, in the end, is how it is possible for Derrida to say *à-Dieu* while rightly passing for an atheist, to say *adieu—sans Dieu.* Something like this has been done before, by Meister Eckhart, a German mystic who prayed God to rid him of God, while rightly passing for a Dominican friar. The Inquisition went after him for that, but the Inquisition is made up of card carriers in the Ecclesiastical Club,[18] of people who invest everything in the name and nothing in the event.

GOD—OR *ADIEU SANS DIEU*

To say adieu *"sans dieu"*—would that not be to pronounce the death of God? Derrida is very close to a certain death of God, not exactly the Nietzschean version, but—however inflammatory this may seem—a death of God of a rather more Levinasian stripe that is of the highest importance to a theology of the event.[19] There is a certain bidding adieu to God, *adieu à Dieu,* if I may say so, to be found in Levinas, at the end of *Otherwise than Being,* for example, *adieu* to a God with respect to whom Levinas, too, rightly passes for an atheist. In the final paragraph of *Otherwise than Being,* in a text that gives us a good idea of what the "kingdom of God" means for him, Levinas says that this work is written "after the death of a certain god inhabiting the world behind the scenes" (*AE, 233/OTB,* 185).[20] However much Levinas would dissociate himself from Nietzsche's interpretation of "bad conscience," he does not hesitate to associate himself with the Nietzschean inversion of Platonism and with Nietzsche's critique of Platonic-Christian metaphysics. *Il n'y a pas d'arrière monde:* there is no *Hinterwelt,* no second world hidden behind the first one. Hence, the "kingdom of God" is not some other place for him, but another time, which means a certain way to live in time. The rule of God, we have been saying all along, is a rule of time, a way that time rules. The kingdom of God for Levinas does not offer the promise of an afterlife to bathe the wounds of mortal strife, an "eternal life" or "eternal reward" to pay us back for the expenditures we have made on behalf of the other in this valley of tears, but a way of being ruled by a command that comes from a time out of mind.

Levinas would accept Nietzsche's critique of Christianity's "stroke of genius" that Derrida mentions at the end of *The Gift of Death,* which sees the crucifixion as the amortization of an infinite debt that merits us all eternal happiness. Although he treasured the Platonic *epekeina tes ousias,* Levinas attacked Platonism from the start. *Time and the Other* is a sustained critique not only of Sartrean freedom and Dasein's *Seinskönnen* but also of the world of Plato, of his "world of light," which is a "world without time" (*TA,* 88/ *TO,* 93).[21] In Levinas's early language, time is not "a fallen form of Being" but "its very event" *(son événement même)* (*TA,* 88/ *TO,* 92). Hence, when Levinas mentions immortality, he treats it as analogous to insomnia, speaking of "this immortality from which one cannot escape" (*TA,* 27/ *TO,* 48), and he refers to the impossibility of death and even of the "horror of immortality" (*DEE,* 103/ *EE,* 63).[22] One does not vanquish death by way of eternal life—Platonism, straight up or Christian—but rather by way of the relation with the other (*TA,* 73/ *TO,* 81–82) and fecundity (*TA,* 85–89/ *TO,* 90–94; *T&I,* 244–47/267–69).[23] For Levinas, being in time is all, but it is not all in all, which would be too totalizing, for the *world,* the *time of the world* is not all, which is why there is always an *au-delà-dans* in any *être-dans-le-monde.* That excess is what we call the event that makes the world restless.

The kingdom of God is a certain excess in the world, not an immaterial world hidden behind the material one. God is a temporal recess, not a spatial transcendence. God—let us say the event that transpires in the name of God—is the event of having always already passed us by, the event of bypassing the visible and present in such a way as to have left God's trace on the face of the stranger. From the point of view of knowledge, this is always an "ambiguous" operation, for the trace is *not* the residue of a presence, not a visible mark that can be traced back to an originary presence and so made the basis of a demonstration (which means "showing") of the existence or being of God. The trace is not a diminished presence or representation that leads us back by a method of discovery to full presence. Rather, the trace is always, structurally, withdrawn *(retrait)* (*AE,* 14–15/ *OTB,* 12); it is the event of withdrawal. After the death of the Christian-Platonic God inhabiting an immaterial *Hinterwelt,* "the hostage discovers the trace . . . of what, always already past, always *'il,'* does not enter into any present," which "marks with its seal" the face of the stranger. God leaves his seal on the face of stranger as he withdraws from the world (*AE,* 233/ *OTB,* 185), like a ripple of water that betrays a recent disturbance.

God's epiphany takes place in the face-to-face relationship with the stranger. "A God invisible," he says, "means not only a God unimaginable, but a God accessible in justice" (*T&I,* 51/78). Theology, which means the thematization, the thematic explication, of a content, *le dit,* "God," as a massive semantic event, has no content; its concepts are empty, like Kantian concepts without intuitions, apart from the ethical relationship that funds them. Everything about the relationship to God that "cannot be led back to an interhuman relation" (*T&I,* 52/79) is a myth. Ethics funds theology the way perception funds theoretical constructs in phenomenology. Such concepts are empty except insofar as they can be led back *(re-ducere)* to the relation to the neighbor. Everything else is a fabrication of an overactive *spatial* imagination that requires demythologizing. No *Aufklärer* could have said it better. For the kingdom of God is not given in another space behind this space, but in another time older than time. It is not a place but a time, not a "where" but a "when." When God rules.

Thus, from the point of view of the theism of immaterial being and another world, of a transcendent being and an afterlife, Levinas too, no less than Derrida, rightly passes for an atheist.[24] For Levinas, God is not an entity but the event of ethics, the ethical order *(ordo ordinans)* that orders me to the stranger and the stranger to me. God is not a supreme being but a certain holy "ought" without being, *der heilige Geist* as *das heilige Sollen,* forged from a covenant between Kant and Torah.

Our major debt to Levinas is that he has translated God into an event, and our major complaint with him is that he has constricted the event to a strictly ethical category that underestimates its excess (since the event contained within this name has to do with more than obligation to others). God's holiness and separation are not that of a *substantia separata,* but are the seat of an ethical call that orders me to the stranger. As such, the name of God can only be uttered in the context of an ethical action. *Stricto sensu,* we would do as well not to say "God" at all, because God is nothing said, and as soon as God is thematized, a disturbance is created in the ethical order that distracts us from the order that orders me to the other. To stay related to God, to maintain a link with God, I should forget about God, bid adieu to God, *adieu à Dieu,* and welcome the stranger. To stay in tune with the event that happens in the name of God, we may need to suspend that very name. For it is only by loving and welcoming the stranger, by responding *in the name of* the God who loves the stranger, that God can be God. I pray God to rid me of God. God can be God only if my relationship to God is oblique, while my relationship to the neighbor is frontal.

God is God only if I am welcoming the stranger, only when I *do* the name of God, *facere veritatem,* as when I say *"adieu"* to the other, where the *"dieu"* disappears into the valediction given the other. That means that the name of God must be *translated into hospitality,* but this translation takes place in an entirely *pragmatic* order, not a *semantic* one. The translation is radical, beyond any semantic transfer, beyond any aligning of meanings in different semantic fields, beyond being and knowledge, because it is a translation into witnessing, into action. The name of God must be translated into an event, and the event must be translated into a deed. This is a translation into justice that precedes truth, or a translation into truth in the Augustinian sense of *facere veritatem,* "in spirit and in truth." The name of God belongs to the sphere of *dire,* not of *dit,* of *dire adieu,* of *dire bonjour* and *adieu,* not to a discourse on or about God. God is structurally absent from theology, has already passed theology by, by the time theology sets up shop. That, indeed, explains my own earlier reservations about the word *theology.*[25]

There is, accordingly, a curious atheism in Levinas's theism, a curious religious atheism in his ethical theism (since ethics, which *is* hospitality and *à-Dieu,* cannot be a-theistic), a curious *sans Dieu* in his *adieu.* For all the world—for all that is visible, existent, and knowable—I am acting on my own, like an autonomous agent, without mention or thought of God, *sans Dieu,* and I might as well be an atheist.[26] For all the world, I pass for an atheist. There is no need to say or to think God, who orders me to the stranger, or to affirm one's belief in God. Indeed, the very moment that God is any way thematized or made an object of belief, the movement of the command, of witnessing, is interrupted, like a surgeon who looks at his hand instead of at what he is doing. It is necessary to rid ourselves of God in order to witness to God. It is all the same whether one speaks *in the name of* God, or commends someone *to* God, or does not so much as mention God at all. That is because the expression *me voici* contains the event that transpires in the name of God, with or without that name. There is a living, working translatability, a pragmatic equivalence, between *me voici, au nom de Dieu* and *me voici, tout court,* which opens up the possibility of a witness to God, and even of a prayer, *without* referring to God, from which the word *God* is absent.[27] *Me voici, tout court—sans Dieu.* In short: *adieu—sans Dieu.* To God without God, *Dieu sans l'être.* As soon as I say *me voici,* God is at work, God is witnessed, and I am answering *in* the name of God, responding to the event that transpires in the name of everything that that name names, whether or not I use this extraordinary name, whether or not I rightly pass for an atheist. As soon as I respond to the provocation of the stranger, the invocation of God has taken place; the event has taken place. Witnessing does not supply evidence for that to which it bears witness, does not make its being or appearance more probable, and cannot be summoned as an argument for the existence of God. Indeed, God is God, and we bear witness to God only if we rid ourselves of God, which was the prayer of Meister Eckhart, although Levinas is not a negative theologian. For God is God only in the event in which God is at work ordering me to the other, in the deep recess of *illeity* prior to all presence and thematization.

For Levinas, the word *God* is just too much, too big and bombastic for ethics; it crowds ethics out, draws too much attention to itself, overwhelming and drowning it out. Of this word *God,* God as something "said," Levinas says that it "is an overwhelming semantic event that subdues the subversion worked by illeity," by turning it from the order of command to the order of something meant, and this subversion is at work "at this very moment," as we speak and use the name God (*AE,* 193/*OTB,* 151), as we move about in the semantic field. The semantics overwhelms the pragmatics and blocks the translation, which occurs in a praxical not in a semantic field. The whole meaning, the living meaning, of this term lies in the witness that is given to it, a meaning that is not translated but is betrayed as soon as "God" is said and thematized in theology, whether that be in a positive theology or even in the most negative of negative theologies. Witnessing is not theology, either negative or positive, but service to the neighbor who regards me. Witnessing is not a thought but a "deed." Becoming a Christian, Climacus said, is not a *what* but a *how.* Just so, *adieu, à-Dieu,* and the name of God in general for Levinas and Derrida, is not a *what* but a *how.* Just so with prayers and tears; they too are a matter of the *how,* not the *what,* so that one could spend all one's days in prayers and tears while rightly passing for an atheist.

RELIGION WITHOUT RELIGION

Levinas is tempted to call the bond of our relation to this illeity "religion," which would then signify a relation to God without being, or to God without being called God (*AE,* 188/*OTB,* 147), and in *Totality and Infinity* that is just what he called it (*T&I,* 10/40). Perhaps it is better called what Derrida calls a "religion without [*sans*] religion," which would fit very nicely with an *adieu sans Dieu,* or even a religion with or without God. We can certainly call it ethics. From a robustly religious point of view, one would say that Levinas has reduced religion to ethics, thinned it out into a purely ethical event, which is what Merold Westphal calls Levinas's "teleological suspension of religion" for the end of ethics.[28] To speak nonreductively, Levinas has *translated* religion into ethics, translated the name of God as wholly other into a wholly ethical name, a name whose whole signification is service to the neighbor and the stranger who regards me.

Now as we have said, a parallel translation has been going on in deconstruction, which is all about messianic peace, so that the two have begun to
converge upon and be translated into each other. Starting out from the opposite shores of theism and atheism, they join rails in the middle. Even as
for Levinas, religion, *me voici, au nom de Dieu,* translates into ethics, *me
voici, tout court,* so for Derrida, for whom deconstruction is justice, messianic peace, and hospitality, deconstruction undergoes a parallel translation
into an ethico-politics[29] and therefore into the name of God, into a working equivalence with speaking *in* the name of God. *Me voici, au nom de
Dieu,* and *me voici, tout court*—these translate into the same thing, into
hospitality, which is not their "common meaning" but the event they share
in common, whether or not one rightly passes for an atheist. *Me voici, au
nom de Dieu,* that is all the meaning the word God *has* for Levinas; *me voici,
tout court,* that is all the meaning the name of God *needs* for deconstruction.[30]

Thus, an odd sort of *sans Dieu* disturbs the Levinasian-Derridean *à-Dieu.*
An odd convergence of two atheisms inhabits their archi-semitic hospitality. There is, accordingly, an unnerving undecidability between theism and
atheism, theology and a-theology, *Dieu* and *sans Dieu, Dieu* and *a-Dieu,*
where the *à* has now become a privative *a,* as in *amorphe.* The first atheism
is that of Derrida, who does not by the most conventional standards "believe in the existence God," for whom God translates *without remainder*
into service to the neighbor. The other atheism is that of Levinas, who is an
atheist about a certain "God," the thematic, mentioned, thetic God, the
said God, the *theos* of theology, including even the being or the entity of
God, the transcendent God of strong theology. The "God" of Levinas who
orders me to the other and "justice" itself, *s'il y en a,* which is undeconstructible, in Derrida each translates into service to the stranger, hospitality.
In this complex *mis en abyme* of translations, *adieu* and the name of God
are finally translated into hospitality. "One belongs to the Messianic order,"
Levinas says, "when one has been able to admit others among one's own.
That a people should admit those who come and settle among them—even
though they are foreigners with their way of speaking, their smell—that a
people should give them an *akhsaniah* [accommodations], such as a place at
the inn, the wherewithal to breathe and to live—is a song to the glory of the
God of Israel."[31] By the same token, we can say, one belongs to the kingdom when one admits others among one's own.

For Derrida, the undecidability between theology and atheology, theism and atheism, *Dieu* and *sans Dieu* or *a-Dieu* (in the privative sense),
transpires in the desert, in the *khora,* in the indeterminate spacing in which
all the nominal unities, the temporary unities of meaning around which we
organize our works and days, are inscribed. Whenever we attempt to seize

the *name,* to swear an oath by the *name,* to enforce the *name* with institutional power, to threaten the other in the name of the *name,* the sands of undecidability shift and the graven images and fragile structures of the *name* crumble under our touch. Thus, those who seat themselves at the head of the table at the messianic banquet just because they subscribe to the *name,* just because they have papers to prove their official status, will find themselves invited to stand down (Luke 14:7–9).

The standard and conventional difference between *theos* and *atheos,* theology and atheists, between the "infidels" and the "believers," is such stuff as war is made of, of which the war over the holy city of Jerusalem, the blood that is currently being shed in and over the "holy land," may be taken as paradigmatic. The *name* always has to do with the meant God, the thetic, propositional God of theology, not with what we are calling the "event." The name has to do with what Levinas calls *le dit,* the "overwhelming semantic" occurrence that for Derrida is a nominal unity, always translatable into something else, around which the powerful institutions of the concrete "messianisms" are erected. But what the biblical tradition calls the living God (*TA,* 9/ *TO,* 31) has to do with the event, or with what Levinas calls *le dire,* with *à-Dieu,* with *dire adieu.*

Adieu means the pre-position before all propositions of being turned to God, practice not thetics, pragmatics not semantics, the praxis of commending the stranger to God, with *saying* adieu, with *doing* adieu, *facere veritatem,* and writing the rest off as semantics. In short, adieu means translating the name of God into events of hospitality. For in the semantic field, which is the field of being and manifestation, of proof and knowledge, of light and visibility, we are, when it comes to the invisible God, left in the dark, and we are all a little lost. We see now, in the *khora,* through a glass darkly, and we are all a little blind. Deconstruction is a memoir of the blind—and so is theology. "Do you believe? I don't know, one has to believe," Derrida says at the beginning and end of *Memoires d'aveugle,* "*Je ne sais pas, il faut croire.*"[32] Of the command that commands me to the other, Levinas says, I do not know whence—*je ne sais d'où*—it arises (*AE,* 189 / *OTB,* 148–49).

That is why *adieu* is a holy word for Derrida, why hospitality is sacred, and why Derrida is a man of prayers and tears, of faith, hope, and loving hospitality, although he lacks a theology of the *Hinterwelt,* does not say *credo in unum deum,* and rightly passes for an atheist. "The *yes* of faith is not incompatible with a certain atheism or at least with a *certain* thought of God's *inexistence* (beyond being)" (*A,* 111 n.1/143 n.6). When I affirm the other, I do not "know" what I affirm, but I pledge myself to the other *sans voir, sans avoir, sans savoir.* What do I love when I love my God? *Je ne sais pas—il faut croire.* What *(quid)* do I love when I love my God? God is not a what, a *quidditas*, but a *how*, even as the kingdom is not a *where* but a *when*. The name of God is not the name of an entity but of an event.

To be sure, in Levinas, the notion of God functions as a kind of *ordo ordinans*, an overarching backup or anchor, which is at least a depth dimension that orders me to the neighbor or the stranger, which somehow or another is an *au-delà dans*, a transcendence in immanence, a God who is, as Levinas says in a remarkable text, a *tout autre*, who is *autre qu'autrui* (*DVI, 115/GWCM, 69*), commanding responsibility and hospitality. In Derrida, on the other hand, there is no such anchor or depth dimension, but if anything, an unnerving desertion, a *khora*, a desert or an abyss that is the very spacing of *différance* that reminds one of the days before creation, *s'il y en a*, which sees to it that every promise is no less a threat. In Derrida, therefore, hospitality is responsive directly and immediately to the *singularity* of the other, so that every other is wholly other, *tout autre est tout autre*, and there is no movement of deflection from the Good to the neighbor, no *ordo ordinans* in the Levinasian sense ordering my desire for the Good into a desire or affirmation of the neighbor. Rather than an overarching transcendence or *ordo ordinans*, Derrida's *adieu* transpires in a *khora* more like the *il y a* of Levinas, with which, Levinas says in this same text, God, illeity, *l'autre qu'autrui*, slips into a "possible confusion," which further weakens any sharp distinction between Levinas and Derrida on this point.[33]

By advocating the free movement of human beings across the face of the earth, by speaking out for a daring politics that puts the various national identities and national languages at risk, which is a madness as mad as the wedding banquet whose doors are open to every passerby, Derrida explicates the politics of the kingdom. The name of God, the rule of God in his kingdom means, for Derrida, open doors *in deed*, not simply as edifying ethical discourse but as a political deed, *facere veritatem*. The kingdom of God is like a wedding feast to whom everyone is invited, and the least likely to be invited is a special guest of honor. Unconditional hospitality requires a politics without sovereignty. The politics of hospitality is not only the word of honor of a personal ethic but a political policy that embraces the unconditional admission of the foreigner into our land, sharing with them our jobs, our schools, the food out of our mouths. Opening national doors and lowering the barriers of sovereign nations would mean that *we* are the ones who are "extradited," driven out from our safe refuges, forced to answer the knock at our door, in order to welcome and make room for the stranger. Derrida would swing wide the gates of Jerusalem in order to make the stranger—the Palestinian—welcome. Indeed, for Derrida the open doors of unconditional hospitality are—to the great irony of what this name means today, in the "world"—the political event that stirs within the name of "Jerusalem," of the heavenly "gates of Jerusalem." That is what the names of "God" and of the "kingdom of God" *mean,* which is to say, that is the event that is provoked and invoked by those holy names.

HOLY UNDECIDABILITY:
BEING INSIDE/OUTSIDE THE KINGDOM

So then, having pursued this little short circuit of the parable of the wedding feast with Levinas and Derrida, who may we now say is in and who is out in the kingdom of God? Has not the whole thing been thrown into a holy undecidability? But what better outcome could one hope for, what better decision procedure to govern the admissions policy in a sacred anarchy?

Who is in? Not the insiders, who take the kingdom for granted and who think it enough to have been invited without having to show up, who are content to have been mentioned on the original guest list of names. Not, let us say, the card-carrying members of the kingdom, who treat the kingdom as if it were an entitative assembly not an event, who have the papers to prove that they are paid-up members, which show their legitimate status, if they are questioned about their status by the powers that be (usually at weddings and funerals!). Of these card carriers, Amos has the Lord say that he does not want to see their papers, he hates their solemn assemblies, their burnt offerings, and the noise of their songs: "But let justice roll down like waters, and righteousness like an ever-flowing stream" (Amos 5:21–24).

Meister Eckhart said that he prays God to rid us of "God," which we might adapt to say, I pray God to rid me of the name of God and to release the event that is sheltered by this name. Or, I pray God to rid us of religion, since, according to Amos, not to mention Isaiah (1:11–17) and Hosea (6:6), or even Karl Barth or Dietrich Bonhoeffer, God is not interested in religion, but in justice. The Lord demands justice, or hospitality—not a new edition of the hymnal, as Johannes Climacus quipped. Doing God, not saying God. Not saying "Lord, Lord"—the name—but opening one's house to the stranger at the door—the event. So then the insiders who swell the church choruses are, if not out, at least not necessarily in. The difference between the kingdom and the world cuts across the difference between those who are and are not card carriers, name bearers. One could be in the church yet still steeped in the world (in salaries and power), which happens all the time, even as the kingdom is filled with people who never heard of the kingdom or do not want to hear about it, but who forswear power and swing wide the doors of hospitality. It happens all the time.

Who then is *in?* According to the beautiful poetics of the impossible, the outsiders are in, the ones who have no papers to present, who cannot prove that they are card-carrying members of the religions of the Book, whose names do not appear on any official guest list, who do not have an official address to which we could have mailed the invitation. Who might even pass for atheists. Rightly pass. But according to the poetics of the impossible, the mad party that is being thrown in the kingdom is for *them*. The oxen and fatted calves have been prepared for "the poor, the crippled, the lame, and the blind," Luke says (14:13); and on Matthew's version, for "all whom they found, both good and bad" (22:10), straight and not so straight (to the chagrin of Peter Damian), gay and not so gay, black and not so black, repentant and unrepentant, male and female, orthodox and heterodox, constructionists and deconstructionists, theists and atheists, religionists and religion-without-religionists.

The kingdom of God is like a feast where everyone is welcomed with a jubilant divine indiscriminacy, like the prodigal son whose return brings tears to his father's eyes, or the lost sheep that counts more than the ninety-nine that never strayed. The kingdom of God is a like a great party that is thrown for everyone, where even slightly seedy characters who were never invited are then compelled to come in and have a drink. The kingdom of God is opened up by the event of hospitality the way the day is opened by the rising of the sun. The kingdom of God is a community without community, a city without walls, a nation without borders, unconditional hospitality without sovereign power, where the decision procedure for admission is based on a holy undecidability between insider and outsider. For all the world, it looks like all hell has broken out, the holy hell that we have been insisting all along is the stuff of a sacred anarchy.

The whole thing reminds us of the first days of creation, of the first big party that Elohim wanted to throw when he first filled up the formless void by making it replete with life of every form, with all things great and small, and then enjoined us all to extend the divine prodigality and, with ample measures of work and love and leisure, to bring to completion the divine work of making the earth swarm with life.

Appendix to Part Two: Newly Discovered Fragments on the Kingdom of God from "The Gospel of Miriam"

My dear friend Magdalena de la Cruz has recently e-mailed me what she calls "Newly Discovered Fragments on the Kingdom of God from *The Gospel of Miriam*." As you may know, Magdalena is quite a prankster and rather an anarchist herself.[1] I have no idea about the source or authenticity of these texts, no original manuscript to submit to the experts, and no idea about the reliability of the translator, since all the texts are in English yet purport to be fragments of a missing gospel. This latter point would be, if true, quite astonishing. The English is middling good, so I conclude that the translator is an Anglophone who has mischievously introduced French and Latin into the text. Unless, of course, this is an alteration made by Magdalena herself, which I would not put past her, since her attitude to the niceties of scholarly protocol is, to say the least, rather casual. I pass them along to the reader, now as in the past, as a courtesy to an old friend, but with this proviso: whatever I receive from Magdalena is always very provocative and heterodox and, although these materials are highly supportive of my projects, I cannot dispel my suspicions about their provenance. I reproduce these texts with the admonition that the reader take them for what they are worth and not attribute too much authority to them or their author. Magdalena is a free spirit, to say the least, a very independent creature who makes me feel quite conservative whenever I am in her company, which I confess I enjoy very much, by the way.

There were two e-mails, the first (as presented here; it was actually received second) containing two parables and a story, all three in answer to the question about the nature of the kingdom of God. I have used the second e-mail—which arrived first, from a different computer, signed only by a "Maude," but I was hardly deceived—as a kind of "concluding prayer," for, whatever its authenticity, it seemed like a suitable way to end Part Two of this study.

FRAGMENT #1: TWO PARABLES ON
THE KINGDOM OF GOD AND A STORY

1. The kingdom of God is like this. Two women went up to the temple one day and stood before the Gift, the one, by any human reckoning, an honorable woman who honors the law, who could, if anyone could, withstand the scrutiny of good and evil, the calculus that weighs them against each other, and the other woman, by anyone's reckoning, a sinner. But they have gone up to stand, not before the Law, which calculates and weighs merits, but before the Gift, where there is no giving and taking of reasons, no weighing or reckoning of comparative merits and demerits, where every human measure and mundane calculation is suspended, and the only rule is the unruly rule of the expenditure without reserve. The law discerns the difference between these two women, but because the Gift makes the sun of its love rise upon the good and the bad, the distance between them is leveled. For the Gift would love the daughter who has been loyal to her all the days of her life even as she would rejoice in a daughter who confesses her sins. The first woman gives the Gift praise for the sins she has escaped, not by her own resources but by the bottomless grace of the Gift; while the other woman, who gives up every defense of her past, casts herself upon the bountiful mercy of the Gift. I say to you, in the kingdom, how could we decide the difference between these two?

2. The kingdom of God is like this. Two young men who had been friends since childhood decided between themselves one day to ask each of their parents for their inheritance so that they could go off together and enjoy it now instead of waiting for their parents to die. Their parents, who loved their sons, gave them what they wanted. Then the two young men went off to a foreign land and consumed their inheritance, spending it foolishly on passing pleasures and false companions who abandoned them when their fortunes were spent. Their money gone, the two sons lived in miserable poverty and destitution for months on end, begging for their food and sleeping in cold and dangerous streets. Then they decided that even the servants in their parents' houses lived better than they and that the humiliation and ignominy of going home and confessing their foolishness was far better than the miserable circumstances to which they had reduced themselves. So they each went back home and begged their parents forgiveness and said that they would be happy to work as servants in their parents'

home. The parents of the first young man remained silent for a long time, considering their son's words, and then, after consulting together behind closed doors, returned this decision: You have wounded us so profoundly, so injured our honor and love, that justice will not be served until your trespass against us is repaid. And since this injury is absolutely unique, the injury of our love for you, only you can pay us back. Hence, as a condition of readmitting you to our love, we require from you a compensation in coin, paying off pain with pain, so that your pain and humiliation will atone for your offense, and your blood and your suffering will purchase your forgiveness. The parents of the other young man, on the other hand, were overjoyed at the return of their son. Our son was lost, they cried, but now has returned. So they commanded their servants to prepare a great feast to celebrate his return, which continued long into the nights of several days. I ask you, in which one of these parents' home does the kingdom of God rule?

3. Once in the days when Jesus was staying in Bethany with Mary and Martha, their brother Lazarus fell ill, but as it happened, Jesus was away at the time. The two sisters sent word to Jesus to come home at once, which Jesus did, dropping everything when he heard the news in order to hasten back to Bethany. Although Jesus came as quickly as he could, it seemed like forever to the two sisters, and they could not help but grow angry with him for being away at such a crucial time. By the time he was spotted coming down the road to Bethany it was too late and Lazarus had died. Martha went out to greet him, but Mary, beside herself with grief and anger, would not bestir herself. But together Jesus and Martha prevailed upon her to come out and to accompany them to the grave site. When they reached the tomb, Jesus could do nothing but weep over his dear dead friend. What else could he do? They stayed up late that night sipping a cool, smooth wine under a bright moon, telling stories long into the morning hours about their dead brother, laughing over the foolish things he did, the way he could do a perfect imitation of his two sisters, his silly jokes, weeping over the love as strong as death that he had for his sisters and for Jesus. Death came to Lazarus as it comes to us all, as it would come to Mary and Martha and Jesus. They sat up late into the night, listening to Jesus tell his beautiful stories under the stars about the coming of the kingdom and the lilies of the field. They felt the comfort of his words and of the wordless silence into which they would sometimes drift, each quietly musing over their lost brother and friend until someone broke the silence with another story. By the time the first signs of morning began to show, they somehow felt the strength return to their limbs and the hope return to their hearts. They talked through the night, and when the morning came they clutched the new day feverishly, for this was a new day, a day that the Lord had made, and their spirits had been raised from the death that threatened to swallow

them. They knew that Lazarus would want them to live the gift of this day that they had been given, this day and every day, to come out of the gloomy grave of their grief and embrace the day. They loved Lazarus dearly and could not let go of him, but they also knew that the best way to remember him was to let the flow of life resume its course through their limbs, to let the pain slowly ease off and let the life return. The kingdom of God, Jesus said, this time with just the slightest hint of a smile crossing his face, is like the vine that dies in the fall and then in the spring rises from its wintry grave, stirring with new life.

FRAGMENT #2. A PRAYER
FOR THE KINGDOM

How then should we pray in the kingdom?

When you pray, say, mother and father of us all, may your name be blessed, may your name be kept safe, and may all things be made new and transformed. May we all be of a new mind.

Give us today the gift of the day, the gift of time, of your own good time.

May your kingdom come, *viens, oui, oui,* may your rule come, may the rule of the gift come, and hospitality. Let it happen. May the wind of your coming sweep over us as over the deep, and may it lift us up in the palm of your hand. May the event of your coming happen, may it break out upon us and wash over us like water over the land.

When will you come?

Viens, oui oui. Bienvenue.

Release us from our faults, wipe them away without a trace, and make us free for the gift. May the evils of the past be made into a past that was never present, that never happened. Release us from our past, even as we shall release others from what they have done against us.

Free us from the evil one and from the meanness of the world's calculations. Let the gift happen in us and open us up, like the lilies of the field, like the birds of the air.

For the kingdom is yours, the time of your rule, and time is yours. Give us your time as long as there is time to give.

Adveniat regnum tuum.
Viens, oui, oui, au nom de Dieu.
Viens, oui, oui.
Tout court.
Yes, I said, yes, yes.
Amen.

A Concluding Prayer—
for Theology, for the Truth,
for the Event

I am praying not to be lost, praying because I am already lost, praying not to get any more lost than I already am, praying that my prayer does not make things worse. I am trying to think while praying, to pray while thinking,[1] praying like mad—for theology, for theology's truth, for the event. The event for me is not an object but a matter for prayer.

But I must make a confession. My central (if decentering) idea, my one contribution to human welfare, the one thing I want engraved on my headstone, is and has always been the modest proposal that if the truth be told, we none of us—neither believers nor nonbelievers, neither believers in this nor believers in that—know who we are. We are always kept in the dark. That unguarded confession is the culmination of a lifetime of study and writing, of a life spent earnestly seeking the light, not to mention a considerable amount of money spent on books, travel to learned conferences, and drinks in conference hotel bars. Indeed, I can barely say *I* confess. For when we speak of the "I" or the "we" or the "self," we are employing a certain shorthand that glosses over the complexities, that hastily summarizes the current state of an inner anarchic conflict in which there are numerous competing forces, constantly shifting, and unsteady alliances and unexpected turns yet to be taken. The "I" is like the reluctant chairperson of a committee who has been pushed out the door to make a progress report and to create the impression of consensus, while behind closed doors the committee itself remains locked in irreconcilable conflict. If such an anarchic state of affairs prevails concerning ourselves, with whom we have some accumulated and hard-earned familiarity, imagine how much more so this holds when it comes to God, who is said to be wholly other!

Hence the ill-advised decision to speak about God, which I would not have done were I not provoked (by who knows what). But it is too late to retract that. The die has been cast. The leap has been made—and it has landed me in the dark, in a kind of night of truth, where the truth is less something I seek than something I cannot escape. So the only thing left to do is pray for help, *de profundis*. Thus, I conclude with a prayer—and what could be more fitting?—a concluding prayer that is a kind of conclusion without conclusion.

HANGING ON BY A PRAYER
TO GOD *(À DIEU)*

I am praying to God, preyed upon by God, turned to God—by God *(à Dieu)*. Each night upon retiring I pray for the truth, for the truth of the event, for the courage of the truth, for the courage to welcome the event. I am praying for a thought, for a thought that is engendered in prayer, praying for theology, for theology's truth, praying for the courage of the truth of theology.

Under the name of one sort of "hermeneutics" or another, hot or cold, radical or more radical, devilish or angelic, I have all my life been saying a little prayer under my breath, while following the faint lines of force of an event that goes under the name of God. I have been all along trying to trace the logos of a prayer, the logos of a desire for the event that theology calls God. I have been haunted and unhinged by the love of an event that is harbored by this name, by desiring and being desired by this event, hoping and praying to be visited by the truth of this event. I am pursued down the lonely labyrinths of this love, down the nights and down the days of this desire, down the arches of the years,[2] by the desire for something beyond desire, by the thought of something beyond thought, by something I know not what.

By God *(à Dieu)*, by desiring and being desired by God, which is the name of a promise to make things new, to set off mutations and transformations most marvelous to behold.

By God *(à Dieu)*, which is the name of a sigh, of the soft whisper of a spirit sighing, breathing over being, softening hardened hearts, loosening lives grown stiff from hatred, wound tight by retaliation and recrimination, breathing hope where things are hopeless.

By God *(à Dieu)*, desiring and being desired by God, by whatever unknown resources stir restlessly in the name of God, by whatever unforeseeable event is coursing through that name, by whatever long-forgotten memories are buried there. Our hearts are restless with the restlessness of God, St. Augustine said, for God makes being restive, unruly, leaving the future gaping wide open, ajar with expectation, even as God opens the graves of long-dead memories. God throws being's house into holy confusion.

By God *(à Dieu)*, desiring and being desired by God, by which I mean a call without causality, a chaosmic, atelic disturbance, the source of anarchizing effects, of divine disruption, the sacred confusion caused in being by the memory and the promise of the good.

By God *(à Dieu)*, who brings not the tranquility of order, *pace* my dear Augustine, but the disturbed, disjointed disorder, the cracks in the surface of too much order through which the shoots of justice spring.

I am shaken by the uncontainability of the event that the name of God contains, by the trauma of the truth promised under the name of God. Under one name or another. I am disoriented by the night of truth that wrings from me the confession, the concession, that if truth be told, I do not know what event stirs within the names I hold most dear, nor do I know what name to save in order to release the event I hold most dear.

I confess the name of God, praying and weeping over the name of God. Like Augustine in the *Confessions* I have all along been offering up a prayer *in litteris*,[3] an intensely private prayer right out in public, an open confession for the benefit of all to see and hear. So if there is so much as a prayer for this theology of the event for which I grope, it will be because it is itself a prayer—a prayer for theology and a theology for prayer, a theology of the event that takes place in prayer, that prays for the coming of the event (come what may).

I begin with God because I begin with prayer. The name of God is linked to prayer as the bird is linked to the air, as its medium or ambience. We are called by God *(à Dieu)*, which is our vocation, even as we call upon God, call to God *(à Dieu)*, which is our invocation, our prayer, like the *tu*, "you," whom Augustine addresses in the *Confessions*. Remember the staging of the *Confessions:* Augustine has his back to us, and he stands, or kneels, *coram deo.* Whenever the name of God is truly used, rather than merely mentioned, it is prayed. God is above all what one prays for, whom one prays to, what one prays about. Just so, this name springs to Derrida's lips irreducibly mingled with his mother's prayers and tears.[4] "God" is not an object but the other end of a prayer,[5] which is the discursive type, the milieu, of this name. "O God, my God." "May God be with you." "If God wills." "God be praised." "Go with God." *"Adieu."* Those are so many ways the name of God springs to our lips, so many ways to lift our heart to God, to someone, something, somewhere, I know not what, God knows. So it is no accident that we have followed the lines of the kingdom by loosely following a very famous prayer. If all theology means is to treat God as the subject matter of an objectifying discourse, then theology is not possible.

For God is only given in prayer. That is one reason I have worried in the past about employing the word *theology*. But I now think that this impossibility should be counted in among the conditions of possibility of theology, a delimiting condition, so that any possible logos of this name, any possible theology, must be a logos of a prayer, the logos of a passion or a desire, where theology is, like prayer, a wounded word.[6]

I am hanging on by a prayer, by a prayer and a tear for the truth, for theology's truth. I am praying for the truth, where the truth is found, not in a proposition but in a confession, a truth that is not a matter of establishing an *adequatio* but of a confession of our inadequacy. Truth means truthfully to confess the poverty of our philosophy, the weakness of our theology, and the humility of our condition.[7] Truth is a matter for prayer, not epistemology.

I am praying where it is impossible to pray, which does not spell the end of prayer but the beginning, which is why even the most classical forms of prayer begin with a prayer for the prayer—*domine, exaudi nos.* Being left without a prayer is the true beginning of prayer. We are always praying in the dark, which is prayer's element. I am praying to be able to pray, praying that someone be there to hear my prayer, concerned like Claudius that although my words fly up, my thoughts stay here below, worrying whether words without thoughts to heaven go (*Hamlet,* III, 3). But my salvation is that praying to be able to pray is already to pray. What better prayer, what better reason to pray, than when we are lost and left without a prayer?

> O Lord, incline your ear and hear our prayer.
> Let the event come.
> *Viens, oui, oui.*
> Thus does my soul magnify the Lord.

PRAYING WITH BOTH HANDS

I am praying with both hands. On the one hand—what is the sound of one hand praying?—to confess the name of God is to profess it and affirm it, endorse it and countersign it, pray and weep it, again and again, yes, yes, for I am turned by God to God *(à Dieu).*

But on the other hand—the sound of the other hand praying—if the truth be told, to be turned in prayer to the event is to risk being overturned and turned out in the cold. I do not think of truth as a flood of light and illumination, which is the figure of truth that dominates the tradition from Plato to the Enlightenment to Husserl. I think of truth as more like a night than a light. Truth is a claim made upon us—a "truth claim" is less an exact claim we make than an exacting claim that is made upon us—that wrests from us an open-ended concession that we cannot contain the event that the name contains within the limits of the name. Truth is less something I seek than something I cannot evade. To pray for the event in all its truth is to ask for trouble. It forces a concession out of us—as when we say "if truth be told" or "in all truthfulness"—that I do not know what lies ahead for this name or what it is capable of becoming or un-becoming.

In this case, a confession is less a profession than a concession. To confess the truth means to own up to our own limits, to face the music about what we know and do not know. That is why truth is always something we can walk away from, ignore, distort, or repress (it's a weak force and lacks an army). To be honest to God, the truth demands an honest concession that we cannot contain the event harbored by the name of God. I pray for the courage to face the truth, to face the music of the truth. If in midnight moments meditating upon the name of God we are visited by the truth of the event, a shudder passes through us, and we are reminded of the darkness of the night, which should give us pause when next we are inclined to use this name, when next we are tempted to wield it like a sword against our enemies.

Indulge for a moment my authorial conceit that the present study is to be viewed as my *Confessions*. If the honest truth be told, I have never done anything memorable enough to be worthy of confession, never even dared to steal pears (I don't even like pears) or to wear my trousers rolled. But I will nonetheless dare here to speak in these concluding pages of my confessions, which are a way of praying and writing with both hands, praying for the truth, praying not to die from the truth, praying that the truth will set me free.

PRAYING FOR THE
TRUTH OF THEOLOGY

I am praying for theology to come true. In my anarchical way of looking at things, which is not without precedent, prayer brings not peace but the sword (Matt. 10:34). To call upon of the name of God is to call for trouble, for it is to call for loosening up the grip of the world, which threatens to be all in all. To turn to God in prayer one must be willing in return to be overturned by God, to be submitted to an infinitely subversive turn in things, which destabilizes the present order. To pray for theology to come true—where theology is taken to be prayer's own thought—is to want to break up the presence of the world, to prevent the world at present from closing over and sealing off an event that the world cannot contain.

To pray for the coming of theology's truth is to ask to be saved but in a very frustrating way. Here being saved by the truth does not mean being made safe, but being turned upside down, turned out in the cold, uprooted and unhinged by the event that stirs restlessly in this name, suffering from a wound that will not heal. Be careful about what you pray for. For after theological thinking has irrupted, after theology's truth has swept over us, nothing is the same again, and one cannot go on as if nothing had occurred, even if from outer appearances one looks as hale and whole as the next chap. The situation of my weak theologian is well described in Johannes de Silentio's famous account of the knight of faith in *Fear and Trembling*. Where would we ever find such a fellow? Is he not as rare as a priceless pearl, even if as a matter of Christian charity we must concede that every second member of the AAR may be an instance of the type? But if, per impossible, we ever came across such a thinker, would we be able to detect the slightest "heterogeneous optical telegraphy from the infinite, a glance, a facial expression, a gesture, a sadness, a smile that would betray the infinite in its heterogeneity from the finite?"[8] Would there be even the slightest outer hint that inwardly this fellow has been snared by the infinite, shaken by a relation to an unconditional claim, that he subsists in virtue of an absolute relation with the absolute? Why the fellow looks like a computer programmer! Inwardly, this man has been completely unhinged by an absolute relationship with the event, yet he saunters about with all the equilibrium of a "mercantile soul" at a computer fair!

In Tillichian terms, we can say that to experience the truth of theology is to be overtaken by questions of "ultimate concern," so that being "in the truth" is not completely unlike being "in the soup." The opposite would be to live in the un-truth, closed off from the truth, tranquilized and thoughtless. To be saved is to be saved from a somnambulant life and awakened to the event. There would be a peace here, but it would be a superficial and somnambulant peace. One would not be astir with deep theological unrest, having turned one's attention entirely to preliminary, proximate, and superficial matters, while never noticing the event, which knows no limits, which is bottomless and indeterminable, hurtling me down endless and labyrinthine paths.[9] The event of theology's truth saves me by wounding me, wounds me by saving me, setting off odd effects that are figuratively clustered together to form a "kingdom" of such anarchic phenomena.

To pray for the coming of the theological event is to know full well, to confess, to circumfess, indeed to insist that, *if the truth be told,* the undecidability and translatability of our most cherished names are endless. To utter a prayer for a "theology" of the event is, *ex professo,* to settle upon the event astir in the name of God, even as it confesses or concedes that it has but historical and contingent reasons for invoking this name rather than another. I make no claim that this is a universal state of affairs, that the name of God is not translatable, or that it belongs to some final and unsurpassable vocabulary. Indeed, for reasons of impartiality and respect for the cold truth—I am praying in a cold, dimly lit, and unheated chapel made of stone—I insist on the opposite, that no historically determinate name could ever contain the event, that no name bound by time and tide and circumstance—and what name is not?—could ever be impartially accessible to everyone or uniformly desirable by everyone.[10]

My prayer proceeds from a faith that simmering within this contingent and historical name is a subversive and anarchizing event, which is why this name should set off sparks whenever it makes contact with the settled orders of presence or finds its way inside the inaccessible corridors of power. This name has come to us from our mother's breast, from the dark waters of the womb, from our unconscious,[11] from the hidden depths of our language, from our most ordinary language, as opposed to a formal or contrived one, from the lost roots of our multiple histories, all the forces of which have been run together in a massive simplification and concentrated shorthand called "God." This name is made to bear the weight of a history it cannot bear, to carry the torch of a desire that it cannot carry, and to contain an event that it cannot contain. Philosophers think it is philosophy that makes everything questionable, while theology puts questioning to sleep, so that theology, like the sermons delivered in church, is most effective among insomniacs. Philosophers think questioning awakens with the provocative poem of Parmenides, with the interrogatory life of Socrates, with the doubt of Descartes, with Kant's critique, or with Heidegger's question of being.

But we advocates of a theology of the event, who have worn out the knees of our trousers from too much kneeling, smile at such uncritical innocence. We partisans of prayer and weak theology, who belong to a different party, advance the hypothesis that theology has the disruptive force to awaken questioning and to stir thought, and this not because of its own resources as a *logos* but just because the name of God is inscribed in theology.[12] *Theo*logy was named after God and is God's word, God's logos, God's namesake, God's desire, the desire for God. Theology is turned by God to God *(à Dieu)*. The desire awakened by the name of God is inscribed deep in our unconscious, leaping to our lips at times of birth and death, of entreaty and gratitude, of desperation and separation, of surpassing joy and heart-rending sorrow, of peace and danger:

"God help us." "Thanks be to God." "May God be with you."
It is even a name we invoke ("O God"), if I may be ever-so-slightly salacious, in moments of explosive, orgasmic joy—and rightly so; that is also good theology.

What do the philosophers have to compete with such a name? What rival do they propose for such occasions? Who can they put up as an opposing candidate in a general election? "Being"? "Consciousness"? "Substance"? The "System"? Are they serious? Is that a joke? The last cloudy streak of evaporating reality, a mummification, a conceptual embalming,

Nietzsche said. "Be a philosopher, be a mummy," he said, as he pointed at such names in ridicule, holding his sides, collapsing with laughter.[13] And sitting at a nearby table, not far off, Kierkegaard has put down his cigar and taken out his handkerchief to wipe the tears of laughter from his eyes as he reads the latest issue of *The Daily Encyclopedia,* in which we are given every assurance that work on the System is expected to be completed no later than the middle of next week.

Consider the claustrophobic catastrophe that would occur were the truth of theology suppressed or closed off, were our lives left un-turned, were we to leave off praying for the event astir in theology. There would be nothing to check the free reign of the "profane," the unbroken rule of the "world," the harsh economy where there are no gifts, where everything has a price. The profane is the degradation of the sacred into acquisitiveness, the truncating of human experience into consumption, leaving us to wander the shopping malls in search of what we desire and relegating us to reality TV to search for what is real. The profane shrinks human life into the surface of the accumulation of as many things as possible, reducing love to sexuality, history to nostalgia, politics to power and violence, religion to hateful self-righteousness,[14] while allowing the poorest people in our society to fend for themselves, even though they are defenseless. The profane takes what is sacred and debases it, puts it on vulgar display, robbing it of its powers. The profane life is flat and thoughtless, shortsighted and mean-spirited—in short, devoid of prayer.

The opposite of the profane is the sacred, which sets off a chain of anarchic effects that interrupt the closure of secularism, piercing its closure by means of the event that stirs within the name of God. By the "secular" world or order I simply mean the condition in which we all live today, believers and nonbelievers, believers in this and believers in that, apothecaries, apostles, and large-animal veterinarians alike. Modernity simply tries to be tidy about the distinction between the sacred and the secular, private and public, which is not entirely possible.[15] But by *secularism* I mean the rule of the world, the regime of the profane, which represents an assault on the event, a reductionistic attack on the excess of the sacred, the attempt to disenchant the world in virtue of which everything we mean by God is reduced to the economy of the *saeculum,* where everything has a market price. A theology of the event is accordingly an exercise in post-secular thinking. It takes up residence within the secular order and, working its way through secularism and the death of God, comes out the other end on the grounds that it has become obvious that the event harbored by the name of God cannot be contained by the "world" *(saeculum).* So when Mark C. Taylor famously said years ago that deconstruction is the hermeneutics of the death of God,[16] I begged to differ. I myself regard this Taylor-made deconstruction as too downbeat a view, since deconstruction is for me rather a hermeneutics of the desire for God and so a certain religion (without religion). The religious dimension in deconstruction—which makes big totalization projects like "secularism" look incredible—is its affirmation of the impossible, of genuine events that cannot be contained within closed borders. Rather than anything final or funereal, deconstruction is a life-giving aeration, giving faith and the spirit of God room to breathe. The post-secular is a celebration of the event, of an excess or transgression of the world by the event, premised on the idea that the name of God is too much for the world to contain.

We weak theologians of the event, who pray and weep for the coming of the event, have found the death of God to be a dead end. We are subscribers to a *new* Enlightenment, one that is enlightened about Enlightenment, one in which we have acquired a renewed appreciation for the dark and have learned something about the dangers of overexposure to the sun. Rather than a secularization of theology, our post-secular theological project undertakes a theologization of the secular. We come *after* secularization breaks down or breaks open, in a time that is torn open and torn apart by the desire for God, and we treat deconstruction as a hermeneutics of the name of God. The death of God *simpliciter* would represent another failed try at pure and perfect presence, at a closure and a totalization every bit as exclusionary as the closure sought by the strongest theocratic advocates of high theology. But that closure would spell the death of desire. The death of God *simpliciter* would mean the death of every possible God, the death of the unconditional event that is astir in the name of God, in a name like God. That would spell the death of prayer, the death of what we love and desire with a desire beyond desire, the death of everything that makes our beliefs and practices tremble, making them open up like an abyss whenever they come in contact with the event, with something, I know not what.[17]

To pray for theology to come true is to call up all the forces of the sacred to scramble the lines of force in the world and give the ordinary surface of things their glow, like the lilies of the field, which is how it is possible to be superficial out of depth. The sacred today is found in the anarchic effects produced by re-sacralizing the settled secular order, disturbing and disordering the disenchanted "world," producing an anarchic chaosmos of odd, brilliant disturbances, of gifts that spring up like magic in the midst of scrambled economies, like sparks given off when wires cross, filling the air with brilliant elliptical, parabolic, and paradoxical effects. The "kingdom of God" is a celebration of the blessed event of the foundering of the "world," of the excess and open-ended shock that is delivered to the world by God *(à Dieu)*. The truth of the event harbored by the name of God triggers the potencies that stir in things, releasing their pent-up charges of divinity, rocking the world with the shock of the divine. The result is the grace, the graciousness, the aleatory gratuitousness of the gift, the water-into-wine madness of the kingdom, the divine sparks of a sacred anarchy.

ADIEU À DIEU

I am praying because I am lost, praying not to get any more lost than I already am, fully conscious that every prayer worthy of the name suffers through a dark night of the soul, suffers a loss of faith and its own kind of prayerful atheism. Not knowing whether anyone hears our prayer, we pray in the dark to cold and indifferent heavens that seem unmindful that we here below beseech them. We pray *sans voir, sans avoir, sans savoir,* every prayer worthy of the name being to an unknown God.

By praying to be visited by the event we put the name of God at risk, for the event not only shocks the closure of the world in the name of God, but it also shocks the name of God itself, exposing the fragility of that name. The ultimate risk that a theology of the event incurs, the ultimate risk incurred by the irruption of theology's truth, is to expose itself to the loss of the name of God itself. In that way we can make Meister Eckhart's magisterial prayer of mystical atheism our own, praying for God to rid us of God, saying, praying, *adieu à Dieu.*

A theology of the event is inevitably a work in progress, an interim theology, a theology for the interregnum between what has been called God in theology and what is coming, for which, of course, we have no name beyond saying that it is "to come." Even if we pray for the "kingdom" to come, we have no assurance that what is coming in the name of the kingdom will bear that name. So in turning to God, in being overturned by God, we reach still another turning point, which forces yet another confession from us, and once again in the name of the truth of the event. (I am praying not to die from the truth, knowing full well, as Nietzsche said, that too much truth can kill you.[18]) For if the truth be told, that is, if we are to be faithful to the distinction we have drawn between the name and the event, we must be prepared to surrender the name—of God or of the kingdom, of justice or of democracy—just in virtue of the event these names contain, the event we have been maintaining all along they cannot contain. As Derrida says, in the "democracy to come," the "to come" is more important than the "democracy." Just in virtue of the unforeseeability and surprise of the event, we cannot see or say that what is coming, that a democracy to come, for example, will still be called "democracy."[19] At best we can say that what we call democracy today is a predecessor form of something to come, that it links up with something coming, I know not what.

A theology of the event is, after all, in one sense a monster, an unnatural being, because it has taken leave of the familiar names that flourish in the natural languages and has occupied itself with the underlying or innermost events sheltered by these names. But our usual practice is to use the names with which we are familiar, to call and be called by name, not by an "event," which sounds a little eerie, like being haunted by a ghost or hearing voices. Still, the name for what is coming must always and in principle be lacking. It is not so much that names fail us as that such names simply have not arrived yet, have not yet been formed or forged in the furnace of historical circumstance so as to have taken shape in (and given shape to) our lives. To speak of an event is already to have assumed a kind of unnatural, dislocated, second-order position, to have engaged a slightly ghostly or hauntological operation that instead of simply using names straightforwardly has inserted a kind of ironic distance between itself and the direct, first-order use of the name. By opening up the distinction between the name and the event, we expose the name of God to the cold, where it will not have the wherewithal to lay down its head, to the possible coming of a name that is at present lacking, or is not yet found, a new name that will emerge from the event in an unforeseen way. We expose the name of God, not to the coming of a new god, but to the coming of something otherwise than God, something new in which the name of God may be displaced, and this just in virtue of the event harbored by the name of God. That is what the deconstruction of the name of God would come down to. That is what the weakness of theology would come down to. Nothing is safe.

That is why the truth for me is a matter for prayer (as are theology and the event). Dealing with the truth of the event is a matter of being painfully honest, honest to the breaking point, being as hard and ruthless as Nietzsche, while hanging on by a prayer. When truth is less a light than a night, confessing the truth of the event is a confession of our blindness, a confession that is a concession that the names I profess are unkept promises that promise I know not what, that the determinate horizons temporarily thrown up by names are overthrown by the open-ended expanse of the unforeseeability of the event.[20]

We are inevitably caught up in and attached to old names. Every time we say or pray "come," we must inevitably draw upon the reservoir of the past, invoking the names we have inherited, lest we have no vocabulary at all with which to pray. But when we distinguish the name from the event it bears, we are preparing for a future for which we cannot prepare, to take leave of our oldest and most revered names. Like "God." There would be no way to make this name or any other name safe. That is why I concede that I write and pray with both hands, that even as I am trying to save the name of God with my right hand I am also conceding with my left that this

name is not safe. I profess the name of God while making a confession that
what is coming might be called something else, anything except (or "save")
God. *Sauf le nom.*[21]

Let us indulge the fiction that in these "post-secular" times the event
that has been harbored in the name of God shows signs of life even as it
shows signs of twisting free from the name of God—and if God, then theology, and if God and theology, then perhaps religion, too—so that perhaps something else is taking shape, something, I know not what, for which
the name "God" will fail, while we live in the interim between the two.[22] A
theology of the event, then, would have been a paleonymic meditation
upon an ancient name that neither guarantees the future of the name nor
manages to proffer a new name in its place but prepares us prayerfully, *per
impossibile,* for the coming of something unforeseeable. Let us say that the
paradox of weak theology is that even as it is a turning to God by God, it is
also praying to be able to pray in the wake of God, in God's aftermath,
preparing for something I know not what, for which we pray to be able to
pray.

When I desire God or love or democracy, democracy or love or God are
not what I desire, because what is desired is an unconditional event, the
event or the advent of the *tout autre* that is astir in these names, which
means the unconditional *promise* of the event contained in these names.
These are at present the least bad names we have, names for the conditioned, empirical counterparts of something unforeseeable, unconditional,
and nameless. There is no term for my prayer, no *terminus ad quem,* no
final terminology or final name, no unsurpassable end point, no ultimate
horizon of prayer, but only a series of horizons that are constantly collapsing under the weight of desire, under what Charles Winquist so much
loved to call the "pressure" of radical theological desire.[23]

The "in-finity" of "God" refers to an unstable situation in which the finite keeps foundering, in which determinate conditions keep collapsing
under the call of the unconditional event, in which constructions keep
falling under the weight of the undeconstructible. That continual collapse
or fall is what funds thinking theologically, keeping the prayer for theology
in motion, the way walking is a kind of continually falling forward. Coming to grips with the fact that this interminable *terminus ad quem* is
nowhere to be attained gives us a certain amount of peace, the uneasy peace
that concedes that there is no peace, even as it fires our passion for something I know not what. If it does only the former, the result will be a knight
of infinite resignation and not a knight of faith, and if it does only the latter, it will produce a destructive fanatic.

I cannot discern the event that concerns me ultimately,[24] and that failure is my success, my most vital sign, my passion, the passion of my non-

knowing *(passion du non savoir),* my prayer. Ultimacy means what comes last, at the end, what cannot be expected anytime soon, the secret about which I am kept permanently in the dark. But in the meantime there is always more time, always a future, always a horizon of expectation; it is always the interim, the meantime, the interregnum between now and the coming of the kingdom. We live always and already among the conditioned, not in a gnostic refusal of its reality, which would be a refusal of our materiality, but with an Augustinian restlessness that confesses our materiality, our khora-poreality. By exposing the always-conditioned to the unconditional, we keep ourselves open to the truth of the event, to what is stirring within the signs and surfaces that surround us, thereby preventing closure, which would itself prevent the event that is astir within the ordinary and daily things around us (the quotidian or epiousiological). The very idea of what is last, what is ultimate, is that the last is still to come and yet to be identified; the final edition of the news will not appear until later in the day; an existential system will never be completed for any existing spirit. That does not diminish daily existence but intensifies it, making of daily life a pearl of great price, making each day precious. The ultimate is in principle unforeseeable, indiscernible, impossible, which does not mean it is just a failure. On the contrary, that is the secret of its success, the secret itself, which keeps the future open, whereas what has failed is the attempt on the part of the world to bottle up the event and drive out every secret.

A PRAYER TO AN
UNKNOWN GOD

Every prayer worthy of the name is a prayer to an unknown god. If I knew and had assurances about the addressee of my prayer, I would be too self-assured to need to pray. To pray to an unknown God is not only possible but it may be, in the end, the only possible prayer. Derrida's *"s'il y en a"* or *"peut-être"* may be the very form of prayer. Oh, God, my God (if you are there). Oh, God, my God, you are all in all (perhaps).

When all is said and done (which it never is!), the meditation upon the name of God conducted in a weak theology is not a simple vigil over an old name, nor does it nod off in nostalgia, that peculiar *jouissance* we give ourselves by thinking wistfully about and grieving over the loss of old names, nor is it a despair that steels itself for a world without God. These would all be negative results, whereas a theology of the event is an affirmation, yes, yes.

In the end, and we are now at the end, I come back to the lilies of the field and to the discourse against anxiety. The upshot of this entire undertaking is to liberate ourselves from the anxious and obsessive search for the name and thereby to win a certain version of the freedom of the children of God. By that I mean the freedom to do the truth, to make the truth, to make the truth come true, *facere veritatem,* free from any anxiety about knowing the name, for the name of what we love is the name of the unknown God. The end effect of this theology of the event is or should be to transform our lives, to transport us to another order, beyond the order of cognition, of nomination and de-nomination, where we may serve the *deus incognitus* in spirit and in truth. In the end, the truth of the event will make us free by freeing us from obsession over the right or proper name.[25]

Behold the lilies of the field; they are not anxious over names or over what they are called, and look how they have been clothed in such glorious raiment.

The very idea of the truth of the event is to explode the notion that there is a name that is above all other names, in the name of which we can and should make war on rival names to the crown. As long as the event that is desired with a desire beyond desire is contracted to the specific terms of a Proper Name, there will be wars of private property, battles over the copyright, over who owns that name, or who gets to speak authoritatively, with all the authority of the Name. That is the sort of thing that prompts authoritative fellows like Peter Damian to commend to the torch anyone who deforms the Proper Name, or who offers a dissident commentary, interpretation, or translation of it. Disputes break out about the difference between the original language and the language of translation, or about whose language gets to be the sacred one, or whose city gets to be the holy one. How in God's name are we going to settle these wars over the name of God? That belligerence, that mundane militancy, arises from reducing an event to a name, from trapping the truth of the event inside a name, which is what happens in a strong theology.

This prayer for theology has all along been harboring a heretical hypothesis about prayer—that the prayer for the event is a prayer to an unknown God—and an equally unorthodox hypothesis about desire—that the desire for the event is a desire for I know not what. Were I a spiritual master (with which no one has confused me so far), I would do everything I could to keep prayer alive in my novices by enjoining prayer to the unknown God (for which I would ask in return only that they remember me in their prayers). Were I a psychoanalyst (of which no one has accused me so far), I would take it as my life's work to keep desire alive and well in my patients (clients!) by counseling them to see their desire as a desire for the event (which is, I would confess, I know not what), and then they will be as happy as the lilies of the field (for which gift I would in turn charge a reasonable hourly sum).

Were the event identifiable with a Proper Name, we would thus far fail to have a future, a real one. By a real future I mean the risky business of a future for which there is no adequate provision, no horizon of expectation or anticipatory forestructures that can absorb the shock of the event. But because there is only a chain of conditioned, substitutable, provisional, preliminary names at the sound of which some knees somewhere should sometimes bend, there is endless prayer and bottomless desire. If the desire for the event is desire itself, the assignation of a Proper Name to the event would be the death of desire. If prayer is a prayer for the event of the unknown God, the assignation of a Proper Name to God would spell the death of the truly divine God. The name of God is auto-deconstructing, a self-displacing name that keeps making way for the event, effacing its own trace, which is what I love about it. It would thus be my counsel that there is nothing determinately, discernibly ultimate, no first or last, no *arche* or *telos*. For as long as we are subject to time and tide, what comes last, *ultima*, is always coming, signifying the very structure of the to-come, *l'à-venir*, which is the very definition of hope and expectation for the future that is built right into the event. Thus would I keep prayer and desire alive.

Were I—never fear—to resort to politics to keep prayer and desire alive, I would tour the country giving a stump speech in which I would say "The only thing in which we have to hope is hope itself." We are saved more by hope itself than by *what* we hope in, which differs from time to time and place to place and is at best a temporary placeholder for something, I know not what, for some more elemental quality of our lives. There is no single and exclusive, no sustainably determinate "what" in hope, no fixed object of hope; for once something is fixed in place, it collapses under the weight of more hope. So just as FDR campaigned on the premise that the only thing we have to fear is fear itself, I will run a more Derridean campaign and proclaim that the only thing in which we always and everywhere have to hope is hope itself, which is not deconstructible. Whatever determinate and identifiable something we hope in, whatever that turns out to be, is and ever will be deconstructible; but hope itself, if there is such a thing, is not deconstructible. My ultimate passion is the passion of nonknowing, the passion that does not know what stirs its passion, the passion for God, for the unknown God, a prayer for the event that is harbored in the name of God, which means the passion for God knows what, the strong passion of weak theology, for which I live unreservedly, for which I pray day and night.

The life of prayer and desire is fed by the event, kept alive and well by the delimitation of the name, which frees us for the truth of event, and it is the truth that sets us free.

The greatest strength of a weak theology is to keep us on our knees before the unknown God. We do not know whether the name of God is a pseudonym for the event, a fantastic concentration into one name of every-thing we desire and that desires us, or whether what we say we desire about the event is a pseudonym for the desire of God. Is God the incognito of the event, or is the event the incognito of God? Does the event belong to theol-ogy, or does theology belong to the event? A theology of the event arises from the confession that it is not possible to arrest this play, that this weak theology is unable to decide between these two, to resolve this fluctuation from on high in some final and decisive way. But that negative result is the doorway to an affirmation and the point of departure for our endless prayer, the reason we keep on praying.

For the point is to live like the lilies of the field, where there is no ques-tion of resolving it, as if some cognitive matter were at stake. Are we to sup-pose that life is a quiz we are asked to take in which the challenge is to dis-cover the identity of a hidden god? Are we to think that life is a gamble in which we had to choose between one name or another, a shell game in which we had better make the right guess or regret it for all eternity? Are we to imagine that our prayer is in vain if we cannot nail down the Proper Name of its addressee?

On the contrary, everything turns on keeping the gap between the name and the event open, on keeping the tension between them strong and alive, and thereby to be transported by that tension into the passion of life. The passion of life, the passion of desire, the passion of prayer, is fueled by revving up this tension to the breaking point. Undecidability fires passion to the limit, feeding the flames of faith in the unknown God by the very fluctuation of names. It is when I truly do not know what I desire that de-sire is fired white-hot. It is when I truly do not know if there is anyone to pray to that I find myself praying like mad. It is when I truly do not know where I am going that I am really faced with making a move.

All that is left to do is to carry out the motion, to make the move, to make the truth. When the Eleatics argued that motion was impossible, Diogenes refuted them by taking a few steps, which is, in the end, what I am recommending.[26] What matters with the event is to take a step. What matters is the passion, the leap, the witness, while leaving the Eleatics to their Greek games.

Who are we? *Quaestio mihi factus sum.* We are the nameless ones who are driven by the undecidability of the desire for God, made restless by the trembling of an indiscernible event, praying not to get any more lost than we already are, praying that our prayers to heaven go, to somewhere go. The works and days of our ordinary life are made to tremble by some ex-traordinary charge that inflicts upon us an invisible wound from which we cannot and do not even wish to be cured. We are incited by the powerless power of some quiet provocation, like the words "good, good . . . very good" sweeping softly across the surface of the deep, making being restless with the good. We are swept up in the winds of solicitation and invitation, of promise and a prayer for the event, our ears pressed close to the name of God, cupped tightly to the force of the event that gathers like a storm in that name and that keeps the world from closing over. We are tuned to the distant but insistent rumbling of the coming of the kingdom, the coming of the event, *viens, oui, oui.*

The world quivers quietly under the weak force of an event, made restless by the silent promptings of God's divinely subversive call. But is it really God who calls? Who knows who is calling? Is the event a breeze blowing out of paradise, the wind that swept across the darkness of the deep (the *ruach Elohim*), or is it only the anonymous rumbling of I know not what? God only knows!

No matter. We have been delivered from the search for the name of God by the event. For the truth of the event does not belong to the order of identificatory knowledge, as if our life's charge were to track down and learn the secret name of some fugitive spirit. The truth of the event releases us from the order of names and transports us to another level, where truth does not mean learning a name but making truth come true, making it happen, *facere veritatem,* letting the event happen, *sans voir, sans savoir, sans avoir,* praying and weeping before an unknown god.

Lord, when did we see you hungry and give you to eat?

Is that you, Lord?

The truth of the event is not a name but a deed.

Amen. Adieu. Go in peace. Shalom. *Viens, oui, oui.*

NOTES

INTRODUCTION

1. In John D. Caputo, *The Prayers and Tears of Jacques Derrida* (Bloomington: Indiana University Press, 1997), 288–89, following both Derrida and Levinas, I preferred the word *religion* and kept my distance from the word *theology* (but note p. xxix) on the grounds that theology suggests the onto-theological project, which takes God as an object of conceptual analysis—rather than the addressee of a prayer—and is awash in institutional power. For Levinas, God is withdrawn from theology and is found only in the relationship with the neighbor, as when I say "bonjour." I will come back to this in chapter 12. See Emmanuel Levinas, *Totality and Infinity: Essay on Exteriority,* trans. Alphonso Lingis (Pittsburgh: Duquesne University Press, 1969), 79. It now seems to me that theology is nothing more or less than a sustained reflection on the name of God. As Charles Winquist suggests to me, "Perhaps Derrida's religion without religion is accompanied by a theology without theology" (*The Surface of the Deep* [Aurora, Colo.: Davies Publishing Group, 2003], 206). See also Jeffrey W. Robbins, *In Search of a Non-Dogmatic Theology* (Aurora, Colo.: Davies Publishing Group, 2003), 43, 77–81, where I am rightly chided about this skittishness about theology.

2. Religious Studies is calm and objectifying—my previous objection to "theology"—while theology itself retains the disturbing passion for God.

3. See Robbins, *In Search of a Non-Dogmatic Theology,* chapter 3, "Theology without Religion," 41–53.

4. Charles Winquist, *Desiring Theology* (Chicago: University of Chicago Press, 1995).

5. For an earlier account of the event, which emphasizes its singularity, see John D. Caputo, *Against Ethics* (Bloomington: Indiana University Press, 1993), 93–98, 220–27. For Derrida's notion of the event, see Caputo, *Prayers and Tears,* 71–76. While I have not here attempted to reconstruct the meaning of "event" and "sense" in Gilles Deleuze, no one familiar with his monumental *The Logic of Sense,* trans. Mark Lester, ed. Constantin V. Boundas (New York: Columbia University Press, 1990) will fail to see the similarites between my idea of "event" and Deleuze's. In an important "sense," *The Weakness of God* is inspired by Deleuze, and this *Theology of the Event* in my subtitle is very much a contribution to a "(theo)logic of sense."

6. Jacques Derrida, *Negotiations: Interventions and Interviews: 1971–2001,* trans. Elizabeth Rottenberg (Stanford, Calif.: Stanford University Press, 2002), 182.

7. If to think theologically arises from the fact that we use the name of God and do not merely mention it, to use J. L. Austin's distinction, we must add that it is not enough to describe it as a performative utterance. As an event that overtakes us, it is more the case that it uses (or performs) us than that we use (or perform) it, and as a dis-ordering event, it is more like what Derrida calls a "perverformative."

8. Or what Jeffrey Robbins calls a "non-dogmatic theology" (*In Search of a Non-Dogmatic Theology*).

9. By a "weak theology" I do not mean a sorry spinelessness. The term is formed on analogy to Vattimo's "weak thought," Derrida's notion of a "weak force," and Benjamin's

"weak messianic force." It is also used by Jeffrey Robbins, "Weak Theology," *Journal of Cultural and Religious Theory* 5, no. 2 (April 2004) (www.jcrt.org); and Ulrich Engel, O.P., "Religion and Violence: Plea for a Weak Theology *in tempore belli*," *New Blackfriars* 82 (2001): 558–60. Citing Derrida's "Faith and Knowledge" essay—in *Religion,* ed. Jacques Derrida and Gianni Vattimo, trans. Samuel Weber (Stanford, Calif.: Stanford University Press, 1998)—Engel argues that in view of the demands of religious tolerance, the great monotheisms must weaken their strong dogmatic traditions in favor of a weak and pacific theology. Engel's piece can also be found at: www.espaces.info/deutsch/artikel/januar/ReligionVilolenceenglish.pdf

10. On the back cover of John Milbank's *Being Reconciled: Ontology and Pardon* (London: Routledge, 2003), Slavoj Žižek praises the book as "a glass of freshly squeezed orange juice after the chemical 'orange drink'" served up by "the post-modern 'post-secular' industry." We should recall, however, the possibility of pulp fiction.

11. See John D. Caputo, "For the Love of the Things Themselves: Derrida's Phenomenology of the Hyper-Real," *Journal of Cultural and Religious Theory* 1, no. 3 (July 2000) (www.jcrt.org).

12. R. Scott Appleby, Gabriel A. Almond, and Emmanuel Sivan very aptly named their book *Strong Religion: The Rise of Fundamentalisms around the World (The Fundamentalism Project)* (Chicago: University of Chicago Press, 2003). I, on the other hand, as a non-foundationalist and a non-fundamentalist, strongly advocate weak religion.

13. See Derrida, "As If It Were Possible, 'Within Such Limits' . . . ," in *Negotiations,* ed. Rottenberg, 343–70. In this connection, I would also recommend Richard Kearney, *The God Who May Be: A Hermeneutics of Religion* (Bloomington: Indiana University Press, 2001). Kearney, whose earlier work on the possible is cited by Derrida (399, n. 5), is also cultivating an idea of God as a possible rather than as a potent present actuality.

14. Had I come up with that exquisite image of theology myself, I would consider my life's work complete; see *Kierkegaard's Writings,* VI, *Fear and Trembling* and *Repetition,* trans. and ed. Howard and Edna Hong (Princeton, N.J.: Princeton University Press, 1983); *Fear and Trembling,* 32.

15. I first worked out something like this in Caputo, "For the Love of the Things Themselves."

16. By hyper-real I do not mean (nor do I mean to underestimate) Jean Baudrillard's conception of what we call "virtual" reality, the electronic reproduction of reality that is so enveloping that it blurs the distinction between the real and the virtual. Nor do I mean (much as I love it) the *hyperousios* of negative theology, for however much a theology of the event has in common with apophatic deferral of a comprehensive divine name, negative or mystical theology is very strong theology indeed, its deferrals serving to strengthen an absolutely central and powerful transcendence accompanied by a strong sense of who is in and who is out of the secret. See Caputo, *The Prayers and Tears of Jacques Derrida,* §1.

17. Hélène Cixous, *Portrait of Jacques Derrida as a Young Jewish Saint,* trans. Beverley Bie Brahic (New York: Columbia University Press, 2004), vii.

18. See the "Series Forward" in Slavoj Žižek, *The Puppet and the Dwarf: The Perverse Core of Christianity* (Cambridge: MIT Press, 2003), vii–viii.

19. See Jacques Derrida, *Voyous: Deux essais sur la raison* (Galilée, 2003), 13; English: *Rogues: Two Essays on Reason,* trans. Pascale-Anne Brault and Michael Naas (Stanford: Stanford University Press, 2005), xiv. See also "The University without Condition," in Jacques Derrida, *Without Alibi,* ed. and trans. Peggy Kamuf (Stanford, Calif.: Stanford University Press, 2002), 202–37.

20. In the study that follows I will tend to follow that usage, but with this large proviso, that this is what Heidegger would call an "ontical" sense of "world," of which our fundamental being-in-the-world is the presupposition. I am not suggesting that we should leave the "world" to itself to run its bloody course; on the contrary, I am seeking to restore the

passion of our being-in-the-world by delimiting the "economy of the world" by means of the passion of the gift.

21. Were I not of such a serious disposition, I would say that the "sacred anarchy" that follows should be considered as my own modest contribution to the hilarious history of *sa*—from *signifians* through *savoir absolute* to Saint Augustine and now, my candidate, Sacred Anarchy. But I will not say such a thing. I do resist some temptations.

22. I am not denying, in fact, I invite proposals for, analogous versions of something like this event in other traditions, upon which I am even less competent to comment.

23. See John Dominic Crossan, *A Long Way from Tipperary: A Memoir* (New York: HarperCollins, 2000), 136 ff.

24. One could, of course, affirm the parables and paradoxes of the kingdom that I am describing under the name of a "sacred anarchy" in Part II without embracing my idea of the weakness of God in Part I. That is what a more enlightened and progressive version of orthodoxy does. In order to show solidarity with the weak, God voluntarily empties Godself of power, freely chooses not to exercise this power, and this divine *kenosis* does not contradict omnipotence but manifests it. I do not travel down that path because it smacks of a ruse, a kind of docetism, in which weakness is an even more profound demonstration of power, and because it re-implicates God in evil. Omnipotence cannot simply wash its hands of evil simply on the grounds that it has chosen not to intervene.

25. Catherine Keller, *Face of the Deep: A Theology of Becoming* (London: Routledge, 2003).

1. GOD WITHOUT SOVEREIGNTY

1. Jacques Derrida, *Voyous* (Paris: Galilée, 2003), 161; English: *Rogues: Two Essays on Reason,* trans. Pascale-Anne Brault and Michael Naas (Stanford: Stanford University Press, 2005), 114.

2. For new readers of Derrida, who need to brush up on what *différance* "means," see *Deconstruction in a Nutshell: A Conversation with Jacques Derrida,* ed. with commentary by John D. Caputo (New York: Fordham University Press, 1997), 99–105. For more on God and *différance,* see John D. Caputo, *The Prayers and Tears of Jacques Derrida: Religion without Religion* (Bloomington: Indiana University Press, 1997), 1–20.

3. That secular ring does not ring true, however, of *écriture,* a word that means both "writing" and "scripture," although the constant rendering of it as "writing" by Derrida's translators tends to efface its theological sense. Most deconstructors are not interested in making deconstruction a study of scripture, although that is a sense that the theologically tuned will hear. See Kevin Hart, *The Trespass of the Sign* (New York: Fordham University Press, 2000), 49–64, who suggests that this oscillation in *écriture* is like the oscillation in *pharmakon* and *supplément,* and hence that *écriture* is an undecidable. Whatever his authorial intentions, Hart continues, "Derrida's text cannot help but signify both 'writing' and 'scripture'" (61).

4. Jacques Derrida, "Circumfession: Fifty-nine Periods and Periphrases" in Geoffrey Bennington and Jacques Derrida, *Jacques Derrida* (Chicago: University of Chicago Press, 1993), 155.

5. Jacques Derrida, *Margins of Philosophy,* trans. Alan Bass (Chicago: University of Chicago Press, 1982), 22.

6. See *Philosophy in a Time of Terror: Dialogues with Jürgen Habermas and Jacques Derrida,* ed. with commentary by Giovanna Borradori (Chicago: University of Chicago Press, 2003), and Derrida, *Voyous.* For "weak force" *(force faible)* see *Voyous,* 13; *Rogues,* xiv. See also "The University without Condition," in Jacques Derrida, *Without Alibi,* ed. and trans. Peggy Kamuf (Stanford: Stanford University Press, 2002), 202–37. For a commentary on *Voyous,* see John D. Caputo, "Without Sovereignty, Without Being: Unconditionality, the

Coming God and Derrida's Democracy to Come," *Journal of Cultural and Religious Theory* 4, no. 3 (August 2003) (www.jcrt.org). On the "democracy to come," see *Specters of Marx: The State of the Debt, the Work of Mourning, and the New International,* trans. Peggy Kamuf (New York: Routledge, 1994), 64–65.

    7. Jacques Derrida, "The Force of Law: 'The Mystical Foundation of Authority,'" trans. Mary Quantaince, in *Deconstruction and the Possibility of Justice,* ed. Drucilla Cornell et al. (New York: Routledge, 1992), 14–15.

    8. This has been going on for a long time. Kierkegaard has been my steadiest companion, and "Paul" was once my name, when I was, epochs ago, a De La Salle Christian Brother.

    9. See John D. Caputo and Yvonne Sherwood, "Otobiographies, Or How a Torn and Disembodied Ear Hears a Promise of Death: A Prearranged Meeting between Yvonne Sherwood and John Caputo and the Book of Amos and Jacques Derrida," in *Derrida and Religion: Other Testaments,* ed. Kevin Hart and Yvonne Sherwood (London: Routledge, 2004), 209–40.

    10. Jacques Derrida, *Of Grammatology,* corrected edition, trans. Gayatri Spivak (Baltimore: Johns Hopkins University Press, 1997), 42.

    11. John Dominic Crossan, *Jesus: A Revolutionary Biography* (San Francisco: HarperSanFrancisco, 1994), 54 ff.

    12. This is strictly "strategic," since reversal is always a provisional and transitional strategy to be followed by displacement; in the end, the idea is that there would be no special favors, but a community of radical equals.

    13. When Augustine defined peace as the tranquility of order, he reflected a world in which Christianity had made its peace with political power, beginning what became a centuries-old collusion with the state, which is why he devised a theory of just war. Christian life after Constantine lost its anarchic and prophetic spirit that distrusts the tranquility of the prevailing order and is bent on disturbing the peace, and this in the name of *shalom. Shalom* is the peace that comes from justice *(sedaqah)* for the poor and the outcast, the peace that comes of God's rule, not the highly hierarchical domestic tranquility prized by the religious and political right wing. In so doing, Christianity had unfortunately lost the anarchic and prophetic spirit that was alive and well in the sayings of Jesus, in Jesus' prophetic discourse on the "kingdom of God," and in the first three centuries. See Jacques Ellul, *Anarchy and Christianity,* trans. Geoffrey W. Bromiley (Grand Rapids, Mich.: Eerdmans, 1991), 27–30.

    14. *Debates in Continental Philosophy: Conversations with Contemporary Thinkers,* ed. Richard Kearney (New York: Fordham University Press, 2004), xx.

    15. *Specters of Marx,* 56

    16. Søren Kierkegaard, *Kierkegaard's Works,* Vol. XIV, *Two Ages: The Age of Revolution and the Present Age,* ed. and trans. H. Hong and E. Hong (Princeton, N.J.: Princeton University Press, 1978).

    17. Heidegger jacked all this up a couple of notches into ontological terms in *Being and Time,* and through parsimonious footnoting succeeded in making it look like he "grounded" it.

    18. Ellul, *Anarchy and Christianity,* 51–52: the prophets spoke for God against the royal misdeeds, and it was their words, not the king's, that were taken as the word of God.

    19. Derrida, "Force of Law," 26.

    20. Jacques Derrida, *Positions,* trans. Alan Bass (Chicago: University of Chicago Press, 1981), 40.

    21. Derrida, *Of Grammatology,* 71.

    22. Commenting on Hegel, who is commenting on Moses Mendelson, Derrida writes: "Since God does not manifest himself, he is not truth for the Jews, total presence or parou-

sia. He gives orders without appearing." *Glas,* trans. Richard Rand and John Leavey (Lincoln: University of Nebraska Press, 1986), 51a., cited by Hart, *The Trespass of Sign,* 62. Yahweh then would be what is "essentially other than truth," not Heideggerian *lethe,* which is the very heart of truth, *pace* John Sallis, "Deformatives: Essentially Other than Truth," *Double Truth* (Albany: SUNY Press, 1995).

23. See Indira Viswanathan Peterson, *Poems to Siva: The Hymns of the Tamil Saints* (Delhi: Motilal Barardsidass Publishers, 1991), "Bhiksatana: The Beggar (Poems 37–39)," 123–26; and the story of Nandanaar in *Periya Puranam* by Sekkizhaar, condensed English version by G. Vanmikanathan (Mylapore, Madras: Sri Ramakrishna Math, 1985), 558–67. My thanks to my colleague Joanne Waghorne for this tip.

24. Daniel Maguire, *The Moral Core of Judaism and Christianity* (Minneapolis: Fortress Press, 1993), 189–90.

25. See Karl Barth, *The Epistle to the Romans,* trans. E. C. Hoskyns (London: Oxford University Press, 1933). Throughout this famous book, Barth delimits "all ethical and religious illusions" (p. 68), in favor of the "impossible possibility" (p. 79) of God.

26. See Ellul, *Anarchy and Christianity,* 32–34.

27. See Hart, *The Trespass of the Sign,* 107 ff.; See Jacques Derrida, "Des tours de Babel," trans. Joseph Graham, in *Difference in Translation* (Ithaca, N.Y.: Cornell University Press, 1985), 209 ff.

28. Jean-Luc Marion, *God without Being: Hors-Texte,* trans. Thomas A. Carlson (Chicago: University of Chicago Press, 1991), 70 ff.

29. I agree that the discourse of mystical theology has a role to play, that it is itself a powerful and disruptive discourse in its own right, which I very much love. See my discussion of Derrida and Meister Eckhart in *More Radical Hermeneutics* (Bloomington: Indiana University Press, 2001), 249–64. This raises the daunting problem of the relation between the discourse of mystical theology and the scriptural discourse on the "kingdom of God."

30. Plato, *Republic,* trans. Paul Shorey, in *The Collected Dialogues of Plato,* ed. Edith Hamilton and Huntington Cairns (New York: Random House, 1961), Bk. VI, 509 (d), p. 745.

31. See Derrida, *Voyous,* 193–94; *Roques,* 139–40.

32. Ibid., 155; *Roques,* 110.

33. In the poetry of the Scriptures, as Abraham Heschel has very nicely shown, God is not an unmoved but very much a moved mover, who suffers with the suffering and grieves with the grieving (see "The Theology of Pathos," in *The Prophets* [New York: Harper & Row, 1962], 2:1–11). When metaphysical theology reaches the point where it finds itself hard-pressed to explain how God can suffer, the whole onto-theological tradition shipwrecks, having drifted out of sight of its biblical shores.

34. If one were willing to surrender the deliciously disruptive effect of "sacred anarchy" *(hier-an-arche),* one might, on strictly Levinasian grounds, prefer to speak instead of a "holy" anarchy (which has the advantage, in American English, of sounding a little like "[raising] *holy* hell"). Levinas distinguishes the holy *(saint)* from the sacred *(sacré),* as the separate or transcendent from the immanent, where the world or the earth, a mountain or a homeland, is "sacred." Levinas is trying to get us to call Heidegger a "pagan." Levinas is more or less right about that, I think, and Heidegger deserves what he is getting from Levinas, because in Heidegger this Hölderlinian economy of gods and mortals, heavens and earth, is all put in the shameful service of poetizing a dangerous Greco-German language and even homeland of Being. But Levinas's contempt for Heidegger's thoroughly contemptible politics should not blind us to the genuine power of the "sacred"—the power, say, of Native American reverence for the earth, which is another form of non-biblical "religion" and a counter to a destructive violence of the technological will-to-power that Heidegger understands extremely well and Levinas ignores (nothing is simple). The "holy," on

the other hand, is, in Levinas's scheme, the power of the transcendent, of the other, of the wholly other, and here the paradigm is not Native American religion but the God of Israel, the transcendent Jahweh, whose unnameable Name is/means "I am who I am and who I will be"—and you, Moses, have enough on your plate as it is and should mind your own business (Exod. 2:14). Still, Levinas would have profited from taking to heart the psalm on the cedars of Lebanon, which has a different sort of transcendence but a real and irreducible one, or the main body of the book of Job, not the theodicy.

35. In this view I have enough textual support in the New Testament to hold off the Grand Inquisitor at least long enough to make a clean escape out the back door. I even have a theologian or two who will give me provisional cover as I quietly make my exit. (For the rest I will concede that my anarchic nature is such as it is; so be it; that is how God made me.) In *Narratives of a Vulnerable God* (Louisville: John Knox Press, 1994), 3–26, William Placher, for example, argues that the God of the New Testament is to be thought in terms of love not power, and that accordingly the sense of God's power must be ordered (or subordinated) to the preeminence of God's love. The power of God in the New Testament is not to be conceived like the pagan Zeus wielding bolts of thunder at anyone who incurs his wrath. Nor is it to be taken as the arbitrary power of a mad Roman emperor like Caligula, who can destroy anything he will with a single imperial edict. These are blasphemous and pagan images that distort the power of God—our dear Peter Damian, whom I have found a way to love, is a good example of this error—that is revealed in the New Testament, as Placher shows. If, as Roger Haight explains so well in *Jesus: The Symbol of God* (Maryknoll, N.Y.: Orbis, 1999), Jesus is the revelation of God, the *eikon* of the Father, the symbol of God, then the God revealed by Jesus is revealed in powerlessness, in suffering and vulnerability, and this not just docetically, as an appearance God assumes, but quite really. If God is a father, then God is, in all fairness, also a mother, and then God is a father and mother weeping over their suffering children whose sorry fate is out of their control. I also see some signs of life in *The Openness of God: A Biblical Challenge to the Traditional Understanding of God,* ed. Clark Pinnock et al. (Downers Grove, Ill.: InterVarsity Press, and Carlisle, U.K.: Paternoster Press, 1994).

2. ST. PAUL ON THE LOGOS OF THE CROSS

1. For a sensitive account of the logic of the cross, see Stanislas Breton, *Word and Cross,* trans. Jacquelyn Porter (New York: Fordham University Press, 2002).

2. Slavoj Žižek, *The Puppet and the Dwarf: The Perverse Core of Christianity* (Cambridge: MIT Press, 2003), 171.

3. God's love, as William Placer argues, makes God vulnerable, because to love is to expose oneself to suffering from or with the suffering of the beloved. If God were absolutely invulnerable, impassible, then God could not love; God would not have the strength to love. Aristotle's unmoved, impassible God, who knew and presumably loved only himself, and who therefore did not suffer from his love or from the sad fates of beings in the sublunary world, has nothing to do with the image of God revealed in Jesus. See William Placher, *Narratives of a Vulnerable God* (Louisville, Ky.: Westminster John Knox Press, 1994), 3–26.

4. If, as Anthony Bartlett, following René Girard, points out in *Cross Purposes: The Violent Grammar of Christian Atonement* (Harrisburg, Pa.: Trinity Press International, 2001), the idea of a sacrificial death, of death as having an exchange value, is what a "hierarchy" or "sacred order" means, then it would belong to what we are calling a sacred *an*archy to renounce this economy of violence. Bartlett's notion of an "abyssal compassion" corresponds to the notion I am advancing here that the central structure in the death of Jesus is not a sacrificial exchange but Jesus' words of forgiveness.

5. This is a little like Heidegger, who, commenting on Heraclitus's saying that the *basileia* is in the hands of a child *(paidos)*, speaks of a child king, a kingdom in the hands of a child at play, of an-archic *arche* (*The Principle of Reason,* trans. Reginald Lily [Bloomington: Indiana University Press, 1991], 113).

6. Alain Badiou, *Saint Paul: The Foundations of Universalism,* trans. Ray Brassier (Stanford: Stanford University Press, 2003) offers a robust challenge to Nietzsche by seeing in Paul a militant who has been galvanized into action by the event of the resurrection and who, like Zarathustra, overcame guilt and a moribund interest in death by way of the new being, the new life effected by the resurrection. "If Nietzsche is so violent toward Paul it is because he is his rival far more than his opponent" (p. 61). For a helpful commentary, see Thomas Flynn, "The Religious Return in Recent French Philosophy," *Philosophy of Religion for a New Century: Essays in Honor of Thomas Eugene Long* (Dordrecht: Kluwer Academic Publishers, 2004).

7. My taste for this kind of critique of philosophy does not mean I am sick of philosophy (or cynical about it) and recommend replacing it with religion. But I do want to jolt philosophy off dead center and give it a new start, which is pretty much what I think Kierkegaard did when he decided to shock the categories of Greek philosophy with biblical categories on behalf of poor existing individuals everywhere. Disciplinary borders need to be crossed and new objects of study invented, the difference being that for most postmodern writers, such crossings generally mean crossing over onto the turf of art and literature, not of religion, religious poetry, or sacred literature. But Derrida himself tells us that "the original, heterogeneous elements of Judaism and Christianity," before they were assimilated by Greek philosophy, belong to the "other" of Greek philosophy and Western civilization, an other that "haunts" the philosophical tradition "threatening and unsettling the assured 'identities' of Western philosophy." See Richard Kearney's interview with Derrida in *Dialogues with Contemporary Thinkers* (Manchester, U.K.: Manchester University Press, 1984), 117. As Kevin Hart says, commenting on this text, Judaism and Christianity—before they are assimilated by Greek philosophy—are part of the process of deconstruction, not part of deconstruction's prey. The idea behind this experiment in a theology of the event is to expose philosophy to its other, to the more scandalous other of the prophetic, messianic, and eschatological lines of force that run through the kingdom and sweep across the surface of biblical texts and then show up again, downstream, in deconstruction, as they rush toward the sea (*The Trespass of the Sign* [New York: Fordham University Press, 2003], 93).

8. John van Buren, *The Young Heidegger* (Bloomington: Indiana University Press, 1994), 167.

9. This need not be an opposition of Christians and the world. It probably was also an opposition within the Christian community. See Dale Martin, *The Corinthian Body* (New Haven, Conn.: Yale University Press, 1995) for an account of the sociology of the Corinthian Christians and their implicit view of the body. Martin argues that though relatively well-off personally, Paul associated himself with the majority who belonged to the lower socioeconomic stratum, as opposed to "the strong," the well-born Christians, and that this distinction, which characterized the Corinthians at large, also obtained within the Christian community, so that Paul is opposing the "strong" among the Christians who associate themselves with Greek wisdom: "Paul takes issue with corporeal hierarchy of upper-class ideology, substituting in its place a topsy-turvy value system that reflects, in his view, the logic of apocalypticism and loyalty to a crucified Messiah" (xvii).

10. Günther Bornkamm, *Paul,* trans. D. M. G. Stalker (New York: Harper & Row, 1969), 210–16.

11. Thomas Ogletree, *Hospitality to the Stranger* (Philadelphia: Orbis, 1985), 128.

12. That is why I object to Vernard Eller in *Christian Anarchy: Jesus' Primacy over the Powers* (Grand Rapids, Mich.: Eerdmans, 1987; reprint: Eugene, Oreg: Wipf and Stock

Publishers, 1999), to whom Jacques Ellul refers us with admiration. While I like Eller's motif of pacifism and nonviolence, in the end it seems to me not merely nonviolent but timid and world-conforming. This brand of "anarchism"—this cannot be the right word—is classic two-worlds theory. On the one hand, theology, which is polite, soft-spoken—this sounds more like a courtier than a saint, and I am not sure that would have been a good description of Jesus in the temple!—which has, on the other hand, nothing to do with politics, which is Godless pride and hubris. Be conformed to the world as much as you can, but in your heart don't be conformed to the world. Eller is baffled by the fact that people get more upset over the possible nuclear annihilation of life on this planet than about illicit sex between consenting adults. Anarchism means private piety; go practice the kingdom of God in your heart, on weekends and after hours, and the rest of the time, march in step with the powers that be. If you speak, please don't drag Christianity into the argument. Do not make a stir about all the violence and injustice in the world, but in your heart know that Jesus loves us and someday you're going to go to heaven. Do not worry about the persecution of the helpless, because God who is a lot smarter than you are has an idea about how to deal with all that in his own good time. In the meantime, keep your hands off the little miss next door.

13. See Karl Barth, *The Epistle to the Romans,* trans. E. C. Hoskyns (London: Oxford University Press Paperbacks, [1933], 1968), 481 ff.; Jacques Ellul, *Anarchy and Christianity,* trans. Geoffrey W. Bromiley (Grand Rapids, Mich.: Eerdmans, 1991), 78–85.

14. Of course, the deeper problem lies in thinking so hierarchically to begin with. If you think of God in terms of hierarchical power, you will naturally be inclined to think of the human order as imaging that order of power. So the more radical solution is to re-imagine God in terms of what is out of power, which is what Derrida is doing by questioning the model of sovereignty. This is also a central theme of Catherine Keller's *Face of the Deep: A Theology of Becoming* (London: Routledge, 2003), 98, which I will take up in chapters 3–4.

15. This line does not generally play well at home. Jerry Falwell made a statement of that sort after 9/11—"I really believe that the pagans, and the abortionists, and the feminists, and the gays and the lesbians who are actively trying to make that an alternative lifestyle, the ACLU, People For the American Way, all of them who have tried to secularize America. I point the finger in their face and say 'you helped this happen'"—and then found it necessary to head for cover for the next few weeks until the storm blew over. See http://www.cnn.com/2001/US/09/14/Falwell.apology/

16. Daniel Maguire, *The Moral Core of Judaism and Christianity* (Minneapolis: Fortress Press, 1993), 159–60.

3. THE BEAUTIFUL RISK OF CREATION

1. Cited by André Neher, "Visions du temps et l'histoire dans la culture juive," in *Les Cultures et le temps,* ed. UNESCO, Introduction by Paul Ricoeur (Paris: Les presses de l'UNESCO, 1975), 179. This text is cited by Catherine Keller, *Face of the Deep: A Theology of Becoming* (London: Routledge, 2003), 193–94, who is citing Ilya Prigogine and Isabelle Stengers, *Order out of Chaos* (Boulder: New Science Library, 1984), 313, whose translation (from the French) we are using.

2. Jacques Derrida, *Voyous* (Paris: Galilée, 2003), 14; English: *Rogues: Two Essays on Reason,* trans. Pascale-Anne Brault and Michael Naas (Stanford: Stanford University Press, 2005), xiv–xv. For Derrida's account of *khora,* see *On the Name,* ed. Thomas Dutoit (Stanford: Stanford University Press, 1995), 89ff., and for a commentary, John D. Caputo, *Deconstruction in a Nutshell* (New York: Fordham University Press, 1997), ch. 3.

3. See *Pentateuch and Rashi's Commentary,* ed. Abraham Ben Isaiah and Benjamin Sharfman (Brooklyn: S.S. & R. Publishing Co., 1949). See the discussion of Rashi's translation in Jon D. Levenson, *Creation and the Persistence of Evil: The Jewish Drama of Divine Omnipotence* (San Francisco: Harper & Row, 1988), 4–5, and E. A. Speiser, *Genesis* (Garden City, N.Y.: Doubleday, 1984), 12–13, to which we are referred by Levenson (157–58, n. 12).

4. I am following Keller's account of Rashi's grammatical analysis of Genesis 1:1–3 in Keller, *Face of the Deep,* 114–16. According to Keller, Rashi held that the first verses are to be read (schematically): (1) *when* Elohim began to create—(2) at which time the earth was a *tohu wa-bohu* . . . (3) then God said. . . . The first draft of the present chapter challenged the theological doctrines of omnipotence and *creatio ex nihilo* by drawing upon the work of Gerhard May's *Creatio ex nihilo: The Doctrine of "Creation out of Nothing" in Early Christian Thought,* trans. A. S. Worrall (Edinburgh: T & T Clark, 1994), and upon a certain Derridean intuition about *khora* and its link to the *tohu wa-bohu* that I had been mulling over for some time. See Caputo, *Deconstruction in a Nutshell,* 95–96, and "God and Anonymity: Prolegomena to an Ankhoral Religion," in *A Passion for the Impossible: John D. Caputo in Focus,* ed. Mark Dooley (Albany: SUNY Press, 2003), 1–19. But it was only after *Face of the Deep* arrived like a gift in the mail that I found what I was looking for, a theologian literate in post-structuralist theory who could mount just the theological argument and scriptural exegesis I needed to lead me through these thickets while reminding me in the process of the watery *tehom* and opening my eyes to the insights of process philosophy. I am also grateful to Prof. Keller for reading the revised version of this manuscript and for her valuable suggestions which more than once saved me from myself.

5. See David Toshio Tsumura, *The Earth and the Waters in Genesis 1 and 2: A Linguistic Investigation* (Sheffield, England: JSOT Press, Supplement Series 83, 1989), 43; see 17–43 generally.

6. Keller, *Face of the Deep,* 15–61, makes this use of Edward Said's distinction between "beginning," a contextually motivated start of a series, and "origin," an absolutely originary source (which Said got from Foucault, who derived it from Nietzsche!) in his *Beginnings: Intention and Method* (New York: Columbia University Press, 1975), 372 ff.

7. See the excellent visual illustration of the first days in Norbert M. Samuelson, *Judaism and the Doctrine of Creation* (Cambridge: Cambridge University Press, 1994), 161–62.

8. "Two and a half millennia of Western theology have made it easy to forget that throughout the ancient Near eastern world, including Israel, the point of creation is not the production of matter out of nothing, but rather the emergence of a stable community in a benevolent and life-sustaining order" (Levenson, *Creation and the Persistence of Evil,* 12). See also Claus Westermann, *Genesis 1–11* (Minneapolis: Augsburg Press, 1984), 92 (cited by Levenson).

9. I do not object that the original narrative has been altered and expanded by later theological reflection. For one thing, this is not the original narrative but a highly redacted narrative of the beginning, the last one that finally got written down after a long oral tradition. It is not an *arche* itself but a highly edited archive, and only one of two, the second one at that, although it comes first. Such revisioning is the name of game in a theological or religious tradition, as it is indeed in *any* tradition ("tradition" means transmission, repeating with a difference). I object to *how* the aboriginal elements in the narrative have been altered.

10. We are hardly alone. This suspicion is basic to the process theologians. See the authors' Foreword to John Cobb and David Ray Griffin, *Process Theology: An Introductory Exposition* (Knoxville, Ky.: Westminster John Knox Press, 1977), and Charles Hartshorne, *Omnipotence and Other Theological Mistakes* (Albany: SUNY Press, 1983).

11. Luce Irigaray, *The Forgetting of Air in Martin Heidegger,* trans. Mary Beth Mader (Austin: University of Texas Press, 1999), cited by Keller, *Face of the Deep,* 41. Irigaray is making this argument against Heidegger.

12. Emmanuel Levinas, *Otherwise than Being or Beyond Essence,* trans. Alphonso Lingis (The Hague: Martinus Nijhoff Publishers, 1981), 20, 94, 167.

13. See Keller, *Face of the Deep,* 84 ff. on Barth's demonization of the aboriginal elements as *das Nichtige,* as a kind of dark and scary nugatory non-being with whom God does battle (as if Genesis were the *Enuma elish*). See Karl Barth, *Church Dogmatics,* ed. G. W. Bromiley and T. F. Torrance, Vol. III, *The Doctrine of Creation* (London: T & T Clark International, 1958, 2004), 1:106 ff.

14. Radical Orthodoxy is a movement that turns on the quaint and (self-)comforting idea that everything is either a Christian metaphysics of participation (that is, Radical Orthodoxy) or nihilism, by which they seem to mean variants of their version of Nietzsche or Derrida, which for them means that human existence is awash in an irrational flux. So Radical Orthodoxy, which gives us a choice between being Cambridge Thomists or nihilists, needs to expand its horizons.

15. The text of *Enuma elish: The Epic of Creation,* trans. L. W. King, from *The Seven Tablets of Creation* (Escondido, Calif.: Book Tree, 1998) is available online at http://www.sacred-texts.com/ane/enuma.htm

16. Keller, *Face of the Deep,* 28–31. The history of the onto-theologic of *creatio ex nihilo* is starting to sound like Dan Brown's *The Da Vinci Code,* a great cover-up of a feminine principle!

17. Tsumura, *The Earth and the Waters,* 62–65, disputes the idea that a Canaanite dragon myth lies behind the use of *tehom* in Genesis; there is no "struggle with the chaos" *(Chaoskampf)* mythology in Genesis, according to him.

18. That Genesis is a cosmogony, not a theogony, is the basis of the claim of Yeheskel Kaufmann, *The Religion of Israel* (New York: Schocken, 1972), that the essence of Israelite religion lies in God's transcendent power over creation. God is not the highest being *in* the world, like a pagan god, but the transcendent maker *of* the world, and it is that claim that Jon Levenson wants to delimit in *Creation and the Persistence of Evil.*

19. This is not as far-flung a suggestion as it might seem. For Samuelson, *Judaism and the Doctrine of Creation,* there is no *creatio ex nihilo* in the metaphysical sense in Genesis—there is consensus among biblical scholars about that—but rather a world formation that goes back to what Samuelson calls a "nothing" in the sense of "no-thing," that is, "a space predisposed to be made into something" (133; cf. p. 226). As Keller says, Samuelson "characterizes this no-thing in khoric/chaotic terms as space itself" (*Face of the Deep,* 184). In my view there is something khoral about the primeval elements in Genesis even as Derrida thinks about this figure from the *Timaeus* with a biblical image in his head. Samuelson is very good at explicating the fit between the *Timaeus* and medieval Jewish accounts of creation in Genesis. To extinguish or literally "annihilate" this figure of *khora* or of the primal elements is to take a metaphysical flight from reality that leaves the rest of us poor existing individuals to face the worst.

20. Conrad Hyers, *The Meaning of Creation: Genesis and Modern Science* (Atlanta, Ga.: John Knox Press, 1984), 63.

21. Elohim makes what is empty filled and what is desolate come alive; see the interesting schema proposed by Hyers, *Meaning of Creation,* 69.

22. Hyers, *Meaning of Creation,* 66. Or imagine the seven days as seven transparencies imposed one upon the other, as suggested by Samuelson, *Judaism and the Doctrine of Creation,* 159–60. The point is that days 1–3 lay out regions that are filled in and populated respectively in days 4–6.

23. Levinas sometimes slips into thinking that being, or *il y a,* is evil! See Emmanuel Levinas, *On Escape,* trans. Bettina Bergo (Stanford: Stanford University Press, 2003), where this tendency is especially pronounced.

24. See Catherine Keller and Anne Daniell, eds., *Process and Difference: Between Cosmological and Poststructuralist Postmodernism* (Albany: SUNY Press, 2002).

25. John D. Caputo, *Radical Hermeneutics* (Bloomington: Indiana University Press, 1987); *More Radical Hermeneutics* (Bloomington: Indiana University Press, 2001).

26. For Hyers, *The Meaning of Creation,* the primeval elements are not evil (as in Gnosticism), just slippery; for Levenson, *Creation,* 17, they are chaotic and inherently resistant to order, and they require God's mastery to keep them in check; for Keller, they are dark, embracing depths of our existence, and we should get beyond the "tehomophobic" idea of a primal war with them *(Chaoskampf),* such as Levenson advocates.

27. Keller's theology of the earth and its becoming and my own modest theology of the event are partners. For her, Tehom, Elohim, and Ruach form a kind of Whiteheadian Trinity, where the "deep" represents neither God nor not-God, but the depths of God, and in which God and creatures mutually imply one another as beings within being. She delimits omnipotence and *creatio ex nihilo* and saves the void and the deep just in order to give the earth the room to breathe and to see to it that the earth, the cosmos, is saturated—or aerated—with the spirit of God. Just so, I save the wind sweeping across the deep in terms of my thematic of the "call" that rolls over the wild and the deep, the call Elohim calls to us in and through and with the elements. I want to save the void and the deep in order to see that the spirit of God settles upon the least of us, insinuating itself into the cracks and crevices of creation, the lowliest creatures made of dust, and calls to us. The spirit of God is not the power that overpowers creatures but the voice of their powerlessness. We both insist upon the uncertainty and frailty of human existence and that this element is preserved in the Hebrew Scriptures. We share a common celebration of incarnation, where for Keller the kingdom of God means celebrating God's incarnation in matter—the world is God's body, to use the language of Sallie McFague (*The Body of God: An Ecological Theology* [Minneapolis: Fortress Press, 1993]), and I see the kingdom in God siding with the carnage that accompanies and menaces incarnation. Healing wounded flesh is the work of the kingdom, a sign of its khora-poreality. We share a celebration of mortal life, of the uncertainty and contingency of life woven of flesh and time and the elements, of earth and water, birth and death, joy and sorrow. Keller broadens and deepens my argument by seeing to it that the kingdom of God is not confined to human bodies but is expanded to all of God's body.

28. The Israelite priesthood composed an "epic myth that incorporates the best of scientific/philosophical opinion of that time to make sense out of the political-moral-religious situation in which Israel and (perhaps more importantly) its ruling religious priesthood found itself" (Samuelson, *Judaism and the Doctrine of Creation,* 164).

29. For a classic account of the historical-critical basics of Genesis that is still highly regarded today, see Bruce Vawter, *On Genesis: A New Reading* (Garden City, N.Y.: Doubleday, 1977); on creation, see 37–163.

30. Jack Miles, *God: A Biography* (New York: Knopf, 1995), chapter 1. I am using this general frame, and I found the general tendency of Miles's contrast between the two narratives helpful. For Derrida's gloss on the creation narratives, which centers on the naming of animals, see Jacques Derrida, "The Animal That Therefore I Am (More to Follow)," trans. David Wills, *Critical Inquiry* 28 (Winter 2002): 369–418.

31. Milan Kundera, *The Unbearable Lightness of Being,* trans. Michael Heim (New York: Harper & Row, 1985), 247–48 (Part 6, ch. 5): "Behind all the European faiths, religious and political, we find the first chapter of Genesis, which tells us that the world was created properly, that human existence is good. . . . Let us call this basic faith a categorical agreement with being." Kundera is being a little cynical because he thinks that if you hold to that faith, you cannot also hold that "shit" happens (next paragraph), which is, of course, a fail-

ure on Kundera's part to read more carefully. It is just *because* "shit" happens (amply illustrated in the second narrative) that we need the Elohist's faith (first narrative); the two stories belong together. That is the difference between being and an event.

32. Franz Rosenzweig, *The Star of Redemption,* trans. William W. Hallow (Boston: Beacon Press, 1964), 151.

33. As Catherine Keller cautions, "dominion" over the earth meant "caretaking," not "exploitation" or "annihilation." Besides, our first parents even appear to have been vegetarians (Gen. 1:29), and we have to wait for the new creation, the new start with Noah, when after repeating P's injunction to be fruitful and multiply, God invites Noah and his sons to add meat to their diets (9:3).

34. Hyers, *The Meaning of Creation,* 152.

35. Curiously, the *Enuma elish* starts out with the fact that Apsu can't get any sleep because of all the noise his offspring are making. Parenting was clearly the model the ancient mythologists had in their mind in describing the original genesis.

36. In the second narrative, life and fertility are less a gift and more an economy of tit for tat. The first story is the prototype of a more open-ended, generous, gift-giving conception of religion, the rule of the good, of gifts giving rise to more gifts; while the second is a prototype of a grimmer kind of religion, which is a radically "economic," book-balancing, sacrificial, authoritarian, archical, and hierarchical conception. (The irony is, of course, that P himself was a priest and liked neat binary pairs.) The first story favors the word "good" to describe God's rule, while the second is concerned with trials, exiles, and regret. Both views of God and "religion" have since flourished. Both views had a future, and both have a basis in Genesis, in the "Lord God," since, whatever their provenance, Elohim and Yahweh are meant to be the same God, not two different Gods, but two different "personalities" of the same protagonist, as Miles puts it so artfully.

The law that governed the formation of monotheism was that many different personal traits, which in polytheism could be subcontracted out to separate deities, were run together, so that one God had to do it all and be all of these things at once, which has put a lot of stress on the idea of God over the epochs. As we will see, both stories were onto something important about religion, but the problem was to find the right mix and to set the tensions between the two just right. Unfortunately, the beneficence of the gift-giving frame of mind embodied in the first account is regularly overshadowed by the economic violence of the second account, which too many lovers of religion have, alas, loved to excess and held like a sword over the head of their fellow human beings. The benign creativity of Elohim is a lofty counterpart to a God imagined in terms of love, but for real love, we need a little more of the intimacy that shows up in J's narrative, however stormy it might be.

The first creation story is a poem that celebrates life on earth and thanks God for his beneficent act in forming things. P never mentions strength or might. Up to the 26th verse, where it starts to sound a little proprietary and anthropocentric to our modern ecological ears, Genesis might even be viewed as one of our earliest essays in "ecology." It is certainly a retrospective illusion to blame the authors of Genesis for suburban sprawl, blacktop, and shopping malls. Viewed historically, P was simply saying that the world is divinely crafted but not divine, that it is altogether good, and we should make ourselves at home and enjoy. Good and beautiful things proceed from bountiful beneficent beauty. The several authors of Genesis, and multiple stratification of authorship and redaction, entertain competing visions of the rule of God that debate whether and what conditions are attached to the first gift. P is strong on God's majesty, J on God's immanence. The upbeat side of J's portrait of Yahweh is that his tale is very earthy. Adam is described, not as the image of God on high, but as made of earth *(adamah),* destined to return to earth and born to work the earth, even as Yahweh enjoys evening strolls in the cool of the garden, which has an actual location on earth, in Mesopotamia, near real rivers like the Tigris and Euphrates. Yahweh talks familiarly with Adam and Eve instead of making majestic pronouncements from the highest heavens to nobody in particular, as does Elohim. Elohim can seem rather distant, while Yahweh, who seems to have a volatile and stormy disposition, is—like anyone with real passion—also capable of being more loving. While Elohim makes pronouncements from on high, what Yahweh says has the ring of real language, spoken on a real earth. Elohim is quite unperturbed by his creation, but like most new parents, the Yahwist is not sure how to have Yahweh handle his first offspring.

37. Levenson, *Creation and the Persistence of Evil,* proposes an interesting alternative. While rejecting *creatio ex nihilo* as later post-biblical theology, Levenson does hold to God's omnipotence, which he claims is held in existential tension with a residual tendency in created things to go wrong. Genesis is a story of God's omnipotent power to bring about order by *confining* the chaos, but not by eliminating it. The primeval chaos is neither created nor eliminated; it was always there and it is always liable to reemerge. So everything depends on God's fidelity to his word to Noah not to let his creation once again be overrun by the primeval waters (17). Life is "precarious," and the "world is not inherently safe; it is inherently unsafe." Psalm 74 "draws attention to the painful and yawning gap between the liturgical affirmation of God's absolute sovereignty and the empirical reality of evil triumphant and unchecked" (19). Jewish life comes down to a dialectical tension between a realism about the persistence of evil and a faith in God's word affirmed in hymn and ritual. Indeed, in Isaiah 51, God is reproached for allowing this tension to persist (23). Logically speaking, Levenson is not warranted to claim "omnipotence" for God, where the lesser and more biblical notion of "almighty"—that is, more powerful than all else—would do. Omnipotence implies unconditional power, not simply a "world-ordering power" (23) conditioned by, and exercised upon, independent, preexisting materials. Once again, the more one emphasizes God's power, the more it makes God responsible for the "persistence of evil."

38. James L. Kugel, *The God of Old: Inside the Lost World of the Bible* (New York: Free Press, 2003).

39. Walter Benjamin, "The Concept of History," IX, in *Walter Benjamin: Selected Writings,* Vol. 4, *1938–40,* ed. Michael Jennings (Cambridge, Mass.: Belknap Press of Harvard University Press, 2003), 392.

40. As Gerhardt May explains, the argument against (what became) the orthodox *creatio ex nihilo* position is nicely formulated by Hermogenes, of whose texts we have preserved only traces from the attacks upon him by critics like Tertullian, who saw him as a defender of the *Timaeus* (read "Athens"), not Genesis (read "Jerusalem"). In the logic of creation, Hermogenes reasoned, God created the world either (1) out of his own substance, which would result in both pantheism and the divisibility of God; or (2) out of nothing, which would make God responsible for everything, evil included. For Hermogenes, denying omnipotence of God does not limit God but protects God from a fatal limit; he was "emphatically anxious to ensure the absolute goodness of God." Finally, but one alternative remains standing: (3) God creates out of something preexistent, which also enjoys the advantage of being what Genesis actually says. This preexistent matter, says Hermogenes, is neither good nor evil in itself, but evil arises from the traces of disorder that still cling to it even after God has formed it. God actualizes its potential for good by creation, but it retains the residual power to resist God. Gerhardt May, *Creatio ex nihilo: The Doctrine of "Creation out of Nothing" in Early Christian Thought,* trans. A. S. Worrall (Edinburgh: T & T Clark, 1994), 140–41, 146; see also Keller, *Face of the Deep,* 48.

41. Kugel, *The God of Old,* 125–36.

42. See Hans Jonas, *Der Gottesbegriff nach Auschwitz: Eine jüdische Stimme* (Frankfurt: Suhrkamp Taschenbuch No. 1516, 1987), where Jonas argues that by creating, God lost control over what he created and has no power to intervene in nature or history to prevent evils like Auschwitz. For a commentary on Jonas, see Hans Hermann Henrix, "The Power-

lessness of God? A Critical Appraisal of Han Jonas's Idea of God after Auschwitz," in *Jewish Christian Relations,* www.jcrelations.net. See also *Mortality and Morality: A Search for the Good after Auschwitz,* ed. Hans Jonas and Lawrence Vogel (Evanston, Ill.: Northwestern University Press, 1996).

43. Keller, *Face of the Deep,* 131, 135. I am encapsulating here her entire chapter 8, pp. 124 ff.

44. Keller is also drawing upon J. William Whedbee, *The Bible and the Comic Vision: Exploring the Depths of a Seldom-Noticed Aspect of Biblical Literature* (Minneapolis: Augsburg Fortress Press, 1992; Cambridge: Cambridge University Press, 1998).

45. Nowadays most philosophers and theologians have sold their shares in metaphysics, cut their losses, and reinvested in phenomenology, pragmatism, or the analysis of language. What Kant proposed to put in the place of speculative metaphysics, an entirely Moral God, was however almost as boring—saying "thou shalt" all day long is at least as boring as saying "Being is." Kant's critique of metaphysical causality proved to be not a setback but an advance for theology, one that up to a point keeps its eye on the ethical side of the Bible and helps to get us out from under the shadow of Greek metaphysics. From a biblical point of view, God is not a "cause" but someone, not a cause but a call who summons the world and us out of the void, the way Jesus called Lazarus out of the grave.

46. May, *Creatio ex nihilo,* 39–40.

47. Ibid., 74.

48. Keller, *Face of the Deep,* 71.

49. The notion is sometimes attributed to 2 Maccabees 7:28, where the mother of the seven martyred sons tries to encourage her seventh son by saying that the God "who did not make them [the heavens and the earth] out of the things that existed" would certainly be able to raise him from the dead and unite her and all her sons. But, as May comments, she is offering encouragement, not a cosmological observation. She is saying that God is almighty in the classical sense, not an *ex nihilo* creator, and she is using a common expression *(ouk ex onton)* for making something new that was not there before (May, *Creatio ex nihilo,* 6–8, 16, 21). The same thing holds true in the New Testament, for example, of Paul's statements in Romans 4:17 and Hebrews 11:3 (ibid., 26–27). By the same token, thinkers like Tatian taught the orthodox doctrine that God created even matter without using the formula "out of nothing" (ibid., 152).

50. May, *Creatio ex nihilo,* 26.

51. Ibid., 74.

52. Ibid., 76.

53. As with most metaphysical assertions, this one yields contradictory conclusions: from the assertion of the sheer transcendence of God one can conclude *either* that the creation of so lowly thing as matter is beneath God's dignity (standard-form Gnosticism) *or* that creating in the lowly manner of a human artist using preexistent materials is beneath God's dignity (*creatio ex nihilo* Gnosticism).

54. May, *Creatio ex nihilo,* 75.

55. Ibid., 84.

56. "To render the biblical 'all-powerful' deity formally omnipotent was to close out the primal space, the *khora* or chaos, of creaturely spontaneity. Without that space, human freedom and natural chance are themselves directed by a Lord—who is thereby responsible for the havoc they wreak. A tehomic theology seeks with Hermogenes (and [David] Griffin) a theological alternative to the dangerously unavowed amorality of omnipotence. The Hemogenean trace indicates a pathway by which the biblical creation from chaos *could* have developed. This would be the imaginary of a divine power that 'lures' goodness from freedom rather than imposes right by might; a third way between gnostic monism and orthodox dualism" (Keller, *Face of the Deep,* 49).

4. OMNIPOTENCE, UNCONDITIONALITY, AND THE WEAK FORCE OF GOD

1. That gap is not my creation, but a growing consensus among biblical scholars. By *ad literam* I do *not* mean fundamentalism, thinking that this story supplies inside information from on high about an actual course of events back at the beginning of the universe in which a snake tricked a naked couple into eating an apple, all this approximately six thousand years ago. The story is to be understood in the narratival terms that befit it, not by the standards of a representational or correspondence theory of truth. By *"ad literam"* I mean read the story and do not drop any of the letters, words, or images because they do not fit into some preconceived post-biblical metaphysical or theological idea that we want to defend. It also means get into the story, and stop worrying about how snakes could talk, or whether there really was an original formless void, the way we do not worry about whether the ghosts seen by Hamlet, Macbeth, or Scrooge were *really there.* Conrad Hyers, *The Meaning of Creation: Genesis and Modern Science* (Atlanta, Ga.: John Knox Press, 1984) is very good on this point.

2. Emmanuel Levinas, *Totality and Infinity: Essay on Exteriority,* trans. Alphonso Lingis (Pittsburgh: Duquesne University Press, 1969) can be read as tracking the movements of Genesis by tracing the emergence from the primal stuff *(il y a)* first of the elements, then of the daily world of work and home, and then of the face, which is the prohibition of murder in the story of Cain and Abel. But the *il y a* seems to be always there and needs always to be overcome, and Levinas does not seem to see the positive role of the elements. "Ethics" for him means the mounting triumph of the human face over the facelessness of *il y a,* of ethical transcendence over the anonymous rustle of the *tohu wa-bohu.* And everything in Levinas leads up to the child, fertility, to generations as numerous as the stars in the sky. I will come back to Levinas and creation in chapter 11, below.

3. Jürgen Moltmann, *The Crucified God,* trans. R. A. Wilson and J. Bowden (Minneapolis: Fortress Press, 1974).

4. I say "emblematize" because in a poetics of creation, reading this story literally is a matter of figuring out what significance we are to attach to each of its literal and narratival components. Catherine Keller, for example, finds a panentheistic story to tell here, and I would concede that panentheism is a possible poem, a possible poetics of Genesis. But I take a different tack, one that turns on the "call" and the weak force of God.

5. See David Ray Griffin, *God, Power and Evil* (Philadelphia: Westminster Press, 1976) and *Evil Revisited: Responses and Reconsiderations* (Albany: SUNY Press, 1991), a classic and closely argued critique of the orthodox position.

6. As Ellul says, God "does not create by some terrible explosion of power but by the simple word: 'God said'—no more" (*Anarchy and Christianity,* trans. Geoffrey W. Bromiley [Grand Rapids, Mich.: Eerdmans, 1991], 33)—although all this dictating does seem to tire him. To which we might add that he says, in the jussive, "let there be" earth, or day, etc. Letting be, not causal production. To which we add again: letting be, letting *go.*

7. I do not deny that "the Bible"—as if there were (just) *one*—is full of talk about God's kingship, lordship, might, and power. That is part of what I have been calling the Bible's "bipolarity." "The Bible" is not one book but a *bibliothèque,* a library of books, with different authors and different theologies, and *the* "biblical view" is a fiction. We must assume personal responsibility for whatever it is *we* say that *the* Bible says. The Bible is a book that, God forbid, goes so far as to have God say this or that, to put words in the mouth of God, which constitutes a permanent structural risk of idolatry, that is, of bibliolatry, of idolizing our own words, which shows up in Protestant "inerrantism," which I place beside Catholic "infallibility," as fundamentally the same idolatry. That runs the risk

of ventriloquism, of having God puppet what we are saying, so that God speaks our language and advocates our property rights over that of our neighbors, has struck a special deal with us, and clearly prefers us to everyone else. The prophets—Amos is a good example—spend a certain amount of time trying to convince the Israelites that that is not how "the God of Israel" works, that God is the God of all the nations, who condemns injustice wherever it is found, including Israel, which enjoys no divine immunity; but too often their words fall on deaf ears (Amos, 9:7–8). See James Luther Mays, *Amos: A Commentary* (Philadelphia: Westminster Press, 1967), 6–7. That is why I adopt a contrarian hermeneutics in which the sign of God is to be sought in the counter-tendencies in such books, their tendencies to brush against the grain. Accordingly, I locate the "word of God," not in power but in powerlessness, not when the name of God is used to support our own claims to power but when it is used to protest on behalf of the victims of our power. Whether here in Genesis or later on in the Hebrew prophets, I take God to be the God of *anawim*, the God who stands by the most powerless and the poorest of the poor, who enjoy the special favor in God's kingdom. As the Scriptures will eventually get around to saying, God is love, and his power is the powerless power, the weak force, of love. In the prophetic texts, it is the earthly powers, the peoples or the kings, who represent the world's *arche;* God stands with those who lack power, and his word is uttered, not by the kings but by the prophets whom the kings kill, if they can get their hands on them. Injustice and oppression is part of the risk God took in creating, but it was not his idea! The collateral risk of creating is to have to stand with those who are done in by God's risky venture. In the New Testament this comes to a head in the shocking and prophetic form of Jesus, who empties himself and takes the form of servant. Here the "power" of God is most clearly identified with the powerlessness of death and a shameful execution, and God shows his face in the *anarchical* because in an important sense, despite the best intentions of God, a lot of things have gone wrong.

8. Slavoj Žižek, *The Puppet and the Dwarf: The Perverse Core of Christianity* (Cambridge: MIT Press, 2003), makes some interesting remarks about evil and divine impotence; see 126–27, 137.

9. See David Ray Griffin, *God, Power and Evil*, 280–81; Keller, *Face of the Deep*, 49.

10. Jacques Derrida, "How to Avoid Speaking: Denials," trans. Ken Friedan, in *Derrida and Negative Theology*, ed. Harold Coward and Toby Foshay (Albany: SUNY Press, 1989), 98.

11. "There is a painting by Klee called *Angelus Novus*. It shows an angel who seems to move away from something he stares at. His eyes are wide, his mouth is open, his wings are spread. This is how the angel of history must look. His face is turned toward the past. Where a chain of events appears before *us*, *he* sees one single catastrophe which keeps piling wreckage upon wreckage and hurls it in front of his feet. The angel would like to stay, awaken the dead, and make whole what has been smashed. But a storm is blowing from Paradise and has got caught in his wings; it is so strong that the angel can no longer close them. This storm drives him irresistibly into the future, to which his back is turned, while the pile of debris before him grows toward the sky. What we call progress is *this* storm" (Walter Benjamin, "The Concept of History," IX, in *Walter Benjamin: Selected Writings,* Vol. 4, *1938–40,* ed. Michael Jennings [Cambridge, Mass.: Belknap Press of Harvard University Press, 2003], 392). I have been greatly aided in my reading by Irving Wohlfarth, "On the Messianic Structure of Walter Benjamin's Last Reflections," *Glyph* 3 (1978): 148–212; see especially 158, 165. See also Peter Szondi, "Hope in the Past: On Walter Benjamin," *Critical Inquiry* 4, no. 3 (1978).

12. *Kierkegaard's Writings*, XVI, *Works of Love,* trans. and ed. Howard and Edna Hong (Princeton, N.J.: Princeton University Press, 1995), IX, "On the Work of Love in Recollecting One Who Is Dead."

13. Benjamin, "The Concept of History," 391.

14. As Jürgen Moltmann says in the beautiful preface to the English translation of *The Crucified God,* trans. R. A. Wilson and J. Bowden (Minneapolis: Fortress Press, 1993), ix: "Hope without remembrance leads to illusion, just as, conversely, remembrance without hope can result in resignation."

15. Benjamin regards history as the storm that howls, the winds that blow from Paradise, which means ruinous effects of having been sent packing by the blast, the outburst, the "blow out" that Yahweh delivered to the snake, the woman, and the man when he drove them all out of Paradise (Gen. 3:14–19). History, the catastrophe of progress, the progress of catastrophe beginning with Cain's murder of Abel, is the distance between the paradise lost and the promised messianic age; history is the between-time of the fall.

16. Wohlfahrt, "On the Messianic Structure of Walter Benjamin's Last Reflections," 165.

17. See Owen Ware, "Dialectic of the Past / Disjunction of the Future: Derrida and Benjamin on the Concept of Messianism," *Journal of Cultural and Religious Theory* 5, no. 2 (April 2004) (www.jcrt.org).

18. That is why, much as I love it, I do not subscribe to "panentheism," which, to the extent that it is something more than a phenomenology of the call, is more a metaphysics, unless it is a poetics, which is perhaps why I love it.

5. THE POETICS OF THE IMPOSSIBLE

1. To be precise, "*the* impossible" refers not to a logical but to a phenomenological impossibility, that is, a radical unforeseeability, where experience is structured around horizons of expectation that Husserl calls protentions and Heidegger calls hermeneutical forestructures.

2. Jacques Derrida, "The Force of Law: 'The Mystical Foundation of Authority,'" trans. Mary Quantaince, in *Deconstruction and the Possibility of Justice,* ed. Drucilla Cornell et al. (New York: Routledge, 1992), 15.

3. On this account, a poetics of the impossible would be more a "possible worlds logic," the logic of an imaginative construction, except that the kingdom is not a construction but a call, or a response to a call.

4. What we are calling, with Derrida, *the* impossible is delineated in Edmund Husserl, *Ideas Pertaining to a Pure Phenomenology and a Phenomenological Philosophy,* Vol. I, trans. Fred Kersten (The Hague: Martinus Nijhoff Publishers, 1983), §§ 47–49, where Husserl distinguished several senses of the possible, including the possibility of the annihilation of the world, which is not a simple *Unsinn,* but would be, were it to come about, a knee-bending surprise that shatters our powers of protention, our horizon of expectations.

5. Søren Kierkegaard, *Kierkegaard's Works,* Vol. VII, *Philosophical Fragments,* ed. and trans. H. Hong and E. Hong (Princeton, N.J.: Princeton University Press, 1985), 37. Whether one is a "believer" or not—or rather whatever it is that one believes—what Derrida calls *the* impossible is, I am arguing, an essential ingredient in the salt of life, an essential component in the passion ingredient in life. Life comes alive, is really living, only when we push past the probabilities of ordinary desires and we find ourselves faced with the impossible, which is what we desire, and this with a desire beyond desire. Among religious believers the impossible goes under the name of God, but no matter under what name it comes or goes, the impossible is what we desire, even and especially when we do not know what we desire. If someone imposed that on all of us as the definition of "religion," *s'il y en a,* I would not take to the streets in protest. As Johannes Climacus said, what thought desires to think is to think what cannot be thought; nothing less will do; anything less has all the makings of mediocrity.

6. Jacques Derrida, "As If It Were Possible, 'Within Such Limits' . . . ," in *Negotiations: Interventions and Interviews,* ed. and trans. Peggy Kamuf (Stanford: Stanford University Press, 2002), 343–70; Derrida, "The University without Condition," in *Without Alibi,* ed. and trans. Peggy Kamuf (Stanford: Stanford University Press, 2002), 234.

7. See John Savard, *Perfect Fools: Folly for Christ's Sake in Catholic and Orthodox Spirituality* (Oxford: Oxford University Press, 1980).

8. *Kierkegaard's Writings,* XVI, *Works of Love,* ed. and trans. H. Hong and E. Hong (Princeton, N.J.: Princeton University Press, 1995), 345–46.

9. Gilles Deleuze, *The Logic of Sense,* trans. Mark Lester (New York: Columbia University Press, 1990), 1, 9, 10, et passim.

10. Ibid., 1.

11. See Ilya Prigogine and Isabelle Stengers, *Order Out of Chaos* (Boulder, Colo.: New Science Library, 1984), to which I was referred by the work of Catherine Keller. Although John Polkinghorne's views are much closer to both a scientific and theological realism than mine, Polkinghorne also thinks that chaos theory creates some interesting openings for theology, and he does not think that God foreknows what has not happened yet. See John Polkinghorne, "Chaos and Cosmos: A Theological Approach," in *Chaos: The New Science,* Nobel Conference XXVI, ed. John Holte (Lanham, Md.: University Press of America, 1993).

6. HYPER-REALISM AND THE HERMENEUTICS OF THE CALL

1. See Martin Heidegger, *Being and Time,* trans. John Macquarrie and Edward Robinson (New York: Harper & Row, 1962), §§2, 31–32, 45, 56.

2. Or, as Heidegger says more soberly, speaking of the call of conscience: "If the caller is asked about its name, status, origin, or repute, it not only refuses to answer but does not even leave the slightest possibility of one's making it into something with which one can be familiar when one's understanding has a 'worldly' orientation. . . . That which calls the call, simply holds itself aloof from any way of becoming well-known, and this belongs to its phenomenal character. . . . The peculiar indefiniteness of the caller and the impossibility of making more definite what this caller is, are not just nothing; they are distinctive for it in a positive way. They make known that the caller is solely absorbed in summoning us to something, that it is *heard only as such,* and furthermore that it will not let itself be coaxed" (*Being and Time,* 319).

3. Jacques Derrida, "Circumfession: Fifty-nine Periods and Periphrases" in Geoffrey Bennington and Jacques Derrida, *Jacques Derrida* (Chicago: University of Chicago Press, 1993), 122. See Augustine, *Confessions,* X, 6–7.

4. In neglecting these other possibilities, I should be accused, not of Christo-centrism but of simple ignorance. I affirm their importance, but I am incompetent enough about the Hebrew and Christian traditions without having to extend my incompetence worldwide.

5. That is what Žižek and Badiou like about the biblical tradition: it constitutes existential subjects, what they would call "militants," which corresponds to what theology calls the "church militant," to which Kierkegaard liked to remind us we still belong. I like all that too, provided that (1) it does not drag me into Leninism, and (2) "militancy" is taken *ironice,* so that forgiveness is a way of being militant. The mistake of Žižek and Badiou is to fail to see how undecidability and a postmodern sensibility can be packed with an existential punch, which I am trying to show in my "anarcho-Danish deconstructive" version of Christianity.

6. See John D. Caputo, *On Religion* (London: Routledge, 2001), 109–17.

7. Once again, I refer to John Dominic Crossan's formulation of the distinction between the parables that Jesus told and the parable that Jesus *is,* that is, the parables that are told *about* him, whose significance exceeds the distinction between fact and fiction. See Crossan, *A Long Way from Tipperary: What a Former Monk Discovered in His Search for the Truth* (San Francisco: HarperSanFrancisco, 2000), 136 ff., 160 ff.

8. As Norbert M. Samuelson, *Judaism and the Doctrine of Creation* (Cambridge: Cambridge University Press, 1994), says, while the Israelite priesthood employed "the best scientific/philosophic opinion of that time," they were engaged in composing an "epic myth" with a "political-moral-religious" purpose (p. 164).

9. See my critique of Marion in this context in "The Hyperbolization of Phenomenology: Two Possibilities for Religion in Recent Continental Philosophy" in *Counter-Experiences: Reading Jean-Luc Marion,* ed. Kevin Hart (University of Notre Dame Press, forthcoming).

10. Edmund Husserl's *Ideas Pertaining to a Pure Phenomenology and a Phenomenological Philosophy,* Vol. I, trans. Fred Kersten (The Hague: Martinus Nijhoff Publishers, 1983), §30.

11. For more on my idea of hyper-realism, see "For Love of the Things Themselves: Derrida's Hyper-Realism," *Journal for Cultural and Religious Theory* 1, no. 3 (August 2000), electronic journal (http://www.jcrt.org). On theological nonrealism, see Don Cupitt, *Is Nothing Sacred?* (New York: Fordham University Press, 2002).

7. METANOETICS

1. Catherine Keller, *The Face of the Deep: A Theology of Becoming* (London: Routledge, 2003), 29.

2. Bruce Chilton, *Rabbi Jesus: An Intimate Biography* (New York: Random House, Doubleday, 2000), 110.

3. See ibid., 49–50, 110, 134.

4. Emmanuel Levinas, *Difficult Freedom,* trans. Sean Hand (Baltimore: Johns Hopkins University Press, 1990), xiv; Theodor Adorno, *Negative Dialectics,* trans. E. B. Ashton (New York: Continuum, 1983), 207. That healing materialism is also why the rabbis thought that if you offend someone you can't just go around saying you are sorry; you should put your money where your mouth is and put up some cash to back up this change of heart.

5. See, e.g., Slavoj Žižek, *The Puppet and the Dwarf: The Perverse Core of Christianity* (Cambridge, Mass.: MIT Press, 2003).

6. James L. Kugel, *The God of Old: Inside the Lost World of the Bible* (New York: Free Press, 2003).

7. Jacques Derrida, *The Gift of Death,* trans. David Will (Chicago: University of Chicago Press, 1995), 10–20.

8. Chilton (*Rabbi Jesus,* 85–90) makes the interesting suggestion that this does not mean that the outer water actually washes us clean, because the people of God are already pure. Contrary to what Christianity later wanted us to think, Jesus did not renounce all concern with purity and uncleanness; rather he redefined the character of that concern. (On the nature of concern with purity, see Mary Douglas, *Purity and Danger: An Analysis of Concepts of Pollution and Taboo* [London: Routledge & Kegan Paul, 1966; London: Routledge, 2002].) Jesus maintained that as the chosen people the Israelites were *always already pure,* that their purity proceeded from within, from their God-relationship in which they are constituted, by which they as the chosen ones are always already defined. They did not need to be made clean by sacrifice or by water immersion. On the contrary, sacrifice was the way that they "expressed" their purity, actualized it in the world. Purity proceeds from within to the without, and is not given from the without by external actions or rites. "Listen

to me, all of you, and understand: there is nothing outside a person that by going in can defile, but the things that come out are what defile" (Mark 7:14–16). Furthermore, he replaces John's water immersion with a meal fellowship, which is the way the Israelites express their sense that the kingdom has come into their midst. For flesh is not only the scene of pain and vulnerability but also of pleasure and good feeling. Everyone has been given this purity by God; it is not mediated to them by rites or priests. But we must find it *entos humon,* which means not so much "within ourselves" as finding "ourselves in its midst," in the midst of the kingdom of God (Luke 17:21). The kingdom is among us, all around us. It is not accessed by rites or rules, by external intermediaries or "brokers." John Dominic Crossan, *The Historical Jesus* (New York: HarperSanFrancisco, 1992), 225 ff., speaks of the "brokerless kingdom" of God, unbrokered by the authority either of the Roman imperium or the high priests, and the preaching of such a kingdom did not of course give much comfort to either authority in the first century (nor does it in the twenty-first). It is not "accessed" at all, because the kingdom is the standing relationship with God, the relationship in which we always already stand with God, unless we close ourselves off from God by sin.

9. The historical Jesus himself likely restricted the kingdom to the Israelites and had a hard time coming to grips with the implication of his own teaching that it belonged to non-Jews as well, as is shown by the famous story of his meeting with the Syrophoenician woman (Mark 7:24–30). She was putting to the test his teaching that there is nothing about one's external situation that makes one unclean, that impurity comes from within, and she seems to have won the day (see Chilton, *Rabbi Jesus,* 181–82). I will return to this story in chapter 12, on hospitality.

10. Although the word *ethos* in the sense of "custom" is found in several places, I cannot find any occurrence of the word *ethike.* Does this mean that the New Testament is "against ethics"?

11. John P. Meier, *Jesus: A Marginal Jew: Rethinking the Historical Jesus* (New York: Doubleday, 1991).

12. *Kierkegaard's Writings,* XVI, *Works of Love,* trans. and ed. H. Hong and E. Hong (Princeton, N.J.: Princeton University Press, 1995), 318.

13. See Emmanuel Levinas, *Otherwise than Being,* trans. Alphonso Lingis (The Hague: Kluwer Academic Publishers, 1981), 114, 142–46, 149–52, 185. For a good account of the grammar of *hineni,* as well as of the story of the binding of Isaac from a feminist perspective, see Phyllis Trible, *Genesis 22: The Sacrifice of Sarah* (Valparaiso, Ind.: Valparaiso University Press, 1990).

14. For more on my attempt to work out a deconstructionist concept of "obligation" in dialogue with the categoriality of the kingdom, see John D. Caputo, *Against Ethics: Contributions to a Poetics of Obligation with Constant Reference to Deconstruction* (Bloomington: Indiana University Press, 1993); for a very Levinasian version of a biblical postmodernism, see Edith Wyschogrod, *Saints and Postmodernism: Revisioning Moral Philosophy* (Chicago: University of Chicago Press, 1990).

15. See Jacques Derrida, "Force of Law: The 'Mystical Foundation of Authority'," in *Deconstruction and the Possibility of Justice,* ed. Drucilla Cornell et al. (New York: Routledge, 1992), 3–67, especially 14–15.

16. Derrida's interest in the "secret" of "singularity" often takes the form of a reading of Kierkegaard; see *Gift of Death,* chs. 3–4.

17. Jacques Derrida, *Negotiations: Interventions and Interviews 1971–2001,* trans. Elizabeth Rottenberg (Stanford: Stanford University Press, 2002).

18. My thanks to John Maraldo for pointing out a prior occurrence of this term in Tanabe Hajime, who used it in the sense of a movement beyond philosophical reason to a more radical letting-go of reason. See John Maraldo, "Metanoetics and the Crisis of Reason: Tanabe, Nishida, and Contemporary Philosophy," in *The Religious Philosophy of*

Tanabe Hajime: The Metanoetic Imperative (Berkeley: Asian Humanities Press, 1990), 235–55.

19. For more on the distinction I draw between *kardia* and *phronesis,* see Caputo, *Against Ethics,* 99–103, 113–17; and John D. Caputo, *Demythologizing Heidegger* (Bloomington: Indiana University Press, 1993), ch. 3.

20. *Otherwise than Being,* 37–38, 45–51.

21. For a beautiful commentary on forgiveness and *metanoia,* see Hannah Arendt, *The Human Condition* (Chicago: University of Chicago Press, 1958), 236–40. For its New Testament occurrences, see *A Greek-English Lexicon of the New Testament and Other Early Christian Literature,* 3rd ed., rev. and ed. Frederick William Danker (based on Bauer's *Wörterbuch*) (Chicago: University of Chicago Press, 2000), 640–41.

22. One could thus rewrite Heidegger's analysis of the principle that "nothing is without a reason" in terms of forgiveness; see Martin Heidegger, *The Principle of Reason,* trans. Reginald Lilly (Bloomington: Indiana University Press, 1991).

23. In "Violence and Metaphysics," *Writing and Difference,* trans. Alan Bass (Chicago: University of Chicago Press, 1978), 83, Derrida refers to "the two Greeks named Husserl and Heidegger"—Greeks vis-à-vis Levinas.

24. See the "Interlude" in the *Philosophical Fragments* in *Kierkegaard's Writings,* VII, *Philosophical Fragments, or A Fragment of Philosophy,* and *Johannes Climacus, or De Omnibus dubitandum est,* ed. and trans. H. Hong and E. Hong (Princeton, N.J.: Princeton University Press, 1985), 72–89. We will revisit this point in our discussion of Peter Damian in chapter 9.

25. Hannah Arendt, *The Human Condition* (Chicago: University of Chicago Press, 1958), 238–42.

26. "*Veni Creator Spiritus* [a ninth-century hymn], the people sing, Come Creator Spirit. This prayer acknowledge the 'not yet' of the Spirit's presence with its cry 'Come': creation is still underway. At the same time it acknowledges that the energizing power of God is in a most profound way already here. . . . Spirit-Sophia is the source of transforming energy among all creatures. She initiates novelty, instigates change, transforms what is dead into new stretches of life" (Elizabeth Johnson, *She Who Is: The Mystery of God in Feminist Theological Discourse* [New York: Crossroad, 1992], 135; see 133–39).

27. The *Augenblick* is a characteristically Kierkegaardian notion—the moment of truth in which the individual, one-to-one with God, acquires a new mind and resolves upon faith—that has been taken up in a number of places by Derrida, where it means the moment of chance, the opening or breach in the system; e.g., see Jacques Derrida, "The Principle of Reason: The University in the Eyes of Its Pupils," trans. C. Porter and E. Morris, *Diacritics,* 11 (1981): 20. Kierkegaard has captured a great deal of what is called here the structure of the temporality of the kingdom, which he opposes to Hegelian history.

28. It was this feature of the experience of temporality in the New Testament, the notion of the kairotic, sudden, and unpredictable coming of the *parousia* in St. Paul that attracted Heidegger's attention in the early Freiburg lectures. See Martin Heidegger, *The Phenomenology of Religious Life,* trans. Matthias Fritsch and Jennifer Gosetti-Ferencei (Bloomington: Indiana University Press, 2004), 67–74; for a commentary, see John van Buren, *The Young Heidegger* (Bloomington: Indiana University Press, 1994), 157–202.

29. Hildegard of Bingen is cited in Johnson, *She Who Is,* 127–28.

30. *Kierkegaard's Writings,* VI, *Fear and Trembling* and *Repetition,* ed. and trans. H. Hong and E. Hong (Princeton, N.J.: Princeton University Press, 1983), 32.

31. My hypothesis is that in the poetics of the kingdom, things look rather more like the way the world comes out in poststructuralist authors like Derrida, Lyotard, and Deleuze, in their philosophy of the *événement,* or in what one might also call the prophetic postmodernism of Levinas, for whom everything is organized around what is otherwise than *ousia.*

In the kingdom, things are endlessly reformable, revisable, reconfigurable—in a word, de-constructible—and a little anarchic. Such a world reminds us of the magic we have lost when we disenchanted the world after the Enlightenment and turned life over to the cost accountants and to the consumption of mass-produced commodities. But we do not have to resurrect magic itself and hope that we will be overtaken by a wave of miracles to under-stand what these stories are telling us about the eventiveness of life, about the need to be-lieve in what Derrida calls the impossible, which is narratively presented in the reversals and transformations described in these famous sacred narratives. Life is shaped by faith in the impossible and to the extent that it is not, life has passed us by, lacking all love and joy and light and help from pain, as Matthew Arnold says in "Dover Beach." (See the elaboration of this citation from "Dover Beach" in George Pattison, *Thinking about God in the Age of Tech-nology* [Oxford: Oxford University Press, 2005], ch. 7.)

To be sure, deconstruction could never be contracted to a specifically Jewish or Chris-tian form, which would make Derrida very nervous, especially the Christian version. The terms of any particular messianism are always too specific to contain the open-endedness of the call to come, the *viens, oui, oui* in deconstruction, which opens out to a future *sans voir, sans avoir, sans savoir.* But were Christian and Jewish thought to sit down to table with de-construction, they would find there a surprisingly amenable table of categories, even as they would thereby be liberated from their own worst, because dogmatic, tendencies. On my hy-pothesis, there is an uncanny communication between the philosophy of *différance,* the thought of the *khora,* the thought of the *event* in deconstruction, on the one hand, and the biblical metanoetics, the sacred anarchy, we sketch here. I suspect that the echo of a certain biblical discourse has wended its way to Paris, that deconstruction has actually turned up something of the kingdom, even as something of deconstruction turns up in the kingdom, something of an anarchic, eventualistic, nominalistic, non-essentialistic open-endedness, a predilection for *ta me onta,* and a sense of radical transformability.

8. QUOTIDIANISM

1. John Dominic Crossan, *In Parables: The Challenge of the Historical Jesus* (San Fran-cisco: Harper & Row, 1973), 35.

2. For something about the oddity of the word *epiousios,* which, if it is constructed out of *epi* and *ousia,* seems to mean "what is directed to the needs of life," see Gerhard Kittel, *Theological Dictionary of the New Testament,* ed. and trans. G. W. Bromiley (Grand Rapids, Mich.: Eerdmans, 1991), 590–99. For help with this word, I thank my friend and former colleague David Marshall.

3. Here you can see the traces of our quasi-medieval *Commentarium in Pater Noster.*

4. Martin Heidegger, *Gesamtausgabe,* B. 60, *Phänomenologie des religiösen Lebens,* ed. Claudius Strube (Frankfurt/Main: Klostermann, 1995), 78; English: *The Phenomenology of Religious Life,* trans. Matthias Fritsch and Jennifer Gosetti-Ferencei (Bloomington: Indiana University Press, 2004), 54.

5. Franz Overbeck, *Über die Christlichkeit unserer heutigen Theologie* (Leipzig, 1903; photographically reproduced: Darmstadt: Wissenschaftliche Buchgesellschaft, 1989). For Heidegger's use of Overbeck, see "Phenomenology and Theology," trans. James G. Hart and John C. Maraldo, in Martin Heidegger, *Pathmarks,* ed. William McNeill (Cambridge: Cambridge University Press, 1998), 39–40; see also Istvan Feher's commentary on Heideg-ger and Overbeck in "Heidegger's Understanding of the Atheism of Philosophy," *American Catholic Philosophical Quarterly* 69 (1995): 202–206.

6. Heidegger, *Gesamtausgabe,* B. 60, §§25–26, pp. 93–105; *Phenomenology of Religious Life,* pp. 65–75. For an excellent and detailed commentary on these texts, see Theodore

Kisiel, *The Genesis of Heidegger's Being and Time* (Berkeley: University of California Press, 1993), ch. 4, "The Religion Courses (1920–21)." Kisiel also reports (p. 529, n. 5) that Heidegger had read a piece by Dilthey some years earlier in which Dilthey claimed that the historical consciousness of the West was a Christian heritage, that it was Christian interest in the theology of salvation history that laid the foundation for historical consciousness and for the philosophy of history itself.

7. All citations from the New Testament are from the NRSV in *The New Oxford Annotated Bible with the Apocrypha* (New York: Oxford University Press, 1991).

8. Kisiel, *Genesis of Heidegger's Being and Time,* 186.

9. *Gesamtausgabe* B. 60, p. 82; *Religious Life,* 57.

10. Heidegger's lectures clearly reflect the state of the art of New Testament research in the 1920s—his students were impressed at how well he knew the literature (Kisiel, *Genesis of Heidegger's Being and Time,* 193)—whose tone had been set by Albert Schweitzer's *The Quest of the Historical Jesus* (1906). Schweitzer held that Jesus was an "eschatological prophet" whose notion that the kingdom of God was about to be realized was in fact a prophetic declaration of the end of time. This view was displaced by C. H. Dodd's notion of a "realized eschatology," according to which the kingdom does not mean an impending earthly cataclysm but rather that the rule of God has already begun, here and now, with Jesus; cf. C. H. Dodd, *The Parables of the Kingdom,* rev. ed. (New York: Scribner, 1961).

11. Martin Heidegger, *Gesamtausgabe, B. 61: Phänomenologische Interpretationen zu Aristoteles: Einführung in die phänomenologische Forschung* (Frankfurt: Klostermann, 1985), 90; English: *Phenomenological Interpretations of Aristotle's Metaphysics,* trans. Richard Rojcewicz (Bloomington: Indiana University Press, 2001).

12. *Kierkegaard's Writings,* VIII, *The Concept of Anxiety,* trans. Reidar Thomte in collaboration with Albert B. Anderson (Princeton: Princeton University Press, 1980), 81–93.

13. Heidegger, *Gesamtausgabe* B. 60, p. 116; *Religious Life,* p. 83.

14. For a nice overview of the various understandings of "eschatology," see John Dominic Crossan, *The Historical Jesus: The Life of a Mediterranean Jewish Peasant* (San Francisco: Harper & Row, 1991), 265–302.

15. Unlike Kierkegaard, Heidegger wrote no edifying discourses on the birds of the air and the lilies of the field and trusting God's rule in the 1920s; it was only later on, as I will discuss below, with his notion of *Gelassenheit,* that Heidegger addressed anything like this question. For Kierkegaard, anxieties are pagan problems, and if there are a lot of anxieties in Christendom, then Christendom is pagan too. Kierkegaard carefully enumerated the anxieties from which one should be free in the kingdom: anxieties about poverty and abundance, lowliness and highness, presumption and self-torment, and finally of irresolution, fickleness, and disconsolateness. See Kierkegaard's *Christian Discourses* in *Kierkegaard's Writings,* XVII, *Christian Discourses* and *The Crisis and a Crisis in the Life of an Actress,* ed. and trans. H. Hong and E. Hong (Princeton, N.J.: Princeton University Press, 1997).

16. On a "mad economy" of time, see Jacques Derrida, *Given Time, I: Counterfeit Money,* trans. Peggy Kamuf (Chicago: University of Chicago Press, 1992).

17. See F. Gerald Downing, *Christ and the Cynics: Jesus and Other Radical Preachers in First Century Tradition,* JSOT Manuals 4 (Sheffield: Sheffield Academic Press, JSOT Press, 1988).

18. *Kierkegaard's Writings,* VII, *Philosophical Fragments, or A Fragment of Philosophy* and *Johannes Climacus, or De Omnibus dubitandum est,* ed. and trans. H. Hong and E. Hong (Princeton, N.J.: Princeton University Press, 1985), *Philosophical Fragments,* 9–22.

19. Hannah Arendt, *The Human Condition* (Chicago: University of Chicago Press, 1958), 238–40.

20. Derrida, *Given Time,* 9.

21. For some of Derrida's more recent statements on the gift, see *Deconstruction in a Nutshell: A Conversation with Jacques Derrida,* edited with a commentary (New York: Fordham University Press, 1997), 15, 18–19; and *God, the Gift and Postmodernism,* ed. John D. Caputo and Michael J. Scanlon (Bloomington: Indiana University Press, 1999), 54–78.

22. Martin Heidegger, *The Principle of Reason,* trans. R. Lilly (Bloomington: Indiana University Press, 1991), 32–40.

23. *Given Time,* 1.

24. My thanks to Robert Sweetman of the Institute for Christian Studies (Toronto) for pointing this out to me.

25. See Derrida, *Given Time,* 9.

26. See Jean-Luc Marion, *God Without Being,* trans. Thomas Carlson (Chicago: University of Chicago Press, 1991), ch. 6.

27. If the kingdom sayings instruct us on how to live in personal time, they are no less instructive about history. While these profoundly sapiential sayings refer principally to the conduct of personal life and not to the conduct of sovereign states or governments, they also contain a view of historical life and of the rule of reason in history. What would it mean to say that history is God's present, not man's future, that the historical event is God's advent? The kingdom sayings suggest a view of history in terms of what Hannah Arendt called the "natality" of "action," the present as the possibility of a fresh start. They tell us to forget the past, to dismiss past trespasses, to let the present be the occasion of a new beginning, let each day be the first.

Sovereign nation states act out of pride, greed, and self-interest in just the same way that individuals do (the wonder would be if they did not!). But imagine what our historical situation today would be like if we could break the cycle of recrimination by which history is vitiated? Is not the logic of nationalist violence that plagues us in northern Ireland, Yugoslavia, and the Middle East, and the logic both of terrorism and of the counter–war on terrorism, to name only the most prominent, in large part a logic of paying back caught up in a *regressus ad infinitum* that refuses to let go of the past? Does it not belong to the logic of violence that there is *always already* a prior, older, past offense that requires retribution, that *there is no originally innocent* party? Is not every horror against the innocent—from the innocents of Sarajevo and Kosovo and Rwanda to the innocents of the West Bank and South Africa to the innocents of the streets of Belfast and Emagh, to the innocents of 9/11, innocents everywhere, above all the innocent children—is this not always justified in the name of the retribution of past offenses, of redressing offenses that have themselves been justified in exactly the same way, which leads to infinite regress, to infinite vengeance and retribution? And when someone like Anwar Sadat does the opposite, when someone dares to lay aside the desire to retaliate, are we surprised that he is killed? But whenever human beings are able to dismiss the past and start over again, is that not what we mean by God's advent, by the surpassing of this human, all too human logic of vengeance, by the surprise of being overtaken by something more than human, by something a little unbelievable, a little impossible, *the* impossible? The meaning of God's rule in time is not to warrant military action in the name of God, *pro deo et patria,* but forgiveness and dismissing all recrimination against the past. Do we not say that in every great work of peacemaking—when the Berlin wall falls, when the reign of Soviet terror collapses, when racial harmony is achieved in south Georgia or South Africa, when Protestant and Catholic, Arab and Jew, or white and black, join hands, when the lamb lies down with the lion—that "reason has prevailed"? But then, do we not add, as a little supplement, "It's a dream," "It is hard to believe," "It is impossible," "It is a miracle." Does that not mean that something else has intervened and lifted the moment up, a little bit of excess that breaks the chain and tears it out of the circle of past and future and frees it up, something that is a little more than reason and more than human, a little impossible, a little mad? Is not this utterly impossible thing possible only because with God all things are possible?

By the same token, do we not require a sense of the openness of the historical field, of the radical reconfigurability of human affairs, the sense of trust in the future that the kingdom sayings enjoin? Do we not need to do what is possible to alleviate misery today without succumbing to anxiety about tomorrow? For if we look ahead and try to predict what will happen, we will lose hope. Our hope for tomorrow—is that not a hope against hope, a mad hope, not quite, not merely, a human hope? Is that hope not God's rule among us, God's advent, beginning today? Does not historical thinking require a little dash of divine madness, a little something of the poetics of the impossible, a bit of worrying without worry? See Desmond Tutu, *No Future without Forgiveness* (New York: Doubleday Image, 2000).

9. BACK TO THE FUTURE

1. See C. Colt Anderson, "An Eleventh Century Scandal," *America* 192, no. 20 (June 6–13, 2005): 20–23.

2. Catherine Keller, *Face of the Deep: A Theology of Becoming* (London: Routledge, 2003), 64.

3. I love him but for four things: (1) His authoritarianism is a paradigmatic case of a form of "anarchy" in which all human archies are leveled precisely in order to exalt the overarching hierarchical patriarchal power of the divine *arche;* ironically his God is very "Yahwist," fiercely unforgiving and retaliatory, where the anarchical is part of a larger design to heighten the supreme power of God and the church. (2) As a strictly logical matter, I doubt that the idea of changing past time is coherent. On the possible scientific coherence of time-travel, and hence of the possibility of altering the past, see Edith Wyschogrod, *An Ethics of Remembering* (Chicago: University of Chicago Press, 1998), pp. 148–52. (3) Were God to annul the past offense, God would thereby also annul the forgiveness, inasmuch as there would then be nothing to forgive, the sinner having become innocent, having never sinned to begin with. Forgiveness requires that the past offense be left standing, lest there be nothing to forgive, even as it requires that it *somehow* be annulled and removed, lest it become a cursed fate and inalterable destiny. (4) Damian exemplifies the precise mistake that I am arguing *against* in these pages—of mistaking an event for an entity, of mistaking a religious poetics for a speculative metaphysics, of mistaking a religious discourse for a realist-representational one that literalizes God's transformative force into a physical or metaphysical power, of mistaking the weak force of God for a strong one, of mistaking the power of powerlessness for sheer unlimited power. He illustrates the need to undertake the "reduction to the event," in virtue of which the name of God is taken as the name of a call that haunts us and provokes us, not a power who bludgeons us.

4. I am following the "Interlude" in *Philosophical Fragments* in *Kierkegaard's Writings,* VII, *Philosophical Fragments, or A Fragment of Philosophy* and *Johannes Climacus, or De Omnibus dubitandum est,* ed. and trans. H. Hong and E. Hong (Princeton, N.J.: Princeton University Press, 1985), 72–89. Johannes Climacus wants to know whether the past is any more *necessary* than the future—that is, whether it becomes necessary after it has occurred, considering that it was contingent at the time of its occurrence—even as Damian wants to know whether it is just as *contingent* as the future even after it has occurred. The Greeks had their doubts about movement and *kinesis,* and, beginning with the Eleatics, tended to deny it ultimate status, either by denying it outright, as in Parmenides, or by making a good faith effort to "save" it by making it a "copy" of something unchanging, as in Plato, or by assigning it a real but subordinate status in the ousiological order, as in Aristotle, who was the most sensible and most phenomenological of all the major Greek philosophers about changing and sensible things. So if there must be motion, as indeed there must, they finally conceded, it would be better for it to go around in a circle, cyclical motion offering us the

best imitation of eternity, which is the motion of the otherwise immutable heavenly bodies, or else, to go backwards, which is the motion of *anamnesis,* which treats the movement from ignorance into knowledge as the recollection of what has already taken place, which is not so upsetting.

But in the religions of the Book, we prefer not to move in circles or to go backwards, as Constantine Constantius said in *Repetition,* but to press forward into new territory, like Abraham setting out to parts unknown, to go where we have not been before, to go where (the Greeks think) we cannot go, to let something new happen. In the more biblical point of view advanced by Constantine Constantius and Johannes Climacus, we think of things on the horizon of that transforming transformation called "creation." Creation for Constantius comes to a head in human freedom, where it has to do with the capacity for re-creation, to make a radical change of course from one direction to another, where the grace of God gives us a second chance, the gift of a new birth or a new time or a new heart, *metanoia,* which turns us around *(teshuvah).* That is why Damian's project is so interesting and misguided all at the same time. Forgiveness is an impossible attempt to repair the irreparable, to make the sinner *new,* to say to the sinner, "It is *as if* it never happened!" (That was Damian's strong suit.) Even and especially if it *did.* For in the world, which is the order of being, of the real, which means the irremissible, time is unforgiving and the present flows off irremissibly into the past, whereas forgiveness is the remission of the past, which means the remission of irremissible. That is accomplished, not by the strong force of an omnipotent Power who alters the real course of the past—which was Peter Damian's weak suit— but by the weak force of forgiveness, which gives the irremissible past a new meaning. Forgiveness is a weak force, not a strong one.

5. In a similar spirit, although the letter of their texts are very different, very early on in his career, Emmanuel Levinas spoke of repairing the irreparable: "Time, which is a condition of our existence, is above all a condition that is irreparable. The *fait accompli,* swept along by a fleeing present, forever evades man's control, but weighs heavily on his destiny. Beneath the melancholy of the eternal flow of things, Heraclitus's illusory present, there lies the tragedy of the irremovability of a past that cannot be erased. . . . Remorse—that painful expression of a radical powerlessness to redeem the irreparable—heralds the repentance that generates the pardon that redeems. Man finds something in the present with which he can modify or efface the past. Time loses its very irreversibility" ("Reflections on Hitlerism," trans. Sean Hand, *Critical Inquiry,* 17 [Autumn 1990]: 65).

6. Luce Irigaray, *An Ethics of Sexual Difference,* trans. Carolyn Burke and Gillian C. Gill (Ithaca, N.Y.: Cornell University Press, 1993), 5–20. See Irigaray's critical appreciation of Levinas, pp. 185–217.

7. References to Damian are to the pagination of the critical edition of Peter Damian's letters, *Die Briefe des Petrus Damiani,* ed. Kurt Reindel (Munich: Monumenta Germaniae Historica, 1983–93), 4 vols., abbreviated "B1," "B2," etc. This is followed by the English translation in Peter Damian, *Letters,* 4 vols., trans. Owen J. Blum, *The Fathers of the Church* (Washington D.C.: Catholic University of America Press, 1989–98), which is abbreviated as "L1" (Letters 1–30), "L2" (Letters 31–60), "L3" (Letters 61–90) and "L4" (Letters 91–120). The last volume, while continuous in its enumeration of the letters with the preceding vol. 3 and identified in the preface as "the fourth volume in this series" (p. vii), is called Volume 5 on the inside cover; I take that to be a mistake and I treat this as "L4." For an earlier critical edition of *De omnipotentia divina* with a French translation and a superb commentary, see Pierre Damien, *Lettre sur la toute-puissance divine: Introduction, Texte critique, traduction et notes,* by André Cantin (Paris: Editions du Cerf, 1972). For a partial and earlier English translation, see *On Divine Omnipotence,* trans. Owen Blum, in *Medieval Philosophers: From St. Augustine to Nicholas of Cusa,* ed. John F. Wippel and Allan B. Wolter (New York: Free Press, 1969). Also, see the older edition by Cajetan in *Patrologia Latina,* ed.

Migne (Paris, 1867), vols. 144–45. *De divina omnipotentia in reparatione corruptae et factis infectis reddendis* is in v. 145, Opuscula XXXVI. For an excellent commentary in English, see Irven M. Resnick, *Divine Power and Possibility in St. Peter Damian's De Divina Omnipotentia* (Leiden and New York: Brill, 1992).

8. He also tells the story of a youngster who mysteriously passes beyond the locked doors of the monastery to gain entrance to the miller's house, the only question being not whether this happened but whether it was a miracle effected by God and a mystical allusion to the virgin birth, or a temptation sent by an evil spirit (B3, 383–84/L4, 385–86).

9. "And, indeed, God could both cause a virgin to become pregnant before she would lose her virginity and restore virginity after it was lost. Each, of course, was good. . . . To be sure, it is more wondrous and more eminently [reading "more eminently excellent," not more "imminently," for *"valde praecellentius"*] excellent that a virgin should remain inviolate after giving birth than that one, after losing her integrity should recover virginal purity after its loss, because it is more difficult for one to enter after the doors were shut than to be enclosed by doors that had just been opened" (B3, 367/L4, 369).

10. Even when Damian is referring to rape *(stuprum)*, he refers to her fall, her need for penance (B3, 348/L4, 351). Sometimes, in an effort to put the best face on Damian's views, Owen Blum translates as "rape" terms that simply mean that a woman's virginity has been spoiled or corrupted and do not suggest that it has been involuntary. Cf. B3, 343/L4, 346 *(ruina);* B3, 349/L4, 352 *(polluta).* Or Blum has Damian refer to a "violated woman *(corrupta)* after she has done penance," whereas it is the violator not the violated who would do penance; Damian simply means here a woman whose virginity has been corrupted, perhaps, as he says in the next line, by fornication, which would be willful (B3, 367/L4, 370).

11. Resnick, *Divine Power and Possibility,* 48–49. *Liber Gomorrhianus,* Opus VII, PL, 145, col. 159–90, which has been edited for reasons of propriety. For a translation of the Migne edition, see *Book of Gomorrah: An Eleventh-Century Treatise against Clerical Homosexual Practices,* trans. Pierre J. Payer (Waterloo, Ont.: Wilfrid Laurier University Press, 1982). The unrevised text is published in *Die Briefe des Petrus Damiani.* For a translation of this edition of the text, see L2, pp. 3–53.

12. This text, which has been analyzed incisively in Mark Jordan, *The Invention of Sodomy in Christian Theology* (Chicago: University of Chicago Press, 1997), is complicated by running together arguments against violations of the religious ideal of chastity with arguments against same-sex desire, even as the later treatise on virginity and divine omnipotence does not sharply distinguish marital and extramarital sex. Damian seems terrified, Jordan shows, by the threat posed to the Church of a homosexual church within the Church, which is a fear besetting churchmen today. Damian feared clerical sodomy as he feared blasphemy (B1, 328/L2, 51). He wants everyone to feel the threatening words of deutero-Paul, "It is a fearful thing to fall into the hands of the living God" (Heb. 10:31), especially sodomites (B1, 320/L2, 42). Jordan (p. 50) underlines the way Damian addresses the sodomite personally (B1, 198/L2, 18). In a way that flatly contradicts the treatise on divine omnipotence, the *Book of Gomorrah* belongs to a world of inviolable natural necessity and impermeable walls, where the hatches of nature are battened tight against unnatural perversity, against any "inflection" of nature, even while the latter treatise rejoiced in everything that is irregular and inflected, and delighted in saying that God himself made nature against nature (B3, 368/L4, 371) (which would put God on the side of you know who!). Perhaps God will pardon the sodomites in heaven, although Damian is not always encouraging about that, but Damian is never going to give them any peace on earth or permit them to hold an office in the church (B1, 290/L2, 10). Their vice merits the harshest earthly punishment and permanent exclusion from the work of the Church. "No subsequent holy life" can make up for what they have done. As Jordan says (p. 57), sodomy seems to be "a sin from which there is no return in this life."

13. Cantin translates *absit autem* as *on se garde:* one must take care or be on guard that one does not deny it; "far be it from us" to deny it. Owen Blum translates it, "God forbid that it be applied to divine majesty" (B3, 368/L4, 370).

14. Cantin (p. 110) thinks Damian took both sides of the response in the spirit of dialectics, both the *sic* and the *non,* but that he hedged his bet. Damian never actually said that God could undo the past, Cantin claims, but every time he got close to saying it, he backed off and simply said, far be it from me to deny it, lest anyone accuse me of speaking impiously about God. Cantin, I think, is closer to the mark when he says that the *sic* and the *non* belong together in a kind of Hegelian dialectic (p. 178). Resnick thinks Damian proved both sides and left it to faith to decide in favor of the divine omnipotence; cf. *Divine Power and Possibility,* 4, 102.

15. Later on, theologians protected God's omnipotence by distinguishing God's "absolute power" *(potentia absoluta),* what God is capable of doing, absolutely speaking, for example, freely creating the world *ex nihilo,* when the canvas is blank, so to speak, from his "ordered power" *(potentia ordinata),* what God is capable of doing within the order of the world he has actually created, once he has started painting. So the mainstream view is that while, from the point of view of his absolute power, he could have created a world in which Rome was not founded, once he has created a world in which it was, then his ordered power operates within those limits, which would mean living with the fact that what is done is done. That, on the whole, is a more sensible way of addressing this issue, but I applaud Damian, not for his sense but for his sensibility, at least on this point of forgiveness, whatever other fires may have roared in his belly.

16. This also resolves the problem of divine alterability. For God would in one eternal act have caused it to be that something was done and that it was not done, inasmuch as both of these possibilities float simultaneously in the timeless present in which all the moments of time are stretched out before him. In one timeless act, God causes Rome to have been founded and then to have its founding annulled. The alteration would be in creation, not in God. In producing two different effects, God did not do two different things. God did not retract something he had done, seeing that it turned out badly. God willed in one eternal will a double result that produces a contradiction in nature, time, and logic, not in God.

17. *Logic.* According to Aristotle *(de interpretatione,* I, 9:18b8), if a thing has actually happened in the past, then that is inalterable; if something exists, then as long as it exists, it is impossible for it not to exist; and if something will be, then it will be. Damian is referring to what Aquinas would later on call contingent necessity: *if* something that is contingent in itself actually comes to be, then insofar as it is, it necessarily is so; "if *p,* then *p,*" which is necessarily true, even though *p* is contingent and dependent upon God. So, if God can alter the future, he can for the same reason alter the past. The problem is that language gives a ring of necessity to something that really is, in itself, thoroughly contingent. The real contingency of things past, present, and future is betrayed by the spell of necessity that language casts over things. In reality, all three moments of time are contingent and alterable and equally present to God, so that Damian adds to the doctrine of future contingents his own account of the contingency of the past. God's power over the past is no different than his power over the future, which everyone who prays for a better future readily concedes (B3, 352/L4, 355). Strictly speaking, we should say not that "Rome was founded," but that "Rome may or may not have been founded," which reflects not a merely epistemic uncertainty on our part, but an ontological contingency in the event itself. Whence Robert McArthur and Michael Slattery, "Peter Damian and Undoing the Past," *Philosophical Studies* (Maynooth) 25 (1974): 137–141, argue that Damian does not violate the principle of noncontradiction by affirming that both *p* and *~p,* but makes a statement in modal logic about past contingents, of the form "it is possible that either *p* or *~p,*" "it is possible either that Rome was founded or it was not"; the contingency does not have to do

with the limits of our knowledge *(modus cognoscendi)* but with the reality of the past *(modus essendi).*

Damian shares Nietzsche's view that grammar is a web of fictions invented by human beings for their own convenience, even as he would agree with Nietzsche that physics too is an interpretation. But unlike Nietzsche, he did not think that we would not be rid of God until we got rid of grammar, but rather that getting rid of grammar is the only way to get open to God's ways, which are not our ways. Nor does he have a doctrine of eternal recurrence, but quite the opposite, a doctrine of eternal non-occurrence, which allows God the freedom to see to it that what happened in the past did not happen; not only did it not happen eternally, but it did not happen at all. The word of God given to us in Scripture does not come into the world in order to be measured by the logicians and mastered by rhetoricians. The results of the work in the liberal arts *(ars humana)* must never be set up in opposition to the divine power. If such techniques must be used at all, they must, like a good handmaiden *(ancilla dominae)* (B3, 354/L4, 356), humbly serve their mistress, lest the superficial logic and rhetoric of language perversely rule the reading of the revealed word of God. The masters of the liberal arts are masters of words, not of things, masters of dialectical prestidigitation, not of the divine majesty, so Damian is happy to concede to them mastery in their illusory domain (B3, 355/L4, 357–58), for the wisdom of this world is, as the Apostle says, foolishness with God (1 Cor. 3:19).

Natural laws. Damian's opponents doubt that God can restore a virgin to pristine integrity on the grounds that the same thing cannot happen and not happen at the same time. But, Damian says, while we may not fear attributing such an impossibility to nature, "far be it from him" to apply this limitation to the divine majesty. "For he who has given birth to nature can easily, when he wishes, take away the necessity of nature" (B3, 368/L4, 370; trans. by Resnick, *Divine Power and Possibility,* 103). "It is at the moment that he makes this distinction," Cantin observes, "that Damian earns his reputation for audacity in the history of philosophy" (p. 101). In Cantin's view, however, Damian is rigorously guarded in never actually saying in so many words that God *can* annul the past. He simply says he is not going to get caught denying it. But if he does not want to deny this, that can only be if he concedes that it is possible and can offer an explanation of how it is possible. Then Damian admits it is possible that it is possible, which is to concede its possibility, which is the question. For the question is not whether God *does* undo the past, but whether God *can.* Better audacity toward logic and nature, Damian might respond, than blasphemy toward almighty God! He who has authored nature can change the order of nature to his liking. Indeed, was not God at work intervening on nature right from the very start? Has not God made nature against nature (B3, 368/L4, 371), by making it out of nothing, creating animals out of the brute elements and a woman out of a man's rib? The only nature that nature has is found, not in nature but in God: "Indeed, the very nature of things," he says, "has its own nature, viz., the will of God *(Ipsa quippe rerum natura habet naturam suam, Dei scilicet voluntatem)*" (B3, 370/L4, 371). Nature has no immanent, eidetic necessity of its own. Nature is more truly defined by its efficient cause, external to itself, than by own immanent formal cause (Resnick, *Divine Power and Possibility,* 106, citing Damian, *Institutio monialis).* Damian cites Augustine in *City of God* (Bk. 21, c. 4: clear flames turn things black, straw keeps snow cold and fruit warm, etc.). Possessed of no account of deeper natural laws, Damian observes only a shallow sequence of events in nature, so that every deviation from this *ephemeral flow* is treated as a natural wonder. What wonder, then, that God, who has permitted Mary to remain a virgin in giving birth, could, if he wished, restore the integrity of any virgin! (B3, 269–74/L4, 371–74).

18. Resnick, *Divine Power and Possibility,* 3.

19. Ibid., 107.

20. Gilles Deleuze, *The Logic of Sense,* trans. Mark Lester, ed. Constantin V. Boundas (New York: Columbia University Press, 1990).

21. Michel Serres, *Angels: A Modern Myth*, trans. Francis Cowper (Paris: Flammarion, 1995), 7.

22. See n. 17 above.

10. FORGIVEN TIME

1. Jean-Luc Marion, *Being Given*, trans. Jeffrey Kosky (Stanford: Stanford University Press, 2002), §20, pp. 189–99.

2. Jacques Derrida, *Given Time*, trans. Peggy Kamuf (Chicago: University of Chicago Press, 1992), 163.

3. This, of course, is the paradox of forgiveness developed by Derrida. See his "To Forgive: The Unforgivable and the Imprescriptible" and "On Forgiveness: A Roundtable" in *Questioning God*, ed. John D. Caputo, Mark Dooley, and Michael Scanlon (Bloomington: Indiana University Press, 2001), 21–72.

4. A. N. Wilson, *Jesus: A Life* (New York: Fawcett Columbine, 1992), 30–31.

5. E. P. Sanders, *Jesus and Judaism* (Philadelphia: Fortress Press, 1985)—hereafter *"JJ"*—regards the parable as a Lucan or pre-Lucan creation (p. 175), and he cites Peter Fiedler, *Jesus und die Sünder* (1976) in support (p. 385, n. 6).

6. To a great extent, Wilson puts the research of the Hungarian Geza Vermes into an accessible and popular form. Like E. P. Sanders after him, Vermes stresses the Jewish context of Jesus' life and teachings and tries to disentangle later Christian polemics against the Jews from Jesus' deeply Galilean spirituality. See *Jesus the Jew: A Historian's Reading of the Gospels* (Philadelphia: Fortress Press, 1973).

7. Hannah Arendt, *The Human Condition* (Chicago: University of Chicago Press, 1958), 236–40.

8. Derrida, *Given Time*, 101, n. 18.

9. Emmanuel Levinas, *Nine Talmudic Readings*, trans. Annette Aronowicz (Bloomington: Indiana University Press), 19.

10. Jacques Derrida, *The Gift of Death*, trans. David Wills (Chicago: University of Chicago Press, 1995), 88 ff.

11. If by divine omnipotence we mean that God can do anything, then to see to it that something was both done and not done, made and not made, is not a "thing," not a possible, but what the medievals called a *flatus vocis*. One's lips—or one's keyboard—are moving but nothing is getting said. It would no more limit God's omnipotence to say that God "cannot" make something to have happened and not to have happened than it would to say that God "cannot" do evil, since even Damian admits that God is "constrained" by the good. What Damian says is long on praise, short on predication.

12. Robert Gibbs, *Why Ethics? Signs of Responsibility* (Princeton, N.J.: Princeton University Press, 1999), 334. See especially chs. 15 ("Why Confess?") and 16 ("Why Forgive?"). The Rosenzweig texts Gibbs is commenting on are from Franz Rosenzweig, *The Star of Redemption*, trans. William W. Hallo (Boston: Beacon Press, 1971), 180–81. I also recommend Gibbs's texts for its insightful excursions into the ethico-religious character of historiography in Walter Benjamin, and Benjamin's relevance to the question of remembering and forgiving.

13. *Kierkegaard's Writings*, IV, *Either/Or, Part II*, ed. and trans. H. Hong and E. Hong (Princeton, N.J.: Princeton University Press, 1987), 349.

14. Rosenzweig, *Star of Redemption*, 180–81.

15. Emmanuel Levinas, *Totality and Infinity*, trans. Alphonso Lingis (Pittsburgh: Duquesne University Press, 1969), 282–83.

16. Levinas, *Totality and Infinity*, 282.

17. Ibid., 283 (emphasis mine).

18. Ibid., 282.

19. Gibbs, *Why Ethics?* 351.

20. Levinas, *Totality and Infinity,* 283. See Gibbs, *Why Ethics?* 351–53.

21. To be sure, by pointing out that, in virtue of the *felix culpa,* it will have been better sometimes to conserve the sin rather than to undo it, lest we prevent in advance the saintly convert or the advent of Jesus himself, we would not be contradicting Peter Damian. Peter would agree that when not to remove the sin is indeed what is better, then that is precisely what God would do, because God, who is constrained only by goodness, not being, always does what it is better to do. But when that is not better, there is nothing about being, past or present, that can check God's power.

22. As Gibbs goes on to point out, we must also take account of "the social construction of time" (p. 355), and hence of the role that forgiveness plays for a community, of the need of the community to repent and be forgiven, to forget and remember. But that is an extension of this topic that I cannot undertake here.

23. Derrida, *Gift of Death,* 114–15.

24. This was one of Paul's views of Christ's death, but not his central view, which was that by his death and resurrection, Christ has initiated a new order, a new life, a life of grace, by which we have been raised into a new creation. See E. P. Sanders, *Paul* (Oxford: Oxford University Press, 1991), 65–76.

25. See Edward Schillebeeckx, *Jesus: An Experiment in Christology,* trans. Hubert Hoskins (New York: Crossroad, 1985), 399–515.

26. That Christology can take a very high form, and it can affirm that Jesus is the Son of God, but in that case, it says that in the incarnation God expresses his solidarity with suffering, and suffers with us, in what has been called "theo-passionism." See John D. Caputo, *The Prayers and Tears of Jacques Derrida: Religion without Religion* (Bloomington: Indiana University Press, 1997), 331–39.

27. "Saint": Hélène Cixious, *Portrait of Jacques Derrida as a Young Jewish Saint* (New York: Columbia University Press, 2004); Caputo, *The Prayers and Tears of Jacques Derrida,* 134 ff. "Reb Rida": Jacques Derrida, *Writing and Difference,* trans. Alan Bass (Chicago: University of Chicago Press, 1978), 78.

11. "LAZARUS, COME OUT"

1. "In what sense is he flesh, who walks on the water and through closed doors, who cannot be captured by his enemies, who at the well of Samaria is tired and desires a drink, yet has no need of drink and has food different from that which his disciples seek? He cannot be deceived by men, because he knows their innermost thoughts even before they speak. He debates with them from the vantage point of the infinite difference between heaven and earth. He has need neither of the witness of Moses nor of the Baptist. He dissociates himself from the Jews, as if they were not his own people, and he meets his mother as the one who is her Lord. . . . And in the end the Johannine Christ goes victoriously to his death of his own accord" (Ernst Kasemann, *The Testament of Jesus,* trans. Gerhard Krodel [Philadelphia: Fortress Press, 1968], 9).

2. See the interesting account of this story in Bruce Chilton, *Rabbi Jesus: An Intimate Biography* (New York: Doubleday Image Books, 2000), 244–46.

3. That is the point of the three highly anarchical and an-economic "lost and found" stories in the New Testament—the lost sheep, the lost coin, and the lost son. In the calculations of the kingdom, each one is a singularity of infinite depth, a precious pearl. These "little ones" cannot be bought or sold or compensated for their time. Each individual is a qualitative infinity that outstrips any mere quantitative accounting. God alone, who knows what is in their heart, who has taken careful account of every hair on their head (Luke 21:18), can take account of their unaccountable worth.

4. Jean-François Lyotard, *The Differend: Phrases in Dispute,* trans. Georges Van Den Abbeele (Minneapolis: University of Minnesota Press, 1988), 100–103.

5. Edith Wyschogrod, *An Ethics of Remembering: History, Heterology and Nameless Others* (Chicago: University of Chicago Press, 1998).

6. See our discussion of this point above, in chapter 4, "Omnipotence."

7. Emmanuel Levinas, *DEE: De l'existence à l'existant* (Paris: Fontaine, 1947); *EE: Existence and Existents,* Eng. trans. Alphonso Lingis (Dordrecht: Kluwer, 1978; Pittsburgh: Duquesne University Press, 2001); *TA: Le Temps et l'autre* (Paris: PUF/Quadrige, 1983), 11; *TO:* Eng. trans. Richard Cohen (Pittsburgh: Duquesne University Press, 1987), 33. Levinas is discussing a kind of phenomenology of the first moment of creation in which the existent rises up from the formless anonymity of "existence" or the *"il y a,"* from the indeterminate sea of being *(il y a de l'être)—tehom* and *tohu wa-bohu*—and seizes upon existence. The victor, the existent, is taken captive by the vanquished in an odd version of the master/slave dialectic. The triumphant existent must now bend all its efforts to "escaping" being—the first piece the young Levinas published, in 1935, was entitled *On Escape [De l'évasion],* trans. Bettina Bergo (Stanford: Stanford University Press, 2003)—in order to break its captivity by that in which it has first established itself by its "virile" efforts. Both of these texts have an unfortunate tendency to describe being or existence as "evil," which is a particularly bad choice of words, given the fact that he is supplying a phenomenological version of Genesis in which all things are made good from something that is innocent of good or evil; this point is criticized rather too enthusiastically by Phillip Blond, "Emmanuel Levinas: God and Phenomenology," in *Post-Secular Philosophy: Between Philosophy and Theology,* ed. Phillip Blond (London and New York: Routledge, 1998), 195–228.

8. Jacques Derrida, "Hostipitality," in *Acts of Religion,* ed. Gil Anidjar (New York and London: Routledge, 2002), 390–91.

9. "Where suffering attains its purity, where there is no longer anything between us and it, the supreme responsibility of this extreme assumption turns into supreme irresponsibility, into infancy. Sobbing is this, and precisely through this it announces death. To die is to return to this state of irresponsibility, to be the infantile shaking of sobbing" (*TA,* 60/ *TO,* 72). Levinas's phenomenological analysis of suffering is strikingly confirmed for us in Elaine Scarry's well-known book, *The Body in Pain* (New York: Oxford University Press, 1985), which I discussed in *Against Ethics* (Bloomington: Indiana University Press, 1993), 205–206.

10. Derrida, "Hostipitality," 391.

11. Note the mistranslation in DEE, 156/EE, 91: "Just as the happiness *(bonheure)* of humanity does not justify the misery *(malheure)*"—not "mystery"—"of the individual." This remains uncorrected in the Duquesne reprint: (Pittsburgh: Duquesne University Press, 2001), 93.

12. See Jacques Derrida, *The Gift of Death,* trans. David Wills (Chicago: University of Chicago Press, 1995), 97–98; and *Voyous,* 14–15; English: *Rogues: Two Essays on Reason,* trans. Pascale-Anne Brault and Michael Naas (Stanford: Stanford University Press, 2005), where Derrida speaks of *salus* without salvation or an economy of redemption.

13. Charles Winquist describes something similar in Tillich's concept of salvation. While Tillich seems to speak of the kingdom of God, eternal life, and judgment as the final conquest of life's ambiguities, we should remember that these are symbols of the quest for an unambiguous life, that he is against literalism, supernaturalism, and magic. There is no revelatory super-knowledge that annuls our finitude. For example, in serious despair over the meaning of life, in which we take a secret pleasure, we experience the seriousness of life and hence the power to affirm life. Despair participates in the power of life. We are blessed/happy in our despair; meaninglessness becomes meaningful in despair, and we affirm a faith in life. Eternal blessedness is the positivity that emerges from negativity. Grace

strikes us in despair when we find the courage to be, to say yes to the finitude of life. A beatific vision, not of God but of the world. The world is divinely ordinary, and life can be lived meaningfully under the conditions of finitude. Theological thinking is unsettling because it unsettles the ordinary, making us think it under the pressure of that than which no greater can be conceived, our ultimate concern and a demand for what does not disappoint. We have the courage to be because we look into the abyss and say yes to life, to its divine ordinariness. See Charles Winquist, *The Surface of the Deep* (Aurora, Colo.: Davies Group Publishing Co., 2003), 221–23.

14. Emmanuel Levinas, *Totality and Infinity,* trans. Alphonso Lingis (Pittsburgh: Duquesne University Press, 1969), 234.

15. Ibid.

16. John D. Caputo, *Against Ethics* (Bloomington: Indiana University Press, 1993), 243–44.

17. The time of salvation is neither Bergsonian duration, in which the present impinges or "encroaches" (DEE, 157/EE, 91–92) upon the future by the sheer precipitancy of the *élan vitale,* nor the headlong rush, the *Vorlaufen,* of ecstatic Dasein's anticipatory projection upon its ownmost possibility to be. Neither Bergson nor Heidegger gives the present its moment in the sun, its time and duration, and so neither allows the future to be truly accomplished as a release from the present. The Levinasian notion of resurrection—we live time and the future more deeply as the resurrection of the present—requires the "indispensable interval of nothingness" (DEE, 158/EE, 93) which separates the instant and allows it to be constituted. The present must first surge up in its discontinuous density, for it is only then that the *exigency* of the present can be nourished and engendered. In just the same way that there is a nourishing of the present in epiousiology, where we are counseled by Jesus to trust, not to worry about what we shall eat or how we shall be clothed, there is a comparable enduring of the hopelessness of the present in all hope. The enchainment to the present needs to be constituted before the need for release is felt. It is not enough to enter the next instant "identical and unforgiven *(impardonné),*" which would be no more than the repetition of the same. This exigency is not a demand for the perseverance of the same but for *dénouement*—for something that unties the knot by which it is tied to itself—and *recommencement,* for a new beginning. The exigency is a demand for a "miraculous" beginning, a "beginning again as other" (DEE, 159/EE, 93), not a beginning from itself *(à partir de soi),* but beginning from the other, from the caress of the other. "Resurrection," Derrida says, commenting on this text, "is the miracle of each instant" ("Hostipitality," 392).

18. While the child is a powerful figure of hope, although this should not be taken sentimentally and in isolation from economic analyses that explain why the lives of children are also rendered hopeless, Levinas was rightly criticized by Irigaray as proposing this as the final word on "love" *(eros),* because love mutually engenders life in the lovers, quite apart from the child. See Luce Irigaray, *An Ethics of Sexual Difference,* trans. Carolyn Burke and Gillian C. Gill (Ithaca, N.Y.: Cornell University Press, 1993), 185 ff.

19. Truly to break outside into the "absolute alterity of another instant" is not possible for the solitary subject. "This alterity comes to me only from the other" (DEE, 160/EE, 93). The ticktock time that flows in "internal time consciousness" is fraudulent for Levinas, amounting only to a repetition of the same in which the instant is "negated" only in order to resurface in the next instant as the same, which is nothing more than simple self-preservation or self-regeneration—as opposed to a new birth. Such internal negation is not true alterity but a self-assertion that deploys the mediation of self-negation. Whether as protention and retention in Husserl, the projection upon death in Heidegger, the dialectical power of the negative in Hegel, or the freedom derived from *le néant* in Sartre's *pour soi,* such time is nothing but monotony in comparison with that genuine alterity that gives time starting from the other, issuing in a false freedom and a false time, altogether different

from the time issuing from pardoning, *pardoner,* from being released by the other *(autrui)* (DEE, 161/EE, 94).

20. The text of *De l'existence à l'existant* concludes with a shift of focus, a reversal of the terms of the self *(moi)* and the other *(autrui).* Up to that point, the subject is one who suffers and is released by the coming of the other, where the other is "the Messiah or salvation." But in the conclusion of the work it is the other who suffers—the other is "the weak one whereas I am the strong," or "the poor one, 'the widow and the orphan,'" or the other is the enemy and stronger (DEE 162–63/EE, 95). In either case, the other is no longer one who alleviates the suffering of the subject. By the same token, the "caress" shifts from the caress *by* the other, by the healer or consoler who alleviates the suffering of the subject, to become the erotic caress, the caress *of* the other by the subject who reaches out into the infinite mystery and exteriority of the feminine other, groping in a distance that cannot be crossed. The caress is not the one by which the subject is lifted out of its misery and misfortune, but the caress whose loving futility would cross the distance of the other that is maintained in the very proximity of the embrace. In these final pages, alterity, salvation, and pardon are quickly sketched in terms of eros and the ethics of the other, terms that will require the lengthy analyses in *Totality and Infinity* to make sense. But what interests me in these pages is their first appearance in the healing gesture of the other, who comes, like the Messiah, to save the subject from itself.

21. For many years, the "Colonial Williamsburg Foundation" in Virginia attempted a nostalgic reconstruction of eighteenth-century Virginia by leaving out the slaves who made that economy run. The Foundation is very good at reconstructing the architecture, paints, and wallpapers of the era, but they wanted to forget the tears.

22. Walter Benjamin, "The Concept of History," IX, in *Walter Benjamin: Selected Writings,* Vol. 4, *1938–40,* ed. Michael Jennings (Cambridge, Mass.: Belknap Press of Harvard University Press, 2003), 392.

23. What I am describing here as a radical historian, Edith Wyschogrod describes as a "heterological historian" in *An Ethics of Remembering.*

24. Benjamin, "The Concept of History," 390.

25. Johann Baptist Metz, *Faith in History and Society,* trans. D. Smith (New York: Crossroad, 1980), 109–15.

26. Levinas, *Totality and Infinity,* 182.

27. Lyotard, *The Differend,* 86–196; *Heidegger and "the jews,"* trans. Andreas Michel and Mark Roberts (Minneapolis: University of Minnesota Press, 1990).

28. Levinas, *Totality and Infinity,* 240–247.

29. Ibid., 55.

12. THE EVENT OF HOSPITALITY

1. Kierkegaard is especially protective of the paradox here: do not try to write this off as an "act of charity" with charity-house food; the Scriptures are explicit: this is a "banquet" and everything is the best. See *Kierkegaard's Writings,* XVI, *Works of Love,* ed. and trans. H. Hong and E. Hong (Princeton, N.J.: Princeton University Press, 1995), 81–84.

2. Under the influence of Paul, the later Christian communities in which the Gospels were composed were enthusiastic about a mission to the Gentiles, but there is good reason to think that Jesus did not see himself as having such a mission. See E. P. Sanders, *Jesus and Judaism* (Philadelphia: Fortress Press, 1985), 218–21.

3. See Bruce Chilton, *Rabbi Jesus: An Intimate Biography* (New York: Doubleday Image Books, 2000), 181–82.

4. Alain Badiou, *St. Paul: The Foundation of Universalism* (Stanford: Stanford University Press, 2003).

5. According to Crossan, the original version of the story in Q, presumably a story of radical egalitarianism and "open commensality," has been retold in terms of the Christian polemic with the Jews. Luke is telling the same story that he tells in *Acts*. First the Jews are invited into the kingdom announced by Jesus, and they decline, and so the invitation goes out to the Gentiles. In Matthew, the king, presumably God, gives a wedding feast for his son, Jesus, which is spurned by the invited guests, the Jews, who also rough up his messengers, the prophets. See John Dominic Crossan, *The Historical Jesus* (New York: HarperSanFrancisco, 1991), 261–62. Sanders thinks the story might mean that Jesus saw his own ministry as supplementing that of John the Baptist: "Those first called—by John—did not come in, and so others were invited" by Jesus (*Jesus and Judaism*, 227). The first debate in Christianity, between Peter and Paul, was a border dispute about whether in order to gain access to the kingdom you had to pass through the door of circumcision and Judaism.

6. For Derrida's account of such aporetic hospitality, see Jacques Derrida, "Hostipitality," in *Acts of Religion*, ed. Gil Anidjar (New York: Routledge, 2002), 356–420, and for a commentary, see *Deconstruction in a Nutshell: A Conversation with Jacques Derrida*, edited with a commentary by John D. Caputo (New York: Fordham University Press, 1997), 109–13.

7. Derrida refers us to the work of Louis Massignon (1883–1962), an intellectual but also an activist who worked on behalf of Algerians and Palestinians, for whom "sacred hospitality" is a central ethical and political concept, one whose roots lie in Genesis 12:1, that is, in Abraham, the father of the three great monotheisms, who came to the earth as a stranger and a "saint of hospitality." See Derrida, "Hostipitality," *Acts of Religion*, 368 ff. Louis Massignon, *L'hospitalité sacrée* (Paris: Nouvelle Cité, 1987); *Testimonies and Reflections: Essays of Louis Massignon*, ed. Herbert Mason (Notre Dame, Ind.: University of Notre Dame Press, 1989). To be sure, the Canaanites might not share this view of biblical hospitality; see Regina M. Schwartz, *The Curse of Cain: The Violent Legacy of Monotheism* (Chicago: University of Chicago Press, 1998).

8. Thomas Ogletree, *Hospitality to the Stranger: Dimensions of Moral Understanding* (Philadelphia: Fortress Press, 1985), 1–9; Ogletree also uses Levinas to develop this biblical paradigm, but not uncritically; see 51–57.

9. *DVI:* Emmanuel Levinas, *De Dieu qui vient a l'idée* (Paris: J. Vrin, 1982); *GWCM:* English: *Of God Who Comes to Mind*, trans. Bettina Bergo (Stanford: Stanford University Press, 1998).

10. *A:* Jacques Derrida, *Adieu: à Emmanuel Levinas* (Paris: Galilée, 1997); the English translation follows a slash: *Adieu: To Emmanuel Levinas*, trans. Pascale-Anne Brault and Michael Naas (Stanford: Stanford University Press, 1999).

11. A discussion of "*A-dieu*" is to be found in "Diachrony and Representation," in *Time and the Other*, trans. Richard Cohen (Pittsburgh: Duquesne University Press, 1987); cited as *TO*.

12. For more on "rogues," see Jacques Derrida, *Voyous* (Paris: Galilée, 2003); English: *Rogues: Two Essays on Reason*, trans. Pascale-Anne Brault and Michael Naas (Stanford: Stanford University Press, 2005); and John D. Caputo, "Without Sovereignty, Without Being: Unconditionality, the Coming God and Derrida's Democracy to Come," *Journal of Cultural and Religious Theory* 4, no. 3 (August 2003) (www.jcrt.org).

13. "By way of discreet though transparent allusions, Levinas oriented our gazes toward what is happening today, not only in Israel but in Europe and France, in Africa, America, and Asia, since at least the First World War and since what Hannah Arendt called *The Decline of the Nation-State:* everywhere that refugees of every kind, immigrants with or without citizenship, exiled or forced from their homes, whether with or without papers, from the heart of Nazi Europe to the former Yugoslavia, from the Middle East to Rwanda, from Zaire all the way to California, from the Church of St. Bernard to the thirteenth ar-

rondissement in Paris, Cambodians, Armenians, Palestinians, Algerians and so many others call for a change in the socio- and geo-political space to a mutation—a juridico-political mutation, though, before this, assuming that this limit still has any pertinence, an ethical conversion" (*A*, 131/71; cf. *A*, 118/64, 175–76/100–101).

14. Strictly speaking, in English usage, according to the *Oxford English Dictionary, adieu* should not be translated as "farewell," because *Adieu* is not directed to the wayfarer, to the one who is leaving, but to the one who remains behind. *Adieu,* to-God, does not mean "farewell, or "go with God," but rather "I commend you to God," like the English "Goodbye," "God be with you," which would in fact be a better translation. *Adieu* was originally said *by* the one *departing* to the one *left behind,* while "farewell" was addressed to the *wayfarer,* to the one departing, by those left behind.

> *The one remaining behind:* "Farewell, fare thee well, go with God, have a safe journey, wherever your travels may take you."

> *The traveler:* "Adieu, I commend you *to God,* to God's loving care while I am gone, God be with you for as long as I am gone. May God's presence fill you in my absence."

So it would be difficult, *stricto sensu,* to say *adieu* to one who has died, the "departed." If death is a journey, it is a journey that the *other* one takes, while we, the living, remain behind, and we should bid "farewell" to him, who has departed. "Fare thee well, wherever you are going," wherever all the departed are going. At the hour of death, the one who is dying should bid *adieu* to those who remain behind, "God be with you after I am gone."

15. Jacques Derrida and Geoffrey Bennington, *Jacques Derrida,* trans. Geoffrey Bennington (Chicago: University of Chicago Press, 1993), 153–55. For a commentary, see John D. Caputo, *Prayers and Tears of Jacques Derrida* (Bloomington: Indiana University Press, 1997), ch. 6, "Confession." *Adieu* is the title of Derrida's book, of the first essay in the book, and the word he addresses to Levinas when he bids adieu to him on December 27, 1995, in the Pantin Cemetery, in the graveside eulogy, which ends very poignantly "Adieu, Emmanuel."

16. See John D. Caputo, "Tears Beyond Being: Derrida's Confession of Prayer," in *Augustine and Postmodernism: Confessions and Circumfession,* ed. John D. Caputo and Michael Scanlon (Bloomington: Indiana University Press, 2005), 95–114.

17. That is one of the theses of Jacques Derrida, *Monolingualism of the Other; or, The Prosthesis of Origin,* trans. Patrick Mensah (Stanford: Stanford University Press, 1998).

18. In Eckhart's case a Franciscan pope was out to get the celebrated Dominican preacher and to divert attention from fellow Franciscan William of Occam!

19. I very much agree with Jacques Rolland's comment that "however provocative such an assertion might be—Levinas should be understood as a thinker of the 'death of God.'" See Emmanuel Levinas, *On Escape,* trans. Bettina Bergo (Stanford: Stanford University Press, 2003), "Annotations," 89.

20. *AE:* Emmanuel Levinas, *Autrement qu'être ou au-delà de l'essence* (The Hague: Nijhoff, 1974); *OTB: Otherwise than Being or Beyond Essence,* trans. Alphonso Lingis (The Hague: Martinus Nijhoff Publishers, 1981).

21. *TA:* Levinas, *Le temps et l'autre* (Paris: PUF, 1983).

22. *DEE:* Emmanuel Levinas, *De l'existence à l'existant* (Paris: Fontaine, 1947); *EE: Existence and Existents,* Eng. trans. Alphonso Lingis (Dordrecht: Kluwer, 1978; Pittsburgh: Duquesne University Press, 2001).

23. *T&I = Totalité et infini: Essai sur l'extériorité,* 2nd ed. (The Hague: Nijhoff, 1965); Eng. trans. *Totality and Infinity: Essay on Exteriority,* trans. Alphonso Lingis (Pittsburgh: Duquesne University Press, 1969).

24. In *Difficult Freedom: Essays on Judaism,* trans. Sean Hand (Baltimore: Johns Hopkins University Press, 1990), 117, Levinas warns against treating the distinction between believer

and nonbeliever too simplistically, as if we were distinguishing a pharmacist and a non-pharmacist; he prefers to distinguish those who regard the Scriptures as a special and irreducible form of the Spirit from those who do not.

25. See above, "Introduction."

26. The glory of God rises up, beyond phenomenality, in my responsibility and anarchic substitution. I do not thereby demonstrate the existence of, or verify my belief in, the infinite—as if this had to do with being or knowledge—but I "bear witness" to it (*AE,* 186/ *OTB,* 146). The *me voici* bears witness, not to something that it knows or represents, not to anything that is or appears or is thematized, but to what commands me. But this command finds words only in the one who is commanded, in my *me voici.* There is thus a curious autonomy in this heteronomy, for my saying is the very way the Infinite passes by, and my obedience the only way the order is known. In a certain way I am the author of the law that I obey, the author of what I have received.

27. "'Here I am, in the name of God,' without [*sans*] referring myself directly to his presence. 'Here I am,' just that [*tout court*]. The word *God* is still absent from the phrase in which God is for the first time involved in words. It does not at all state 'I believe in God.' To bear witness to God is precisely not to state this extraordinary word. . . . As a sign given to the other of this very signification, the 'here I am' signifies me in the name of God, at the service of the human beings who regard me. . . . Witness is humility and admission, it is kerygma and prayer, glorification and recognition" (*AE,* 190/ *OTB,* 149).

28. Merold Westphal, "Levinas' Teleological Suspension of the Religious," *Ethics as First Philosophy: The Significance of Levinas for Philosophy, Literature, and Religion,* ed. Adriaan T. Peperzak (New York and London: Routledge, 1995), 151–60.

29. See Derrida's discussion of the ethical core or ethicity of ethics in Jacques Derrida, *On the Name,* ed. Thomas Dutoit (Stanford: Stanford University Press, 1995), 133.

30. The God beyond being not only does not have to be, but he does not have to give to me or pardon me. What sort of faith or devotion would there be if I were sure that God could not abandon me (separate himself)? Does Levinas think, Derrida wonders, that the *à-Dieu* is a prayer or a greeting addressed to a God who must respond, or might God abandon me? What elicits our admiration in this beautiful word *adieu,* Derrida says, is its desire or love of the stranger, its disproportion (*A,* 182/104). The "God who loves the stranger," beyond being, is not there. "Before and beyond the 'existence' of God, outside of his probable improbability, right up to the most vigilant if not the most desperate, the most 'sober' [*dé-grisé*] [Levinas loves this word 'sober'] of atheisms, the Saying *à-Dieu* would signify hospitality." Not an abstract "love of the stranger," but the God *who* loves the stranger (*A,* 182/104–105).

31. Emmanuel Levinas, *In the Time of the Nations,* trans. Michael B. Smith (Bloomington: Indiana University Press, 1994), 98.

32. Jacques Derrida, *Mémoires d'aveugle: L'autoportrait et autres ruines* (Paris: Éditions de la Réunion des musées nationaux, 1990), 9, 130. Eng. trans: *Memoirs of the Blind: The Self-Portrait and Other Ruins,* trans. Pascale-Anne Brault and Michael Naas (Chicago: University of Chicago Press, 1993), 1, 129.

33. Furthermore, while Levinas always denounces the narcissism of the same, Derrida thinks—to Derrida's credit—there is always a residual narcissism in the deconstructive notion of hospitality. There is no one narcissism, Derrida says, but varying degrees of narcissism, from the most close-fisted and mean-spirited narcissism up to the most open-ended, "hospitable" narcissisms. See Jacques Derrida, *Points . . . Interviews, 1974–94,* ed. Elisabeth Weber, trans. Peggy Kamuf (Stanford: Stanford University Press, 1995), 199. Finally, as the text of *Adieu* makes especially clear, Derrida presses the political paradox of hospitality more radically than does Levinas, presses all the more insistently to translate this ethics of hospitality into politics, to open the doors of this ethics to the demands of political hospi-

tality—in particular, as regards the modern state that answers to the biblical name of Israel. Derrida wants to sound an international alarm about the demands of hospitality, to stress national and international political structures to the precise point at which, short of breaking, they become more porous. He wants to break down the walls and barriers that nations build against the strangers whose weary faces glow, not with visible beauty—on the contrary!—but with God's glory, upon whom God makes his face to shine. Throughout the pages of *Adieu* migrant and immigrant bodies pass us by, pressing their faces against the windows of our quiet academic studies, regarding us as we write and talk and think in the comfort of our academic refuges, soliciting not words but deeds, not the word *God* but Godliness. For God is not a semantic event, however overwhelming, but a deed. Derrida would finally demand a more or less direct political translation of the ethics of hospitality, and hence of the name of God, a risky and formidable translation that fills us with fear and trembling, like daring to hold a dagger over one's own, which would result in open doors, in nations without borders or national barriers. He said this before September 11 and he is still saying it.

APPENDIX TO PART TWO

1. The record of my first communications from Magdalena is to be found in John D. Caputo, *Against Ethics: Contributions to a Poetics of Obligation with Constant Reference to Deconstruction* (Bloomington: Indiana University Press, 1993), 134–93.

A CONCLUDING PRAYER

1. While I do not mean to encourage the Heideggerians, I like the way the German words *Andenken* and *Andacht* unite "thinking" *(Denken)* with devotional prayer.
2. A poor paraphrase of the famous opening verse of Francis Thompson, "The Hound of Heaven."
3. Augustine, *Confessions,* Book IX, c. 12; Jacques Derrida, "Circumfession: Fifty-nine Periods and Periphrases" in Geoffrey Bennington and Jacques Derrida, *Jacques Derrida* (Chicago: University of Chicago Press, 1993), 47.
4. Derrida, "Circumfession," 118.
5. Were God a large green bird, Kierkegaard once quipped, God would have less difficulty gaining acceptance, although this ease might come at the price of faith. God is a spirit, not a sensible being, a promise, not a readily available, medium-size object of ordinary perception. Removed from the sensible order, God can only be called for, called to, called upon, structurally and not just as a matter of fact, which requires a certain faith, and which takes the form of a certain kind of prayer. If God is unknown to the sphere of sensible appearances, then the expression "the unknown God" is a truism, and praying to the unknown God, which Luke has St. Paul (supposedly) denouncing in the Acts of the Apostles, is the only kind of prayer there is. See John D. Caputo, "Tears Beyond Being: Derrida's Confession of Prayer," in *Augustine and Postmodernism: Confession and Circumfession,* ed. John D. Caputo and Michael Scanlon (Bloomington: Indiana University Press, 2005), 95–114.
6. Jean-Louis Chrétien, "The Wounded Word: The Phenomenology of Prayer," trans. Jeffrey Kosky, in *Phenomenology and the "Theological Turn": The French Debate* (New York: Fordham University Press, 2001), 147–75.
7. In *Radical Hermeneutics: Repetition, Deconstruction and the Hermeneutic Project* (Bloomington: Indiana University Press, 1987), 156, I said, "The truth is there is no

Truth," by which I meant to imply not skepticism but that, if the truth be told, we have no overarching capitalized *grands récits* that catch up everything in their sweep, and so we should settle for smaller lowercase truths, more quotidian varieties of truth. For a good commentary on my point, see Merold Westphal, "The Cheating of Cratylus (Genitivus Subjectivus)," in *Modernity and Its Discontents,* ed. James Marsh, John D. Caputo, and Merold Westphal (New York: Fordham University Press, 1992), 163–82.

8. *Kierkegaard's Writings,* VI, *Fear and Trembling* and *Repetition,* ed. and trans. H. Hong and E. Hong (Princeton, N.J.: Princeton University Press, 1983), 39.

9. While I treasure the spirit of this Tillichian line about theological questioning, we should avoid theological chauvinism. Tillich is rehearsing the idea of a "fundamental ontology," which I think is overreaching. Any discipline can break wide open under the press of the questions it itself is raising. Even veterinary science, which Kierkegaard liked to make fun of, will lead you up, or down, to animal suffering, landing you right at the door of the problem of evil. Tillich tried too hard to reconcile the kingdom of God with the vocabulary of being; see Paul Tillich, *Biblical Religion and the Search for Ultimate Reality* (Chicago: University of Chicago Press, 1955).

10. One could be tossed and turned by the turmoil of the event without ever having heard the name of God. I simply propose that this is one of the most prestigious, promising, and threatening names we know, where by "we" I mean highly miscegenated jewgreek Westerners who have descended from a long line of prolific, polyvalent, and polymorphic monotheists and polytheistic Greco-Romans.

11. It resists assimilation by both the symbolic and imaginary orders, and if you say then that by the process of elimination it must belong to the "real," we will say that it also twists free of the real and belongs to the hyper-real.

12. *Pace* the deeply modernist *and* Heideggerian dogma that the name of God shuts thinking down and closes us off from the question of truth and the truth of the question, we maintain that this name makes everything about the world questionable.

13. Friedrich Nietzsche, *Twilight of the Idols* in *Twilight of the Idols and The Anti-Christ,* trans. R. J. Hollingdale (London: Penguin Books, 1968), 35, 37.

14. Alain Badiou delineates four domains of truth—politics, art, science, and love. But despite writing an interesting book on St. Paul, Badiou omits mention of the event of truth, or the truth of the event, in the theological or religious order, which is peremptorily dismissed as simply not true, as simply "mythological" without trying to understand the event of truth harbored in these narratives. See Alain Badiou, *St. Paul: The Foundation of Universalism,* trans. Ray Brassier (Stanford: Stanford University Press, 2003), 107.

15. There are incursions on the public sphere from the religious right, which is what is all around us today, to which we on the left object, but also from the religious left, which is what drove Martin Luther King and Bishop Tutu, Mahatma Gandhi and Dietrich Bonhoeffer, to which we do not object.

16. Mark Taylor, *Erring: A Postmodern A/theology* (Chicago: University of Chicago Press, 1984), 6.

17. The death of God, as Nietzsche well realized, would be a mind-numbing event, compared to which the death of anything else would receive only passing notice in the obituary section. The bipolar name of God is capable of irrupting with shocking force and power, with violence and bloodiness; it has accumulated all the power and prestige of the worldly institutions that have taken it over, which makes for a strong force, while the event it harbors is the weak but unconditional force of a poor perhaps *(peut-être).*

18. Friedrich Nietzsche, *Beyond Good and Evil,* trans. R. J. Hollingdale (London: Penguin Books, 1972), No. 39, 50.

19. Jacques Derrida, *Negotiations: Interventions and Interviews: 1971–2001,* trans. Elizabeth Rottenberg (Stanford: Stanford University Press, 2002), 182.

20. Please note: By exposing the name, which is always concrete, contingent, and con-structed, that is, historical, to the truth of the event, I am not trying to slip in some overar-ching a-historical essence, but to confess the anti-essentialist restlessness that inhabits historical names. By the truth of the event I do not mean a divine illumination or the light of pure reason or the truth of some underlying *Wesen*. I mean the truthful confession, the honest (to God) concession, that we do not know who we are or what future is harbored by the event that stirs restlessly within the name.

21. That is the dynamics of the *sauf* (safe/except) in Derrida, which also shows up in the English "save." So we have endeavored to keep the name of God *safe* even as we have put it at *risk*. Our confession is a profession and a concession, a way to both save and sur-render the name of God.

22. We flatter ourselves with the conceit that the present time is a turning point, a cru-cial moment in which all the forces that have organized things up to now are undergoing a deep shift. That is probably not true, and if it were true, it would be too soon to tell; at best one would have made a lucky guess. But it is a useful heuristic device that is afoot in the talk these days of "post-this" and "post-that."

23. Parts of this "Conclusion" were first presented in a commentary on Charles Win-quist, *The Surface of the Deep* (Aurora, Colo.: Davies Group, 2003), in a memorial session at the American Academy of Religion after Charlie's untimely death. It has been rewritten so extensively since then that it is no longer a commentary of that sort, but it owes a debt to that work that, being now unidentifiable, is even deeper.

24. I am spicing up Tillich with a little dash of deconstruction: in the desire for God, for the unconditional event, there is no identifiable ultimate concern, for that identification would immediately turn the gold of ultimacy into the lead of something proximate, thereby locking the event inside a name and confining the unconditional to something con-ditioned. There is nothing determinately, decisively, discernibly ultimate that could possi-bly bear that much weight or support that much pressure. There is no name that once proposed could not be deposed, no *one* name that can be affirmed without ironic distance to be above every other name, at the sound of which every knee everywhere should bend (although everyone is entitled to their opinion). There is no god that can bear the weight of the name of God, no historical name that can contain the event that is gathering force there.

25. In that sense, then, our theology of the event has been a liberation theology. Fur-thermore, making or doing the truth is a way of giving "testimony" to the truth, which is what *martyros* means in Greek. So the ideal knight of faith in a theology of the event would be both a confessor and martyr.

26. See the last paragraph of *Fear and Trembling* and the first paragraph of *Repetition* in *Kierkegaard's Writings,* VI, *Fear and Trembling and Repetition,* 123,

GENERAL INDEX

Abel, 60, 63, 74, 96, 176, 178, 181, 254, 315n2, 317n15

Abraham, 70, 137, 138–39, 150

Adam, 65, 66, 69, 71, 73, 186, 231, 313n36

Adam and Eve, story of, 65. *See also* creation narratives

adieu, 264, 274, 275, 289, 292–95, 299, 336n14; and Derrida, 265–69, 276; and Levinas, 269, 272; in prayer, 284–86; *sans dieu*, 269–73, 274

Against Ethics (Caputo), 103, 301n5

Alcoholics Anonymous, 226

Alice in Wonderland (Carroll), 109, 112, 184, 203–204, 206

alterity, 72, 136, 137, 138, 143, 252, 333n19; of death, 250; of the past, 253; and sexual difference, 186

Amos, 28, 31, 107, 136, 316n7. *See also* the separate Scriptural Index

anarche, 14, 17, 27, 58, 76, 139, 237. *See also arche*

anarchism, 308n12

anarchy, 8, 10, 26–27, 31, 37, 51, 156, 183–85, 216. *See also* sacred anarchy

angels, 205

animals, suffering of, 339n9

Annunciation, 102

Anselm, 215–16, 232

Antigone, 221

Anti-Oedipus (Deleuze), 204

anxiety, 160–61, 163–65, 169–70, 175, 233, 295–96, 323n15. *See also* worry

aporia, 186; of forgiveness, 210–13

arche, 14, 33, 37, 134, 135, 139, 176, 237, 297, 309n9, 316n7; and creation, 58, 76; Damian and, 196, 202, 325n3; Derrida and, 26, 27, 29, 266; and *différance*, 25, 30; and event, 34; and future, 165; and kingdom of God, 48; and Lazarus, 238; and prophets, 31; and radical history, 254; and responsibility, 137; and

time, 156, 160; and world, 51. *See also anarche*

Arendt, Hannah, 19, 65, 145, 148, 169, 217, 233

Aristotle, 46–47, 93, 328n17; and being, 196; and creation, 76; and God's love, 306n3; and metaphysics, 73, 158; and *ousia*, 201; and reason, 142, 143; and time, 146, 147, 150, 174. *See also* ethics

atheism, 25, 136, 269, 271, 272, 274, 275, 292

atheists, 265–66, 268, 273, 275, 278

Attack Upon Christendom (Kierkegaard), 135

Augustine, St., 39, 252, 284–85; and desire, 111; and evil, 193; and forgiveness, 215; and innocence, 186; and love of God, 115; and name of God, 88; and order, 30; and quotidianism, 160–61; and truth, 268, 272; and will, 143

authority, 49–50, 51, 53, 70, 105, 116

axiomatics, 203–207

Babel, tower of, 35, 216

Babylonia, 61, 62

Badiou, Alain, 134, 261, 307n6, 318n5, 339n14

Bartlett, Anthony, 306n4

Barth, Karl, 33, 51, 61, 196, 277

Basilides, 81–82

being, 9, 15, 35–36, 39, 40, 47, 53, 67, 107, 121, 154, 174, 178, 180, 202, 224, 246–48; beyond, 5, 37–38, 86, 124, 187; and call, 105; in creation, 58–59, 82, 86, 178; and event, 5, 216; and good, 187, 196, 204; and kingdom of God, 37, 107, 153; logic of, 109; and name of God, 9, 10, 11, 13; and sovereignty, 38; and thinking, 187; and time, 149, 151, 187, 241, 253; and truth, 16. *See also* reduction

Being and Time (Heidegger), 174

Benjamin, Walter, 7, 173, 244, 252; and
creation, 74, 75, 176, 178, 180; and the
dead, 257; and history, 74, 77, 94, 128,
149–50, 253, 254; and hope, 95–96;
and weak theology, 7, 244
Bible, 315n7
bodies, as events, 204–205
body, the, 129–31, 163–64. *See also* flesh
Bonhoeffer, Dietrich, 51, 277
Book of Gomorrah (Liber Gomorrhianus)
(Damian), 185, 190–91
Bornkamm, Günther, 50
The Brothers Karamazov (Dostoevsky), 17,
162–63

Caesar, 51–52
Cain, 63, 74, 96, 176, 178, 181, 254,
315n2, 317n15
call, 15, 18, 38, 40, 41, 53, 201, 299; and
creation, 93, 137, 178, 180, 203,
311n27; event and, 5, 53, 96–97;
hermeneutics of, 102–103, 113–24,
207; and hyper-realism, 11; and justice,
13, 28, 141; and the kingdom of God,
15, 39, 104, 105, 206; and logos of the
cross, 44, 45; and name of God, 8, 12,
94, 314n45; and poetics, 103, 107;
power of, 41, 43, 91, 176; and prophets,
30; and truth, 16. *See also* responsibility
Carroll, Lewis, 20, 112
causality, 36, 40, 41
chance, 60, 64, 73–74, 75
chaos, 313n37, 314n56
chaos theory, 64, 111, 112, 318n11
children, 228–29, 252, 257, 333n18
Chilton, Bruce, 129
Christendom, 48, 133
Christianity, 130, 217, 233, 270, 307n7;
and creation, 62; and Jesus, 136,
304n13; Kierkegaard on, 48, 133;
and logos of the cross, 42, 43, 44
Christians, 50, 307n9
church and state, 50
Circonfession (Derrida), 235, 265
circumcision, 335n5
circumfession, 4, 115
Clement of Alexandria, 81
clergy, 183, 189, 201
Climacus, Johannes, 1, 9, 104, 273, 277,
325n4; on faith, 11, 223; on Greeks,
143, 167; on history, 256; on name of
God, 267
Clinton, Bill, 212

community, 262, 278
"The Concept of History" (Benjamin), 94
confession, 4, 28, 115, 225–31
Confessions (Augustine), 88, 89–90, 199,
215, 285
Constantine Constantius (Kierkegaard),
161, 326n4
conversion, 167
creatio ex nihilo, 59, 62, 75–83, 85, 86–87,
102, 146, 310n19; Damian and, 19,
146, 183, 203; Keller and, 63, 311n27;
and omnipotence, 71, 186, 240,
311n27, 313n37; and transformation,
147, 207
creation, 18, 55–83, 122, 127–29, 137,
142, 147–49, 151, 152, 176–78, 183,
194–95, 233, 278, 332n7; and *arche,*
58, 76; and being, 58–59, 82, 86, 178;
and call, 93, 137, 178, 180, 203,
311n27; Damian and, 185; and *différance,* 276; *ex nihilo,* 59, 63, 71,
75–83, 85; and faith, 89, 93, 181; good
in, 53, 58, 62–63, 67–72, 75–81,
87–90, 92–93, 106, 129, 132, 148,
248; Levinas and, 18, 58, 60, 64, 229;
and omnipotence, 18, 73, 86, 237; poetics of, 177; and power, 56, 59, 72, 73,
82, 85, 86, 87; theology of, 63, 67, 110;
and time, 57–58, 85, 87, 89, 109; as
transformation, 147, 326n4. *See also* re-
creation; risk
creation narratives, 65–75, 88–89, 91–93,
120, 127–29, 132, 133, 138, 148, 172,
176, 178, 237, 238, 312n36. *See also* J
(author of creation narrative); P (author
of creation narrative)
Critique of Practical Reason (Kant), 131,
134
cross, the, 15, 16, 17, 26, 118; logos of,
42–54; theology of, 41
Crossan, John Dominic, 30, 155, 156
crucifixion, 42, 43, 44, 118–19, 135, 232,
234, 270
Cynics, 166

Damian, Peter, 86, 181, 182–207, 225,
228, 235, 253, 296; and changing past
time, 145–46, 147, 184–86, 192–93,
195–99, 205–206, 208–209, 224, 226,
229, 230, 242, 244, 249, 251, 325n4;
on *creatio ex nihilo,* 19, 146, 183, 203;
on creation, 185; criticisms of, 325n3;
on death, 218; on divine omnipotence,

35–36, 37, 47, 174, 289; and death,
130; and hermeneutics, 112, 113; and
Jesus, 161; and metanoetics, 153; and
name, 11; and quotidianism, 158–63;
and reason, 321n22; and time, 160,
163, 171, 173; and translation, 266;
and truth, 5; and world, 302n20
Heidegger and "the jews" (Lyotard), 255
Heraclitus, 133
hermeneutical situation, 113–15
hermeneutics, 2, 6, 7, 18, 40, 101–12,
154, 207, 228, 230; of the call, 113–24,
207; of the event, 208; of facticity,
158–61; and quotidianism, 158–63;
radical, 60, 64, 101
Hermogenes, 313n40, 314n56
heteronomy, 137, 138
Hildegard of Bingen, 152
history, 95, 160, 178, 180, 186, 244,
321n27, 323n6; Benjamin on, 74, 77,
94, 128, 149–50, 176, 178, 253–57;
and creation, 57, 70, 71, 96; as dangerous memory, 253–57; and event, 5;
Joyce on, 77, 128; and the kingdom of
God, 324n27; messianic, 253; philosophy of, 174; radical, 254, 256; revisionist, 230; and salvation, 153; and suffering, 253–57
Hobbes, Thomas, 70, 74
holy, 305n34
Holy Spirit, 149, 152, 187–88
homosexuality, 184, 189, 190, 327n12
hope, 75, 94, 104, 118, 124, 159, 246,
249, 297, 324n27; and the dead, 256;
Derrida and, 252; and event, 5; and the
impossible, 244, 249; and kingdom of
God, 16; and name of God, 88; and the
past, 95–96; Paul on, 96, 160; and the
present, 246–47, 251; and quotidianism, 165, 179; and time, 149, 248, 257
horizon, 4–5
hospitality, 13, 20, 29, 96, 111, 112, 136,
137, 138, 166–67; event of, 259–78;
and Kierkegaard, 334n1; as law of God,
263–64; sacred, 263, 275; as weak force,
262
Humeanism, holy, 201–203
Husserl, Edmund, 10, 121, 154, 199, 230;
and call, 115; and logic, 200; and phenomenology, 119, 192, 197, 209, 224,
229, 246; and time, 109, 146, 162, 174,
228; and truth, 286. *See also epoche;* retention

hyperousios, 37–38, 302n16
hyper-realism, 9–12, 102, 113, 121–24
hyper-reality, 11–12, 18

illeity, 273, 276
image: in creation, 177; of God, 60,
67–68, 69, 70–71, 72, 128, 306n3
immortality, 270
impossible, the, 5, 16, 18, 88, 96, 115–16,
157, 182, 244; axiomatics of, 203–207;
Damian and, 186, 192–93, 199,
202–203, 251; and deconstruction,
141, 239; definition of, 317n1; Derrida
and, 16, 102, 111, 240, 331n31; and
event, 5, 109–10, 228, 238; and forgiveness, 111, 209, 228; and history, 128;
and kingdom of God, 16, 30, 102–12,
132, 206; and logic, 206, 266; and
Pharisee and tax collector, 215; and
quotidianism, 172; and time, 109, 150,
157. *See also* poetics
infinity, 294
innocence, 186, 189, 195
Inquisition, 269
intensity, 11, 40
intervention, 77–78, 93, 94, 102, 105,
176, 178, 200, 202, 313n42
Irenaeus, 80, 183
Irigaray, Luce, 60, 63, 64, 186
irreparable loss, 242–44

J (author of creation narrative), 66, 67, 69,
71, 148, 312n36. *See also* creation
Jacob, 73
Jacques, St. (Derrida), 235
Jairus, 249
James, William, 199
Jeremiah, 52–53. *See also the separate Scriptural Index*
Jeroboam, 31
Jerome, St., 188
Jerusalem, 276
Jesus, 17, 19, 51, 52, 102–103, 107, 135,
136, 142, 166, 167, 169, 187, 188,
215, 316n7, 323n10; attack on the
temple, 53, 222; crucifixion of, 15, 49;
death of, as sacrificial, 232–34, 331n24;
divinity of, 43; and event, 128–29; and
forgiveness, 44, 144, 169, 190, 212–13,
217, 306n4; and healing, 128, 129–30,
139–40, 143, 149, 150, 232, 261; and
kingdom of God, 261; and Lazarus,
236–58; and logos of the cross, 42–45,

hospitality, 272, 274, 275, 337n33; and kingdom of God, 38–39, 89, 101, 115–16; reduction of, 115–17, 121; in weak theology, 295. *See also* event; reduction

narcissism, 337n33
National Socialism, 5
Neher, André, 57
Neoplatonism, 111
New Testament, 15, 48, 81, 130–31, 132, 139, 153, 184, 306n35; and deconstruction, 212; and ethics, 134–41; family values in, 135; and healing, 140, 144; Heidegger and, 161; and law, 111, 133; and logic, 106; and omnipotence, 112; and time, 174; and truth, 16; and world, 50, 107, 134
Nicomachean Ethics (Aristotle), 158
Nietzsche, Friedrich, 44, 46, 114, 119, 269, 270, 329n17; and creation, 61, 63, 178; and Peter Damian, 328n17; and justice, 221, 232; and kingdom of God, 134; and name of God, 289–90; and New Testament, 15, 103; and past, 145; and truth, 292, 293
nihilism, 82, 87, 310n14
Nine Talmudic Lectures (Levinas), 220
Noah, 70, 312n33, 313n37
nous, 142–43, 145

object, 4
Ogletree, Thomas, 50, 263
omnipotence, 12, 55, 65, 75, 79, 84–97, 314n56; and *creatio ex nihilo*, 71, 186, 240, 311n27, 313n37; and creation, 18, 73, 86, 237; Damian and, 146, 152, 184, 187, 188, 190, 191, 193, 195–97, 202, 203, 207, 209, 240; and death, 16, 237; and evil, 76, 303n24, 330n11; and history, 244; and the impossible, 103; logic of, 18; metaphysics of, 77, 80, 102, 105, 112, 183, 240; and New Testament, 112
On the Divine Omnipotence in the Restoration of What is Destroyed and in Rendering what is Done Undone (Peter Damian), 188
order, 29, 30–37, 45, 50, 59, 313n37
Otherwise than Being (Levinas), 269
ousia, 32, 46, 47, 105, 107, 110–11, 134, 150, 151, 152, 162, 168, 173–74, 185, 188, 201, 205, 227

ousiology, 111, 173, 202, 204
Overbeck, Franz, 158

P (author of creation narrative), 65, 66, 69, 71, 75, 88, 128, 148, 176, 178, 312n36
pain, 245–46, 247, 249, 251, 252
panentheism, 317n18
pantheism, 85, 315n4, 317n18
papal infallibility, 76–77; as idolatry, 315n7
parables, 13, 14, 16, 106–107, 129, 215, 231, 280–82, 303n24, 319n7; wedding feast, 259–78
paradox, 106, 204–206, 215, 234, 303n24; of forgiveness, 229–30
Pardonner le temps (Derrida), 235
Parmenides, 110, 133, 152, 153, 289
parousia, 31, 32, 159, 161, 168
passion, 1, 104, 108–109, 294–95, 298
The Passion of Christ, 131
past, 153, 170, 254, 256, 257, 293; changing of, 19, 182–207, 230–31; Damian and, 145–46, 147, 208–209, 224, 226, 229, 230, 242, 244, 249, 251; forgetting of, 169, 223–25, 228; and forgiveness, 94, 146, 147, 148, 202, 230–31, 325n3; Levinas and, 253; Nietzsche and, 145; and quotidianism, 171, 175, 180; and sinners, 228; undoing of, 191–201, 205, 227, 229
pathos, 104, 144
patience, 15
Pattison, George, 322n31
Paul, St., 7, 17, 26, 32, 33, 40, 103, 107, 232, 261; and Derrida, 12–13; and hope, 96, 104, 160, 256; and Jesus, 161; and Kierkegaard, 28, 31; and kingdom of God, 133–34; and logos of the Cross, 42–54; and the sacrificial interpretation of death of Jesus, 331n24; and the second coming, 120
perhaps, the, 105, 108, 180–81, 295, 339n17
Phaedo (Plato), 130
Pharisee and tax collector, story of, 214–16, 222–25, 227, 231, 234–35
Pharisees, the, 139–41, 141, 218, 219, 248, 261
phenomenology, 115–16, 117, 119, 121, 131, 146–47, 154, 162, 188, 192, 197, 209, 210, 224, 228, 229, 240, 242,

246, 249, 271, 332n7. *See also epoche;*
Husserl, Edmund; Marion, Jean-Luc;
reduction
philosophy, 120, 136, 152, 153, 289;
Greek, 46, 47, 131, 132, 138
phronesis, 46–47, 142–46
physis, Heidegger's view of, 171
Placher, William, 306n35, 306n3
Plato, 47, 56, 73, 81, 130, 133, 152–53,
196, 286
Platonism, 3, 5, 269, 270
poetics, 4, 103–104, 107, 118, 119, 204;
of creation, 177; Damian and, 182,
183, 199, 202, 203; and deconstruction, 18; and *epoche,* 119; and ethics,
252; of the event, 4, 208, 210, 238–39,
248, 262, 264; and forgiveness, 208,
220; of the gift, 217; and heart, 142; of
the impossible, 101–12, 134, 172,
199–200, 255; of the kingdom of God,
118, 119, 120–21, 239, 277–78,
321n31; Levinas and, 248, 254; and
logic, 105; and *metanoia,* 143, 145, 149,
154; and miracles, 238; and quotidianism, 156, 172; and sin, 227; and transformation, 132
politics, 26, 265, 268, 297; and hospitality,
276, 337n33
Polkinghorne, John, 318n11
polytheism, 177, 312n36
possibility, 4–5. *See also* impossible, the
power, 9, 12–13, 16, 36, 43, 75, 79, 80,
84, 136, 154, 308n14; Basilides and,
82; and being, 105; and call, 41, 43,
91, 176, 180; and creation, 56, 59, 72,
73, 82, 85, 86, 87; Damian and, 19,
135, 152, 186, 187, 201, 202, 229,
230; and deconstruction, 32; divine,
12, 44, 77, 102, 154, 183, 184, 188,
195, 196, 224; ecclesiastical, 183; and
event, 5, 34, 90; fantasy of, 78–79;
from God, 13, 48–54; human, 84,
183; Jesus and, 150; in Job, 78; and
kingdom of God, 135; and love, 34,
185, 316n7; messianic, 95; metaphysical, 187, 325n3; and name of God,
7–8, 9, 23, 88; of names, 2; ordered,
328n15; St. Paul and, 42, 45; political,
52, 304n13; of powerlessness, 13–14.
16, 23, 26, 29, 40, 43, 53, 90, 96;
Roman, 15, 43, 50; sovereign, 13, 32,
33, 35, 37, 38, 90, 186, 196, 203, 278;
and theology, 15, 33, 40; of transfor-

mation, 151; unconditional, 313n37;
unlimited, 203; and world, 12, 17, 39,
46, 48, 94, 110, 162; worldly, 29, 37,
44, 49, 52
powerlessness, 23, 40, 90, 93, 96, 298,
316n7; and alterity, 138; and call, 13,
176; Damian and, 146, 183, 203; Derrida and, 27, 29; and the impossible,
105; and kingdom of God, 15, 16, 17,
26, 234; and Lazarus, 238; Levinas and,
254; and logos of the cross, 43, 44, 53;
and *metanoia,* 143; and quotidianism,
180; and religion, 91; in *Republic,*
37–38; and sacred anarchy, 137; and
world, 12–13
prayer, 1, 18, 20, 79, 95, 106, 154, 158,
254, 277, 282, 283–99, 337n30; Derrida and, 265, 266, 273, 295; and event,
2, 5, 6, 122, 286–92, 295–99; and history, 253, 254, 255, 257; and the impossible, 157; and Jesus, 156; and kingdom of God, 108; Levinas and, 264,
272, 273; Lord's, 18–19, 127, 168–69,
201; and the name of God, 286; and remembrance of the dead, 95; for truth, 6,
383–84
preaching, 129, 131
presence, 33, 35, 36, 37, 173
present, 31–32, 246–47, 251, 252, 256,
340n22
"The Present Age" (Kierkegaard), 33
principium, 25, 29, 34, 135
Prodigal Son, 215, 232, 233
promise, 2, 5, 38, 90, 92, 93–94, 121–24,
294
prophetic, 30–32, 48, 51, 53
prophets, 30–31, 32, 34, 48, 52, 53,
223–24, 316n7
Psalms, 151. *See also the separate Scriptural
Index*
purity, 319n8

quotidianism, 19, 155–81, 295

Radical Orthodoxy, 310n14
rape, 189
Rashi, Rabbi, 57
realism, 102, 123
Realpolitik, 268
reason, 80, 114, 119, 142, 143–44, 145
rebirth, 20, 236–58
reciprocity, 262, 264
reconciliation, 211, 212, 231

SCRIPTURAL INDEX

JOHN D. CAPUTO has been, since 2004, the Thomas J. Watson Professor of Religion and Humanities and Professor of Philosophy at Syracuse University. He is also David R. Cook Professor Emeritus of Philosophy at Villanova University, where he taught from 1968 until 2004. His most recent book is *Augustine and Postmodernism: Confessions and Circumfession,* co-edited with Michael Scanlon (Indiana University Press, 2005). Recent publications include *On Religion* (Routledge, 2001), *More Radical Hermeneutics: On Not Knowing Who We Are* (Indiana University Press, 2000), and *The Prayers and Tears of Jacques Derrida: Religion without Religion* (Indiana University Press, 1997). Two books have recently appeared about his work: *Religion With/out Religion: The Prayers and Tears of John D. Caputo,* ed. James H. Olthuis (Routledge, 2001); and *A Passion for the Impossible: John D. Caputo in Focus,* ed. Mark Dooley (SUNY Press, 2003). Caputo serves as editor of the Fordham University Press book series Perspectives in Continental Philosophy and as chairman of the board of editors of *Journal of Cultural and Religious Theory.*

www.ingramcontent.com/pod-product-compliance
Ingram Content Group UK Ltd.
Pitfield, Milton Keynes, MK11 3LW, UK
UKHW020004100525
458410UK00005B/83